COUNTERING TAX CRIME IN THE EUROPEAN UNION

This book seeks durable solutions for tax crime and is a great resource for the development of knowledge, policy and law on tax crime. The book uniquely blends current practice with new approaches to countering tax crime. With insights from the EU-funded project, PROTAX, which conducts advanced research on tax crimes, the book comparatively analyses the EU's tax crime measures and the Ten Global Principles (TGPs) on fighting tax crime by the Organisation for Economic Cooperation and Development (OECD).

The study critically examines how the TGPs can serve as minimum standards for the EU to counter tax crime such as tax evasion and tax fraud. The study also analyses how the anti-tax avoidance package can be graduated to fight tax crime in the EU. When escalated, the strengths of the EU tax crime measures and TGPs can form a fortress in which criminal law can be empowered to mitigate tax crimes with greater effect.

This book will be particularly useful for end-user stakeholders such as tax policy makers, LEAs, professional enablers as well as academics and students interested in productive interaction between tax, criminal and administrative laws.

Countering Tax Crime in the European Union

Benchmarking the OECD's Ten Global Principles

Umut Turksen

·HART·

OXFORD · LONDON · NEW YORK · NEW DELHI · SYDNEY

HART PUBLISHING

Bloomsbury Publishing Plc

Kemp House, Chawley Park, Cumnor Hill, Oxford, OX2 9PH, UK

1385 Broadway, New York, NY 10018, USA

29 Earlsfort Terrace, Dublin 2, Ireland

HART PUBLISHING, the Hart/Stag logo, BLOOMSBURY and the Diana logo are
trademarks of Bloomsbury Publishing Plc

First published in Great Britain 2021

A catalogue record for this book is available from the British Library.

Library of Congress Cataloging-in-Publication data

Names: Turksen, Umut, author.

Title: Countering tax crime in the European Union : benchmarking the
OECD's ten global principles / Umut Turksen.

Description: Oxford, UK ; New York, NY : Hart Publishing, an imprint of
Bloomsbury Publishing, 2021. | Includes bibliographical references and index.

Identifiers: LCCN 2020051777 (print) | LCCN 2020051778 (ebook) |
ISBN 9781509937950 (hardback) | ISBN 9781509946150 (paperback) |
ISBN 9781509937967 (pdf) | ISBN 9781509937974 (Epub)

Subjects: LCSH: Tax evasion—Law and legislation—European Union countries. |
Taxation—Law and legislation—European Union countries—Criminal provisions.

Classification: LCC KJE7475 .T87 2021 (print) | LCC KJE7475 (ebook) | DDC 345.24/02338—dc23

LC record available at https://lccn.loc.gov/2020051777

LC ebook record available at https://lccn.loc.gov/2020051778

ISBN:	HB:	978-1-50993-795-0
	ePDF:	978-1-50993-796-7
	ePub:	978-1-50993-797-4

Typeset by Compuscript Ltd, Shannon

To find out more about our authors and books visit www.hartpublishing.co.uk.
Here you will find extracts, author information, details of forthcoming events
and the option to sign up for our newsletters.

ACKNOWLEDGEMENTS

This book could not have been possible without generous help from many colleagues, friends and organisations.

First of all, I would like to thank Dr Adam Abukari. I owe an enormous debt of gratitude for his generosity, dedication and intelligence which contributed greatly to this book.

I am also immensely grateful to my fellow researchers and colleagues including Dr Stuart MacLennan, Dr Donato Vozza, Dr Reinhard Kreissl, Dr Fanou Rasmouki, Dr David Wright, Dr Matthew Hall, Dr Franz Reger, Stephanie Öner, Peeter Paisuots, Dr Daniel Frendo, Daniel MacGinty, Cristina Farinha, Berta Santos, Rui Felix, Ana Djakovic, Engin Erken, Nilimesh Baruah, Dr Hieke Luecke. Prof Brigitte Unger, Prof Nicholas Ryder, Dr Alison Lui, Sam Bourton, Dr Lorenzo Pasculli, Dr Stuart MacLennan and Dr Costantino Grasso. It has been a great pleasure to work with them all, who are genuinely interested in and happy to render a constructive critique for the pressing global issues which this book aims to tackle. Thank you for being there through the extraordinary and hard times which COVID-19 has imposed on us.

Finally, I want to thank my wife, Jo, and my children for tolerating my anti-social working hours and disappearances in the process of writing yet another book.

CONTENTS

LIST OF ABBREVIATIONS

AML	Anti-Money Laundering
APCTC	Action Plan to Combat Tax Crimes
AEOI	Automatic exchange of information
BEPS	Base erosion and profit shifting
BZSt	Bundeszentralamt für Steuern
CJEU	Court of Justice of the European Union
CRS	Common Reporting Standard
ECRIS	European Criminal Records Information System
EFECC	European Financial and Economic Crime Centre
EPPO	European Public Prosecutor Office
EU	European Union
FIU	Financial Intelligence Unit
FTC	Forum on Tax and Crime
GDP	Gross domestic product
GST	Goods and services tax (GST)
HMRC	Her Majesty's Revenue and Customs
IFFs	Illicit financial flows
LEAs	Law enforcement agencies
MLAT	Mutual Legal Assistance Treaty
MNCs	Multinational corporations
MTIC	Missing trader intra-community
OCG	Organised criminal group
OECD	Organisation for Economic Cooperation and Development
OLAF	European Union Anti-Fraud Office
PROTAX	European Union Horizon 2020 project on countering tax crime in the EU

SDGs	Sustainable Development Goals
STRs	Suspicious Transaction Reports
TFTC	Task Force on Tax Crimes and Other Crimes
TGPs	Ten Global Principles
UNODC	United Nations Office on Drugs and Crime
VAT	Value added tax

LIST OF FIGURES

LIST OF TABLES

TABLE OF CASES

TABLE OF LEGISLATION

France

Germany

Ireland

Italy

Switzerland

1

Introduction

Tax offenders can evade reality but they cannot evade the consequences of evading reality.[1] The legal framework against tax crimes such as tax fraud and tax evasion, that paints this reality, must make tax criminals face the full rigour of the law.

Background

Markets and finances have become more globalised than ever. Countries across the world continue to increase their appetite for gaining a useful foothold against criminal exploitation of the increasing complexities associated with their interconnected systems and interests in the global marketplace. One of the critical areas of mutual concern and interest among jurisdictions is the complex disposition of tax crimes – including tax fraud, tax evasion and related financial crimes such as money laundering and fiscal corruption.

Indeed, tax crimes have notoriously taken an aversive international dimension, yet they continue to have national relevance since they are committed within the jurisdiction of states. With the international dimension, taxpayers leverage international opportunities to commit tax crimes in the national jurisdictions that provide the launching path opportunities. With the local dimension, resident taxpayers (both natural and legal persons) exploit the weaknesses in the law formulation and enforcement architecture to commit tax crimes, hoping that the long arm of the law will not catch them.

Essentially, tax criminals adeptly exploit loopholes and weaknesses (eg, the lack of a common definition of tax crimes) in local and international systems to commit tax crimes. As the loopholes are being closed and weaknesses are being addressed, tax criminals develop more sophisticated methods to override the efficacy of tax law enactment and enforcement strategies. These have serious social and economic consequences such as widening inequality and inadequate revenue for much-needed public services and socioeconomic development projects. Because of the huge adverse socioeconomic implications of tax crimes, it has become obvious that the search for remedies thereof must continue unabated.

---

[1] This proposition is drawn from 'The Objectivist Ethics (1961)' wherein Ayn Rand is said to have averred that man 'is free to evade reality, he is free to unfocus his mind and stumble blindly down any road he pleases, but not free to avoid the abyss he refuses to see'. In effect, 'we can evade reality, but we cannot evade the consequences of evading reality'. See Working Minds. 'Quotations from Ayn Rand [1905–1982]', www. working-minds.com/ARquotes.htm, accessed 20 April 2020.

The fight against tax crimes must use more sophisticated strategies, which are based on tenets such as effective and resilient principles, standards and enforcement mechanisms. These must stand the test of time and effectively counter the vagaries of sophistication of tax criminals. For instance, by virtue of the global and local disposition of tax crimes, there is the need for stronger inter-agency collaboration and cooperation – both domestically and internationally- in fighting tax crimes.

EU Member States appear to be individually demonstrating the desire, even if with unsettled political will, to take effective measures in countering tax crimes. Collectively too, under the umbrella of the OECD and the EU and as part of bilateral and multilateral cooperation, measures are being designed and implemented to counter tax crimes. For instance, the publication, in 2017, of the OECD's Ten Global Principles (TGPs) for fighting tax crimes, with a claim to be global in nature, is a good example of such collective initiatives.

The TGPs were designed to be representative of essential international principles that could be effectively used to combat tax crimes. These principles, imbued with the strategic inputs from over 200 countries, do address pertinent concerns ranging from legal, administrative, institutional to operational areas that are germane to establishing a system that is, at least, efficient, in countering tax crimes. The disposition of the principles is designed in a way that gives space or opportunity for different countries to 'benchmark their legal and operational framework and identify areas where improvements can be made'.[2]

The TGPs are situated within the framework of 'a whole of government approach to fighting tax crimes'.[3] It is premised on the understanding that tax crimes are dynamic, and criminals easily adapt themselves to generously benefit from any financial opportunities. Leveraging every available benefit any tax crimes can chance on, tax criminals also, all the more, usually outpace the legislative and enforcement modifications that have been put in place by the state machinery to effectively prevent, detect and prosecute these crimes. It is due deliberation to establish this framework that brought out the TGPs on countering tax crimes, which have three-layered purposes:

(i)   to allow countries to be able to benchmark their legal and operational framework so as to identify tax practices that are deemed successful for the improvement of relevant systems in the areas that are essential 'for an effective system to fight tax crimes';
(ii) to allow progress of countries to be measured 'through regular updates'; and
(iii) to allow countries to 'articulate their needs for training' or capacity-building on fighting tax crimes.[4]

The TGPs have established 10 global principles, covering the legal, strategic, administrative and operational aspects of addressing tax crimes.[5] The TGPs include criminalisation

---

[2] OECD, 'Strengthening the global response to tax crime' (8 November 2017), www.oecd.org/tax/crime/strengthening-the-global-response-to-tax-crime.htm, accessed 25 March 2020.
[3] OECD, 'About tax and crime', www.oecd.org/tax/crime/about-tax-and-crime.htm, accessed 25 March 2020.
[4] OECD, *Fighting Tax Crime: The Ten Global Principles* (OECD Publishing, 2017), www.oecd.org/tax/crime/fighting-tax-crime-the-ten-global-principles.htm, accessed 26 October 2019.
[5] Ibid.

of tax offences, effective strategies against tax crimes, adequate and effective resources and powers for LEAs, inter-agency and international cooperation, organisational structure with defined responsibilities, classificatior of tax crimes as predicate offences for money laundering as well as protection of fundamental rights of tax offenders.[6] With their crosscutting and complementary nature, the TGPs can, at least, serve as a 'minimum standard' to finding durable solutions for tax crimes, internationally.

These set of principles, if implemented and practised accordingly, can act as a strong lever for success. This is partly because the OECD has made provision for the continuous improvement of the principles through a framework of broadening jurisdictional and institutional participation in the OECD forum on tax and crime (FTC).[7] The FTC also fosters efforts towards developing more tools for countering tax crimes and money laundering.[8]

The OECD Task Force on Tax Crimes and other Crimes (TFTC),[9] which prepared the TGPs, is expected to take stock of the TGPs in collaboration with the FTC[10] and other partners. The TGPs have drawn on the experience of TFTC's members and additional survey data provided by the 31 jurisdictions in Table 1.

Table 1 Countries surveyed by OECD to draw on for the TGPs[11]

Europe		American countries	Asia-pacific countries	African countries	Total
EU countries	**Other European countries**				
Austria	Georgia	Brazil	Australia	South Africa	
Czech Republic	Iceland	Canada	Indonesia		
Denmark	Norway	El Salvador	Japan		
Finland	Switzerland	United States	Malaysia		
France	United Kingdom		New Zealand		
Germany			Singapore		

(continued)

---

[6] Ibid.

[7] OECD, 'About tax and crime'.

[8] Ibid.

[9] TFTC holds two meetings in a year. Participation in the meetings of the TFTC is stricter than participation in the meetings of the FTC. One of the objectives of the TFTC is centred on international policy and standard setting – which is one of the pillars of the Oslo Dialogue. The TFTC mobilises financial crime policy makers and law enforcement authorities just like FTC does but this activity is restricted to OECD member countries and jurisdictions that have been listed in the Participation Plan of Committee on Fiscal Affairs (CFA) (see OECD, 'Global Affairs: Participation plans', www.oecd.org/global-relations/partnershipsinoecd-bodies/participations-plans.htm, accessed 15 May 2020) (OECD's project assistant at the Centre for Tax Policy and Administration, Eunkyung Shin, was kind enough to provide the author with some email clarification notes on TFTC and FTC – thank you, Eunkyung).

[10] The FTC gathers senior policy makers from different government agencies around the globe including those from the tax, anti-money laundering and anti-corruption communities. The forum holds meetings every two years 'to explore approaches for closer cooperation at domestic and international levels to more effectively fight financial crime and showcase certain key risks in the tax and crime area, allowing countries to target resources and learn from the experience of others'.

[11] OECD, *Fighting Tax Crime.*

Table 1 *(Continued)*

EU countries	Europe	American countries	Asia-pacific countries	African countries	Total
	Other European countries				
Greece					
Italy					
Lithuania					
Luxembourg					
Netherlands					
Slovak Republic					
Slovenia					
Spain					
Sweden					
15	5	4	6	1	31

Although the TGPs could become popular amongst OECD countries and their associates, the extent to which tax crime measures of various countries in the EU are effectively harmonious with the TGPs is unclear. This requires a critical analysis to determine:

i.   if and to what extent the OECD countries are integrating the minimum standards of fighting tax crimes into the legal framework of their jurisdictions; and
ii. which robust pathways can effectively and sustainably counter the menace of tax crimes in OECD countries.

Meanwhile, as it were, in the archetypical legal framework of the European Union (EU), several tax crime counter-measures have been developed for its members, many of which are also members of the OECD.[12] These measures include legal approaches to countering tax crimes in the EU. The EU Directives designed to harmonise the anti-money laundering regulations and anti-tax avoidance practices are typical of the legal approaches adopted by the EU.

   In fact, in the past decade or so, there has been a degree of intensification in designing and developing policy, legislative and administrative initiatives that are geared towards fighting tax crimes in Europe. It is within the competence of the EU to facilitate cooperation and exchange of information among its Member States on diverse taxes, especially savings taxation and VAT.[13] In this regard, tax authorities of EU Member States are being given the legal tools to collaborate in the exchange of information on matters relating to tax crimes. This is achieved through legal instruments such as the Directive on Administrative Cooperation (DAC) (2011/16/EU) regarding

---

[12] Of the 27 EU members, only five are not members of the 37-member OECD; see OECD, 'Where: Global reach', www.oecd.org/about/members-and-partners/ accessed 29 April 2020; European Union, 'EU member countries in brief' (last published 1 February 2020), https://europa.eu/european-union/about-eu/countries/member-countries_en, accessed 13 April 2020.

[13] European Commission, 'Role of the EU: An action plan to combat tax fraud and evasion', https://ec.europa.eu/taxation_customs/fight-against-tax-fraud-tax-evasion/role-eu_en, accessed 14 March 2020.

direct taxation,[14] Anti-Tax Avoidance Directive (EU) 2016/1164 to protect the performance of the internal market,[15] and Council Directive 2006/112/EC on VAT.[16]

Apart from utilising the legislative competences, the EU has also established expert groups such as the Code of Conduct Group on Business Taxation[17] – which provides the platform for EU Member States to make assessment on the tax regimes of each other so as to discover any 'harmful tax measures', to seek for the abolishment of existing harmful tax measures, and to ensure that Member States do not introduce any new harmful tax measures. In the same vein, the EU has set up the Tax Policy Group,[18] which provides the platform for discussions by representatives of EU finance ministers on double taxation, tax avoidance and related concerns on tax malpractices.[19] There are also many groups such as the VAT forum, VAT Committee, VAT expert group, and the Group on the future of VAT in the EU[20] that work to unite the EU, its Member States and/or representatives of business in discussing means by which the operationalisation of the tax systems in the EU can be effectively improved.[21] In addition, there is the Fiscalis Programme[22] which enables tax officials to pay working visits to other EU Member States and facilitates 'joint actions' amongst the tax officials of EU Member States.

More recently, the European Commission has observed that these current arrangements on competences of the EU in matters of tax must be reinforced and the EU is determined to continue to engage in effective monitoring and improvement of its current operations in countering tax crimes. The adoption of the 'action plan to combat tax crimes' (APCTC)[23] by the EU Commission in 2012 has been one of such efforts to counter tax evasion and fraud. The APCTC consists of over 30 measures aimed at combatting tax crimes now and in the future. These 30 measures capture steps which

---

[14] Council Directive 2011/16/EU of 15 February 2011 on administrative cooperation in the field of taxation and repealing Directive 77/799/EEC, [2011] OJ L 64/ 1–12.

[15] Council Directive (EU) 2016/1164 of 12 July 2016 laying down rules against tax avoidance practices that directly affect the functioning of the internal market, [2016] OJ L 193/1–14.

[16] Council Directive 2006/112/EC of 28 November 2006 on the common system of value added tax, [2006] OJ L 347/1–118; see consolidated version as of 1 January 2020 at: Council Directive 2006/112/EC of 28 November 2006 on the common system of value added tax, https://eur-lex.europa.eu/legal-content/EN/TXT/PDF/?uri=CELEX:02006L0112-20200101&from=EN accessed 8 January 2020.

[17] ECOFIN, 'The code of conduct for business taxation – Conclusions of the Council of Economics and Finance Ministers' (ECOFIN) on 1 December 1997', 98/C 2/01.

[18] European Commission, 'Commissioner Šemeta launches Tax Policy Group to push forward fundamental issues in taxation' (Press Release Database, Brussels, 12 October 2010, IP/10/1312), http://europa.eu/rapid/press-release_IP-10-1312_en.htm, accessed 8 January 2020.

[19] European Commission, 'Role of the EU: An action plan to combat tax fraud and evasion', https://ec.europa.eu/taxation_customs/fight-against-tax-fraud-tax-evasion/role-eu_en, accessed 14 March 2020.

[20] European Commission, 'VAT', https://ec.europa.eu/taxation_customs/business/vat_en, accessed 8 January 2020.

[21] European Commission, 'Role of the EU: An action plan to combat tax fraud and evasion', https://ec.europa.eu/taxation_customs/fight-against-tax-fraud-tax-evasion/role-eu_en, accessed 14 March 2020.

[22] European Commission, 'The Fiscalis 2020 Programme', https://ec.europa.eu/taxation_customs/fiscalis-programme_en, accessed 8 January 2020.

[23] European Commission, 'Communication From the Commission to the European Parliament and the Council: An Action Plan to strengthen the fight against tax fraud and tax evasion' (SWD (2012) 403 final) (SWD(2012) 404 final) (Brussels, 6.12.2012 COM(2012) 722 final, https://ec.europa.eu/taxation_customs/sites/taxation/files/resources/documents/taxation/tax_fraud_evasion/com_2012_722_en.pdf, accessed 8 January 2020.

aim to ensure that tax revenues of MS are protected against aggressive tax planning,[24] tax havens in respect of good governance[25] and unfair competition.[26]

With the gamut of legal and technical measures, the EU appears to have developed a near-effective European toolbox that, when applied and harnessed by the EU Member States, can enhance the effectiveness of taxation in the EU Member States. In this regard, the EU has currently prioritised three targets:

- Member States of the EU should endeavour to 'make the necessary improvements to their national tax administrations and systems'.

- The second priority is to ensure that Member States of the EU fully utilise the current European toolbox.

- The third priority target is to see how new rules and instruments will be agreed upon by Member States to enhance the effectiveness of the current EU toolkits on tax crimes.

Research projects, financed through EU Horizon 2020 programme,[27] such as PROTAX,[28] which generates policy guidelines and toolkits to harmonise the treatment of tax crime and enhance information sharing across different European jurisdictions,[29] and COFFERS (Combatting Fiscal Fraud and Empowering Regulators)[30] are part of ground-breaking initiatives that can help EU in developing more effective toolkits for fighting tax crimes in EU Member States.

Although the EU has these measures, three key concerns arise from them. In the first place, there is much concentration on the administrative law measures than the core tax crime measures – in fact, the core measures that can meet the standards of criminal law are very limited and/or fairly weak in the anti-tax evasion and tax fraud dispensation of the EU. The approach of the EU to tax measures is to prefer administrative and technical tax crime counter-measures, rather than core criminal law measures. The second concern is that even though most of the measures are technical and administrative in nature and application, there is still a challenge of adequacy and effectiveness of these non-criminal law tax measures. The third concern is that there have been *no* clearly defined or organised principles for fighting tax crimes in the EU. The first and second concerns can be addressed by this book by isolating the criminal and administrative law elements and smartly examining the best pathways to effectively use them alongside each other. The third concern is addressed by this book by interfacing the TGPs with the EU tax crime measures to assess whether there are durable solutions for tax crimes in the horizon.

---

[24] European Commission, 'Commission Recommendation of 6.12.2012 on aggressive tax planning' (Brussels, 6.12.2012 C (2012) 8806 final, https://ec.europa.eu/taxation_customs/sites/taxation/files/resources/documents/taxation/tax_fraud_evasion/c_2012_8806_en.pdf, accessed 8 January 2020.

[25] Ibid.

[26] European Commission, 'Role of the EU: An action plan to combat tax fraud and evasion', https://ec.europa.eu/taxation_customs/fight-against-tax-fraud-tax-evasion/role-eu_en, accessed 14 March 2020.

[27] U Turksen and others, 'D1.2: Case Studies of Tax Crimes in the European Union' (EU PROTAX, 2018).

[28] PROTAX, 'PROTAX provides solutions for the prevention and prosecution of tax crimes' (EU Horizon 2020 Project), https://protax-project.eu/, accessed 16 March 2020.

[29] Ibid.

[30] COFFERS, 'About Coffers' (EU Horizon 2020 Project: Combating Fiscal Fraud and Empowering Regulators), https://coffers.eu/, accessed 16 March 2020.

However, while further remedies are being sought and current measures are being tried by the EU, the TGPs have brought forth an emerging global rule order (as minimum standards) on combating tax crimes. The existing EU measures and the measures being sought for could strategically adopt the principles into its delivery framework.

It is imperative that tax crime solutions are not made to be short-lived or temporary, or confined to EU borders. They must be designed with durability and global reach in mind. This is because tax offenders use complex and international processes and tools such as modern technology, aggressive tax planning and professional enablers to avoid and evade taxes in ways that require the proactive development of multifaceted approaches by political actors, law enforcement agencies (LEAs) and tax authorities to find durable solutions for such offences.[31] It is not yet clear if and to what extent the OECD's TGPs provide durable solutions for fighting tax crimes in the EU. However, they can be seen to provide the right direction.

From the foregoing, the subject area of this book focuses on the best solutions the TGPs can provide for efforts at generating the needed tax crime measures of the EU. The underlying question which the book presents for critical analysis is this: can the OECD global principles provide durable solutions for EU tax crime measures?

It will be interesting to see how the EU has incorporated the TGPs in its legal framework for finding durable solutions against tax crimes in the EU Member States. To enliven the uniqueness of this book, findings and data from empirical research are interspersed with academic rigour to generate germane perspectives on the interrelationship between the legal frameworks of the EU and OECD with respect to countering tax crimes.

Taxation is here to stay. As rightly posited by Benjamin Franklin (in a letter to M Leroy in 1789), 'in this world nothing is certain but death and *taxes*'.[32] It is argued in this book that, just as taxes have become a permanent feature in policy and legal frameworks, so will be most tax crimes and related resistance against payment of taxes. In effect, while tax crimes exist wherever there are taxes, tax evasion, tax fraud and related tax crimes are global phenomena which require global solutions.

This chapter provides the context, overview, and general approach of the book.

Understanding the Basics of Tax

Tax is a 'compulsory and unrequited payment made by a legal or natural person to the general government which includes supra-national authorities such as the EU, the central administration and the agencies whose operations are under its effective control, state and local governments and their administrations, social security schemes and autonomous governmental entities, excluding public enterprises'.[33] Tax is, thus, a levy that is imposed by the state upon the taxpayer.[34]

---

[31] G Gimdal, 'Aggressive tax planning' (The TAX 2 report, DG EPRS, EU Parliament, July 2016).

[32] D White, 'Taxes in the Ancient World' (2002) 48(28) *University of Pennsylvania Almanac*, https://almanac.upenn.edu/archive/v48/n28/AncientTaxes.html 20 March 2020.

[33] OECD, 'Negotiating Group on the Multilateral Agreement on Investment (MAI)' (Expert Group No 3 on Treatment of Tax Issues in the MAI, 19 April 1996), www.oecd.org/daf/mai/pdf/eg2/eg2963e.pdf, accessed 21 December 2019.

[34] Ibid.

Frunza adds that tax refers to 'a financial liability established and collected by a government or an equivalent agency', which has the mandate to impose tax levies on 'income, capital, resources, labour, goods and services'.[35] Dobrovič, Korauš and others further provide that, in formal and legal contexts, taxes can be seen as 'mandatory and statutory payments that taxpayers pay to the relevant public budget in a specified amount and by set deadlines'.[36] This definition adds emphasis to time, which obviously is implicitly recognised by other definitions of tax. In the financial and economic contexts, Dobrovič et al indicate the need to also appreciate taxes as characterising 'a fiscal relationship between a taxpayer and a state'. It is also imperative to define taxes from philosophical, cultural and humanistic perspectives, which would enable a holistic relationship to be built around tax law and enforcement in such a way as to integrate qualitative features of taxation.[37]

In fact, the ecosystem of tax is broad and varied across national, regional and international frontiers. Any tax system provides for institutional arrangements that seek to effectively administer taxes.[38] The tax system contains legal, regulatory, and technical institutions as well as 'tools, practices and methods' that are used in administering, assessing, enforcing and inspecting matters on taxes.[39] Kreissl reveals that the tax environment provides for interconnected elements.[40] The payments made by the taxpayer exclude fines that are not related 'to tax offences and compulsory loans paid to government'.[41] In terms of being unrequited payments, taxes are so because the contention by some taxpayers and critics in many countries is that the 'benefits provided by government to taxpayers are not normally in proportion to their payments'.[42] The tax law compels applicable persons to make payments to the government treasury. Failure to pay taxes will attract sanctions and/or penalties.[43]

Direct and indirect taxes are the two main categories of taxes. Direct tax is simply a levy on income or profits of a person (whether legal or natural) who directly makes payment thereof to the responsible government institution, while excluding levies on goods or services. The imposition of the levy affects only the final supply to the consumer. The tax imposing or receiving institution receives the payment directly from the person upon whom the tax has been levied.

---

[35] M-C Frunza, *Value added tax fraud* (Routledge, 2019) 1.

[36] J Dobrovič and others, 'Action plan on sustainability of fight against tax fraud and tax evasion: EU countries comparison' (2019) 12(4) *Journal of International Studies* 272, 274; A Korauš and others, 'The impact of monetary variables on the economic growth and sustainable development: case of selected countries' (2017) 6(3) *Journal of Security and Sustainability Issues* 383.

[37] Ibid.

[38] Ibid.

[39] Ibid.

[40] R Kreissl and others, 'D1.1 – The Case Study Design: Guideline and template for case studies on tax crimes in Europe' (PROTAX, 2018).

[41] See OECD, 'Negotiating Group on the Multilateral Agreement on Investment (MAI)' (Expert Group No 3 on Treatment of Tax Issues in the MAI, 19 April 1996), www.oecd.org/daf/mai/pdf/eg2/eg2963e.pdf, accessed 21 December 2019.

[42] Ibid.

[43] Ibid.

Direct taxes include personal income tax, capital gains taxes, inheritance/estate taxes, admission fees to national parks, gift taxes, real property tax and corporate taxes. Income tax is a particularly prominent example of direct tax. This is because the person that earns the income is immediately responsible for paying the tax. Corporate taxes, which are taxes that corporations and other businesses (usually other than sole proprietorships and partnerships in a number of jurisdictions) are required to pay on earned profits to the government, have gained a lot of attraction due to the growth of businesses over time. Essentially, direct taxes are either directly levied on/and paid by an individual or a business of corporate nature. Thus, direct taxes can be either corporate taxes or personal taxes.

Indirect taxes are taxes levied or imposed on goods/products and services while excluding income or profits from the goods/products or services. However, the consumer eventually pays for the tax levied. Thus, the amount of tax that is levied on goods or services is passed on to the consumer as part of the purchase price of the good/product or service. Indirect taxes include:

- Import duties (very common form), which impose an obligation on an importer of a good to pay a duty at the time the good makes entry into the destination country. This payment is hidden in the price of the product that is sold to the consumer. Even if it is indicated as part of the selling price to the consumer, the consumer ultimately buys the good as a whole without necessarily considering the cost contribution of the import duty.

- Tax on carbon emissions by manufacturers.

- Excise taxes or 'sin taxes', such as taxes on fuel, tobacco, gambling and liquor.

- Consumption taxes, such as value added tax (VAT) charged on most goods and services traded.[44]

- Indirect sales taxes, which are imposed as VAT in the course of the production.

VAT is a prominent indirect tax. The OECD defines VAT as:[45]

> Any national tax by whatever name or acronym it is known, such as Goods and Services Tax (GST), which embodies the basic features of a value added tax, i.e. a broad-based tax on final consumption collected from, but in principle not borne by, businesses through a staged collection process, whatever method is used for determining the tax liability (e.g. invoice-credit method or subtraction method).[46]

Thus, whereas direct taxes are those that are directly imposed on the income or wealth of a person, indirect taxes are those that are levied on the price of goods and/or services.

---

[44] Frunza, *Value added tax fraud*, 1.

[45] For details about the tax system in EU legislative framework on VAT, see Council Directive 2006/112/EC of 28 November 2006 on the common system of value added tax ([2006] OJ L 347/1–118; see also consolidated version as of 1 January 2020 at: Council Directive 2006/112/EC of 28 November 2006 on the common system of value added tax, https://eur-lex.europa.eu/legal-content/EN/TXT/PDF/?uri=CELEX:02006L0112-20200101&from=EN, accessed 8 January 2020.

[46] Recommendation of the Council on the Application of Value Added Tax/Goods and Services Tax to the International Trade in Services and Intangibles, adopted on 27 September 2016, art I, https://legalinstruments.oecd.org/en/instruments/OECD-LEGAL-0430, accessed 7 May 2020.

The levy of a tax can generally be computed by using two key elements: 1) the tax base, representing the nominal value upon which the assessment of tax liability is made, and 2) the tax rate, which is presented generally as a percentage.[47]

Whether a tax is direct or indirect, the framework that operationalises the rates, rules, limits and dimensions of every tax is founded on law. Thus, a legal and regulatory framework for taxation is established and regularly refreshed in every country to reflect current trends and public policy priorities. In tax law, levying of taxes is done in accord with fundamental principles of taxation and after the legislature and the executive make careful policy choices from array of alternative courses of action that can address the purpose the tax seeks to achieve.[48] Governments face difficult law and policy choices in not only levying taxes but also in countering criminal offences on these taxes.

The complexities that come with these taxes contribute to the difficulties faced by tax authorities and other law enforcement agencies (LEAs) in countering tax crimes. Tax fraud such as VAT fraud, which refers to a conduct whereby taxpayer(s) take steps to illegally evade their tax liability,[49] is one of the critical features of tax crimes[50] that would require proactive and adjustable measures in both the EU and OECD countries.

The nature and variety of the taxes and the crimes associated with them are historically, culturally and politically driven.[51] This disposition is a product of many years of experience, which taxpayers and tax authorities have developed within culturally acceptable frameworks[52] that generate relevant legitimacy for authorities and tax morale for taxpayers.

Historical Context of Tax and Tax Crimes

Taxes started with direct taxation (later expanded to many variants thereof)[53] and indirect taxes.[54] It is not settled,[55] but the history of taxes can be traced back to the Assyrian Empire. There is evidence of taxation in tablets from as far back as the eighth century BC, whereby the Assyrian Empire levied taxes on caravans entering its territory.[56]

---

[47] Frunza, *Value added tax fraud*,1.

[48] Fiscalis Tax Gap Project Group (FPG/041), 'The Concept of Tax Gaps Report on VAT Gap Estimations' (Brussels, European Commission, March 2016) 13, https://ec.europa.eu/taxation_customs/sites/taxation/files/docs/body/tgpg_report_en.pdf, 20 March 2020.

[49] J Dvořáček and L Tyll, *Outsourcing and offshoring business activities* (CH Beck, 2010).

[50] OECD, 'Technology Tools to Tackle Tax Evasion and Tax Fraud' (2017) 6, www.oecd.org/tax/crime/technology-tools-to-tackle-tax-evasion-and-tax-fraud.pdf, accessed 25 February 2020.

[51] T Besley, A Jensen and T Persson, 'Norms, Enforcement, and Tax Evasion' (NBER Working Paper No 25575, February 2019), www.lse.ac.uk/economics/Assets/Documents/personal-pages/tim-besley/working-papers/norms-enforcement-and-tax-evasion.pdf, accessed 15 March 2020.

[52] EA Posner, 'Law and Social Norms: The Case of Tax Compliance' (2000) 86 *Virginia Law Review* 1781–1819.

[53] Direct tax is simply a levy on income or profits of a person (whether legal or natural) who directly makes payment thereof to the responsible government institution.

[54] Indirect taxes are taxes levied or imposed on goods/products and services while excluding income or profits from the goods/products or services.

[55] Different accounts have been given of the earliest date of taxes in ancient times.

[56] See AJ Dani and J-P Mohen, *History of Humanity: From the third millennium to the seventh century BC* (Vol II, Routledge, 1996); P Steinkeller and M Hudson, *Labor in the Ancient World* (Vol V, ISLET-Verlag,

However, ancient Egypt arguably has been deemed to be the place where the first modern taxation happened. This was around 3,000–2,800 BC, in the Old Kingdom of Egypt.[57] The *corvée* and tithe were the earliest and most common forms of taxation. Whereas the *corvée* was a forced labour of peasants[58] for the state, the tithe was one-tenth of something that was paid as a compulsory tax to the government or a religious contribution to a religious entity.[59] In ancient Egypt, Pharaoh was said to lead forces to collect tithes from the public in his kingdom.[60] These were essentially direct taxes. With time, various kingdoms, subsequently, countries and related jurisdictions, developed their own forms of taxation.

In the United States, for example, in 1913, the modern differentiation between direct taxes such as personal income tax and latter-day indirect taxes was occasioned by the enactment of the 16th Amendment.[61] Hitherto, tax law only recognised direct taxes which needed to be apportioned directly to the population in a given jurisdiction. With the 16th Amendment, the tax law was changed to ensure that both direct and indirect taxes were levied. Other jurisdictions in the world increasingly saw the need to expand the tax basket to include indirect taxes. One of the indirect taxes that later received a lot of patronage in tax law was the VAT.

France is said to have introduced the 'first modern VAT' on 10 April 1954. Although the initial idea of VAT came from Germany in 1918, the nature of VAT introduced in France saw 'for the first time in the modern economy a situation where tax collection burden was taken off from tax authorities and retailers and placed upon taxpayers'.[62] By the 1960s, many European countries were attracted by the VAT concept and started its implementation in earnest. Essentially, VAT is a levy on 'the difference between the total turnover and total purchases from another business'.[63] It measures 'the added value at an aggregate level over a period of time'.[64] What happens, in effect, is that the charge of VAT is imposed on 'registered businesses and final non-business customers … [who] do not pay the VAT directly to the government but to B-to-C [business to client] companies'.[65] Given the dimension of fraud, some argue that the current rules that define VAT 'are not fit for purpose'.[66]

2015); see also C Michel, 'The Old Assyrian Trade in the light of Recent Kültepe Archives' [2008] *Journal of the Canadian Society for Mesopotamian Studies* 71–82.

[57] D White, 'Taxes in the Ancient World' (2002) 48(28) *University of Pennsylvania Almanac*, https://almanac.upenn.edu/archive/v48/n28/AncientTaxes.html, accessed 20 March 2020.

[58] These peasants were deemed so poor that they could not pay other forms of tax. The synonym for labour in ancient Egypt was taxation.

[59] DF Burg, *A World History of Tax Rebellions: An Encyclopaedia of Tax Rebels, Revolts, and Riots from Antiquity to the Present* (Taylor & Francis, 2004) vi–viii.

[60] M Olmert, *Milton's Teeth and Ovid's Umbrella: Curiouser and Curiouser Adventures in History* (Simon and Schuster, 1996).

[61] United States Senate, *Constitution of the United States* 1788, www.senate.gov/civics/constitution_item/constitution.htm#amdt_16_%281913%29, accessed 20 March 2020.

[62] J Dobrovič and others, 'Action plan on sustainability of fight against tax fraud and tax evasion: EU countries comparison' (2019) 12(4) *Journal of International Studies* 272, 274; R Arp, *1001 Ideas that Changed the Way We Think* (Atria Books, 2013).

[63] Dobrovič and others, 'Action plan on sustainability', 274; RF van Brederode, *Systems of General Sales Taxation: Theory, Policy and Practice* (Kluwer Law International, 2009).

[64] Ibid.

[65] Frunza, *Value added tax fraud*, 1.

[66] Frunza, *Value added tax fraud*.

The primary and traditional aim of tax is to raise the needed revenue for financing the expenditures of the public (in fact, aside credit, taxes are historically the most critical source of raising revenue for the general government).[67] In the nineteenth century, the notion of tax mainly serving as a source of finance to the government was particularly prevalent. Hitherto, and up to today, governments have been predisposed to using taxes for both fiscal purposes and other purposes such as trade competition, public policy (eg, high tax on tobacco and alcohol to reduce consumption), which altogether can be categorised into five main purposes – allocation of resources, income redistribution, economic stability, economic growth or development, and international competitiveness.[68] Taxes are, by these objectives, a means through which government can achieve its goals.[69]

Thus, taxation has historically been linked to a source of power and sovereignty for governments to generate revenues from the economic activities and possessions of people associated with their jurisdictions to enable them finance public budget which pays for the goods and services that the state offers. Taxes, therefore, serve as the principal revenue source for funding national budget of countries such as Malta, Italy, Estonia, Austria, Ireland, Portugal, Spain, France, Germany, the United Kingdom and United States or a region such as the EU.[70] The Declaration of the Rights of Man and the Citizen 1789 provides that taxes are 'indispensable for the maintenance of the public force and for the expenses of administration; it ought to be equally shared between all citizens, according to their means'.[71]

This declaration articulates the 'ability to pay', as an important feature of taxation which can contribute to the level of compliance by taxpayers. Thus, imposition of taxes must take cognisance of the capacity of the taxpayer to pay the levied amount without being unduly affected adversely – such as making the taxpayer increasingly worst off. One of the salient elements in this declaration is, therefore, the emphasis placed on the principle of equality in taxation. The declaration also reinforces taxation as a resource for social and economic development. Integral to the relationship in taxation is also the collaborative (solidarity) principle, which appeals to authorities to consult, partner and cooperate with taxpayers in designing and enforcing tax rules. If served well by governments, the overarching purpose of taxes regarding public financing and economic management is evidently aligned to the stitching realities of public good.

A couple of strategic interests and drivers have been attributed to growth of patterns and size of taxes over time. Throughout history, at the heart of the concern taxpayers mull over is that taxes impose an additional financial burden on their assets, capital and profits, thereby adversely affecting desirable outturns of their financial plans. The constellation of forces surrounding the diversity associated with complexities,

---

[67] MS Cox, CE McLure and F Neumark, 'Taxation' (*Encyclopædia Britannica*, 18 October 2019), www.britannica.com/topic/taxation, accessed 14 April 2020.

[68] Ibid.

[69] Dobrovič and others, 'Action plan on sustainability', 274; A Krauš and others, 'The impact of monetary variables on the economic growth and sustainable development: case of selected countries' (2017) 6(3) *Journal of Security and Sustainability Issues* 383.

[70] Frunza, *Value added tax fraud*, 1.

[71] The Declaration of the Rights of Man and of the Citizen, 26 August 1789 (French: *Déclaration des droits de l'homme et du citoyen de 1789*), art XIII.

justification, legitimacy and effects of taxes have brought into its fold a long-standing history of resistance by many taxpayers to meet their tax obligations. This resistance has usually escalated to contravene the tax laws of jurisdiction(s) in question – both by the process of failing to pay and by the failure to pay taxes to the general government. The reluctance to pay tax, together with the conduct of taxpayers hiding their income and wealth so as not to pay taxes on them, are ancient phenomena popularly known, today, as tax evasion and tax fraud.

Techniques Employed in Tax Crimes

The techniques of evading taxes, such as misreporting, under-reporting, over-reporting, falsification of documents, using tax havens and employing offshore bank accounts, started a long time ago in many jurisdictions.[72] One of the countries that first provided infrastructure for secrecy in banking, which created a convenient hidden place and escape route for tax criminals, was Switzerland in the eighteenth century around 1713, when 'The Great Council of Geneva' enacted legislation which sought to prevent banking institutions from sharing information on clients with others.[73] Switzerland is famous for its pioneering role in protecting secrecy for tax havens.[74]

By the end of the nineteenth century,[75] Switzerland allowed banks to offer numbered bank accounts.[76] Numbered bank accounts characterised a system whereby the account holder's identity was substituted with a multi-digit number, which was known only to the client and the specified private banking personnel handling the client in question. The introduction of the numbered bank accounts added another layer of secrecy to banking in Switzerland, which enabled bank clients in Europe to evade the payment of taxes.[77]

This banking practice became widespread in Swiss banks when the Federal Act on Banks and Savings Banks of Switzerland 1934 (the Swiss Banking Law 1934)[78] was enacted. When, in the 1980s, Germany and France applied pressure on Switzerland to allow disclosure of customer information, in the midst of capital flight in Europe, Switzerland rather heightened the cord of sovereignty by enacting this legislation that

[72] OECD, 'Technology Tools to Tackle Tax Evasion and Tax Fraud' (2017) 6, www.oecd.org/tax/crime/technology-tools-to-tackle-tax-evasion-and-tax-fraud.pdf, accessed 25 February 2020.

[73] M Koba, 'Swiss Bank Accounts: Separating Fact from Fiction', *CNBC* (Fat Cat Living, 20 August 2008), www.cnbc.com/id/26182063, accessed 11 July 2020; Tax Justice Network, 'Financial Secrecy Index 2020: Narrative Report on Switzerland', https://fsi.taxjustice.net/PDF/Switzerland.pdf, accessed 24 March 2020.

[74] Tax Justice Network, 'Financial Secrecy Index 2020', www.taxjustice.net/2020/02/18/financial-secrecy-index-2020-reports-progress-on-global-transparency-but-backsliding-from-us-cayman-and-uk-prompts-call-for-sanctions/, accessed 15 May 2020.

[75] LY Gelemerova, *The anti-money laundering system in the context of globalisation: a Panopticon built on quicksand?* (Wolf Legal Publishers, 2011) 30, www.semanticscholar.org/paper/The-anti-money-laundering-system-in-the-context-of-Gelemerova/0ed482bb1b4cc02aba0ecaa7b20ef8c898ccf4bb, accessed 14 April 2020; see also J Robinson, *The sink: Terror, Crime and Dirty Money in the Offshore World* (Constable & Robinson, 2003).

[76] Ibid.

[77] D Schütz, *The Fall of UBS: The Forces that Brought Down Switzerland's Biggest Bank* (Pyramid Media Group Inc, 2006).

[78] Swiss Federal Act on Banks and Savings Banks (Banking Act) of 8 November 1934.

made divulging of customer information a criminal offence. This protective position for banks' clients was supported, in 1984, by a majority of Swiss citizens, about 73 per cent of whom voted in favour of maintaining the secrecy regime in Switzerland.[79]

As time went by, some of the Swiss banks began to supplement clients' numbered accounts with code names, such as 'Octopussy',[80] 'Cardinal',[81] or 'Cello',[82] which alternatively identified the client, but could still only be understood by those bankers close to the client's banking transactions. These accounts did not provide complete anonymity for the client, since the client's name would be saved by the bank while being subject to a disclosure that is limited and reasonable or justifiable. Yet, ultimately, banking clients found this a useful platform to hide their wealth and income, and thereby to evade payment of taxes.

Albeit with some minor improvement in transparency, the numbered bank account system still exists in Switzerland along with other countries in Europe such as Austria, Luxembourg and Cyprus. In order to register a numbered or alternatively code named bank account,[83] Swiss law now requires banks to conduct a multi-stage clearance investigation of clients in order to ascertain, among other things, the lawful origins of clients' assets.[84] In most cases, thus, a customer background check is required to be conducted by the bank to ascertain and confirm who the customer really is. In other parts of Europe and countries in the EU, the Americas (including Panama, Cayman Islands and Belize), Asia-Pacific (including Hong Kong, Singapore, UAE and Lebanon) and Africa (eg, Liberia) that provide legal space for the operation of numbered accounts,[85] banks are required to ensure that their clients go through strict vetting processes and to declare who the beneficial owner is.[86]

In almost all countries that permit this practice of numbered bank accounts, clients are prohibited from using fake names to open numbered bank accounts. This is particularly so in Switzerland, the United States, some countries in the EU, and other offshore financial centres. Other formalities such as signing of document that seal the relationship between the bank and the account holder are a requirement for opening the numbered bank account in most cases.[87]

However, because numbered bank accounts are often linked to the proclivity for clients to minimise monitoring by government and to evade or avoid payment of taxes, there are many jurisdictions that have prohibited banks from operating such accounts.

---

[79] Koba, 'Swiss Bank Accounts'.
[80] L Browning, 'Names Deal Cracks Swiss Bank Secrecy', *The New York Times* (Global Business, August 2009), www.nytimes.com/2009/08/20/business/global/20ubs.html, accessed 11 March 2020.
[81] D Enrich 'A Swiss Banker Helped Americans Dodge Taxes. Was It a Crime?' *The New York Times* (6 January 2018), www.nytimes.com/2018/01/06/business/stefan-buck-tax-evasion.html, accessed 11 March 2020.
[82] Browning, 'Names Deal'.
[83] Offshore Manual, 'Swiss Numbered Bank Account', www.offshore-manual.com/SwissNumbered.html, accessed 11 March 2020.
[84] Koba, 'Swiss Bank Accounts'.
[85] See 2019 numbered bank accounts across the world at: GT Offshore Shield, 'Numbered Bank Account in Andorra 2020: Asset Protection', https://offshoreshield.globaltradersacademy.org/en/numbered-bank-accounts/andorra/, accessed 26 March 2020.
[86] Koba, 'Swiss Bank Accounts'.
[87] Offshore Manual, 'Swiss Numbered Bank Account'.

The existing numbered bank accounts in some jurisdictions are usually fraught with laws and regulations, but the deeply private nature of the accounts provides layers of opportunities to be used to compromise tax system – unlike the normal or traditional bank accounts which are not as heavily private.

For instance, in Switzerland, it remains unlawful for bankers to make a disclosure to any government agency or other persons of whether a bank account is numbered or not until proof of deliberate fraud has been established and/or a permission is sought from the client. If there is a failure to report assets so as to avoid or evade the payment of taxes (as long as no intentional fraud is detected), bankers are still not required to make a disclosure, due to client confidentiality requirements. A banker can risk being sentenced to prison if s/he discloses client information or whistle-blows without their consent or without detection of deliberate fraud. The numbered accounts are only part of a cocktail of financial secrecy protection measures in Switzerland and other countries that provide safe havens for hiding of assets that make it possible for tax crimes to be committed.

As it stands, Tax Justice Network's Financial Secrecy Index (FSI), which measures the level of protection given to bank secrets or the lack of financial transparency, has consistently placed Switzerland as one of the top secrecy regimes for banks in the world. The 2020 FSI, for instance, ranked Switzerland as the third out of 133 countries in the world for protecting financial secrets – on account of Switzerland's 'high secrecy score of 74 and a large global scale weight for the size of offshore financial services (4.12 per cent of the global market).'[88] The FSI analysis shows that the popular banking secrecy laws continue to operate even though Switzerland's move towards automatic exchange of information on tax (AEOI) through the Common Reporting Standard (CRS) has begun to vitiate the Swiss banking secrecy regime.[89]

For instance, PROTAX research into the tax crimes related whistle-blower legal framework in Switzerland highlighted the peculiar case of Hervé Falciani, whose status as whistle-blower was arguable because of the whole financial secrecy architecture and the lack of any definition of a whistle-blower in the Swiss legal framework.

Box 1 The Falciani Case

In 2014, the Swiss Criminal Federal Court held against Falciani for four offences:

1. *Aggravated economic/industrial espionage.*[90]
2. *Unauthorised obtaining of data.*[91]
3. *Breach of business secrecy.*[92]
4. *Violation of banking secrecy.*[93]

(continued)

---

[88] Tax Justice Network, 'Financial Secrecy Index 2020'.
[89] Ibid.
[90] Swiss Criminal Code of 21 December 1937 (Status as of 3 March 2020), Art 273(2).
[91] Ibid, Art 143(1).
[92] Ibid, Art 162.
[93] Ibid, Art 47.

Box 1 *(Continued)*

Disclosing confidential employer information or trade secrets is viewed by the Swiss Courts as a criminal offence.[94] This is particularly so in the case of bank secrecy in Article 47 of the Swiss Banking Act 1934.

In 2016, the Swiss Supreme Court sentenced Falciani in absentia to a five-year jail term for aggravated economic espionage,[95] which provides that: 'Any person who seeks to obtain a manufacturing or trade secret in order to make it available to an external official agency, a foreign organisation, a private enterprise, or the agents of any of these, or, any person who makes a manufacturing or trade secret available to a foreign official agency, a foreign organisation, a private enterprise, or the agents of any of these, is liable to a custodial sentence not exceeding three years or to a monetary penalty, or in serious cases to a custodial sentence of not less than one year. Any custodial sentence may be combined with a monetary penalty.'[96]

The accused had pleaded guilty to breaching Swiss law: 'Yes, I broke the law. But I broke a law that harms all of us.'[97] In effect, Falciani was a criminal who stole HSBC's confidential client data, thereby breaching Swiss criminal law and the Swiss Code of Obligations. He did not utilise HSBC's whistle-blowing hotline and passed the data to French and German authorities.

Essentially, revealing secrets of financial institutions has been criminalised in Switzerland. In this case, Falciani was, however, cleared of data theft, breach of business and banking secrecy.[98] The prohibitions are formulated in a way that makes protection of financial secrets extreme, as found in the 2020 Financial Secrecy Index (FSI) by Tax Justice Network.[99] According to the French prosecutor, Eric de Montgolfier, for the Swiss, 'Falciani's attack on the data was not merely an attack on the bank. It was an attack on the whole of Switzerland.' The disclosure enabled exposure of tax evasion and fraud in Europe and beyond.

The Swiss Code of Obligations 1911[100] bolsters this protective culture of bank secrecy. Article 321a of the Swiss Code of Obligations states that: 'The employee must perform the work assigned to him with due care and loyally safeguard the employer/'s legitimate interests.' This duty of loyalty continues after termination of contract under Article 334 of Swiss Code of Obligations 1911. As such, the

(continued)

---

[94] Turksen and others, 'D1.2: Case Studies'.

[95] Swiss Criminal Code 1937 (Status as of 3 March 2020), Art 273(2).

[96] Ibid, Art 273 (subject to amendments regarding sanctions: Penalties revised by No II 1 para 16 of the FA of 13 Dec 2002, in force since 1 Jan 2007 (AS 2006 3459 3535; BBl 1999 1979); Turksen and others, 'D1.2: Case Studies'.

[97] Turksen and others, 'D1.2: Case Studies'.

[98] Ibid.

[99] Tax Justice Network, 'Financial Secrecy Index 2020'.

[100] Federal Act on the Amendment of the Swiss Civil Code (Part Five: The Code of Obligations) of 30 March 1911 (Status as of 1 January 2020), www.admin.ch/opc/en/classified-compilation/19110009/202004010000/220.pdf, accessed 11 February 2020.

Box 1 *(Continued)*

> *inherent ethos of Swiss legislation has been very protective of the employer and secrets thereof. Recently however, there have been marginal improvements in data transparency and whistle-blower protection in Switzerland.*[101]

As far back as 1932 in France, when a political scandal concerning the French elite broke out, large-scale tax evasion was exposed and the wide utilisation of the secret Swiss banking system was highlighted. Known as the 'Paris affair' or the 'Basler Handelsbank affair', this case was investigated by the French police who 'discovered a list with about 2000 names of French citizens, including politicians, judges, bishops, generals and wealthy industrialists, who were hiding their money in Switzerland'[102] as a safe haven for possible evasion of taxes. What this implies is that the recent upsurge in tax evasion cases, such as the Liechtenstein case,[103] has historical undertones.

Box 2a The Liechtenstein Accounts Case

> *This case occurred in Liechtenstein, which is a microstate bordering Switzerland from the east. Since 1868, this Swiss neighbour has 'become a close appendage of Switzerland in terms of the mechanics of secrecy structures'.*[104] *The exposure in question revealed that hundreds of wealthy German tax evaders had hidden millions of euros in bank accounts in Liechtenstein. The German intelligence service was reported to have made payments to an informant amounting to EUR 4.2 million. The informant was a former employee of Liechtenstein banking group, LGT. The purpose of the payments to the informant was to obtain the incriminating list of tax evaders that was alleged to have been stolen from LGT. In the same vein, it was reported that the United Kingdom also made payments to a whistle-blower amounting to £100,000. The whistle-blower was tasked to extract details of Liechtenstein accounts held by Britons. This move came after earlier refusing to make payment for relevant information. This case brought up a scandal which raised the issue of the ethics and accountability of the highly paid business elite in Germany and other places. The case also ignited a debate about the way information was obtained and then shared with the authorities of other countries. LGT appeared to be displeased with the methods, 'describing [them] as illegal and extremely offensive'.*[105] *In view of the complexities associated with tax crimes and secrecy regimes, the questionable methods for detecting the offences sometimes become potent tools to close in on the tax criminals, even if some fundamental rights may have been adversely impacted in doing so.*

---

[101] Turksen and others, 'D1.2: Case Studies'.
[102] Gelemerova, *The anti-money laundering system*; DW staff (sp), 'Liechtenstein Tax Scandal Spreads across Europe' (Business, 25 February 2008), www.dw-world.de/dw/article/0,3148308,00.html accessed 11 March 2020.
[103] DW staff (sp), 'Liechtenstein Tax Scandal'.
[104] Tax Justice Network, 'Financial Secrecy Index 2020'.
[105] Gelemerova, *The anti-money laundering system*; DW staff (sp), 'Liechtenstein Tax Scandal'.

Essentially, citizens of many countries that seek to evade taxation have continued to find the Swiss banking secrecy protection regime and that of related safe havens highly attractive. However, the banking secrecy regime in Switzerland (conveniently located in the middle of Europe) and along with other such secrecy jurisdictions offer a bad standard all too well and good for tax offenders. Any traces of the kind of Swiss financial sector secrecy in other jurisdictions offer an attractive platform for proceeds from tax crimes to flourish – making the fight against tax crimes challenging across many jurisdictions. Looking to the future, the nature of resilience shown by tax crimes can still present a threat to policy and law[106] – including their effects on LEAs, whistle-blowers and the media investigators.

Government Response

Governments have increasingly sponsored tax policies, laws and enforcement mechanisms that suppress and/or eliminate the resistance of taxpayers to the discharge of their tax obligations. Across time, both criminal and civil laws have been used to address infractions and delinquencies in the tax justice administration framework.

From the traditional standpoint, tax offences were not always classified as crimes as such, therefore were dealt with under administrative/civil law provisions and processes. It was not until the beginning of the twentieth century that authorities, particularly in the United States, found it necessary to assign a penal criminality to tax evasion and tax fraud.

When the Chicago Crime Commission published a list of 28 notorious gangsters in 1930, Alphonse Capone was top on the list. The Chicago Crime Commission demanded the prosecution of these gangsters, regarded as public enemies, using 'all possible legal means'.[107] This step characterised an initiative that was significant in the personification of organised crime, primarily due to how the Commission made reference to the public status of the gangsters as criminals, instead of referring just to the specific crimes of the gangsters. While the intention was to explore different criminal offences from the gangsters' public status as criminals, at this point in time, it was likely 'less possible to prove any crime other than tax evasion'.[108]

The effectiveness of tax evasion prosecution had begun to take shape after the US Supreme Court's decision in 1927 to the effect that illegal earnings were also subject to taxation. It was on the back of the 1927 Supreme Court's decision, and the the work of Chicago Crime Commission, that the popular Al Capone case was prosecuted. Al Capone was indicted with tax evasion amounting to more than $250,000 on unreported income between 1924 and 1929.[109] Prosecution in the case, therefore, argued that Al Capone should be convicted as a tax evader – rather than the gangsterism Al Capone was known and pursued for.[110]

---

[106] Ibid.
[107] Ibid.
[108] Ibid.
[109] Ibid. Also see, D Larry Crumbley and N Apostolou, 'America's first (and most fearless) high-profile forensic accountant' (September/October 2007) *The Value Examiner* 16, 18, www.bus.lsu.edu/accounting/faculty/lcrumbley/AlCapone.pdf, accessed 11 March 2020.
[110] Gelemerova, *The anti-money laundering system?*.

In 1931 Al Capone was prosecuted, convicted and sentenced to 11 years in prison with fines amounting to $250,000 (around $4 million in today's value) and costs totalling $30,000. Prosecutors succeeded in demonstrating that Al Capone lived lavishly, although he claimed he did not earn any income and had never filed tax returns. Prosecutors were also able to link Al Capone with proceeds from a gambling operation.

From the 1990s, the scope for governments to counter crime was widened to significantly encapsulate the establishment of deterrent measures such as the confiscation of proceeds of crime and imposition of stiffer punishments. Further steps have since been taken by many governments to include crime prevention and early detection measures. For instance, suspicious transaction or activity reporting systems by the regulated sectors have made it possible for the investigation of illicit financial flows (IFFs) to detect the potential occurrence of underlying criminal offences such as tax crimes and money laundering even before such crimes are committed.[111]

Hitherto, criminal law had concentrated efforts in trying to solve crimes. That is, instead of preventing and discouraging crime, it was traditionally the preoccupation of governments to seek to bring culprits to book without necessarily considering the whole ecosystem of countering the intricacies surrounding the crime. More recently, tax offences have been included as criminal acts in the penal code of many countries (including the OECD and EU Member States) and designated as predicate crimes under the anti-money laundering legal frameworks.[112] Tax evasion and tax fraud have thus been integrated into the ecosystem of criminal or penal law in order to enhance the integrity and wealth of taxation.

All forms of tax non-compliance, including tax fraud, tax evasion, tax avoidance and aggressive tax planning exist across all types of taxpayers and taxes.[113] They also can easily extend across frontiers without being noticed.

Historically, the OECD has been one of the key international institutions responding to challenges posed by tax crimes. In particular, the OECD Oslo Dialogue launched the first Forum on Tax and Crime, in March 2011. The second International Forum on Tax and Crime was held in Rome between 14 and 15 June 2012. The third International

---

[111] OECD, *Money Laundering and Terrorist Financing Awareness Handbook for Tax Examiners and Tax Auditors* (OECD, 2019), www.oecd.org/tax/crime/money-laundering-and-terrorist-financing-awareness-handbook-for-tax-examiners-and-tax-auditors.pdf, accessed 19 December 2019; The World Bank, 'Illicit Financial Flows (IFFs)' (Brief, 7 July 2017), www.worldbank.org/en/topic/financialsector/brief/illicit-financial-flows-iffs, accessed 12 December 2019.

[112] Directive (EU) 2018/1673 of the European Parliament and of the Council of 23 October 2018 on combating money laundering by criminal law, PE/30/2018/REV/1 [2018] OJ L 284/22–30; Directive (EU) 2018/843 of the European Parliament and of the Council of 30 May 2018 amending Directive (EU) 2015/849 on the prevention of the use of the financial system for the purposes of money laundering or terrorist financing, and amending Directives 2009/138/EC and 2013/36/EU, [2009] OJ L 156/43; Council Framework Decision 2001/500/JHA of 26 June 2001 on money laundering, the identification, tracing, freezing, seizing and confiscation of instrumentalities and the proceeds of crime, [2001] OJ L 182/1–2; see also U Turksen, 'Implications of Anti-Money Laundering Law for Accountancy in the European Union – A Comparative Study' in N Ryder and others (eds), *Fighting Financial Crime in the Global Economic Crisis* (Routledge, 2015) 75–109; E Savona and M Riccardi, 'Assessing the risk of money laundering in Europe' (Final Report of Project IARM, April 2017); C Collovà, 'Prevention of the use of the financial system for the purposes of money laundering or terrorist financing' (DG EPRS, EU Parliament, October 2016).

[113] HM Treasury and HM Revenues & Customs, *Tackling tax avoidance, evasion, and other forms of non-compliance* (Crown, March 2019) 7, https://assets.publishing.service.gov.uk/government/uploads/system/uploads/attachment_data/file/785551/tackling_tax_avoidance_evasion_and_other_forms_of_non-compliance_web.pdf accessed 18 July 2020.

Forum on Tax and Crime was held in Istanbul between 7 and 8 November 2013. The fourth OECD Forum on Tax and Crime was held in Amsterdam between 16 and 17 September 2015. The fifth OECD Forum on Tax and Crime took place in London from 7 to 8 November 2017.[114] Essentially, these five forums, so far within a decade, have advanced the need for executing the operational theme known as 'a whole of government approach to fighting tax crimes and illicit flows'. This theme is partly built on the following proposition:

> Countering these activities requires greater transparency, more effective intelligence gathering and analysis, and **improvements in co-operation and information sharing between government agencies and between countries** to prevent, detect and prosecute criminals and recover the proceeds of their illicit activities.[115]

In effect, the Oslo Dialogue is an international policy initiative by the OECD in partnership with international platforms such as the G20 and the World Bank. It aims at promoting a 'whole-of-government approach' (ie considering all competent agencies of the general government) to countering tax crimes and other financial crimes in the world. The Dialogue has since held five additional meetings with a focus on two key items:

i.   To tackle issues at the forefront of the global fight against illicit financial flows.[116]
ii.   To focus on practical measures governments can take to ensure cross-agency implementation of the Ten Global Principles for combatting tax crimes and other financial crimes.[117]

The second item is very germane to this book, since it will zero in on the TGPs with regards to the additional measures which jurisdictions can practically take to enhance inter-agency collaboration in the implementation of the TGPs. The first item is equally critical because it will further give opportunity for practitioners to see how the illicit financial flows – which provide a complicated ecosystem for tax crimes – can be effectively countered.

The publication of the TGPs in 2017 thus followed many years of efforts by the OECD to establish a robust framework for fighting tax crimes. The Fifth OECD forum on tax and crime produced the report that established the TGPs, along with the publication of a second report, titled 'Effective Inter-Agency Cooperation in Fighting Tax Crimes and Other Financial Crimes'[118] that narrates and offers recommendations on the present situation of successful law and practice in 51 states regarding 'domestic inter-agency cooperation to combat tax crimes and other financial crimes such as corruption' (or bribery).[119] Over 200 experts on tax and economic crimes from across the globe in

---

[114] OECD, 'Save the date: Sixth OECD Forum on Tax and Crime: Strengthening our Foundations: Intensifying the Global Response to Tax Crimes and Other Financial Crimes, 15–17 December 2020, Ottawa, Canada', www.oecd.org/tax/forum-on-tax-and-crime.htm, accessed 28 March 2020.

[115] OECD, 'About tax and crime', www.oecd.org/tax/crime/about-tax-and-crime.htm, accessed 25 March 2020.

[116] Ibid.

[117] Ibid.

[118] OECD, *Effective Inter-Agency Co-operation in Fighting Tax Crimes and Other Financial Crimes*, 3rd edn (OECD Publishing, 2017), www.oecd.org/tax/crime/effective-inter-agency-co-operation-in-fighting-tax-crimes-and-other-financial-crimes.htm, accessed 12 March 2020.

[119] Ibid.

the fields of 'tax, customs, anti-corruption, anti-money laundering, policing, and pros-ecution'[120] attended the forum. While discussing measures to more effectively counter tax and economic crimes in the world, the experts took 'stock of the threats of tax crime, progress in countering tax crimes and priorities that required action'.[121] Priorities that required action were noted as follows:

> Professional enablers must be supported to assist tax debtors to settle their tax obligations and that they should, on their part, do all they could to tackle tax crimes;
>
> The level of international and cross-government co-operation has to be increased in order to develop a comprehensive and global counter measures against tax crime;
>
> Countries should make effort to learn from the lessons across the world on the best way to address tax crimes by getting to implement the Ten Global Principles;
>
> The ability of countries to globally collaborate should be strengthened and capacity of experts to quickly and securely share intelligence and data be developed; and
>
> Every county's capacity should be built in order to fight financial crimes so much so that tax criminals would not have a place to hide.[122]

Supporting, cooperation, collaboration, sharing and capacity-building in the value chain of the ecosystem of international tax crime measures, led by the OECD, are key terms that resonate across the above five priority areas. These priorities draw attention to the current needs in the counter-tax crime environment after years of efforts to help effectively counter tax crimes in the OECD member countries and internationally.

Cultural Context of Tax and Tax Crimes

One of the challenges of countering tax crimes has been the cultural orientation and attitudes of the public in Member States of EU and OECD towards paying tax. Culture is a human factor that defines many elements of human behaviour or construction, including that which encapsulates 'shared elements that provide the standards for perceiving, believing, evaluating, communicating, and acting among those who share a language, a historical period, and a geographic location'.[123] As a social construct, culture can be observed from individual, group, national and international angles. There can be significant or minor variations across these domains in the same way that there can be huge, little or moderate converging points.[124] From every way that culture is observed, culture has significant 'implications for advertising content, persuasiveness of appeals, consumer motivation, consumer judgment processes, and consumer response styles'[125] and this is also true in the context of countering tax crimes.

---

[120] OECD, 'Fifth OECD Forum on Tax and Crime' (2017), www.oecd.org/tax/crime/forum-on-tax-and-crime.htm, accessed 25 March 2020.

[121] OECD, 'Strengthening the global response to tax crime' (8 November 2017), www.oecd.org/tax/crime/strengthening-the-global-response-to-tax-crime.htm, accessed 25 March 2020.

[122] Ibid.

[123] S Shavitt, AY Lee and TP Johnson, 'Cross-cultural consumer psychology' in CP Haugtvedt, PM Herr and FR Kardes (eds), *Handbook of consumer psychology* (Routledge, 2008) 1103.

[124] Ibid.

[125] Ibid.

Markus and Kitayama add that culture can be seen as 'a stand-in for a similarly untidy and expansive set of material and symbolic concepts such as world, environment, contexts, cultural systems, social systems, social structures, institutions, practices, policies, meanings, norms, and values, that give form and direction to behaviour'.[126] While underscoring the verbose and dynamic nature of culture, Markus and Kitayama note that culture 'is not a stable set of beliefs or values that reside inside people' but resides 'in the world, in patterns of ideas, practices, institutions, products, and artifacts'[127] or human attributions. This view of culture not only characterises culture as an evasively dynamic concept but also as something that locates itself in attributions other than in human beings or people. This position is not entirely accurate, since human behaviour and world view ought to be substantively acknowledged in the holistic understanding of culture. Markus and Kitayama do not adequately recognise how culture intrinsically originates from a key human factor – human behaviour and world view. Thus, culture also resides in the people. Therefore, tax crime counter-measures considering culture as a factor ought to also recognise the role human beings play in modelling and exhibiting culture both in terms of tax compliance and tax enforcement practices.

However, it does not take away the fact that culture can be demonstrably seen in the human attributions as advanced by Markus and Kitayama. It can, therefore, be averred that culture can be observed as a concept involving people, attributions and dynamism. In a continued flux, as can be seen in Figure 1, human beings are affected by their environment (particularly, social) just as they affect or influence the outlook of this environment. For instance, every potential taxpayer can be influenced to pay tax by the way of life and behaviour they are accustomed to either through their personal mental outlook and/or that of their family, ethnic, regional, and country. At the same time, the taxpayer and tax authorities can also help in shaping how people perceive and respond to tax system in a given jurisdiction.

Figure 1 Cultural Structure

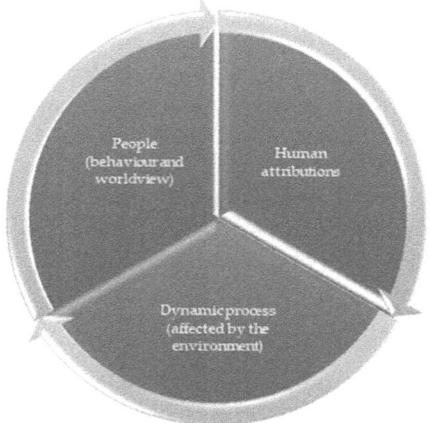

---

[126] HR Markus and S Kitayama, 'Cultures and Selves: A Cycle of Mutual Constitution' (2010) 5 (4) *Perspectives on Psychological Science* 420–30.
[127] Ibid.

Culture is a crucial concept for the understanding and responding or reacting to behaviour of people since it provides the personalised lens by which the people view or perceive messages and outputs.[128] Within the context of EU's multicultural fabric, culture is, therefore, critical in understanding how and why taxpayers approach tax crimes and how to address their concerns using socio-legal approach and design measures to counter tax crimes.

The two definitions of culture essentially provide germane areas of generally agreed understanding of culture which incorporate factors that are both external and internal:[129]

- external to people, such as societal values or similar cultural dimensions, social practices, and artefacts,[130] and

- internal to people, such as independent/interdependent, self-construal or other traits, including the overlooked aspect of language.[131]

Viewing culture from the perspective of society and individual levels, a conceptual framework can be formed 'to review an extensive but fragmented literature from fields as diverse as psychology, sociology, anthropology, linguistics, medicine, marketing, and business'[132] as well as criminology and law. No matter the nature of diversity, culture is largely framed on perception and cognition to take effect.

Table 2 Attributes of Perception and Cognition in Relation to Culture[133]

Perception	*Cognition*
▪ Self-perception	▪ Perspective-taking
▪ Perception of groups & others	▪ Attributions & causal judgements
▪ Perception of emotions	▪ Self-esteem
▪ Perception of the environment and aesthetic preferences	▪ Cognitive style (information processing)
▪ Sensory perceptions	▪ Categorisation
	▪ Memory
	▪ Processing of persuasion messages and decision-making

The perception and cognition attributes of individuals depend upon cross-cultural differences or similarities in two interconnected poles or streams. On one hand, these differences are dependent upon:

- the relationship between individualist and collectivist values;

- the relationship between independent and interdependent self; and

- the language applied.

---

[128] Shavitt, Lee and Johnson, 'Cross-cultural consumer psychology', 1103.
[129] MN Kastanakisa and BG Voyerab, 'The effect of culture on perception and cognition: A conceptual framework' (2014) 67(4) *Journal of Business Research* 425–33.
[130] Ibid.
[131] Ibid.
[132] Ibid.
[133] Ibid.

On the other side of the pole, the perception and cognition attributes are influenced by cross-cultural differences or similarities in *behaviour* of people.[134] The focus of this book is to utilise this framework in the context of how perceptual and cognitive orientation by culture of taxpayers and counter-tax crime ecosystem influences tax crime and compliance.

This framework and accompanying literature review afford us the opportunity to understand the way in which culture conditions perception and cognition especially as they relate to taxation and tax crime. In particular, cultural elements such as norms and values have a way of affecting perception and cognition, which eventually lead to behavioural differences.[135]

For instance, elements of perception such as self-perception, emotional perception, sensory perception, environmental perception and group perception about taxation and tax crime on one hand have a direct vertical relationship with cognition or understanding of the significance of taxation and the damage of tax crimes and why taxes must be paid. Coming to terms with this significance involves cognitive elements such as processing of persuasion messages and decision-making, self-esteem, information processing, memory, as well as attributions and causal judgements about issues surrounding taxation and tax crimes. These components can have cross-cultural differences or similarities in:

- language, independent versus interdependent self, and individualist versus collectivist values, on one hand; and
- behaviour of the taxpayer (the public) and authorities such as tax administrations and other LEAs, on the other hand.

Differences in culture in EU and OECD countries can, for instance, result in 'notorious misunderstandings' in relation to approaches to investigating and prosecuting tax crimes. For example, whereas some cultures may influence tax authorities to concurrently investigate and prosecute tax offences under both administrative and/or criminal laws, some other authorities see wisdom and value in clearly demarcating administrative tax offences from criminal tax offences and thereby investigating and prosecuting them separately.

Cultural tenets such as positive norms, attitudes, values and worldviews have long provided stitching threads for holding together the human factors of tax crimes such as competence/skills and approaches of LEAs. Posner[136] makes an interesting point about the role of norms in defining the unpredictable or unmeasured contours of tax compliance:

> A widespread view among tax scholars holds that law enforcement does not explain why people pay taxes. The penalty for ordinary tax convictions is [relatively] small; the probability of detection is trivial; so, the expected sanction is [relatively] small. Yet large numbers of Americans [and citizens of other OECD countries as well as citizens of many other countries including those in EU countries] pay their taxes. This pattern contradicts the standard

---

[134] Ibid.
[135] Ibid.
[136] Posner, 'Law and Social Norms'.

economic model of law enforcement, which holds that people violate a law if the benefit exceeds the expected sanction. Some scholars therefore conclude that the explanation for the *tendency to pay taxes must be that people are obeying a norm – presumably a norm of tax payment or a more general norm of law-abiding behaviour.*[137]

However, culture identified across institutions, the public and law has also long been presented as a source for disintegration of the fibres of tax crime counter-measures in both OECD and EU countries. Looking at cultural contexts from legal-institutional-public orientation, PROTAX research highlighted cross-cutting insights from 10 EU jurisdictions[138] which reveal how cultural orientation of the institutions (LEAs in particular) and the public does negatively and/or positively influence the effectiveness of tax crime counter-measures in the EU. Whereas from the public point of view, some EU countries have the attitude of seeing tax crimes as lesser crimes, which do not attract as much attention as the traditional crimes such as robbery and murder, the professional attitudes in the prosecution of tax crimes were also found to be indifferent and sometimes lack the necessary coordination or organisational competence across LEAs. Rasmouki et al have uncovered 'problems and controversies as they emerged [from legal-institutional eco-systems of] different national jurisdictions, with regard to the practicalities and professional attitudes in the prosecution of tax crimes'.[139]

The differences between jurisdictions are more striking when a cross-country perspective is taken into consideration and when jurisdictions with different cultural attitudes and perceptions towards tax policy and tax crime are carefully examined. For instance, while Scandinavian societies are considered as having a culture of trust and transparency and traditionally score highly in comparative studies on tax honesty,[140] the same cannot be said of many OECD and EU countries outside the Scandinavian area.

Kadriann Ikkonen from the Tallinn Administration Court in Estonia advocated the need to zero in on the domestic context in the fight against tax crimes.[141] In this regard, Ikkonen highlighted two principal reasons for paying or not paying taxes.

i.   Paying taxes is beneficial to individual taxpayers as long as it is not too costly to pay taxes.
ii. Tax payment is regarded as 'a pro-social activity, or moral duty'.[142]

To address these two factors, Estonia conducts 'positive tax campaigns to improve the moral sense of duty and pro-social culture of paying taxes, and by improving the efficiency of the tax ecosystem and producing disincentives to not paying

---

[137] Ibid.

[138] Austria, Czech Republic, Estonia, Finland, Germany, Ireland, Italy, Malta, Portugal and the United Kingdom.

[139] F Rasmouki and others, 'D2.3 Approaches to tax crimes in the European Union' (EU PROTAX, 2019) 7.

[140] B Rothstein, 'Trust, Social Dilemmas and Collective Memories' (2000) 12(4) *Journal of Theoretical Politics* 477–501.

[141] PROTAX Conference, 22 November 2019, Brussels, https://protax-project.eu/protax-conference-report/ accessed 15 May 2020.

[142] Ibid.

taxes. These types of measures involve making cash payments less desirable, laws compelling invoices over €1,000 to be declared and hotlines to report suspicious tax activity'.[143]

Undoubtedly, the legal factor in terms of the motivation to obey the law and the instilling of fear that the penal provisions the law brings can be hurtful or discomforting to the taxpayer are presented as a push factor for compliance. But the uses to which taxes are put, and the degree of accountability, can inspire or demotivate taxpayers in the payment of taxes. This point may well be captured by the imperative of the 'pro-social activity', or moral duty'. There are several related factors which can push or pull taxpayers in tax payment. However, the culture of criminalisation of tax offences, attitude, awareness of tax offences (nature, effects and damages), perception and interest of taxpayers and professionals (including those in LEAs) is a critical driving force in the metrics of the counter tax crime ecosystem.

PROTAX research on the perception of the public and authorities revealed an apparent major pattern across the 10 selected EU jurisdictions. With respect to perceptions of authorities in charge of investigation and prosecution of tax crimes, although they see tax crimes as 'one of the most serious issues facing the authorities', the 'type of sentencing received by tax offenders does not seem to reflect the seriousness of the crime'. The judiciary in many jurisdictions, for instance, does not apply maximum sentences in cases involving tax crimes. At the same time, the legal framework largely does not provide stringent punishments to deter potential tax offenders. With respect to public perception, the following pattern was observed:

> The public does not perceive tax evasion as a serious crime compared to more tangible crimes such as theft or narcotic crimes. This perception stems from a lack of awareness of the public about the direct and tremendous damage caused to society by tax crime. In turn, this lack of awareness is due to two major factors. Firstly, the type of sentencing applied to various tax offences leads to the public perception that this white-collar crime is a 'lesser crime' than a mainstream crime. In other words, the discrepancy between the magnitude of the crime and the underlying sentences does not contribute to conveying its seriousness and threats. One participant [in the PROTAX focus groups] likened white-collar crimes to crimes involving footballers. [He observed for instance that] nobody is going to [likely] switch off the TV because Ronaldo, who is a tax criminal,[144] is playing. Secondly, the difficulty to attract the interest of the media to cover tax crime cases given that media show more interest towards other type of crimes. It appears that what determines the degree of interest of the media and public is not the case itself, but the individuals involved in the case. Stories of tax offences are reported from an angle of scandal, but the media fail to understand and convey the scope and implications of tax offences and other financial crimes. As a result, the public does not see how a drug dealer, or human trafficker employs tax evasion and money laundering.[145]

The focus group held in Finland revealed that it was hard to attract the interest of the media in tax crime matters, which thus limited exposure of such crimes and criminals

---

[143] Ibid.
[144] BBC, 'Ronaldo fined €18.8m over tax evasion', *BBC News* (22 January 2019) www.bbc.co.uk/news/world-europe-46957605, accessed 6 February 2020).
[145] Rasmouki and others, 'D2.3 Approaches to tax crimes', 9.

to the public. In the focus group in Ireland, it was stated that tax criminal issues are generally embedded in the public consciousness. The public perception, in terms of sentencing, is that tax crimes are 'poorly sentenced'. There is also a curious attention of the public on what the Irish tax authority (Revenue) publishes regarding 'who paid most tax and who paid civil penalty'. With regards to Finland, 'the public is against tax evasion because of the awareness that the Finnish welfare state is funded by tax revenues'. This underscores the value of authorities ensuring that the public is regularly updated about what use they are putting taxes to. The media in Estonia 'are keen to cover tax crime cases involving corporations or those cases perpetuated as part of an organised crime'. The public in Germany sees tax crime as an issue for society, but the seriousness with which they attach to tax crimes is limited in nature. In fact, at the individual level regarding personal taxes, taxpayers in Germany appear not to be significantly aware of tax crimes and the seriousness thereof. In the case of Portugal, the recent financial and sovereign debt crises that plagued the country presented a significant watershed moment 'in shifting the interest of the public opinion towards tax crimes and raising its awareness of its threats and impacts on society'.[146]

In effect, across EU and OECD countries, it would appear that there is increasing shifting of mentality of taxpayers on tax crimes and tax payment, especially on the back of the emergence of large-scale cases brought to lights and evidenced by exposés such as the 'LuxLeaks',[147] 'Football Leaks',[148] 'SwissLeaks',[149] 'Panama Papers',[150] 'Paradise Papers',[151] and other prominent national cases or government initiatives.[152]

Public perception, modelled on the cultural conceptual framework, can have many adverse consequences on tax crime counter-measures. The 'specific infrastructure and the unnoticed cultural factors are important for enforcement of tax crime'.[153] Different jurisdictions have different perceptions and different approaches to tax crimes. Efforts are being made to domestically leverage opportunities in the tax system to turn opportunities into tangible benefits. Table 3 provides examples of tax crime measures to address the problem of public perception.

---

[146] Ibid, 10.

[147] S Bowers, 'European Authorities Launch Probe into Secret Lux Leaks Tax Deal' (ICIJ, 7 March 2019), www.icij.org/investigations/luxembourg-leaks/european-authorities-launch-probe-into-secret-lux-leaks-tax-deal/, accessed 2 March 2020.

[148] See European Investigation Collaborations, 'About us', https://eic.network/, accessed 2 March 2020.

[149] ICIJ, 'An ICIJ Investigation Swiss Leaks: Murky Cash Sheltered by Bank Secrecy: Private Bank Secrets Revealed' (2015), www.icij.org/investigations/swiss-leaks/, accessed 2 March 2020.

[150] ICIJ, 'The Panama Papers: Exposing the Rogue Offshore Finance Industry' www.icij.org/investigations/panama-papers/#_ga=2.246748164.1276343162.1584385292-1381287180.1584385292 accessed 2 March 2020.

[151] W Fitzgibbon and D Starkman, 'The "Paradise Papers" and the Long Twilight Struggle against Offshore Secrecy' (27 December 2017) www.icij.org/investigations/paradise-papers/paradise-papers-long-twilight-struggle-offshore-secrecy/ accessed 2 March 2020.

[152] Rasmouki and others, 'D2.3 Approaches to tax crimes' 10.

[153] M Hall and others, 'D2.4 – Conference Report summarising and documenting contributions from T2.7' (EU PROTAX, 2020) 7.

Table 3 Examples of Measures to Sensitise the Public about Tax Offences in the EU[154]

Estonia	• The Tax and Customs Board pursues 'voluntary tax compliance' by making payment of tax and collaboration with the authorities as easy as possible. This reduces the inconvenience and cost associated with tax compliance, thereby increasing the appetite of taxpayers to comply with tax laws.
	• Estonia celebrates companies that pay most tax by publishing the information to the public. This enhances transparency and builds public confidence in the tax system.
Finland	• The authorities publish data about tax revenues and their sources. The effect of this transparency is that Finnish citizens know that tax should be paid. This translatable public education can increase the culture of accountability and consequent confidence and trust in the tax system.
Germany	• Germany acquired CDs containing data about tax evaders, which in turn resulted in an increase in the number of people declaring themselves to the authorities. Thus, indirect awareness is created about effort of government to counter tax crimes but this effort and related measures are approached with some indifference and thereby making Germany one of the major tax evasion centres in the EU.
Portugal	• There is a programme entitled 'tax citizenship 2.0' which was presented by the tax authority whereby the tax authority signed protocols with the Ministry of Education with the purpose of educating young children about tax crimes and their impact. This initiative appears to be a very relevant measure to raise tax awareness.
Ireland	• Even if tax offenders may not spend time in jail or not a lot of time, on the newspaper they are declared guilty and they get a criminal record. Names are published even when a punitive penalty is paid.
	• Revenue publicise information about who pays most tax as well as large excise seizure.
	• The tax regime system in Ireland is a self-assessment system which helps in bringing about compliance.

Perceptions of taxation and tax crimes by the public and professionals are culturally rooted, which needs comprehensive education and sensitisation. These must be aligned to individualist and collectivist values with new or repackaged values attached to tax payment and approaches to countering tax offences. This requires the use of appropriate narrative or messages that can motivate taxpayers to appreciate tax value in compliance, impact of tax crimes and to adjust their behaviours accordingly. It also requires 'a change in the sentencing culture of the judiciary and more transparency regarding the underlying data of cases in order to convey the seriousness of' tax crimes.[155] The media is a powerful platform that presents potent instruments for modelling and remodelling culture towards a given end. The media can, therefore, contribute significantly to cultural change of tax resistance and tax inaction. This can be achieved by adopting

---

[154] Rasmouki and others, 'D2.3 Approaches to tax crimes' 10.
[155] Ibid, 98.

a more informed reporting style about the topic as opposed to the need to share (or disseminate) those cases that carry scandalous elements.

It suffices to assert that the cultural environment, just like the historical underpinning of tax, leaves behind certain sentiments, attitudes and a general way of life or approach of the people to tax law and economic issues that require deconstructing and unpicking in ways that can mitigate their impeding effects such as corruption, low tax morale and fraud.

The Foundation of EU Tax Law Relative to OECD Tax Rules

The OECD and its Legal Framework

Established on 30 September 1961,[156] the OECD is an intergovernmental organisation and association of 37 jurisdictions across the world which represents a combined population of 1,291,087,000[157] excluding Colombia[158] which recently became a member of the organisation. The OECD members (Australia, Austria, Belgium, Canada, Chile, Colombia, Czech Republic, Denmark, Estonia, Finland, France, Germany, Greece, Hungary, Iceland, Ireland, Israel, Italy, Japan, Korea, Latvia, Lithuania, Luxembourg, Mexico, Netherlands, New Zealand, Norway, Poland, Portugal, Slovak Republic, Slovenia, Spain, Sweden, Switzerland, Turkey, the United Kingdom, the United States) account for a significant share of global GDP[159] and market share.

Usually, OECD tax measures tend to assume a global dimension partly due to the inputs and interests of the 37 industrialised nations and institutions therein, the majority of which are also members of another powerful intergovernmental and supranational organisation, the EU. Of the 27 EU members, only five (Romania, Malta, Cyprus, Croatia and Bulgaria) are not members of the OECD.[160] Thus, the remaining 22 EU Member States in effect make up 59.5 per cent of the OECD membership.

Key industrialised nations outside the EU such as the United Kingdom, the United States, Australia, Japan, Canada, Norway and Switzerland also participate as members of the OECD. Additionally, three of the five permanent members of the United Nations (UN) Security Council (France, the United Kingdom and United States) are members of the OECD.

In tandem with mobilising a global consensus on fighting tax evasion, through forums such as the Global Forum on Transparency and Exchange of Information for Tax Purposes, the Forum on Tax and Crime (to which many non-OECD members

---

[156] OECD, 'History' www.oecd.org/about/history/, accessed 7 May 2020.

[157] OECD, 'Population and Migration', www.oecd.org/sdd/01_Population_and_migration.pdf, accessed 13 May 2020.

[158] OECD, 'Where: Global reach', www.oecd.org/about/members-and-partners/, accessed 29 April 2020.

[159] See OECD, 'Gross domestic product (GDP)', https //data.oecd.org/gdp/gross-domestic-product-gdp.htm, accessed 22 July 2020.

[160] European Union, 'EU member countries in brief' (1 February 2020), https://europa.eu/european-union/about-eu/countries/member-countries_en, accessed 13 April 2020; OECD, 'Where: Global reach'.

are also party), as well as the TFTC, tax policies and recommendations of the OECD are usually backed by powerful institutions such as the G20, the IMF, the World Bank and Financial Action Task Force (FATF).[161] For instance, the dialogue and cooperation which the Committee on Fiscal Affairs of OECD usually has with FATF (which has 38 members wherein the EU Commission is a party) goes to reinforce the international standing of OECD policies on countering tax crimes and money laundering. Indeed, FATF's Recommendations are complemented by the OECD's work to counter tax crimes and money laundering. Subsequently, the tax measures recommended by the OECD have a critical driving force in tax decision-making among the EU Member States as well as among other prominent global economic players.

One of the main aims of the OECD is to 'build strong economies and improve efficiency in its member countries by promoting free market policies and trade using normative measures'. With this disposition, the implementation of the OECD's principles (ie, TGPs) on countering tax crimes is based largely on the goodwill of its members and their mutual respect for each other. This is not necessarily like the EU, which has stronger supranational legal structure where its treaties and secondary legal instruments regarding tax crimes oblige its members to implement and enforce such legal provisions.[162]

The legal framework of the OECD has had about 450 substantive legal instruments since the organisation was founded in 1961. The legal framework comprises of:

- Acts: the Decisions and Recommendations adopted by the OECD Council[163] (in accordance with the OECD Convention).[164] These are generally binding on Member States.[165]

- Other legal instruments that have been developed within the OECD framework, including declarations and international agreements as well as Arrangements, Understandings and others. These are generally not binding but have normative value.[166]

In this regard the legal instruments are often categorised into five areas of the OECD legal framework:

i.   Decisions. These are legal instruments of the OECD which are legally binding on all Member States with exception of the members that abstain at the time of adop-

---

[161] OECD, 'Global Forum on Tax Transparency marks a dramatic shift in the fight against tax evasion with the widespread commencement of the automatic exchange of financial information' (2018), www.oecd.org/tax/transparency/global-forum-marks-a-dramatic-shift-in-the-fight-against-tax-evasion-with-the-widespread-commencement-of-the-automatic-exchange-of-financial-information.htm, accessed 11 March 2020; OECD, 'Strengthening the global response to tax crime' www.oecd.org/tax/crime/strengthening-the-global-response-to-tax-crime.htm, accessed 11 July 2020.

[162] C Barnard, *The Substantive Law of the EU: The Four Freedoms Paperback,* 4th edn (OUP, 2013); C Tobler and J Beglinger, *Essential EU Law in Chart,s* 4th edn (HVG-ORAC, 2018).

[163] 'A Council composed of all the Members shall be the body from which all acts of the Organisation derive. The Council may meet in sessions of Ministers or of Permanent Representatives'; see Convention on the Organisation for Economic Co-operation and Development of 14 December 1960, Art 7.

[164] Convention on the Organisation for Economic Co-operation and Development of 14 December 1960, www.oecd.org/general/conventionontheorganisationforeconomicco-operationanddevelopment.htm, accessed 14 March 2020.

[165] OECD, 'Legal Instruments', www.oecd.org/legal/legal-instruments.htm, accessed 7 May 2020.

[166] Ibid.

tion. These instruments are not necessarily international treaties, but 'they entail the same kind of legal obligations'. The countries that adhere to (the adherents) have an obligation 'to implement Decisions and must take the measures necessary for such implementation'.[167]

ii.   Recommendations. These are legal instruments which do not legally bind members of the OECD. However, practice has accorded the Recommendations 'great moral force as representing the political will of Adherents'. The expectation is 'that Adherents will do their utmost to fully implement' these instruments. What this means is that OECD Member States that intend not to implement the Recommendations 'usually abstain when a Recommendation is adopted, although this is not required in legal terms'.[168]

iii. Declarations. These 'are prepared within the Organisation, generally within a subsidiary body' and often 'set general principles or long-term goals, have a solemn character and are usually adopted at Ministerial meetings of the Council or of committees of the Organisation'.[169]

iv.   International Agreements. These legal instruments are 'negotiated and concluded within the framework of the Organisation' and 'are legally binding on the Parties'. These instruments usually have a strong global force.[170]

v.   Arrangement, Understandings and Others. These are the many ad hoc substantive legal instruments that 'have been developed within the OECD framework over time, such as the Arrangement on Officially Supported Export Credits, the International Understanding on Maritime Transport Principles and the Development Assistance Committee (DAC) Recommendations'.[171]

The material OECD legal instruments relating to tax and crime include the following:[172]

- Declaration on Automatic Exchange of Information in Tax Matters, adopted on 6 May 2014 (EU has adhered this instrument);

- Recommendation of the Council to Facilitate Co-operation between Tax and Other Law Enforcement Authorities to Combat Serious Crimes, adopted on 14 October 2010;

- Multilateral Convention to Implement Tax Treaty Related Measures to Prevent Base Erosion and Profit Shifting, adopted on 24 November 2016;

- Recommendation of the Council on the Application of Value Added Tax/Goods and Services Tax to the International Trade in Services and Intangibles, adopted on 27 September 2016;

- Recommendation of the Council on the Standard for Automatic Exchange of Financial Account Information in Tax Matters, adopted on 15 July 2014;

---

[167] Ibid.
[168] Ibid.
[169] Ibid.
[170] Ibid.
[171] Ibid.
[172] OECD Legal Instruments, https://legalinstruments.oecd.org/en/instruments/OECD-LEGAL-0309, accessed 24 July 2020.

- Recommendation of the Council on Tax Measures for Further Combating Bribery of Foreign Public Officials in International Business Transactions, adopted on 25 May 2009;
- Recommendation of the Council on the Use of the OECD Model Memorandum of Understanding on Automatic Exchange of Information for Tax Purposes, adopted on 22 March 2001;
- Recommendation of the Council on Implementing the Proposals contained in the 1998 Report on Harmful Tax Competition, adopted on 16 June 2000;
- Recommendation of the Council on Counteracting Harmful Tax Competition, adopted on 9 April 1998;
- Recommendation of the Council on the Granting and Design of Tax Sparing in Tax Conventions, adopted on 23 October 1997;
- Recommendation of the Council concerning the Model Tax Convention on Income and on Capital, adopted on 23 October 1997;
- Recommendation of the Council on the Use of Tax Identification Numbers in an International Context, adopted on 13 March 1997;
- Recommendation of the Council concerning an OECD Model Agreement for the Undertaking of Simultaneous Tax Examinations, adopted on 23 July 1992;
- Recommendation of the Council concerning Tax Treaty Override, adopted on 2 October 1989;
- Convention on Mutual Administrative Assistance in Tax Matters, opened for signature on 25 January 1988;
- Protocol amending the Convention on Mutual Administrative Assistance in Tax Matters, noted by the Council on 18 February 2010;
- Recommendation of the Council concerning the Avoidance of Double Taxation with respect to Taxes on Estates and Inheritances and on Gifts, adopted on 3 June 1982;
- Recommendation of the Council on Tax Avoidance and Evasion, adopted on 21 September 1977;
- Recommendation of the Council concerning Guidelines for Protecting Consumers from Fraudulent and Deceptive Commercial Practices across Borders, adopted on 11 June 2003;
- Declaration on Trans-border Data Flows, adopted on 11 April 1985; and
- Recommendation of the Council concerning Guidelines Governing the Protection of Privacy and Trans-border Flows of Personal Data, adopted on 23 September 1980.

It is evident that there are more recommendations than any other legal instruments. Notably, there are no decisions, which are the binding legal instruments in the OECD legal framework. However, there are also few conventions that provide more binding imperatives for members of the OECD. The declarations, which also have strong normative force, are also few. However, it is not necessarily about how many or few the binding instruments are, but how potent and/or substantive the few are. At the same time, those non-binding instruments usually have moral force beyond the OECD members to command respect of the international community. One such instrument which is not even directly found in any of the legal instruments but which provides respectable normative force is the OECD report on global principles for fighting against tax crime – of course, under the auspices of the taskforce on tax crime and other crimes of the OECD (which are examined in detail later in the book). All the instruments above do contribute, in one way or the other, to the counter tax crime endeavours in OECD countries.

The EU and its Legal Framework

The EU and OECD have legal and policy frameworks and recommendations that inform decision-making and actions regarding the fight against tax crimes. The EU and OECD play leading roles not only for their Member States but also for the world at large – especially in terms of setting standards and championing the course of socioeconomic development.

The EU is essentially an intergovernmental and supranational organisation and a union of 27 Member States with about 446 million people,[173] located on over 4 million km² in Europe and with the world's third largest population after China and India.[174] The EU's GDP equally has strong showing in the global sphere.[175] In effect, the EU not only has population, land and standards as essential assets, the EU also has a huge market share and potential – with significant prospects and opportunities for taxation.

The legislation of the EU has two main divisions: primary and secondary. While the primary legislation is the treaties which form the basis or the ground rules upon which all actions of the EU are taken, the secondary legislation comprises of regulations, directives and decisions, which are drawn from the principles and objectives embedded in the treaties[176] which collectively form the EU's *acquis communautaire*. There are also non-binding instruments (namely, communications, resolutions, and opinions), and other instruments (namely, EU institutions' internal regulations, EU action programmes, and others).[177]

There have been several treaties since the EU was founded which bind members of the Union, and establish 'EU objectives, rules for EU institutions, how decisions are made and the relationship between the EU and its member countries'. No action

---

[173] Current population figure provided by OECD is 514,513,000 in the 27 country EU; see OECD, 'Population and Migration', www.oecd.org/sdd/01_Population_and_migration.pdf, accessed 13 May 2020.

[174] European Union, 'Living in the EU' (last published 29 April 2020), https://europa.eu/european-union/about-eu/figures/living_en, accessed 7 May 2020.

[175] Eurostat, 'Gross domestic product at market prices', https://ec.europa.eu/eurostat/tgm/refreshTableAction.do?tab=table&plugin=1&pcode=tec00001&language=en, accessed 7 May 2020; International Monetary Fund, '4. Report for Selected Country Groups and Subjects', www.imf.org/external/pubs/ft/weo/2016/02/weodata/weorept.aspx?pr.x=56&pr.y=8&sy=2016&ey=2016&scsm=1&ssd=1&sort=country&ds=.&br=1&c=001,998&s=NGDPD&grp=1&a=1, accessed 17 May 2020.

[176] European Union, 'EU law', https://europa.eu/european-union/law_en, accessed 22 July 2020. For detailed information see, The EU Parliament, Sources and scope of European Union law, www.europarl.europa.eu/factsheets/en/sheet/6/sources-and-scope-of-european-union-law, accessed 22 July 2020.

[177] Eur-lex, 'Legal Acts', https://eur-lex.europa.eu/collection/eu-law/legislation/recent.html, accessed 8 May 2020.

is expected to be conducted outside of the areas specified in the treaties. Therefore, all EU actions that are carried out are founded on the treaties 'that have been approved voluntarily and democratically by all EU member countries' in the light of the Union's operations according to the rule of law. For instance, 'a policy area that is not cited in a treaty, cannot have the European Commission propose a law in that area.[178] Through the treaties, the EU institutions are granted the mandate to adopt legislation, which the Member States then implement'.[179]

The key treaties[180] which form the primary sources of EU law (along with the general principles of Union law and fundamental rights) include:

- Treaty on European Union (Consolidated version 2016);
- Treaty on the Functioning of the European Union (Consolidated version 2016);
- Treaty establishing the European Atomic Energy Community (Consolidated version 2016);
- Charter of Fundamental Rights of the European Union (2012).[181]

The competence of the EU in tax matters is derived from the Treaty on the European Union 2012 (TEU),[182] the Treaty on the Functioning of the European Union 2012 (TFEU),[183] and secondary legislation as delegated to the EU by these treaties, as well as the European Convention on Human Rights 1950[184] as stipulated by the Lisbon Treaty 2007. EU tax law, thus, refers to as the legal provisions in the aforementioned instruments that could mount some effects on taxation[185] in the Union. In particular, the legal framework of taxation in the EU is founded on Articles 110–13 of the TFEU. Article 110 provides that it is not permissible for any Member State of the EU to impose any national tax on other members' products which exceeds 'that imposed directly or indirectly on similar domestic products' (EU, 2010/115).[186]

Per this provision, the EU Member States are not allowed to 'impose on the products of other Member States any internal taxation of such a nature as to afford indirect protection to other products'. Even though it is settled case law of the EU that Member States have exclusive competence over domestic direct taxation issues, on tax matters that concern two or more countries of the EU with cross-border activity, the legal

---

[178] European Union, 'EU treaties', https://europa.eu/european-union/law/treaties_en, accessed 18 May 2020.
[179] Ibid.
[180] Eur-lex, 'Treaties currently in force ', https://eur-lex.europa.eu/collection/eu-law/treaties/treaties-force. html, accessed 8 June 2020.
[181] Charter of Fundamental Rights of the European Union [2012] OJ C 326/391.
[182] Consolidated version of The Treaty on the Functioning of the European Union [2012] OJ C326/13.
[183] Ibid 47.
[184] European Court of Human Rights (ECHR) and Council of Europe (COE), *European Convention on Human Rights* (4 November 1950) as amended by Protocols Nos 11 and 14; supplemented by Protocols Nos 1, 4, 6, 7, 12, 13 and 16.
[185] C Barnard and S Peers (eds), *European Union Law*, 2nd edn (Oxford University Press, 2017); M Horspool and others, *European Union Law*, 10th edn (Oxford University Press, 2018); R Schütze, *European Union Law*, 2nd edn (Cambridge University Press, 2018).
[186] Consolidated Treaties, Charter of Fundamental Rights (2010/115), https://europa.eu/european-union/ sites/europaeu/files/eu_citizenship/consolidated-treaties_en.pdf, accessed 18 June 2020.

provisions on taxes do limit the sovereign taxing rights of the EU Member States and give jurisdiction to the EU. Yet, Article 10 and cases in *Royal Bank of Scotland Plc v Elliniko Dimosio (Greek State)*,[187] *Manninen v Finnish Government*,[188] and *Marks & Spencer v United Kingdom Tax Authority*[189] support the settled jurisdiction of Member States over direct taxation.

The challenge regarding jurisdiction is how it is reconciled between the EU and its Member States on topical issues such as VAT. For instance, VAT is a crucial source of national revenue. But 'the VAT system, which is based on legislation adopted at European level and applied at national level, suffers from numerous shortcomings which do not make it fully efficient and compatible with the requirements of a true single market'.[190]

Articles 111 and 112 of the TFEU build on the fair taxation principle established in Article 110. Article 113 gives competence to the Council to adopt, in unanimity, legal instruments to harmonise tax legislations regarding 'turnover taxes, excise duties and other forms of indirect taxation' as long as this endeavour is 'necessary to ensure the establishment and the functioning of the internal market and to avoid distortion of competition'.[191]

There are a number of EU tax measures the enforcement of which are also based on mutual understanding, respect and commitment of Member States. These are usually carried forward by the recommendations and opinions of the EU.[192] But they appear to be subjected to quasi-legal enforceability than most of the legal instruments of the OECD due to the nature of foundational legal instruments and established EU institutions that undertake monitoring exercises on both normative and legal compliances.

It has to be recognised, however, that even in the absence of greater legal force, the OECD's 10 global principles have a huge virtuous and normative prominence among its members. For the purposes of legal analysis, the OECD's tax measures, that have been identified to be effective, will best resonate well in the EU if such measures are codified in the EU legal framework or drafted into the EU tax system.[193] The same can be said in regards to the FATF Recommendations,[194] which have been transposed into the EU *acquis* by a series of Anti-Money Laundering (AML) Directives, including the Fifth (Directive (EU) 2018/843) and Sixth (Directive (EU) 2018/1673) AMLDs.[195]

---

[187] Case C-311/97 *Royal Bank of Scotland* [1999] ECR I-2651.

[188] Case C-319/02 *Manninen* [2004] ECR I-7477.

[189] Case C-446/03 *Marks & Spencer* [2005] ECR I-10837.

[190] European Commission, 'Green Paper on the future of VAT – Towards a simpler, more robust and efficient VAT system', https://ec.europa.eu/taxation_customs/consultations-get-involved/tax-consultations/green-paper-future-vat-towards-a-simpler-more-robust-efficient-vat-system_en, accessed 16 March 2020.

[191] Consolidated Version of the Treaty on the Functioning of the European Union [2008] OJ C 115/47.

[192] P Craig and G De Burca, *EU Law: Text, Cases and Materials*, 6th edn (Oxford University Press, 2015).

[193] OECD, 'About tax and crime'.

[194] See FATF, *International Standards on Combating Money Laundering and the Financing of Terrorism & Proliferation* (FATF, 2012–19), www.fatf-gafi.org/recommendations.html, accessed 24 March 2020.

[195] Directive (EU) 2018/843 of the European Parliament and of the Council of 30 May 2018 amending Directive (EU) 2015/849 on the prevention of the use of the financial system for the purposes of money laundering or terrorist financing, and amending Directives 2009/138/EC and 2013/36/EU, https://eur-lex.europa.eu/legal-content/EN/TXT/?uri=CELEX%3A32018L0843, accessed 12 January 2020.

There are a number of legal acts that are germane to the criminal tax regime in the EU:

- Directive (EU) 2015/849 of the European Parliament and of the Council of 20 May 2015;[196]

- Directive (EU) 2017/1371 of the European Parliament and of the Council of 5 July 2017 on the fight against fraud to the Union's financial interests by means of criminal law by 6 July 2019;

- Directive (EU) 2018/1673 of the European Parliament and of the Council of 23 October 2018 on combating money laundering by criminal law by 3 December 2020;

- Directive (EU) 2018/843 of the European Parliament and of the Council of 30 May 2018 amending Directive (EU) 2015/849 on the prevention of the use of the financial system for the purposes of money laundering or terrorist financing and amending Directives 2009/138/EC and 2013/36/EU;

- European Parliament Resolution of 26 March 2019 on financial crimes, tax evasion and tax avoidance;

- Directive (EU) 2019/1937 of the European Parliament and of the Council of 23 October 2019 on the protection of persons who report breaches of Union law;

- Council Framework Decision 2001/500/JHA of 26 June 2001 on money laundering, the identification, tracing, freezing, seizing and confiscation of instrumentalities and the proceeds of crime;

- Council Directive 2011/16/EU of 15 February 2011 on administrative cooperation in the field of taxation and repealing Directive 77/799/EEC;[197]

- Anti-Tax Avoidance Directive (EU) 2016/1164 to protect the performance of the internal market;[198] and

- Council Directive 2006/112/EC on VAT.[199]

These EU legal instruments are discussed in subsequent chapters of the book.

Approach and Scope

The book has adopted a mix of empirical and theoretical approaches to communicate the essentials. In particular, the author has led an EU-funded project on investigating,

---

[196] Directive (EU) 2015/849 of the European Parliament and of the Council of 20 May 2015 on the prevention of the use of the financial system for the purposes of money laundering or terrorist financing, amending Regulation (EU) No 648/2012 of the European Parliament and of the Council, and repealing Directive 2005/60/EC of the European Parliament and of the Council and Commission Directive 2006/70/EC OJ L 141/73.

[197] Council Directive 2011/16/EU of 15 February 2011 on administrative cooperation in the field of taxation and repealing Directive 77/799/EEC [2011] OJ L 64/1–12.

[198] Council Directive (EU) 2016/1164 of 12 July 2016 laying down rules against tax avoidance practices that directly affect the functioning of the internal market, [2016] OJ L 193/1–14.

[199] Council Directive 2006/112/EC of 28 November 2006 on the common system of value added tax ([2006] OJ L 347/1–118; see consolidated version as of 1 January 2020 at: Council Directive 2006/112/EC of

preventing and prosecuting tax crimes in the EU (namely PROTAX)[200] whereby some of the early and publicly available findings of this research are integrated in the critical analysis within this monograph.

The book is guided by approaches of research drawn from criminal law and justice, public regulatory theory, tax law, economic law and governance.[201] The research approach that is used employs mainly doctrinal (black letter law or law in books) and socio-legal (law in action) methodologies.

The scope of the book is within the interactions between countering tax criminal laws, regulations, rules and principles in the EU and OECD as well as the views and perceptions of tax enforcement agencies in at least 10 Member States of the EU. The TFTC has recommended in its guide on fighting tax crimes (the TGPs)[202] that countries should endeavour to benchmark the frameworks in their jurisdictions against each of the TGPs. This is a welcome move. The TFTC sees the benchmarking as including identification of 'areas where changes in law or operational aspects are needed, such as increasing the type of investigative or enforcement powers, expanding access to other government-held data, devising or updating the strategy for addressing tax offences, and taking greater efforts to measure the impact of the work they do'.[203] This benchmarking is, thus, anchored on comparative, synergetic and integrative examination and adaptation of the TGPs by jurisdictions globally especially the OECD member countries. This book focuses on the extent to which the TGPs can be benchmarked with the EU legal framework on countering tax crimes. The book is, thus, limited to the TGPs and associated tax crime instruments of the OECD as they relate to the anti-tax crime measures of the EU. Attention is paid to measures that are directly or indirectly related to tax crimes. Therefore, pertinent tax avoidance, tax planning and tax abuse measures which strictly may not address the problem of tax crimes are considered. Thus, the non-criminal issues addressed in this book is due to the unavoidable or the integrated role they play in helping or providing the festering environment for tax crimes to be committed. The primary focus, however, is on measures relating directly to criminal offences or tax crimes such as tax evasion and fraud.

In the end, the book not only gives perspectives on counter tax crime measures in the EU and OECD, but also provides a global view of countering tax crimes and avoidance in the context of the EU.

There are seven chapters in this book. This first chapter has given a general introduction to the key issues surrounding the fight against tax crimes. Firstly, it does this by immersing the reader in the background, historical and cultural underpinnings of tax and tax crime counter-measures. Secondly, as an introductory chapter, it provides for the foundation of legal frameworks of OECD and the EU and drives down to the approach and scope of the book. Chapter two critically examines the various definitions of tax crimes in the EU and the OECD. Chapter three looks at the substantive

---

28 November 2006 on the common system of value added tax, https://eur-lex.europa.eu/legal-content/EN/TXT/PDF/?uri=CELEX:02006L0112-20200101&from=EN, accessed 8 January 2020.

[200] PROTAX Project website: www.protax-project.eu.

[201] S Douma, *Legal Research in International and EU Tax Law* (Kluwer, 2014).

[202] OECD, *Fighting Tax Crime: The Ten Global Principles* (OECD Publishing, 2017), www.oecd.org/tax/crime/fighting-tax-crime-the-ten-global-principles.htm, accessed 26 October 2019.

[203] Ibid.

principles of tax crimes, while Chapter four addresses the procedural/structural issues in the fight against tax crimes in the OECD and the EU. Chapter five takes a critical look at the interrelationships between the administrative tax measures such as the Directive on Administrative Cooperation (DAC) and the criminal tax measures explored in the preceding chapter. Chapter six explores other components of the tax crime countering ecosystem such as whistle-blowing and corruption. Chapter seven (the last chapter) provides a conclusion and recommendations.

2

Defining Tax Crimes
in the OECD and the EU

Introduction

Following historical and cultural contexts, Member States of the EU and the OECD have engineered different approaches to and understanding of tax crimes, thereby making cross-border identification and responses to tax crime (eg, investigation, prosecution and asset recovery) difficult. This chapter analyses the diverse formulations of tax crimes in the OECD and EU. It also explains the relationships between tax evasion, tax fraud, tax avoidance, tax abuse and aggressive tax planning.

Providing clear definitions of tax offences creates a critical path for effectively countering tax crimes generally. The focus group discussions held by PROTAX in 2019 revealed a wide spectrum of perspectives on areas such as the adequacy and clarity of the legal definitions of tax crimes in these jurisdictions relating to criminal tax offences. The case studies of PROTAX in 11 European jurisdictions also provided diverse perspectives of criminal tax offences involving court cases. While adequacy of the definition of tax offences was characterised as 'when a legal system ensures that tax violations are punished as crimes',[1] clarity of the definition was contextualised as when the definition 'allows citizens and businesses to determine whether their behaviours comply with or breach criminal law'.[2]

Furthermore, an important element to consider is that definition of tax crimes should be considered as adequate if there is sufficient acceptance or legitimacy of the definition in theory and operation. Additionally, an adequate definition of tax crime should not just be sufficiently comprehensive to capture all essential parameters of existing methods and strategies of tax crimes, but should also be reasonably futuristic in developing an adjustable trap for the constantly changing and sophisticated operations of tax criminals. While in the EU, the definition of tax crimes and their accompanying sanctions are mainly within the competence or jurisdiction of EU Member States, except if a specific competence is granted to the European Union, while mutatis mutandis, the same applies to the Member States of the OECD. These dispositions inform the definitions and analysis in this section.

---

[1] F Rasmouki and others, 'D2.3 Approaches to tax crimes in the European Union' (EU PROTAX, 2019) 12.
[2] Ibid.

Every tax is vulnerable to some form of criminal machinations by the taxpayer. This vulnerability affects direct taxes such as income or profit taxes, and indirect taxes such as VAT (which is particularly affected by widespread fraud, with a strong connection to organised crime) in the EU and OECD countries.[3]

Tax crime is old, yet continues to be a developing concept – with many loose ends and adaptations in tandem with opportunities offered by technology, liberalisation of trade and free movement of goods, services and capital. Although tax crime simply concerns criminal offences in the legal framework of a given jurisdiction, region or internationally, the concept of tax crime is befuddled with uncertainties in tax law and jurisprudence.

One of the reasons that account for this unsettled nature of tax crimes is the cross-border nature of the phenomenon where differences in legal frameworks of jurisdictions give variegated treatment to the understanding of the phenomenon. Another reason is rooted in tax policy objectives that do not see criminalisation of tax offences as a productive path to achieving tax goals such as raising and optimising revenue from taxes and tax liabilities. At the same time, criminal tax offences are also linked to the threshold of tax liability – where a number of jurisdictions set high thresholds at which a tax liability offence can be qualified as a crime; or even when such thresholds are reasonable and harmonised, the way by which they are calculated may differ from one country to another. Uncertainties surrounding tax crimes are also occasioned by the interconnected nature of financial crimes in which tax offences have the singularity of navigating between the frontiers of civil or administrative law and criminal law. For instance, terrorist financing and money laundering are financial crimes that can have straightforward relationship with criminal law without undue ambivalence to apply civil law[4] whereas tax offences traditionally have been dealt with administrative law and processes.

However, in all EU Member States, tax crimes such as tax fraud and tax evasion are designated as predicate offences for money laundering that can be defined and prosecuted under both civil and criminal law. Usually, thresholds of tax liability, seriousness of the fraud and attenuating predisposition of the taxpayer are used to determine whether criminality should be attached to tax offences. Some countries, however, pursue criminal investigation and prosecution alongside administrative/civil investigation and prosecution.

Tax fraud and tax evasion are broad critical elements and/or typologies of tax crimes in both OECD and EU countries. These two concepts are also interrelated. The analysis below shows, in detail, what these terms are, and how they are interrelated with each other and with other elements of tax crime.

---

[3] OECD, *Fighting Tax Crime: The Ten Global Principles* (OECD Publishing, 2017), www.oecd.org/tax/crime/fighting-tax-crime-the-ten-global-principles.htm, accessed 26 June 2020.

[4] Directive (EU) 2015/849 on the prevention of the use of the financial system for the purposes of money laundering or terrorist financing and amending Directives 2009/138/EC and 2013/36/EU (PE/72/2017/REV/1 [2018] OJ L 156/43-74), https://eur-lex.europa.eu/legal-content/EN/TXT/?uri=CELEX%3A32018L0843, accessed 12 January 2020; OECD, *Money Laundering and Terrorist Financing Awareness Handbook for Tax Examiners and Tax Auditors* (OECD, 2019), www.oecd.org/tax/crime/money-laundering-and-terrorist-financing-awareness-handbook-for-tax-examiners-and-tax-auditors.pdf, accessed 19 December 2019.

Fraud

There are many controversies surrounding the definition of fraud. It hardly has a single definition.[5] The phenomenal research by Levi and more recently by scholars such as Doig has thrown significant light on the landscape of fraud. The works by Levi[6] have particularly helped in shaping the contemporary study and understanding of fraud at both academic and practitioner levels. Fraud can generally be defined as 'an intentional act by one or more individuals among management, those charged with governance, employees, or third parties, involving the use of deception to obtain an unjust or illegal advantage'.[7] Levi notes that fraud is a word that is 'deceptively simple'. It is so because fraud is not only built on dishonesty but it also appears, on the surface, that it is easy to identify or know what it is. However, fraud covers 'a very broad territory' and has many complexities – sometimes so difficult for auditors and other investigators to use standard procedures to detect that misconduct. And within this scope, fraud is identified by Levi as:

> A way of making money illegally via deception, whether that deception is directly person-to-person in real space or in virtual space; operates by false stories alone or via the use of deceptive real or e-documents or via Personal Identification Numbers; or uses genuine or phoney business as tools of fraud.[8]

Falsification or false accounting and/or deception are particularly critical ingredients for committing fraud. False accounting refers to the act or process engaged in by a legal and/or natural person to alter, falsify or hide accounts or documents in order to execute deception. Accounts or documents are broad, but can be referred to as 'anything that provides the record of the action or transaction that would form part of any accounting process'.[9] False accounting has extensive particularities, across varied spheres. With respect to the legal person or corporations, the United Kingdom's Theft Act 1968 provides some interesting specifics of false accounting and corporate offences characterising fraud:

(1) Where a person dishonestly, with a view to gain for himself or another or with intent to cause loss to another,

    (a) destroys, defaces, conceals or falsifies any account or any record or document made or required for any accounting purpose; or

    (b) in furnishing information for any purpose produces or makes use of any account, or any such record or document as aforesaid, which to his knowledge is or may be

---

[5] A Doig, *Fraud* (Routledge, 2008); see also A Doig (ed), *Fraud: The Counter Fraud Practitioner's Handbook* (Routledge, 2012).

[6] See M Levi, *The Phantom Capitalists: The Organisation and Control of Long-Firm Fraud* (Heinemann, 1981); M Levi, *Regulating Fraud: White-Collar Crime and the Criminal Process* (Routledge, 1987); M Levi (ed), *Fraud: Organisation, Motivation and Control* (Dartmouth, 1999); M Levi, 'The Investigation, Prosecution, and Trial of Serious Fraud' (Royal Commission on Criminal Justice Research Study No 14, 1993).

[7] Financial Reporting Council (FRC), 'International Standard on Auditing (UK and Ireland) 240: The auditor's responsibilities relating to fraud in an audit of financial statements' (October 2009) 35, www.frc.org.uk/getattachment/6cb0c88e-b11e-4b03-81b6-527e992d4f0e/ISA-240.pdf, accessed 13 December 2019.

[8] M Levi, 'Trends and costs of Fraud' in A Doig (ed), *Fraud: The Counter Fraud Practitioner's Handbook* 7.

[9] Doig, *Fraud*.

> misleading, false or deceptive in a material particular; he shall, on conviction on indictment, be liable to imprisonment for a term not exceeding seven years.

> (2)   For purposes of this section a person who makes or concurs in making in an account or other document an entry which is or may be misleading, false or deceptive in a material particular, or who omits or concurs in omitting a material particular from an account or other document, is to be treated as falsifying the account or document.[10]

False accounting thus includes 'faking, altering, and hiding accounting documents'.[11] Other elements of fraud in the Theft Act 1968 concern corporate offences which are: liability of company officers for certain offences by company;[12] false statements by company directors and others (including misleading, false or deceptive written statements;[13] and suppression and others of documents. With respect to suppression and others of documents, section 20 of the Theft Act 1968 provides that:

> (1)   A person who dishonestly, with a view to gain for himself or another or with intent to cause loss to another, destroys, defaces or conceals any valuable security, any will or other testamentary document or any original document of or belonging to, or filed or deposited in, any court of justice or any government department shall on conviction on indictment be liable to imprisonment for a term not exceeding seven years.[14]

Thus, dishonest destruction, defacement, or concealment of official documents or accounts in order to gain or benefit therefrom is a fraudulent conduct and a criminal offence in the United Kingdom. In the same vein, Article 1 of the EU Council Act of 26 July 1995,[15] defines fraud along five baselines that affect the financial interests of the European Communities. Thus, regarding expenditure, fraud is any intentional act or omission relating to:

> i.   The use or presentation of false, incorrect or incomplete statements or documents, which has as its effect *the misappropriation or wrongful retention of funds from the general budget of the European Communities or budgets* managed by, or on behalf of, the European Communities;
> ii.   Non-disclosure of information in violation of a specific obligation, with the same effect, the misapplication of such funds for purposes other than those for which they were originally granted;
> iii.   The use or presentation of false, incorrect or incomplete statements or documents, which has as its effect *the illegal diminution of the resources of the general budget of the European Communities or budgets* managed by, or on behalf of, the European Communities;
> iv.   Non-disclosure of information in violation of a specific obligation, with the same effect as in iii above (the illegal diminution of the resources);

---

[10] The Theft Act 1968 c 60, s 17.
[11] Doig, *Fraud.*
[12] The Theft Act 1968 c 60, s 18.
[13] Ibid, s 19.
[14] Ibid, s 20.
[15] Council Act of 26 July 1995 drawing up the Convention on the protection of the European Communities' financial interests (95/C 316/03), Official Journal of the European Communities, C 316/48, https://eur-lex.europa.eu/legal-content/EN/TXT/PDF/?uri=CELEX:31995F1127%2803%29&from=EN, accessed 23 March 2020.

v. Misapplication of a legally obtained benefit, with the same effect as in iii above (the illegal diminution of the resources).[16]

The definition in Article 1 of the Council Act[17] provides for familiar elements such as the intentional preparation, supply or use of false, incorrect or incomplete statements or documents and 'non-disclosure of information', but goes to further highlight another leg to the definitions provided beforehand: when a lawful benefit that is misapplied has the effect of illegal diminution of the resources of the general budget of the European Communities or budgets. Misappropriation or wrongful retention are elements that have also been modelled as providing details for the definition of fraud. There is also emphasis given to how incorrect, irregular or mistaken conduct on documents or accounts can amount to fraud when it is found to be intentional and/or benefiting the culprit. The test for determining intentional nature of a conduct is domiciled in Article 4 of Council Act of 26 July 1995,[18] as to 'be inferred from objective, factual circumstances'. Article 1(2) criminalises the fraudulent conducts in Article 1(1) above and Member States are required to transpose them into national laws.[19]

Following the provisions in Article 1 of Council Act of 26 July 1995,[20] the EU's Anti-Fraud Office (OLAF) summarises fraud as 'a deliberate act of deception intended for personal gain or to cause a loss to another party'. It also includes intentional or deliberate irregularity. Irregularity is defined in Article 1 of the Council Regulation 2988/95[21] as:

> Any infringement of a provision of Community law resulting from an act or omission by an economic operator, which has, or would have, the effect of prejudicing the general budget of the Communities or budgets managed by them, either by reducing or losing revenue accruing from own resources collected directly on behalf of the Communities, or by an unjustified item of expenditure.[22]

Therefore, an intentional 'act which does not comply with EU rules and which has a potentially negative impact on EU financial interests, but which may be the result of genuine errors committed both by beneficiaries claiming funds and by the authorities responsible for making payments'[23] can be classified as a fraudulent act.

Furthermore, OECD simply defines fraud as 'the acquisition of another person's property by deception'.[24] Thus, any deceptive act that results in acquiring someone's property is understood by OECD to be a fraudulent act or omission. This definition

---

[16] Council Act of 26 July 1995 drawing up the Convention on the protection of the European Communities' financial interests (95/C 316/03), Official Journal of the European Communities, C 316/48.

[17] Ibid.

[18] Ibid.

[19] Ibid, Art 1.

[20] C 316/48.

[21] Council Regulation 2988/95 of 18 December 1995 on the protection of the European Communities financial interests, Official Journal of the European Communities, L 312/1, https://eur-lex.europa.eu/legal-content/EN/TXT/PDF/?uri=CELEX:31995R2988&from=EN, accessed 23 March 2020.

[22] Ibid.

[23] OLAF, European Anti-Fraud Office, 'Report fraud', https://ec.europa.eu/anti-fraud/olaf-and-you/report-fraud_en, accessed 23 March 2020.

[24] OECD, 'Glossary of statistical terms: Fraud', https://stats.oecd.org/glossary/detail.asp?ID=4781, accessed 23 March 2020.

is directly drawn from the definition provided by the Council's[25] definition of fraud above.

Integral in the foregoing definitions are:

- A dishonest intention to commit fraud. It is an imperative qualification to know that the conduct is illegal.
- A guilty act or omission to commit fraud. For instance, a manoeuvre, manipulation, falsification or deception to commit fraud.
- Usually involving illegal monetary gain or financial benefit (but not limited to finances).
- The advantage obtained must be illegal or unjust, regardless of the form it takes.[26]
- Can involve a legal person(s) and/or natural person(s).
- Both illegal and legal businesses can be used to commit fraud.
- Can involve a shared responsibility – conspiracy, concealment of fraud and decision or action not to report fraud.

These definitions of fraud articulate a 'huge range of contexts in which frauds, large and small, lasting milliseconds (like unauthorised electronic funds transfers) or many years (like the Madoff Ponzi scheme), are perpetrated'.[27] Fraud can be committed in many diverse fields such as finance, education, technology, health, sports, manufacturing, marketing, commerce, geography and construction. Whereas some frauds are planned as scams right from beginning – sometimes as part of an organised crime group activity – other frauds (with or without outsider involvement or participation) are occasioned by insiders who spot or identify certain loopholes 'which, if undetected, may spread from there into much larger schemes'. These tenets of fraud find expression in EU and OECD legal frameworks.

More often than not, it is after a fraudulent event has taken place that an assessment can be made whether the act is a fraud or the extent to which it is a fraud. Its interpretation would determine the planning category into which a given fraud falls.[28] As a result of the broad, evasive and technical nature of fraud, knowing what it is and mechanics of committing the fraud has become a cumbersome enterprise in many fields of endeavour.

Levi has outlined six issues on the study of fraud, as follows:

i. The limited academic interest in fraud in the United Kingdom and the absence of empirical studies.
ii. The changes to economic activity which result in shifts in patterns of crime.
iii. The cost of fraud against the cost of crime, particularly at the higher end of the value scale where fraud easily outstrips armed robbery on a case-by-case basis.

---

[25] Council Act of 26 July 1995 drawing up the Convention on the protection of the European Communities' financial interests (95/C 316/03), Official Journal of the European Communities, C 316/48.

[26] C Allain, J Fraudeau and A-G Martin, 'Facing tax fraud in the European Union – Challenges and perspectives' (European Judicial Training Network, International Cooperation in Criminal Matters, 2016) 3.

[27] M Levi, 'Trends and costs of Fraud' in Doig, *Fraud: The Counter Fraud Practitioner's Handbook* 7.

[28] Ibid.

iv. Fraud may be linked to a number of other crimes, such as money laundering, and involves the use of professionals to facilitate them.

v. The multiplicity of agencies and the variations in powers of the agencies dealing with fraud.

vi. The trial process and the issue of jury trials.[29]

The first point or issue is not the case today as it was in 1987 and 1993 when Levi was presenting these issues and when Doig first analysed the issues in 2006. The fourth point especially highlights the interconnection between fraud and other crimes such as tax crimes and related financial crimes – including money laundering.[30] Understanding the ecosystem of fraud will be appropriate for a better comprehension of the defining limits of fraud.

The fraud treated in this section is by no means anywhere near a comprehensive outlook on fraud. These dimensions of fraud treated are for the purpose of providing a reasonable background for defining and understanding tax fraud and tax evasion.

Tax Fraud and Tax Evasion

The definitions of fraud above act as a springboard to defining tax fraud and evasion. The EU and OECD are among the international organisations concerned about the threat of tax fraud and evasion to the financial stability and economic development of their members.

Tax Fraud

In the EU legal framework, definition of tax fraud finds general expression in Council Act of 1995[31] and Directive (EU) 2017/1371.[32] In furtherance to the Council Act of 1995, as discussed above, Article 3 of Directive (EU) 2017/1371[33] provides the following key elements as characterising fraud affecting the Union's financial interests in four respects:

i. non-procurement-related expenditure;
ii. procurement-related expenditure;

[29] Doig, *Fraud*; see M Levi, 'The Investigation, Prosecution, and Trial of Serious Fraud' (Royal Commission on Criminal Justice Research Study No 14, 1993); M Levi, *Regulating Fraud: White-Collar Crime and the Criminal Process* (Routledge, 1987).

[30] See N Ryder, U Turksen and S Hassler (eds), *Fighting Financial Crime in the Global Economic Crisis* (Routledge, 2014); U Turksen and N Ryder, 'The fight against fraud: A critical review and comparative analysis of the Labour and Conservative governments' anti-fraud policies in the United Kingdom' (2015) 4(2) *Law and Economics Yearly Review* 369; K Harrison and N Ryder, *The Law Relating to Financial Crime in the United Kingdom*, 2nd edn (Routledge, 2016).

[31] Council Act of 26 July 1995 drawing up the Convention on the protection of the European Communities' financial interests (95/C 316/03), Official Journal of the European Communities, C 316/48.

[32] Directive (EU) 2017/1371 of the European Parliament and of the Council of 5 July 2017 on the fight against fraud to the Union's financial interests by means of criminal law [2017] OJ L 198/29–41.

[33] Ibid.

iii.   revenue other than revenue arising from VAT own resources; and
iv.   revenue arising from VAT own resources.[34]

These four perspectives bring the understanding of fraud to the doorstep of tax fraud – particularly VAT fraud. In the context of Article 3, fraud is used from the financial perspective – thus, financial fraud. The particulars of the four areas provided by Article 3(2)[35] that can be affected by fraud are illustrated below:

Article 3 (2)(a)	*Further particulars*
In respect of non-procurement-related expenditure, any act or omission relating to either of the following:	(i) The use or presentation of false, incorrect or incomplete statements or documents, which has as its effect the misappropriation or wrongful retention of funds or assets from the Union budget or budgets managed by the Union, or on its behalf.
	(ii) Non-disclosure of information in violation of a specific obligation, with the same effect.
	(iii) The misapplication of such funds or assets for purposes other than those for which they were originally granted.

The particulars provided in Article 3(2)(a) of the Directive only apply to non-procurement-related expenditure, any act or omission. The particulars that stand out in Article 3 (2)(a)(i) are *falsification, usage of incomplete or incorrect materials*. However, these must have effects, which are engineered by ill motives. The effects of these flawed actions must be *misappropriation* or *wrongful retention* of funds or assets. The other qualifier is that the assets or funds affected by flawed actions should emanate from the budget of the EU or budgets that are managed by the EU or managed on behalf of the EU. This qualifier brings into focus the context of fraud.

Article 3(2)(a)(ii) adds *failure to disclose* relevant information as an ingredient of fraud. This is conditioned upon the fact that such a failure should violate a particular legal obligation to qualify as an ingredient of fraud. Here also, context is required to qualify non-disclosure of relevant information as a fraudulent act. Article 3(2)(a)(iii) directs our attention to purposeful use of assets or funds – acting contrarily is fraudulent. Thus, misapplying funds or assets counts as a prohibitive act denoted as fraudulent conduct.

In determining financial fraud from Article 3(2)(b), therefore, objective element or *actus rea* (guilty act) does play a more significant role than the mental element or *mens rea* (guilty mind), which can be reasonably deduced from the cause and effect analysis.[36] In fact, in imposing on the EU Member States the obligation to counter financial fraud, Article 3(1) also emphasises intention or guilty mind as an essential ingredient for determining fraud. It thus states, 'Member States *shall* take the necessary measures to ensure that fraud affecting the Union's financial interests constitutes a criminal offence when committed *intentionally*.'[37]

---

[34] Ibid.
[35] Ibid.
[36] Ibid.
[37] Art 3(1) of Directive (EU) 2017/1371 (emphasis added).

Article 3(2)(b) of the Directive[38] below provides for particulars of fraud in procurement related expenditure:

Article 3(2)(b)	Further particulars
In respect of procurement-related expenditure, at least when committed in order to make an unlawful gain for the perpetrator or another by causing a loss to the Union's financial interests, any act or omission relating to either of the following:	(i) The use or presentation of false, incorrect or incomplete statements or documents, which has as its effect the misappropriation or wrongful retention of funds or assets from the Union budget or budgets managed by the Union, or on its behalf.
	(ii) Non-disclosure of information in violation of a specific obligation, with the same effect.
	(iii) The misapplication of such funds or assets for purposes other than those for which they were originally granted, which damages the Union's financial interests.

The particulars that stand out in Article 3(2)(b)(i) contain the same elements as Article 3(2)(a)(i) above. The same applies to Article 3(2)(b)(ii) and Article 3(2)(a)(ii). However, the difference between the ingredients of Article 3(2)(b)(iii) and Article 3(2)(a)(iii) is that in Article 3(2)(b)(iii), there is an explicit qualification – *damage caused to the financial interests of the EU*. Thus, for procurement-related expenditure, the non-purposeful use of funds or assets is qualified as fraud if the conduct causes damage to the Union's financial interests. This implies that, for the non-procurement-related expenditure, even if the conduct does not damage the financial interest of the EU, the misapplication will, all the more, still qualify as a fraudulent conduct.

The particulars that stand out in Article 3(2)(c)[39] are provided below:

Article 3(2)(c)	Further particulars
In respect of revenue other than revenue arising from VAT own resources referred to in point (d) below, any act or omission relating to either of the following:	(i) The use or presentation of false, incorrect or incomplete statements or documents, which has as its effect the illegal diminution of the resources of the Union budget or budgets managed by the Union, or on its behalf.
	(ii) Non-disclosure of information in violation of a specific obligation, with the same effect.
	(iii) Misapplication of a legally obtained benefit, with the same effect.

The particular wording in Article 3(2)(c) is almost the same as that of the particulars in Article 3(2)(a) above. The only minor exception is that whereas a misappropriation or wrongful retention is taken as an effect of falsification or incomplete/incorrect

---

[38] Ibid.
[39] Ibid.

statements/documents as appertained in Article 3(2)(a)(i), in Article 3(2)(c)(i) the effect is in respect of the illegal diminution of the resources – implying any illegality that reduces the resources of the Union. In effect, Article 3(2)(c)(i) can encapsulate Article 3(2)(a)(i), since misappropriation or wrongful retention are contributory factors for diminution of resources.

Considering the particulars of Article 3(2)(d), however, a noticeable difference can be seen in relation to the previous three subsections of Article 3(2). Article 3(2)(d) focuses on VAT. The previous subsections present a framework of misconduct that can capture not only VAT and other taxes but also other financial crimes such as corruption and money laundering. However, Article 3(2)(d) also has common features with the other subsections such as falsification, incorrect or incomplete information, and failure to disclose information.

However, unmerited claim of or right to claim VAT refunds using correct VAT statements to fraudulently disguise non-payment is a clear feature that sets apart Article 3(2)(d) from Article 3(2)(c), Article 3(2)(b), and Article 3(2)(a).[40]

Article 3(2)(d)	Further particulars
In respect of revenue arising from VAT own resources, any act or omission committed in cross-border fraudulent schemes in relation to either of the following:	(i) The use or presentation of false, incorrect or incomplete VAT-related statements or documents, which has as an effect the diminution of the resources of the Union budget.
	(ii) Non-disclosure of VAT-related information in violation of a specific obligation, with the same effect.
	(iii) The presentation of correct VAT-related statements for the purposes of fraudulently disguising the non-payment or wrongful creation of rights to VAT refunds.

The above illustrations have presented particulars for the financial fraud that can be committed in the four areas. These four areas touch on strategic poles upon which criminals can commit any fraud. However, what can be gleaned from Article 3(2)(d) is that there appears to be some special treatment or attention given to VAT fraud primarily due to the prominence it assumes in EU policy priorities[41] given its large scale.[42] In proclaiming the serious offences relating to fraud against tax, the EU has thrown further light on the outlook of VAT fraud, noting in Recital 4 of Directive (EU) 2017/1371 that:

> Offences against the common VAT system should be considered to be serious where they are connected with the territory of two or more Member States, result from a fraudulent

---

[40] Directive (EU) 2017/1371 of the European Parliament and of the Council of 5 July 2017 on the fight against fraud to the Union's financial interests by means of criminal law [2017] OJ L 198/29–41.

[41] Ibid.

[42] The VAT gap in the EU was estimated to be around €137.5 billion, representing a loss of 11.2 per cent of the total expected VAT revenue. EU Commission, 'Study and Reports on the VAT Gap in the EU-28 Member States: 2019 Final Report' TAXUD/2015/CC/131, https://ec.europa.eu/taxation_customs/sites/taxation/files/vat-gap-full-report-2019_en.pdf, accessed 22 July 2020.

scheme whereby those offences are committed in a structured way with the aim of taking undue advantage of the common VAT system and the total damage caused by the offences is at least EUR 10 000 000.[43]

The above provision highlights the organised or structured nature of fraud, cheating or undue advantage-taking of the common VAT system of the EU – which are regarded as serious offences. Additionally, this fraudulent disposition is considered a serious offence if the total damage caused thereof amounts to, at least, €10,000,000 – thus establishing (a rather high) threshold in the definition of tax crimes in the EU. The threshold regime is used, albeit on different scales, by almost all EU and OECD Member States. In the event that the EU Member States do not put in place a legal instrument or provision for punishing VAT fraud involving a total damage of less than this amount, this would not constitute a breach of EU law. Moreover, the Directive has also introduced a territorial threshold which obliges Member States to criminalise serious VAT fraud committed in one or more states. This means that the EU has decided to not criminalise serious VAT fraud committed in a single jurisdiction.

It is worth noting here that there are not only different threshold amounts for criminalisation of tax offences in EU Member States, but also different ways to calculate them. That is why even if two countries provide for the same threshold fiscal value for criminalisation of tax offences, very different consequences and results can occur. For example, Austria defines a threshold of €100,000 for criminal court prosecution. The same amount is applicable in Greece (however, in the case of VAT fraud, the threshold is only €50,000). Despite the same threshold in Austria and Greece, there is a fundamental difference in regards to how the threshold is determined. According to Austrian law, the threshold is connected with the overall sum of taxes evaded, stemming from all deeds prosecuted within the same proceeding,[44] whereas Greek law calculates the threshold for each fiscal year and each kind of tax separately.[45] So, the limits for criminalisation in Greece can be much higher than in Austria – even if it involves VAT fraud.

Beyond descriptions of the concepts in EU legislation, the European Commission has defined both tax fraud and tax evasion in its publications. These definitions are operational and simplified versions of the prescriptions given in the legislation. In this regard, the European Commission defines tax fraud as 'a form of deliberate evasion of tax which is generally punishable under criminal law. The term includes situations in which deliberately false statements are submitted or fake documents are produced.' The key constituents of this definition include:

- intention, wilfulness;
- evasion;
- illegal conduct as recognised by criminal law; and
- falsification.

---

[43] Directive (EU) 2017/1371 of the European Parliament and of the Council of 5 July 2017 on the fight against fraud to the Union's financial interests by means of criminal law [2017] OJ L 198/29–41.

[44] As well as in Bulgaria and Hungary.

[45] As well as in Estonia and Italy.

Subsequently, in effect, both the *mens rea* or the mental element/intention, and *actus reus* or guilty act or the objective element (evasion, falsification) are counted as two critical elements of a tax crime from the fraud perspective.[46] Interestingly, one of the constituents in the above definition of tax fraud by the European Commission is evasion – which simply means to escape doing something, particularly by means of deceit or trickery. Therefore, tax fraud is referred to as wilful and intentional falsification, suppression, and such manipulation of tax information in order that the individual and/or the corporate entity involved in this conduct reduces or fails to pay the required tax liability.

In France, Article 1741 of the French General Tax Code 2016 makes tax fraud a criminal offence. The criminal conduct to limit tax liability can be:

- a misrepresentation of the true affairs of the taxpayer;
- a wilful concealment of income or profits of the taxpayer; and/or
- organising the taxpayer's own insolvency.

However, France's criminal code has no explicit provision prohibiting tax fraud. Thus, tax fraud is criminalised under the tax/fiscal law, not by the criminal code. At the same time, investigative procedures are set out in the French Tax Procedure Code rather than the Penal Procedure Code. Therefore, the provisions for criminalisation and procedures are found in codes that are distinct from the traditional criminal offences such as robbery. This again highlights the complex nature and peculiarity of tax fraud and evasion in France. However, this is not peculiar to France only. A number of other countries in the EU also have complex cross-cutting identification and administration of tax offences.

In Luxembourg, paragraph 396 of the General Tax Law 1931 prohibits tax fraud. It provides that tax fraud can be ascertained: 'If the tax fraud concerns a significant amount of taxes and was committed through the systematic use of fraudulent manoeuvres or manipulation in order to conceal pertinent facts from the authority or to persuade it into the existence of false facts.'[47] Thus, tax fraud is taken into account for enforcement depending on the magnitude and systematic nature of the fraudulent conduct to conceal facts or profits from the tax authorities. Technically, tax fraud in Luxembourg is closely linked to counterfeit accounting of legal persons.[48]

In France, there is individual liability other than corporate liability. Therefore, the law differentiates between the moral or legal person and the physical or natural person. In this regard, if a natural person commits tax fraud in a company (legal person), prosecutors would pursue the physical person who committed the tax fraud such as concealing the profits of the legal person from the tax authorities. Conversely, in Luxemburg, the legal person can be held criminally liable for a tax fraud. Such differences exist across the 27 EU Member States, making a uniform definition of tax fraud and evasion more complicated.

---

[46] European Commission, 'Time to get the Missing Part Back: What does it mean – Tax fraud', https://ec.europa.eu/taxation_customs/fight-against-tax-fraud-tax-evasion/missing-part_en, accessed 25 March 2020.

[47] Allain, Fraudeau and Martin, 'Facing tax fraud in the European Union'.

[48] Ibid.

To this end, the following examples provide further evidence of personal tax fraud:

i. intentional failure to file personal income tax return;
ii. usage of false or fake social security number; or any such unique number for employees;
iii. making claim for personal expenses as business expenses;
iv. intentional overstatement of expenses or deductions;
v. deliberately failing to report all the income received;
vi. preparing and filing a false tax return;
vii. misrepresenting situational facts with the intention to falsify in order to claim tax deductions or tax credits; and
viii. intentionally failing to pay tax debt.[49]

Some of the fraudulent activities above can also be carried out by corporate entities too, especially via the last five examples of fraud on the list. For businesses or corporate entities, there are complex examples or methods for tax fraud, including the following:

- wilful failure to file payroll tax reports;
- intentional failure to report some or all of cash payments made to employees;
- hiring 'an outside payroll service that doesn't turn over funds' to the tax authority,
- failure to withhold income tax or such other taxes from employee earnings or pay-cheques within the tax year; and
- failure to report and pay to the tax authorities any payroll taxes that have been collected.[50]

The methods of tax fraud also exemplify tax evasion for individuals and businesses. These effectively align with the legal provisions of many jurisdictions in the EU and beyond. For instance, they are in sync with Spanish tax law, particularly so as Article 305 *bis* of the Spanish Criminal Code 2015 situates tax evasion as fraudulent conduct. But a threshold regime applies to Article 305 *bis* in the amount of €120,000.

Tax Evasion

Another formation of tax crime is, thus, looked at from the evasion perspective. Tax evasion is generally defined as comprising 'illegal arrangements where tax liability is hidden or ignored, ie the taxpayer pays less tax than s/he is supposed to pay under the law by hiding income or information from the tax authorities.'[51] However, there are instances where some taxpayers completely fail to pay all tax liabilities. Thus, it is also

---

[49] U Turksen and others, 'D1.2: Case Studies of Tax Crimes in the European Union' (EU PROTAX, 2018).

[50] Ibid; see also Murray J, 'What Is the Difference Between Tax Avoidance and Tax Evasion? How to Avoid Tax Fraud Charges', *The Balance – Small Business* (29 April 2020), www.thebalancesmb.com/tax-avoidance-vs-evasion-397671, accessed 8 October 2020.

[51] European Commission, 'Time to get the Missing Part Back: What does it mean – Tax evasion', https://ec.europa.eu/taxation_customs/fight-against-tax-fraud-tax-evasion/missing-part_en, accessed 25 March 2020.

possible for the taxpayer to completely refuse to pay the required tax liability. That would obviously be illegal under either civil or criminal laws of the country. Therefore, when taxes are illegally underpaid or illegally not paid under the circumstances described by the European Commission immediately above, tax evasion would have occurred. In effect, tax evasion is a deliberate failure of 'people or businesses to declare or account for what they owe'. This 'includes the hidden economy, which is when someone [completely] hides taxable activity' from the tax authority. Frunza adds that tax evasion is characterised by the use of illegal methods to partially or totally reduce taxpayer's liability, or to fraudulently access tax reimbursement from the national tax office.[52]

We can decipher at least two key constituents of this tax crime formation:

- the illegal conduct as recognised by criminal law; and
- hidden and/or ignored tax liability.

In this definition of tax evasion, the European Commission does not specifically indicate the inclusion of intention on the part of the taxpayer. However, it is difficult to hide or ignore something without first forming the intention to do so. Therefore, both guilty act or objective element (ie, ignoring or hiding tax liability) and intention or guilty mind (subjective element) are material elements to consider in determining a tax crime in the context of tax evasion. With respect to the subjective element of tax offences, it does require, depending on the legal system, an intention and/or dishonesty [to prove]. PROTAX research outputs highlighted the limits of this notion of dishonesty.[53] Moreover, the definition of these elements is also affected by the case law' in the EU and its Member States.

In this vein, tax evasion can be referred to as the application of illegal methods and processes (i.e. by fraudulent acts and deception) to avoid paying taxes.[54] These illegal methods or examples of tax evasion include:

- underreporting of income;
- complete failure to report any income to tax authorities; and
- conduct of a similar nature which may be deemed to be intentional means to illegally avoid paying taxes due to a taxpayer.[55]

Hybrid Nature and Differentiation of Tax Fraud and Tax Evasion

It will be clear, by now, that tax evasion and tax fraud are difficult to differentiate. In Spain, for instance, tax evasion is 'an illegal act of evading taxes by concealing income, earned either legally or illegally, from detection and collection by the tax authorities'.[56] The objective element therein as tax crime is when the taxpayer seeks to *defraud* 'the

---

[52] M-C Frunza, *Value added tax fraud* (Routledge, 2019) 1.
[53] Rasmouki and others, 'D2.3 Approaches to tax crimes'.
[54] Turksen and others, 'D1.2: Case Studies'.
[55] Ibid.
[56] Art. 305 and 305 *bis* (Organic Law No 1/2015 of March 30, 2015, amending Organic Law No 10/1995 of 23 November 1995, of the Criminal Code).

state, community, regional and local tax authorities, evading the payment of taxes, amounts which were withheld or which should have been withheld [for] tax payments, irregularly receiving rebates or enjoying tax benefits in the same way, provided that the sum of the defrauded payment, the unpaid sum of retentions or payments or of rebates or tax benefits irregularly obtained or enjoyed are in excess of €120,000'.[57] If it is tax infringement, the objective element of tax evasion therein is connected with the 'intentional or unintentional act or omission of any degree of negligence that is categorised and sanctioned as such in this or another law'.[58] The tax evasion mental element as a tax crime, thus, has two parameters to test: the intent of the taxpayer and any omission by the taxpayer.[59] It is clear that a number of stakeholders in the tax enforcement community have misgivings about the subjective or mental element of the prohibited act that identifies guilt of a criminal tax offence based on intention and/or dishonesty, as the legal framework of a jurisdiction would dictate.[60]

In effect, since fraud can be any 'act of deception or misrepresentation', part of what tax evasion involves is fraud and that is what someone evading taxes does – thus, deceiving tax authorities through misrepresentation of their tax status and liability.[61] For instance, tax fraud and tax evasion are both integrated in the following scheme: getting VAT-free goods imported into another EU country (sometimes in a scheme involving fictitious companies), sell the goods to clients, charge the customers VAT, and then vanishing with the proceeds without submitting the tax, or alternatively submitting suppressed or falsified VAT accounts to the national tax authority. This illustration connotes missing trader VAT fraud and VAT carousel fraud.[62] In fact, both the EU and OECD treat tax fraud and tax evasion as if they are the same thing, complementary or interchangeable.

It may be argued that trying to differentiate these terms is pointless since they can be used as joint concepts and given a joint meaning. However, this argument appears pale or vitiated, almost without firm legs to stand on, in the face of the varied ways in which EU and OECD Member States have deployed the concepts in their jurisprudence. As indicated earlier, taxation connotes a symbol of sovereignty of a given jurisdiction. Therefore, in the EU, tax regulation in which the EU has competence usually receives a unanimous vote from EU Member States. At the same time, each EU Member State defines tax fraud and tax evasion based on their legal framework, tax policy direction and political priorities. The absence of a common EU definition of tax fraud and tax evasion that can find expression in national legal frameworks makes the definition of tax crime for investigation, prosecution, conviction and asset recovery purposes a lingering challenge.[63]

---

[57] Art. 305 and 305 *bis* (Spanish 2015 Criminal Code).

[58] Art 183 of General Taxation Law (*Ley General Tributaria*) 58/2003 of 17 December (BOE of 18 December).

[59] Turksen and others, 'D1.2: Case Studies'; see Europarl, 'Member States capabilities in fighting tax crimes: Relevant legal definition(s) of tax-related offences' (Spain fiche), www.europarl.europa.eu/cmsdata/124716/Spain%20fiche.pdf, accessed 12 January 2020.

[60] Ibid.

[61] Turksen and others, 'D1.2: Case Studies'.

[62] P Cannon, 'What are the penalties for tax evasion (UK)?', www.patrickcannon.net/tax-evasion-penalties-uk/, accessed 27 March 2020.

[63] Turksen and others, 'D1.2: Case Studies'.

Both tax fraud and tax evasion possess a hybrid nature in the light of tax law and criminal law.[64] This is because these terms, in many jurisdictions and the *acquis communautaire* of the EU, are partly administrative and partly criminal, which are respectively governed by tax/administrative/civil law and tax/criminal/penal law.

In one of its technical reports,[65] the OECD has identified both tax fraud and tax evasion as 'illegal and intentional misrepresentation of tax obligations' involving 'deliberate omission or falsification of income or revenue, as well as efforts to be invisible to tax authorities altogether'. These offences involve cheating the public of revenue that is to be used for public goods and puts compliant taxpayers (individuals and businesses) that obey the law at a disadvantage.[66] Just as in the EU, there is hardly any commonly transferable definition of either 'tax fraud and tax evasion' or tax crimes, generally, which effectively find expression in the national criminal laws and/or tax laws.

Panayi[67] and Turksen[68] add their voices to the challenge of finding a 'unified definition'[69] of tax crime as expressed 'in the inconsistencies of [tax crime] variants even as used by the Court of Justice of the European Union (CJEU) including the use of "'abuse', 'evasion', 'avoidance' and 'fraud' interchangeably in the tax case law"'.[70] Obviously, it is a settled understanding among a majority of scholars, governments, other policy makers and LEAs that tax avoidance and, to some extent, tax abuse and aggressive tax planning should not necessarily compete for space with tax evasion and tax fraud when it comes to establishing their boundaries.

With respect to tax abuse and tax crime, it has been observed that:

> There is a thin line between abuse and crime. This is a problem of definition. It is difficult to assess which cases the tax authorities classify as abuses. Even the EU and the OECD have no uniform understanding of tax abuse/clear boundaries between avoidance and evasion.[71]

It can only be added, as a peculiar exception – and a term that denotes a process of not following certain paths, in order not to be confronted with what someone does not want to see, do or be affected by – that, tax avoidance is the baseline for beginning to describe the mechanics or strategy to achieve any of the tax crime variations. Panayi points out that the challenge about the differences in graduating tax avoidance to tax fraud or tax evasion has more to do with the transactions that are considered legitimate tax planning measures and the transactions that have not been considered as illegitimate tax avoidance.

Panayi's argument is that the lack of unified definition is also due to 'linguistic discrepancies associated with the translation of the Court's judgements'. Related to the

---

[64] R Boadwaya, M Marchand and P Pestieau, 'Towards a Theory of the Direct–Indirect Tax Mix' (1994) 55(1) *Journal of Public Economics* 71.

[65] OECD, 'Technology Tools to Tackle Tax Evasion and Tax Fraud' (2017) 6, www.oecd.org/tax/crime/technology-tools-to-tackle-tax-evasion-and-tax-fraud.pdf, accessed 25 February 2020.

[66] Ibid.

[67] CHJI Panayi, *Advanced Issues in International and European Tax Law* (Hart Publishing, 2015).

[68] Ibid.

[69] U Turksen, 'The Criminalisation and protection of whistle-blowers in the EU's counter financial crime framework' in Ligeti and Tosla (eds), *Economic and Financial Crime in Europe* (Hart Publishing, 2018).

[70] Turksen and others, 'D1.2: Case Studies'; Panayi, *Advanced Issues in International and European Tax Law*.

[71] R Kreissl and others, 'Austrian Focus Group – Synthesis of discussions: Focus groups to explore institutional practices in anti-money laundering and tax evasion' (EU PROTAX, 2019).

linguistic differences in the EU, the interpretations of these terms tend to be different across EU Member States. There is also 'no clarity between the perimeters of these terms being assigned to tax crime in these jurisdictions'.[72] For example, the discussion so far in this section has attempted to establish borderlines between fraud, tax fraud and tax evasion.

Although fraud and tax fraud can be defined with relatively high degrees of similarity around a central point, tax evasion has no such unification of definition in the criminal law landscape. So even though tax evasion is considered by many scholars and jurisdictions to be a tax crime, the concept has been treated as part of the main tax concepts that generate controversies. For instance, according to Turksen, 'There is no unified definition of tax evasion across the EU.' Member States and in general, the counter tax crime laws in the EU have significant variations.[73]

Arguably, one of the drivers for these variations is the respect for principle of the extreme *ratio* of criminal law: the criminal penalty should only be applied to the extent that other instruments, including administrative law, cannot effectively prevent and deter citizens from committing offences. If a country is able to optimise tax collection in tandem with minimising tax offences, it is unlikely to emphasise criminalisation of tax offences.

With respect to corporate tax liability in 10 selected EU jurisdictions, evidence from the PROTAX studies indicates that the main differences in the legislation of these jurisdictions relate to the nature of the responsibility in question, the entities that can be liable, the tax offences envisioned, the structure of the liability regime of the entities, types and degrees of sanctions, and the rules concerning prosecution.[74] With the adoption of Directive (EU) 2017/1371 of 5 July 2017 on the fight against fraud to the Union's financial interests by means of criminal law (the PFI Directive), there is to be an improved alignment of the criminal tax regime, at least in the context of cross-border VAT fraud, in EU Member States – the destination of having a harmonised legal framework appears to be long way off. In regards to the OECD countries outside the EU, they will continue to be guided by TGPs, with their currently varied criminal tax legal frameworks.

Corporate Liability

Following the main categories or forms of taxes, two principal kinds of tax crime are found. These are tax crime committed by an individual, and tax crime committed by a business or firm (ie, corporate tax fraud). Corporate or business tax crime has had wide coverage by the media recently. However, corporate tax crime, especially involving multinational corporations (MNCs) appears to be both evasive and pervasive. The idea of corporate tax offence has actually been where the line between tax fraud or evasion and tax avoidance appears thinnest. This is because firms not only adopt many schemes

---

[72] Turksen and others, 'D1.2: Case Studies'); Panayi, *Advanced Issues in International and European Tax Law*.
[73] Turksen, 'The Criminalisation and Protection of Whistleblowers'; Turksen and others, 'D1.2: Case Studies'.
[74] F Rasmouki and others, 'D2.3 Approaches to tax crimes'.

and strategies, permitted by law or tax agreements, to reduce their tax liabilities, but also benefit from secrecy jurisdictions and subsidiary presence in multiple jurisdictions with the assistance of various enablers. At the heart of the challenge is that the defining limits of these concepts depend highly on the nature of legal frameworks of different jurisdictions and the kind of interpretations attached to the respective national laws and regulations.

MNCs are always attempting to exploit differences in tax policies, laws and rates in different jurisdictions by locating or moving their business branches around, to avoid being heavily taxed and optimise profits. This seemingly permissible exploitation of tax laws, of course, sits well within a given legal framework but it can sometimes be seen by the authorities and the public as immoral, unethical or offensive, thus attracting huge media attention. For instance, the media popularised and created intense public debate over the so-called 'double Irish' or 'Dutch sandwich' arrangements[75] (and the huge potential tax liabilities involved) that were associated with popular multinational tech companies such as Microsoft, Google, Apple or Amazon or Microsoft. However, these arrangements were not considered fraudulent or criminal.[76]

Illegal Acts and Tax Liability

In evaluating tax liability, it does not matter whether the income, profit or transaction is connected with an illegality or legality. Legal and illegal transactions are, in principle under most national legislation and/or case law, taxable. The fundamental argument that underlies this position is that 'taxation should be neutral to the legal character or morality of the activity'.

Box 2b   Taxability of Illegal Activities

> *Illegal or immoral activities should not have the benefit of non-taxability as this situation would result in an economic disadvantage of legal activities. Hereby, the taxation of illegal and immoral activities is not considered as legalisation or approval of these activities. This is controversial. In practice the tax liability occurred by illegal activities is likely to be entirely concealed from the (tax) administration, when illegal activities are subject to tax.*

In the EU, because of the differences between national legal frameworks relevant to tax crimes, it is difficult to pin down the definition of illegal acts or otherwise. While some

---

[75] Hakelberg aptly summarises these cases: 'With the complicity of several small EU member states, these companies set up tax-planning schemes like the "Double Irish with a Dutch Sandwich" to minimize the taxable profits of their subsidiaries in large EU member states. They achieved this through cost-sharing arrangements allowing them to transfer the rights to the foreign use of their IP from the US to subsidiaries in Ireland, Luxembourg, or the Netherlands.' See L Hakelberg, 'The power of states and business: Explaining transformative change in the fight against tax evasion and avoidance', COFFERS Project, D3.2, p 29, http://coffers.eu/wp-content/uploads/2019/11/D3.2-Conference-Paper.pdf, accessed 22 July 2020.

[76] Allain, Fraudeau and Martin, 'Facing tax fraud in the European'.

activities can be legal in one jurisdiction, the same activities can be recognised as illegal in another jurisdiction.

Essentially, whether in the EU or OECD countries, tax evasion and tax fraud are complementing and sometimes substitutive bedfellows in the domain of tax crimes – whereby there are, at least, working definitions for the two terms. Tax evasion appears more to be a subset of tax fraud within the reasonable limits of linguistic barriers, interpretation differences, legal framework differences, tax policy choices, socio-economic and political considerations, building of common ground, and related pressures that hinder cooperation and collaboration. Tax evasion and tax fraud, together, form the spine of tax crimes, no matter where they are found in the EU and OECD countries. But tax fraud and tax evasion in the legal frameworks of these jurisdictions contain some of the key defining elements of tax fraud and tax evasion articulated above – which can reasonably be placed in the criminal law domain. Indeed, most EU Member States have criminalised tax fraud and tax evasion, albeit in different formations.

Tax Crimes? In Search of Further Particulars

The difficulty in defining tax fraud and tax evasion dovetails into the challenge that is posed in defining tax crimes in general – it becomes even more complex. A survey of many jurisdictions and publications on tax crimes returns a varied understanding of tax crimes just like it is with tax fraud, tax evasion and tax abuse (to some extent). The following different terminologies of the main tax crimes are in the legal frameworks of ten EU jurisdictions[77] reveal that such provisions are imbedded in mainly tax legislation and/or criminal codes of these Member States:

Table 4 Different Terminologies of Tax Crimes in 10 EU Jurisdictions

Country	Statutes and tax offences
Austria	Tax evasion (Article 33 of the Fiscal Offences Act 1958)
	Tax fraud (Article 39 of the Fiscal Offences Act 1958)
Czech Republic	Evasion of taxes, fees and similar compulsory payment (section 240 of the Penal Code 2009)
	Evasion of taxes, social security insurance fee and similar compulsory payment (section 241 of the Penal Code 2009)
Estonia	Concealment of tax liability and unfounded increase of claim for refund (§ 389 of the Penal Code 2001)
Finland	Tax Fraud (section 1, Chapter 29, of the Penal Code 1889)
	Aggravated tax fraud (section 2, Chapter 29, of the Penal Code 1889)
	Petty tax fraud (section 3, Chapter 29, of the Penal Code 1889)

(continued)

---

[77] Turksen and others, 'D1.2: Case Studies'.

Table 4 *(Continued)*

Country	Statutes and tax offences
Germany	Tax violation (section 4, Chapter 29, of the Penal Code 1889)
	Tax crimes (section 369 of the Fiscal Code 2002)
	Tax evasion (section 370 of the Fiscal Code 2002)
Italy[78]	Fraudulent return by using invoices or other documents for non-existent operations (Article 2 of Legislative Decree no 74/2000)
	Fraudulent return by using other artifices (Article 3 of Legislative Decree n 74/2000)
	False tax returns (Article 4 of Legislative Decree no 74/2000)
	Failure to file tax returns (Article 5 of Legislative Decree no 74/2000)
	Issuing of invoices or other documents for non-existent operations (Article 8 of Legislative Decree no 74/2000)
	Concealment and destruction of accounting records (Article 10 of Legislative Decree no 74/2000)
	Failure to pay withholding tax due or certified (Article 10 *bis* of Legislative Decree no 74/2000)
	Failure to pay the value added tax (Article 10 *ter* of Legislative Decree no 74/2000)
	Undue offsetting (Article 10 *quater* of Legislative Decree no 74/2000)
Malta	Fraudulent subtraction of tax payments (Article 11 of Legislative Decree n 74/2000)
	Penal provisions relating to fraud, etc. (Article 52 of Chapter 372 – Income Tax Management Act 1994)
Portugal	Tax Scam (Article 87 of the General Regime of Tax Infringements)
	Tax Fraud (Article 103 of the General Regime of Tax Infringements)
United Kingdom	Conspiracy to defraud (Common law offence preserved by the Criminal Law Act 1977, section 5(2))
	Cheating the Public Revenue (Common Law offence, preserved by Theft Act 1968, section 32(1)(a))
	Untrue Declarations (Customs and Excise Management Act 1979, section 167)
Ireland	Revenue Offences (section 1078 of the Taxes Consolidation Act 1997)

This by no means exhaustive list of legal sources, with the variety of terminologies of tax crimes in these jurisdictions, illustrates how extensively varied the connotations of tax crimes in different jurisdictions are.

A common feature of all the legislation in these jurisdictions is that it generally fails to provide a straightforward definition of tax crimes – instead, offences are articulated as being exhibited in prescribed list of prohibited behaviours or conduct of the taxpayer.

---

[78] Law Decree No 124 of 26 October 2019 has introduced some amendments to the scope and dimension of some of these offences.

Ireland, Italy, Finland and the United Kingdom exemplify countries in Europe that have given very extensive lists of behaviours, which though they provide more specifics also present a tale of overlapping behaviours. For instance, section 1078 of the Taxes Consolidation Act 1997 of Ireland outlines revenue offences drawn from several statutes as follows:

> A person shall, without prejudice to any other penalty to which the person may be liable, be guilty of an offence under this section if the person – (a) *knowingly or wilfully* delivers any incorrect return, statement or accounts or knowingly or wilfully furnishes any incorrect information in connection with any tax, (b) *knowingly aids, abets, assists, incites or induces* another person to make or deliver knowingly or wilfully any incorrect return, statement or accounts in connection with any tax, (c) claims or obtains relief or exemption from, or repayment of, any tax, being a relief, exemption or repayment to which, to the person's knowledge, the person is *not entitled*, (d) *knowingly or wilfully issues or produces* any incorrect invoice, receipt, instrument or other document in connection with any tax, (e) (i) fails to make any deduction required to be made by the person under section 257 (1), (ii) fails, having made the deduction, to pay the sum deducted to the Collector-General within the time specified in that behalf in section 258 (3), or (iii) fails to pay to the Collector-General an amount on account of appropriate tax (within the meaning of Chapter 4 of Part 8) within the time specified in that behalf in section 258 (4), (f) (i) fails to make any deduction required to be made by the person under section 734 (5), or (ii) fails, having made the deduction, to pay the sum deducted to the Collector-General within the time specified in paragraph 1(3) of Schedule 18, (g) *knowingly or wilfully fails to comply* with any provision of the Acts requiring – (i) the furnishing of a return of income, profits or gains, or of sources of income, profits or gains, for the purposes of any tax, (ii) the furnishing of any other return, certificate, notification, particulars, or any statement or evidence, for the purposes of any tax, (iii) the keeping or retention of books, records, accounts or other documents for the purposes of any tax, or (iv) the production of books, records, accounts or other documents, when so requested, for the purposes of any tax, (h) *knowingly or wilfully and within the time limits specified for their retention, destroys, defaces or conceals* from an authorised officer – (i) any documents, or (ii) any other written or printed material in any form, including any information stored, maintained or preserved by means of any mechanical or electronic device, whether or not stored, maintained or preserved in a legible form, which a person is obliged by any provision of the Acts to keep, to issue or to produce for inspection, (i) *fails to remit any income tax payable* pursuant to Chapter 4 of Part 42, and the regulations under that Chapter, or value-added tax within the time specified in that behalf in relation to income tax or value-added tax, as the case may be, by the Acts, or (j) *obstructs or interferes with any officer* of the Revenue Commissioners, or any other person, in the exercise or performance of powers or duties under the Acts for the purposes of any tax.[79]

The elements in the above provision of the Taxes Consolidation Act 1997 make a series of references to other statutes in a way that makes it difficult for appropriate borderlines to be drawn for tax crimes that can be reasonably aligned with the dimensions of tax crimes in legal frameworks of other countries.

In the legal framework of Austria, Articles 33 and 39 of the Fiscal Offences Act 1958 attempt to differentiate between tax evasion and tax fraud. Article 33(1) provides that: 'Guilty of tax evasion shall be anyone who in violation of a fiscal duty of

---

[79] Taxes Consolidation Act 1997, Number 39.

notification, disclosure or trueness intentionally brings about a reduction of taxes ...'. In Article 39(1)(a), 'guilty of tax fraud' refers to a situation where an offence of tax evasion is committed through things such as falsification of documents. These mean that, in the Austrian tax legal regime, tax evasion is used to define tax fraud via falsification and deception and related dishonest behaviours.

In the legal framework of Finland, sections 1 and 4 of Chapter 29 of the Penal Code 1889 attempt to distinguish tax fraud from tax violation – yet the terms are used interchangeably or complementarily in section 4(a)–(c). Section 1 provides that:

> (1) A person who (1) gives a taxation authority false information on a fact that influences the assessment of tax, (2) files a tax return concealing a fact that influences the assessment of tax, (3) for the purpose of avoiding tax, fails to observe a statutory duty pertaining to taxation that is of significance in the assessment of tax, or (4) otherwise acts fraudulently, and thereby causes or attempts to cause a tax not to be assessed, a tax to be assessed too low or a tax to be unduly refunded, shall be sentenced for tax fraud.

Sections 2 and 3 of the penal code address aggravated tax fraud (in which considerable financial benefit is sought or the offence is committed in a particularly methodical manner), and petty fraud (depending on the smallness of the amount of financial benefit sought and other circumstances connected with the offence). Section 4 of the penal code focuses on tax violation and provides that:

> (1) A person who, in order to gain financial benefit for himself or herself or another, fails to pay in time one of the following for a reason other than insolvency or a stay on payments imposed by a court: (1) a withholding tax, a tax-at-source or a conveyance tax, (2) a turnover tax calculated per calendar month or a comparable tax payable on certain insurance premiums, (3) a value-added tax, or (4) an employer's social security contribution shall be sentenced, unless the act is punishable as tax fraud, for a tax violation ... (2) However, a slight failure which has been rectified without delay is not deemed a tax violation.

The challenge of finding common grounds in tax crime definitions is compounded by the tax liability thresholds used by some jurisdictions to qualify a tax offence as a crime. In Spain, for instance, tax fraud is an offence but it is qualified as a crime if the amount defrauded reaches €120,000. But there are instances where criminal offences are established beyond the consideration of a threshold. Thus, both the threshold and non-threshold considerations are run side by side. This applies to many jurisdictions both in the EU and OECD. In Italy, for instance, provision is made for both tax liability threshold and the non-threshold regime tax offences to be qualified as criminal offences requiring investigation and prosecution. Law Decree No 124 of 26 October 2019 made significant amendments to the tax penal regime in Italy by reducing the thresholds and improving on the sanctions regime. In the Czech Republic, it can be seen that:

> Sections 138 (on Thresholds) and 240 ('Evasion of taxes, fees and similar compulsory payments') of the Czech Penal Code mention three thresholds: CZK 50,000 (about €1,956); CZK 500,000 (about €19,566.25); and 5,000,000 CZK (about €195,662.50). Consequently, this criminal offence is punished as follows: imprisonment ranging from six months to 3 years or prohibition of activity (if the damage is more than CZK 50,000 but less than CZK 500,000); imprisonment ranging from 2 to 8 years (if the damage is more than CZK 500,000, but less

5,000,000 CZK or the tax crime has been committed by at least two persons); imprisonment ranging from 5 to 10 years (if the damage is more than 5,000,000 CZK).[80]

There are many variations in tax liability thresholds that qualify as criminal tax offences warranting investigation and prosecution in different jurisdictions. So even if the technical/legal definitions of the terminologies and related identifiers of tax offences were to be similar, the thresholds would still have provided a significant basis for discrepancy and a source of worry for not just EU countries but also the OECD countries, given the cross-border nature and fluidity of tax offences as well as the interconnected nature of economic, institutional and legal systems particularly among the 27 EU Member States and the United Kingdom. The different threshold regimes tie in with the varied sanctions in different jurisdictions of the EU and OECD countries.[81] While all EU Member States criminalise tax crimes and/or designate them as predicate offences under their anti-money laundering regulations, it is not expected that all these jurisdictions must have uniform sanctions. However, if the set of sanctions in one country is far lower or higher than in another country, it provides opportunities for potential tax offenders to take locational decisions (forum shopping) that would ensure that they shift their activities to a regime that provides lower sanctions or in which they would escape conviction altogether. Having asserted this, it is possible to have uniform or near-uniform tax liability thresholds and a common definition of tax fraud across EU countries and, to some extent, the OECD countries if there is a collective political will to do so.

The foregoing has sought to establish common grounds for defining tax crimes across EU and OECD countries. It is important to reckon that, integral in this process is the question surrounding the adequacy and clarity of definition of tax offences. It is obviously difficult to find common grounds if respective definitions in different EU jurisdictions are neither adequate nor clear enough. Tax experts, LEAs and related professionals who participated in the empirical research conducted by PROTAX across several jurisdictions of the EU opined on whether or not the definition of tax crimes in the criminal legal framework of their respective jurisdictions are adequate and clear.[82] Table 5 highlights the perspectives that were gathered.

Table 5 Clarity and Adequacy of Tax Crimes – Opinions of Focus Groups

Country, Focus groups	Synthesised views of participating experts in the focus groups
Austria	The participants' view of the legal definitions in Austria were distributed between low, medium, high and very high levels. However, the majority of the participants observed that there was neither adequacy nor clarity in the legal definition of tax offences in Austria – nor even in the OECD and the EU as a whole.

(continued)

---

[80] Czech Penal Code, 2009, www.ejtn.eu/PageFiles/6533/Criminal%20Code%20of%20the%20Czech%20Republic.pdf, accessed 25 September 2020.
[81] Rasmouki and others, 'D2.3 Approaches to tax crimes'.
[82] Ibid.

Table 5 *(Continued)*

Czech Republic	There was a consensus among the participants in the Czech Republic that the legal definitions of tax crimes in their jurisdiction were of high adequacy and clarity.
Estonia	There was a consensus among the participants in Estonia that the definitions of tax crimes are highly adequate and clear (level 4), with one participant of the view that there is always potential for fine-tuning a definition, rating it as adequate.
Finland	There was a consensus among the participants in Finland that the legal definitions of tax crimes in their jurisdiction were of very high adequacy and clarity (level 5).
Germany	Half of the participants in Germany considered the definitions of tax offences as of very high adequacy and clarity (level 5), while the other half rated tax crime definitions as of high adequacy and clarity (level 4).
Italy	The participants' views of the legal definitions in Italy were divided between medium (level 3) and high level (level 4) of adequacy and clarity. The majority agreed that adequacy and clarity of tax crime definitions was at the medium level.
Malta	Apart from one participant, there was a consensus in Malta that the legal definition of tax crimes in their jurisdiction is of medium adequacy and clarity (level 3).
Portugal	The participants in Portugal agreed that the definitions of tax crimes in their jurisdiction were highly clear and adequate (level 4).
United Kingdom	The participants' view of the legal definition in UK was evenly distributed between low (level 2), medium (level 3) and high (level 4). Most of the tax offences require proof of dishonesty but participants observed that there is no definition of what is meant by dishonesty.
Ireland	There was a consensus among the participants that the legal definitions of tax crimes in their jurisdiction were of very high adequacy (level 5).

While six groups of stakeholders (Finland, Ireland, Germany, Estonia, Portugal and Czech Republic) considered the definition of tax crimes to be very high and/or highly adequate and clear, four (Austria, Italy, the United Kingdom and Malta) essentially argued that the legal definition was approximately at an average level.[83] This anecdotally suggests that clarity and adequacy of the definition of tax offences in these jurisdictions are moderately high. That is to say that there is a favourable perception of the clarity and adequacy of tax crimes in these EU jurisdictions and that there is equally a good number of experts and practitioners who view the adequacy and clarity of tax crimes with both mixed feelings and outright dissatisfaction with the status quo. Thus, it was revealed that:

> Even in the focus groups that expressed a positive opinion on the adequacy and clarity of the definitions of tax offences, some participants considered that the descriptions could be

[83] Ibid 23.

improved further. Moreover, the various definitions contained in the multiple laws include concepts or conditions that can give rise to misinterpretations or can be challenging to prove. For instance, the Finnish focus group highlighted the limits in proving intent in tax crimes committed by omission; one participant [in] the Estonian focus group expressed the view that there is always the potential for fine-tuning a definition of tax crime and rating it as adequate.[84]

Tax offences affect taxpayers, whose understanding of the clarity and adequacy of tax crimes is critical for compliance This is because some taxpayers may be committing tax crimes due to their limited understanding of the tax crime provisions (thus, potentially making unintentional errors) or their full understanding of the legal provisions and using such understanding to their advantage (thus, exploiting the tax system due to the taxpayer's identification of lacunae in the law). Future research involving the perception and understanding of the scope, limitations and dangers of tax crimes in the EU and OECD can help accumulate significant public knowledge that can support legal reforms in tax crimes. Even though the general public was not directly engaged in the PROTAX study, the expert participants used their experience to make a point that the views of the public in regard to the clarity of tax crime definitions sometimes appear opposed to the views of tax experts and practitioners. Thus 'definitions of tax crimes could be considered clear by authorities but unclear by citizens'. In particular, 'participants of the Italian and German focus groups stressed that there is a problem of clear identification of prohibited acts by citizens due to the complexity of tax and criminal legislation'.[85]

Figure 2 Opposite Views on Clarity of Tax Crime Definition

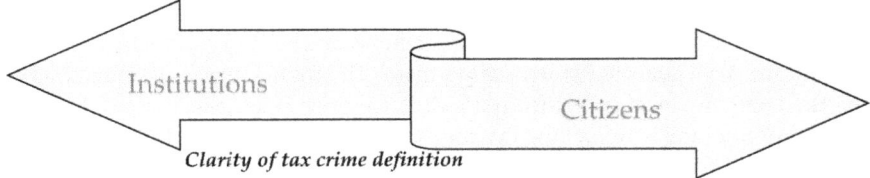

It is, therefore, imperative that the criminal legal provisions on tax are clear to both professionals and the public – it cannot be 'enough that the law is clear [or not clear] to the professionals and institutions' only.[86]

VAT Fraud – A Typical EU Tax Crime

According to the European Commission, VAT fraud is regarded as one of the most widespread tax frauds in EU Member States. Indeed, evasion of VAT is so pervasive that it affects every country in the world with indirect taxation systems such as VAT and

[84] Ibid.
[85] Ibid.
[86] Ibid.

goods and services tax (GST).[87] In spite of the fact that VAT presents a real source of structural risk for trade in the world, due to its persistent exposure to evasion activities, it is settled that VAT is one of the stable sources of income for financing national budgets in most countries. Considering that VAT is about 20 per cent of the tax revenue of EU Member States and about 12 per cent of the budget of the EU, the widespread nature of tax fraud must be seriously countered. More often than not, taxpayers use the simple VAT fraud or 'missing trader intra-community' (MTIC) or VAT carousel to defraud the public treasury.

The effectiveness of VAT is, by nature, dependent upon 'the integrity and loyalty of various intermediaries that collect and pay the tax along the economic chain'. Without integrity, loyalty and needed enforcement and deterrent infrastructure, VAT will become limiting and ineffective owing to its exposure to two sources of evasion. The two factors below contribute to integrity issues in VAT system:

- Hidden or black markets provide opportunities for taxpayers to refuse to submit their undeclared trades to VAT. As a result, the VAT base is reduced in ways that culminate in evasion of VAT.

- Deserting or paying little attention to 'intermediaries in distressed financial situations or traders who are unfaithful (usually become 'missing' ones) relating to a tax discipline' is a characteristic source for VAT evasion.[88]

VAT fraud occurs when a business collects VAT from its buyer, is required to pay this amount to the tax authority, and fails to make the payment thereof.[89] Instead, the company goes into liquidation and the owner or manager of the company vanishes or 'walks away with the money', in no time. It must be noted that the company will have paid input VAT if it 'purchased the goods in its own Member State'.[90] This means that this type of fraud is 'limited to the difference between the VAT paid when buying the goods and the VAT collected when selling them'. The money involved is much greater 'when the company buys goods from another Member State, because purchasing the goods is VAT free, and when selling the goods, the company receives VAT, and therefore has the entire VAT'. In proportional terms, the company can steal a lot of money. But the company would disappear and therefore this type of fraud is labelled the *missing trader fraud*.[91]

Adding to the catalogue of fraudulent acts, companies also engage in carousel fraud, which goes even further in terms of its complexity. What happens is that 'the same goods are bought and resold by the fraudster via middlemen several times. Each time the amount of collected VAT increases and the company goes into liquidation before the tax authority can collect the accumulated VAT'. The process is known as carousel fraud because of 'the way the same product goes around several times before the

---

[87] GST is a dimension of VAT that is imposed on most goods and services traded by businesses for domestic consumption – principally paid by consumers through the businesses.

[88] Frunza, *Value added tax fraud*.

[89] See Directive (EU) 2017/1371 of the European Parliament and of the Council of 5 July 2017 on the fight against fraud to the Union's financial interests by means of criminal law [2017] OJ L 198/29–41.

[90] European Commission, 'Single VAT Area', https://ec.europa.eu/taxation_customs/business/vat/action-plan-vat/single-vat-area_en#heading_3, accessed 13 July 2020.

[91] Ibid.

fraudsters disappear'.[92] So in effect, the carousel fraud is a kind of complex missing trader VAT fraud.

VAT Fraud Typologies

Just as with tax fraud and evasion generally, it is a challenge to provide universal typologies for VAT fraud. This challenge is further compounded by the lack of or limited statistics on tax fraud in general and VAT fraud in particular.

Because of the unsettled definition of VAT fraud across the legal frameworks of different jurisdictions, it is plausible to base analytical and empirical classifications of VAT fraud typologies on two major silos of an economy:

i. *The shadow economy*: The shadow economy constitutes informal transactions that encapsulate trade in goods and services that is carried out outside the remits or boundaries of relevant laws and regulations of a nation. It is difficult to assess the scale of transactions in the shadow economy since state authorities mostly cannot or find it difficult to directly observe the volumes and values of the goods and services traded therein. As a result, the base of the tax (no matter the form) does not include the output coming from the shadow economy. Even though heavily industrialised countries such as those constituting the bulk of the membership of EU and OECD have less of a shadow economy, this informal economy still possesses threatening underlying forces that operate on the blind side of the authorities.[93]

ii. *The formal economy*: The formal economy is characterised by recognised economic activities under national law whereby turnover figures are not only observable and quantifiable, primarily because the transactions are conducted by registered establishments, but also processes and outputs are supposed to document turnover figures. In the formal silo, the economy's size can be measured through business records – particularly mandatory reports from businesses to government institutions including annual financial statements and regular tax filings. The output from the formal economy is, therefore, included in the national tax base.[94] For the purposes of VAT, the turnover of the formal economy has a direct proportional relationship with the VAT base.

Thus, these segments of the economy are not mutually exclusive, since almost every jurisdiction has both shadow and formal economies operating simultaneously – most of the time. From a criminal law perspective, the shadow or hidden economy poses constraints that are more serious for investigators and prosecutors of tax crime to present indictable and convictable facts and evidence in court. As it were, in this segment of the economy, exchange of documents and transactions is informal, leaving it with faint traces that can hardly be pursued confidently by LEAs. Expert underground or undercover work, for a long time, together with upscale investigative tools such as

---

[92] Ibid.
[93] Frunza, *Value added tax fraud.*
[94] Ibid.

technology relating to artificial intelligence and related tools with high-resolution secret audio-visual cameras with long-life batteries may be required.

In the light of the informal and formal silos, Frunza has proposed four empirical classification of typologies of VAT fraud: Shadow-economy-based VAT fraud, missing trader fraud, misrepresenting the figures from the trading book of an organisation, and misrepresenting the type of traded goods or services.

Shadow Economy-Related VAT Fraud

This formation of fraud entails trades of goods and services from both domestic and cross-border platforms that have neither been declared to authorities nor submitted to VAT. There is an inevitable link between tax fraud (particularly VAT fraud) and the shadow economy. This is because since trade and transactions in the shadow economy are not declared by the businesses for tax purposes, it becomes difficult if not impossible for the government to charge tax on such transactions. If the figures related to the taxation base or to the appropriate tax rate of a given company are not accurate, the amount of the collected tax will not be genuine. The observability and the accuracy of the figures reported within the formal economy rely on the robustness of the collection processes of accounting data from the organisations included in the national business registry. The extent to which the accounting data collection processes from formalised businesses[95] are robust determines the level of observation conducted and accuracy of figures submitted by the businesses. It therefore implies that without registered businesses reporting to relevant authorities, as obtained in the shadow economy, it is difficult to observe and report accurate figures for VAT purposes. In effect, without accurate taxation base, the amount of tax that will be collected is most unlikely to be genuine or accurate.

Misrepresentation of Figures from the Trading Book of a Business

This misrepresentation is achieved through accounting shenanigans, which are geared toward artificial reduction of the amount of VAT liabilities, while ensuring that the rest of the accounting figures remain unaltered. More often than not, these malfeasant activities are employed for an extended period, without ceasing the business – as pertains to transactions in missing trader.

Misrepresentation of the Type of Traded Goods or Services

This activity seeks to ensure that the VAT liability of the business is reduced using an inappropriate VAT rate that is lower than the required rate. The activity is characterised by tax declaration of an item in a category different from the correct one to arbitrate the percentage of the VAT rate. VAT evasion in the shadow economy is therefore more prevalent, but difficult to grapple with.[96]

---

[95] Businesses that have been duly registered and embedded in the national business registry or such related national register are formalised businesses.

[96] Frunza, *Value added tax fraud* 1.

Missing Trader Fraud

Missing trader fraud is a dissimulation or concealment of trade from the formal economy. This activity is aimed at hiding part or total turnover to secure underestimation of the base of the VAT and payment of less or non-payment of full value of the liability to the national treasury. The process is smartly designed in such a way that the missing trader will disappear within a short period after the actors are convinced that transaction process is matured to enable them to make a safe exit. The missing trader completes the process by closing, abandoning or even making the business bankrupt in order to prevent authorities to trace the transactions.

Missing trader encapsulates diverse types of VAT fraud, such as carousel fraud, MTIC fraud, cross-invoicing, contra-trading and barter trading. Just like the VAT carousel fraud, the MTIC fraud is also one of the most popular and damaging types of VAT fraud.[97] The underlying mechanism of the MTIC is informed by the measure that intra-Community trades are not submitted to VAT. The basic form of the MTIC fraud is illustrated as follows: A trader from one EU country buys a commodity from another country of the EU without being charged VAT. The trader goes on to sell the commodity domestically with VAT charged. However, the trader fails to pay the VAT charged to the local tax authority.

Recital 4 of Directive (EU) 2017/1371 of the European Parliament provides that:

> The notion of serious offences against the common system of value added tax ('VAT') as established by Council Directive 2006/112/EC (8) (the 'common VAT system') refers to the most serious forms of VAT fraud, in particular carrousel fraud, VAT fraud through missing traders, and VAT fraud committed within a criminal organisation, which create serious threats to the common VAT system and thus to the Union budget.[98]

VAT fraud is obviously cross-cutting. Whether in formal or non-formal settings, transactional relationships among economic actors have the propensity to result in non-compliant behaviour with respect to the relationship between businesses (ie, taxable persons: B2B) on one hand and between business and households (ie, taxable person and consumer: B2C) on the other hand.[99] Tax evasion carried out by businesses often concerns the segments of the value chain in which the right to deduct VAT is limited and the business practically assumes the position of the final consumer.[100]

As with tax evasion and tax fraud in general, there is no generally applicable definition of VAT evasion. Its meaning is dependent upon national legal frameworks, general

---

[97] Europol estimates that €40 to €60 billion is lost annually to MTIC fraud schemes taking place in the EU; See Europol, 'MTIC Fraud Investigation and LEA's Cooperation Improving' (6 March 2018), www.europol.europa.eu/publications-documents/mtic-fraud-investigation-and-leas-cooperation-improving, and EU Commission, 'The concept of the Tax Gap' (2018), https://ec.europa.eu/taxation_customs/news/vat-gap-report_en%20-%20accessed%20at%2001/06/2020, accessed 22 July 2020.

[98] Directive (EU) 2017/1371 of the European Parliament and of the Council of 5 July 2017 on the fight against fraud to the Union's financial interests by means of criminal law [2017] OJ L 198/29–41.

[99] See Council Directive 2006/112/EC of 28 November 2006 on the common system of value added tax ([2006] OJ L 347/1–118; see also the consolidated version as of 1 January 2020 at: Council Directive 2006/112/EC of 28 November 2006 on the common system of value added tax, https://eur-lex.europa.eu/legal-content/EN/TXT/PDF/?uri=CELEX:02006L0112-20200101&from=EN, accessed 8 January 2020.

[100] Fiscalis Tax Gap Project Group (FPG/041), 'The Concept of Tax Gaps Report on VAT Gap Estimations' (Brussels, European Commission, March 2016), https://ec.europa.eu/taxation_customs/sites/taxation/files/docs/body/tgpg_report_en.pdf, 20 July 2020.

context of application and the kind of interpretation the local tax administration bring to the concept. However, VAT evasion is often defined as the deliberate under-declaration of taxable transactions, as well as non-declaration of taxable transactions relating to concealed legal and illegal economic activities.

Four of the 14 case studies from 11 European jurisdictions conducted by PROTAX research involved VAT carousel fraud. See the illustration in Box 3.

Box 3 VAT Carousel – The Missing Trader

With a VAT carousel (Missing Trader), the simple illustration is as follows: At least three companies are required to successfully operate a VAT carrousel. Two of these companies can be located within the EU while the other firm should be located outside of the EU. Company one, or Q, located in Italy purchases goods such as electrical products or services from company two, or X, located in Austria. Because the two firms are in the EU, firm Q would not or is not expected to pay relevant taxes. Company Q then goes on to sell the electrical products to a third company, company Y, which is based in a country such as Brazil (a country outside the EU). Company Q gets VAT from company Y after selling the electrical products. In this case, company Y, an EU non-resident, can reclaim the amount of VAT from Italy. Company Q is required to pay the VAT amount to the Italian tax authorities in three months. However, by that time, company Q has disappeared. Thus, the wheel or carousel upon which this fraud rides is known as Missing Trader. It happens because, company Q can be a paper or phoney company and can reach out to similar phoney firms (say company X and Y or more) to turn the carousel around many times before the three months end. By the time any control on VAT by the tax authorities comes along, the trail of the transactions would become cumbersome if not almost impossible to trace. In order to effectively seal the fraud, company X will ensure that the same kind of electrical products are sold back to company Y, in such circumambulatory manner until the electrical products are made to move out of the circuit or transaction chain.

For a more complex Missing Trader VAT fraud, the following case study in Estonia presents a typical example: The modus operandi of the Estonian case study was found to be as follows.

An import and export company, AS Spratfil, which was led by Boris Ustinovs, organised fish trade from companies in Norway. A fictitious acquisition chain was used in a way that would allow the companies to declare the VAT that could be recovered from the state. On presentation of tax declarations, only the data of transactions which took place between the two transaction partners was to be allowed as basic documents. The criminal investigations however detected that real transactions between AS Spratfil and OÜ Trigend did not take place. They were fictitious and such transactions were not allowed to be enclosed to tax declarations, to include an input VAT.[101]

---

[101] Turksen and others, 'D1.2: Case Studies'.

In order to execute the tax fraud scheme, AS Spratfil needed a chain of missing traders. To build that scheme up, an organised criminal group (OCG) was utilised in Estonia, who helped to organise the necessary missing traders and organised their further activities, formalising fictitious documents, performing bank transfers etc. A similar chain of missing traders was created in Latvia and was led by Latvia's OCG. The Estonian OCG was led by Arlet Martinson, Latvia's by Igors Kuzmans. It is noteworthy that the same fish and supply chain with missing traders was also conducted for similar tax fraud in Latvia, thus the criminal income was doubled.

The cooperation between the two groups helped to organise an 'assignee on business' trustee in Estonia, specifically from Latvia, a so-called liaison officer, Andris Punans. His tasks were dealing with frontmen, managing the establishment of missing traders, communicating with banks on behalf of frontmen, entering contracts to cover crime by shadow activities (hiring rooms, equipment) and so on; he had rented residential and office premises in Tallinn for that purpose.

The fish purchase and sales chain took place between the various Latvian and Estonian companies in the scheme. Such a long supply chain in itself is neither economically reasonable nor credible. In fact, the purchases of fish from Norwegian companies were organised by AS Spratfil itself: traded over prices, agreed on quantities and terms of delivery.[102]

In order to criminally evade the tax liability and avoid excessive attention from the tax administration, the tax liability of fictitious transactions was kept close to zero for the missing traders participating in the tax fraud. In order to reduce the tax liability, the missing traders declared fictitious acquisitions. With the documents relating to the goods delivered, trucks moved in across the Estonian-Latvian border. However, they pretended to be empty vehicles. The same fraud was used in both directions, ie the carriage of goods was shown in the direction of both Estonia and Latvia. For instance, based on documents assessed, the same truck fictitiously brought yarn to Estonia from Latvia, and wooden rods were taken back to Latvia from Estonia.

The truck made a stop of specific duration in a specially rented premises in order to deceive Estonian authorities – a stop that would fit with the time spent to load the goods. Evidence presented and accepted in court however indicated that there was no real loading and unloading of goods. During the criminal investigation, this was detected by surveillance operation, using cameras installed at the loading site. The truck was repeatedly checked during so-called routine road inspections by the LEAs and it was always empty. However, in the case of potential tax control, the goods were always present in the rented truck at the shadow companies' warehouses.[103]

In effect, it was only strict surveillance by the LEAs that could unpack the complexities in the tax fraud, which was an intentional scheme to push missing traders through the circuit – in order to smartly but criminally evade taxes.[104] This criminal scheme is illustrated in Figure 3.

Complex VAT carousel frauds have also been found in Italy and Austria, which highlights just how widespread VAT carousel fraud is in the EU. Essentially, in all the VAT carousel case studies, there was a cross-border dimension, which involved actors from many jurisdictions. In the Austrian case study, for instance, the Missing Trader

---

[102] Ibid.
[103] Ibid.
[104] ibid.

Figure 3 Complex Arrangement of Missing Trader in PROTAX Estonia Case Study

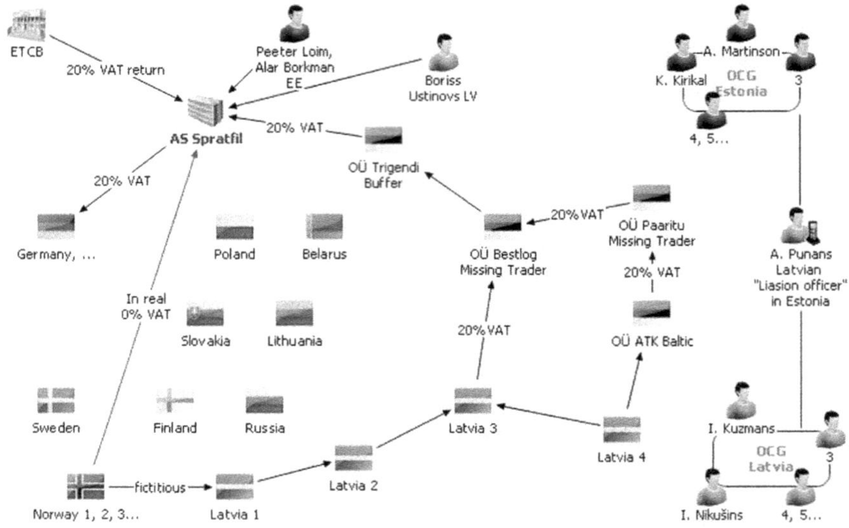

VAT Fraud scheme was organised in an international context in relation to EU Member States as well as third countries. The focus of criminal investigation in Austria, however, involved only the tax evasion committed in Austria. Therefore, little was known about the ties that existed between the criminal actors in the various countries involved.[105]

In demonstrating the internalised nature of VAT fraud, the European Union has put out an interesting diagram as to the outlook of VAT operations internationally. This buttresses the above complex VAT carousel and is shown in Table 6.

Table 6 International VAT Fraud[106]

VAT fraudsters and how they defraud:	It is settled that well-established criminal networks mainly commit cross-border VAT fraud. Often, the act of defrauding involves, at least, two or more Member States of EU, can involve extremely complicated schemes and may target specific sectors of the economy, including electronics and cars. Proceeds of the activities have even been used to finance terrorist activities.[107]
How international VAT fraud works:	VAT is presently charged on sales of goods between businesses in the same country. Meaning, businesses are given the incentive to collect VAT on their onward sales to the final consumer or to another company (so they can deduct the VAT paid by them to their suppliers of goods or services). But the goods sold cross-border between businesses are exempted from VAT at the moment.

(continued)

---

[105] Ibid.

[106] European Commission, 'Single VAT Area', https://ec.europa.eu/taxation_customs/business/vat/action-plan-vat/single-vat-area_en#heading_3, accessed 13 April 2020.

[107] Ibid.

Table 6 *(Continued)*

	In effect, transactions on goods or services between country A and country B of the EU attract a zero VAT charge.[108]
What does the difference in cross-border zero charge and in-country charge do?	The difference makes committing VAT fraud just so easy. In the sense that, a company from country A lacking integrity may purchase goods in another EU country B without being subject to VAT and legally sell them onwards in their own country and charge VAT.
What happens to VAT charged?	The business collects the cash from the sale without paying the collected VAT on the sale to its tax administration. And very often, these companies vanish, without even being audited.[109]
How often does this activity happen?	This fraudulent behaviour does happen over and over in which the same goods can be moved back and forth across borders between the same shady companies and at each time, fraudsters fraudulently pocket the VAT. This back and forth fraudulent activity is referred to as carousel fraud.[110]
Any remedy?	It is imperative that the way VAT is collected in the EU is changed. This can be done through the introduction of VAT on cross-border sales between companies in the EU.

Because of the complexities involved in transnational business arrangements by the MNCs, even if they fraudulently avoid paying tax in a given jurisdiction, it is difficult for authorities to detect whether a crime has been committed. Actually fraudulent avoidance of tax is thus often characterised as legal avoidance of tax. The ease with which businesses can take advantage of this delineation challenge does not apply to individuals, since wealthy individuals cannot always create branches of themselves as can be done by business entities.[111]

Tax Avoidance and Tax Planning

Tax avoidance and tax planning have been intermittently used in the foregoing attempt to unpack the intricacies surrounding tax crimes. Thus, tax fraud and tax evasion have been frequently used – both clearly denoting a criminal conduct and recognised as punishable offences in different formations across EU and OECD countries. Tax avoidance and tax planning are, however, lawful tax measures by taxpayers – with exceptions when there is abuse or aggressiveness that appears to extend into tax evasion and tax fraud and related criminal conduct. The underlying difference between tax fraud and tax evasion on one hand and tax avoidance and tax planning on the other hand is that, while the latter can be procured entirely through legal means whereby the tax/administrative/fiscal law and/or criminal law does not automatically provide punishment

---

[108] Ibid.
[109] Ibid.
[110] Ibid.
[111] Allain, Fraudeau and Martin, 'Facing tax fraud in the European Union'.

thereof, the former is automatically criminalised and may accordingly be sanctioned and/or punished.[112]

The EU has considered tax avoidance as one of the 'missing parts' that must be brought back, and paid attention to. This is also especially so because there is often a fine line that separates tax evasion, tax fraud, tax planning and tax avoidance.[113]

Tax Avoidance

In this regard, tax avoidance refers to a situation where the taxpayer is acting 'within the law, sometimes at the edge of legality, to minimise or eliminate tax that would otherwise be legally owed. It often involves exploiting the strict letter of the law, loopholes and mismatches to obtain a tax advantage that was not originally intended by the legislation.'[114] In this definition, the key constituents include:

- legal conduct;
- minimisation and/or elimination of tax liability; and
- exploitation of the inadequacies in the law.

Tax avoidance often involves bending and/or exploiting the rules of the tax system to gain a tax advantage which had not been intended by the legislature or the tax authorities. Usually, tax avoidance is characterised by 'contrived, artificial transactions that serve little or no purpose other than to produce this advantage'[115] for the taxpayer. This action operates within the letter, but not the spirit, of the law. An interesting observation made by the HMRC is that 'most tax avoidance schemes simply do not work, and those who use them may end up having to pay much more than the tax they tried to avoid, including penalties'.[116] It is not clear however, what calculus or criterion has been used to determine the limited success of tax avoidance schemes. What is clear is that tax avoidance adds to the complexity in identifying and confronting tax evasion and tax fraud, since its operations are legal but can mimic or provide foundational layers or a launch pad for tax evasion and tax fraud or related non-compliant conduct.

Since the actions and intention therewith in tax avoidance are entirely recognised by the law as lawful, and these actions sometimes bear similarities to tax evasion (apart from the illegal component), it is always possible for taxpayers to collaborate with professional tax enablers such as accountants, lawyers and tax consultants to identify unsuspecting legal lacunae. This can eventually make the work of the tax authorities and other LEAs cumbersome whereby the general red flags would not be automatically raised.

---

[112] European Commission, 'Time to get the Missing Part Back: What does it mean – Tax fraud, https://ec.europa.eu/taxation_customs/fight-against-tax-fraud-tax-evasion/missing-part_en, accessed 25 March 2020.

[113] Ibid.

[114] Ibid.

[115] HM Treasury and HM Revenues & Customs, *Tackling tax avoidance, evasion, and other forms of non-compliance* (Crown, March 2019) 7, https://assets.publishing.service.gov.uk/government/uploads/system/uploads/attachment_data/file/785551/tackling_tax_avoidance_evasion_and_other_forms_of_non-compliance_web.pdf, accessed 18 July 2020.

[116] Ibid.

In effect, tax avoidance constitutes legal steps taken by a taxpayer to reduce tax liability by claiming deduction or refunds. In an attempt to smartly exploit the tax loopholes, taxpayers can make use of professional enablers (eg, accountants, lawyers, tax advisors), complex structures such as offshore holdings in secrecy jurisdictions and structured financial products such as insurance or derivatives, which are put in place to enhance tax avoidance.[117] With international tax avoidance, which is popular with multinational corporations and wealthy individuals, the taxpayer moves their holdings, their interests or their property in one jurisdiction to another to minimise their tax liability in the country of origin. Shifting the registered beneficial ownership and the location of the assets are also common methods to evade and/or avoid taxes. The country of destination usually has advantageous tax policies and laws which are favourable to the taxpayer.[118]

When tax avoidance is abused in a way that overstretches legality, it can be prosecuted as a civil offence and/or as a criminal office – as long as the legal regime provides containment for such overlaps.

Tax Planning

Tax planning, on the other hand entails the use of 'tax reliefs for the purpose for which they were intended'. For instance, typical forms of legitimate tax planning in the United Kingdom include 'claiming relief on capital investment, saving in a tax-exempt ISA or saving for retirement by contributing to a pension scheme'. With tax planning, taxpayers ingeniously plan to use allowances, deductions, or tax exemptions to their advantage. The taxpayers effectively work within the regulatory framework to plan their way out of certain avoidable burdens or liabilities in the tax system.[119] In this way, tax planning is not considered to be tax avoidance – they are different from each other but belong to the same legal realm.[120]

When tax planning is aggressively used in a way that overstretches legality, it can be prosecuted as a civil offence and even as a criminal offence as long as the legal framework makes provision for such trapping of aggressiveness to amount to a breach of tax law.

In effect, even though tax fraud and tax evasion define the criminal domain of tax offences, tax avoidance and tax planning can contribute to enhancing tax crimes in the EU. According to the European Commission, the money that is lost to tax fraud/tax evasion and avoidance in the EU, estimated at €1 trillion, occurs in ways such as:

- tax fraud and evasion, which illegally deprive public budgets of money;[121]
- tax havens, which facilitate tax evaders and avoiders by storing money offshore, often unreported and untaxed;[122] and

---

[117] Frunza, *Value added tax fraud* 1.
[118] Allain, Fraudeau and Martin, 'Facing tax fraud in the European Union'.
[119] European Commission, 'Time to get the Missing Part Back'.
[120] HM Treasury and HM Revenues & Customs, *Tackling tax avoidance* 7.
[121] European Commission, 'A huge problem: How big is the tax fraud and tax evasion problem?', https://ec.europa.eu/taxation_customs/fight-against-tax-fraud-tax-evasion/a-huge-problem_en, accessed 14 March 2020.
[122] Ibid.

- aggressive tax planning by big businesses or individuals, which exploits the limits of the law with the aim of minimising taxes paid.[123]

Thus, as indicated above, tax evasion, tax fraud, tax avoidance, tax abuse and tax planning are critical elements that contribute to the huge problem posed by tax crimes in the EU. It is, however, only tax fraud and tax evasion that have been clearly defined as criminal behaviours and subjected to criminal investigation and justice processes.

Ramifications and Measurement of Tax Crimes

Tax crimes have many ramifications. In particular, when tax evasion is high, it can significantly create many economic effects including:

- suddenly reducing the value of tax incentives, affecting allocative behaviour;
- creation of artificial biases in macroeconomic indicators that could result in inappropriate policy responses;
- affecting income redistribution; and
- impeding attempts or measures to monetise and digitise economies.[124]

From the legal point of view, a high degree of tax evasion creates effects such as:

- increase in other tax crimes such as tax fraud;
- increase in other financial crimes such as money laundering, corruption and terrorism financing;
- difficulty in enacting effective legislation and regulations to comprehensively counter the crimes; and
- difficulty in enforcing effective legislation and regulations to comprehensively counter the crimes.

Every jurisdiction tolerates, to a certain degree, the existence of tax evasion. What this implies is that more often than not, the existence of tax evasion is not necessarily of great concern to policymakers, mainstream LEAs and tax administrators, but the extent, magnitude or degree of tax evasion has always been. That is why it is imperative for jurisdictions to possess the capabilities in measuring the size of tax evasion.

A good measure of tax evasion 'gives policymakers an idea about the reliability of their policy analysis and the expected effectiveness of their policy prescriptions' – including legal frameworks and enforcement practices. What has, however, been a serious challenge is the inherent difficulty in establishing and operationalising the instruments for measuring tax evasion – particularly the direct measurement of tax evasion. This can be attributed to a number of reasons including the illegal nature of tax evasion that always requires and maintains secrecy and the conceptual problems

---

[123] Ibid.
[124] S Richupan, 'Measuring tax evasion: A brief description of the major techniques' (International Monetary Fund, External Relations Dept, December 1984) 38.

that make tax evasion challenging to define. Suffice to underscore that it is possible to analyse and, to some extent, measure the traces that tax evasion leaves. But because tax evasion traces tend to be manifold, the corresponding measurement approaches used to measure these traces result in many different estimates of tax evasion.[125]

Ultimately, while it is not necessarily within the remit of law to provide statistical measures of tax evasion, the scale of tax evasion size remains a paramount concern. In both OECD and EU countries, law can only competently leverage human factors to support the conceptual and operational frameworks for countering tax crimes. Other forms of tax crime such as tax fraud face the same measurement and definition issues as tax evasion. These, thus, generally apply to tax crimes. Figure 4 shows key tax evasion or fraud measurement approaches.

Figure 4 Tax Fraud and Tax Evasion Measurement Approaches[126]

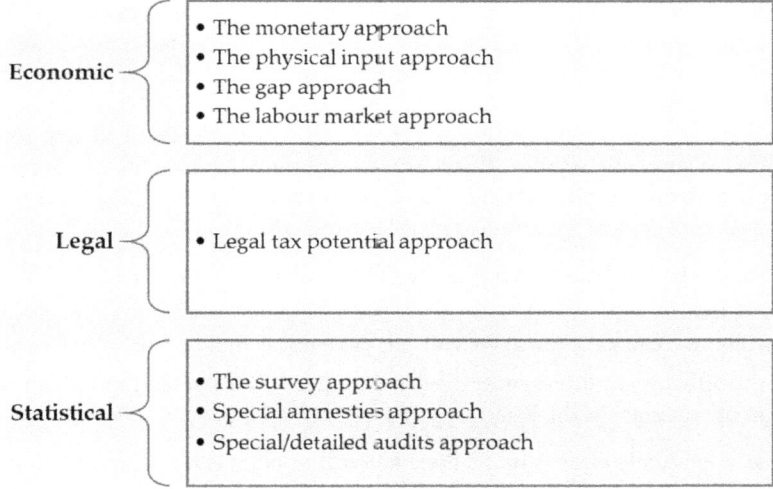

Without going into details about these approaches, an important point to make is that all these approaches suffer from the slippery or evasive nature of tax crimes. Each of the approaches puts emphasis on 'a different aspect of tax evasion or the underground economy, and each has its own strengths and weaknesses'.[127] But it is usually through special/detailed auditing mechanisms that some near-precise data is revealed about the scale of tax crimes, tax gaps and related parameters that help to determine the magnitude of tax crimes. The essence of getting proper measurements about tax crimes relates to how they can effectively inform policy and legal decision-making towards countering tax crimes.[128]

---

[125] Ibid.
[126] Ibid.
[127] For further details, see Richupan, 'Measuring tax evasion' 38.
[128] Ibid.

Tax Crimes and Illicit Financial Flows

Tax crimes and related financial crimes such as money laundering[129] and corruption find their comfort zone in factors such as 'secrecy, inadequate legal frameworks, lax regulation, poor enforcement, and weak inter-agency co-operation'.[130] These have been exploited by criminals to transfer huge amount of money and assets across multiple jurisdictions with relative ease and great speed especially with the support of the advances in technology and enabling environments. These underlie the sophistication and threat associated with illicit financial flows, which are not proportionally aligned to the vitality and speed of law enforcement structures across the world.[131]

Tax crimes and related financial crimes pose a serious threat to the strategic, political, and economic interests of all countries. Huge sums are lost to tax crimes and related financial crimes that characterise illicit financial flows. The VAT gap[132] in the EU has, for instance, been staggering – although it is in decline. Whereas the VAT gap in 2015 was €153.2 billion (13 per cent of VAT revenue), it was reduced to €145.4 billion (12.2 per cent of VAT revenue) in 2016.[133] The VAT gap further declined to €137.5 billion (11.2 per centof the total expected VAT revenue) in 2017.[134] Given the consistent downward trajectory, it was expected that the VAT gap would further decline in subsequent years. This has been especially so since the EU stepped up measures to address tax crimes, which significantly contribute to the high VAT gap in the EU. A number of critical issues are at play here, including:

- the controversies surrounding the determinants of VAT by each EU Member State;
- the late estimation and reporting of the VAT gap by the EU (as of February 2020, it is still not clear what the 2018 VAT gap was, nor is that of 2019 known); and
- the difficulty in finding more reliable figures about the tax gap (which would factor in other taxes) in the EU.

What is evidently clear is that a huge amount of taxes is not collected, that might have enhanced socioeconomic development of the EU, because of the prevalence of tax crimes across EU Member States. Furthermore, it is not clear if and to what extent the current COVID-19 crisis and its evident negative impact on the economy will fuel fraud in general and tax fraud in particular. Past studies indicate that there is a direct and cyclical correlation between economic crisis and financial crime.[135] At a time of such crisis,

---

[129] J Spreutels and C Grijseels 'Interaction between money laundering and tax evasion' (2001) 10(1) *EC Tax Review* 3–12.

[130] APEC/OECD, *Combatting Tax Crimes More Effectively in APEC Economies, Organisation for Economic Co-operation and Development and Asia-Pacific Economic Cooperation* (OECD, 2019), www.oecd.org/tax/crime/combatting-tax-crimes-more-effectively-in-apec-economies.htm, accessed 12 January 2020.

[131] Ibid.

[132] The difference between the expected or estimated tax revenue and the tax revenue that has actually been collected by tax authorities.

[133] Bonch-Osmolovskiy and others, *Study and Reports on the VAT Gap* 76, 77.

[134] Ibid.

[135] M Deflem, *Economic crisis and crime* (Emerald Publishing, 2011); N Ryder and others (eds), *Fighting Financial Crime in the Global Economic Crisis* (Routledge, 2015); N Ryder, *The financial crisis and white-collar*

investment by the state is paramount and much needed. At the same time, optimisation of tax revenues is mutually essential which provide the funds for this investment.

As established earlier, individual personal taxes and corporate-related taxes are the two categories of tax which can be vulnerable to tax evasion or fraud. These criminal activities – as accordingly defined – are illicit financial flows that have been identified as being not only rife in the EU but also linked with organised crime.[136] The World Bank has done a lot of work on illicit financial flows[137] and one can notice how broad the concept is and how challenging it is to define without situating it in a context. According to Everest-Phillips, illicit financial flows are associated with earnings and transfers that are illegal and/or immoral such as tax crimes and/or tax avoidance respectively.[138] Reed and Fontana emphasise the illegal dimension by proffering that the 'illegally earned and transferred' funds are illicit financial flows if the following conditions are deemed to be fulfilled:

- the transfer itself is illegal;
- the funds are proceeds of illegal activity;
- legal obligations relating to the funds, such as payment of tax, have not been observed.[139]

These illegal activities are usually sourced from the hidden economy and are of various forms. Global Financial Integrity (GFI) has classified transactions of illicit nature that criss-cross international borders unnoticed in three forms. These are: 'Corruption, Criminal and Commercial'.[140] Even though GFI has classified proceeds from tax malpractices under the 'Commercial' dimension, it is instructive to note that tax crimes can cut across all the three dimensions, depending on the legal regime and the definition given to tax crimes.

The wide-ranging nature of tax crimes could be significantly part of the basis upon which the OECD denotes tax evasion as the majority shareholder in the business of illicit trading. In large part, especially in this context, illicit financial flows are unlawful earnings, transfers or expenditures that form a huge component of financial crimes. According to the OECD, tax crimes, in the form of tax evasion, constitute two-thirds of all illicit financial flows.[141] And granted that 95 per cent of illicit activities such as drug

---

crime: The perfect storm? (Edward Elgar, 2014); and W Black, *The Best Way to Rob a Bank is to Own One: How Corporate Executives and Politicians Looted the S&L Industry* (University of Texas Press, 2013).

[136] The World Bank, 'Illicit Financial Flows (IFFs)' (Understanding Poverty Financial Sector, Brief, 7 July 2017).

[137] Ibid.

[138] M Everest-Phillips, 'The Political Economy of Controlling Tax Evasion and Illicit Flows' in P Reuter (ed), *Draining Development? Controlling Flows of Illicit Funds from Developing Countries* (The World Bank, 2012) 69–107.

[139] Q Reed and A Fontana, 'Corruption and Illicit Financial Flows: The Limits and Possibilities of Current Approaches' (U4 Anti-Corruption Resource Centre, U4 Issue, January No 2, CMI, 2011) 6–8, www.u4.no/publications/corruption-and-illicit-financial-flows-the-limits-and-possibilities-of-current-approaches-2.pdf, accessed 4 December 2019.

[140] GFI, 'Illicit Financial Flows Analytical Methodologies Utilized', www.gfintegrity.org/wp-content/uploads/2014/09/GFI-Analytics.pdf, accessed 4 December 2019.

[141] OECD, 'About tax and crime', www.oecd.org/tax/crime/about-tax-and-crime.htm, accessed 25 March 2020.

trafficking is annually said[142] to penetrate through borders undetected by LEAs, this certainly underlies the magnitude of tax crimes in most parts of the world, including the EU and OECD countries. It especially becomes acute because tax avoidance strategies such as aggressive tax planning are also employed to avoid tax payment of huge sums in the formal economy.[143]

Although business-related tax crimes are the most challenging to address owing to the complex strategies and schemes they employ with assistance from professional enablers, these crimes have been made easier to commit than individual tax crimes in the EU. One of the challenges arises from the fact that corporations can have networks and branches in multiple EU countries and beyond the EU whereby they can exploit the differences in the rates, secrecy laws, taxation policies and law enforcement practices between these countries. The modus operandi of some MNCs, in this regard, has been particularly questionable legally, ethically and morally. The highly publicised leaks, in recent times, such as SwissLeaks,[144] Paradise Papers,[145] Panama Papers,[146] Football Leaks[147] and LuxLeaks,[148] have not only shaken the corridors of EU leaders and incensed the public, but also have confirmed the large scale of corporate tax crime in the world.[149] The ecosystem of illicit financial flows is such as to make the isolation of tax crimes, to better understand and address them, difficult.

The Varied Sources of Tax Crimes

Legal provisions dealing with tax crime may be scattered across the legal framework of a jurisdiction and may be informed by multiple sources of tax offences.[150] In common law jurisdictions, the main tax crimes are defined in legislative acts, although certain relevant criminal offences derive from common law (eg, the common law offence of cheating the public revenue in the United Kingdom). In the 10 EU countries examined by PROTAX research, the main criminal offences are placed in criminal and/or tax legislation. This is particularly so with respect to the following.

---

[142] R Mazur, 'A Plan to End Global Money Laundering: Whitepaper' (KYC360, RiskScreen), www.riskscreen.com/kyc360/requestamlwhitepaper/, accessed 4 December 2019.

[143] OECD, 'About tax and crime'.

[144] D Reuter and others, 'Explore the Swiss Leaks Data', *60,000 Leaked Files* (ICIJ, 2015), www.icij.org/investigations/swiss-leaks/explore-swiss-leaks-data/, accessed 4 December 2019.

[145] A Wilson-Chapman and W Fitzgibbon, 'The Paradise Papers: What do you want to know?' (Question Time, ICIJ, 2018), www.icij.org/blog/2018/10/the-paradise-papers-what-do-you-want-to-know/, accessed 4 December 2019.

[146] ICIJ, 'Giant Leak of Offshore Financial Records Exposes Global Array of Crime and Corruption' (*The Panama Papers*, 2016), www.icij.org/investigations/panama-papers/20160403-panama-papers-global-overview/, accessed 4 December 2019.

[147] T Morgan, 'Football Leaks revelations: The standout stories broken down', *Telegraph* (2018), www.telegraph.co.uk/football/2018/11/09/football-leaks-series-defining-headlines-may-happen-next/, accessed 4 December 2019.

[148] A Fitzgerald and WM Guevara, 'New Leak Reveals Luxembourg Tax Deals for Disney, Koch Brothers Empire', (LuxLeaks expands, ICIJ, 2014), www.icij.org/investigations/luxembourg-leaks/new-leak-reveals-luxembourg-tax-deals-disney-koch-brothers-empire/, accessed 4 December 2019.

[149] EU Parliament, 'The Impact of Schemes revealed by the Panama Papers on the Economy and Finances of a Sample of Member States' (DG IPOL 2017).

[150] Rasmouki and others, 'D2.3 Approaches to tax crimes' 15.

The first group of countries has included main tax crimes in their penal or criminal codes. For example, Articles 240 et seq of the Czech Republic's Penal Code, Article 389 of Estonia's Penal Code, sections 1 et seq of Chapter 29 of Finland's Penal Code locate the main provisions regarding tax crimes in the criminal code.[151]

The second group of countries has adopted ad hoc legislation on tax crimes or offences.[152] This is evident, for example, in the case of Articles 33 et seq of the Austrian Fiscal Offences Act, Articles 1 et seq of Italy's Legislative Decree of 10 March 2000, no 74 concerning the new discipline of crimes related to income tax and value added tax, and Articles 87 et seq of Portugal's Law 15/2001 of 5 June concerning the General Regime of Tax Infringements.[153]

In other countries the main tax offences are stipulated in tax laws. This can be seen in countries such as Germany (sections 370–71 of the Fiscal Code), Ireland (section 1078 of the Taxes Consolidation Act 1997), Malta (Part IX of Chapter 372, Income Tax Management Act and Part X of the Chapter 406 of Value Added Tax Act), and the United Kingdom (section 106A of the Taxes Management Act 1970).[154]

Despite the proclivity of jurisdictions in the EU to include significant tax offences in one or two sources, particularly in criminal or tax legislation, it is still an open issue regarding sources of tax offences in many jurisdictions. For instance, fragmentation of the legal texts in certain countries can make the identification of tax offences a problematic task for both citizens and some practitioners.[155]

Conclusion

This chapter has demonstrated the lack of unanimity in the definition of tax crimes by EU and OECD Member States. It has also articulated the varied nature of tax crimes across jurisdictions, positing that the differences in definitions of tax crimes depend upon the drafting technique used by each national lawmaker. Largely, there can be general definitions aimed at criminalising conduct that violates tax obligations related to any type of tax. There can also be specific tax crimes that incriminate behaviour that infringes upon tax obligations related to specific types of tax. The differences may also concern the definition of the material element or guilty act (*actus reus*), and the mental element or guilty mind (*mens rea*) as well as the definition of thresholds for the punishment of the tax crimes.[156] Turksen et al also noted that:

> The criminal burden of proof is often difficult to satisfy. This makes civil or administrative action a more attractive option for tax officials. Apart from some of the regulatory challenges associated with the proving of *actus reus* or 'criminal act' against tax laws, prosecutors often find it difficult to demonstrate *mens rea*, 'a guilty mind' or intention of tax offenders to evade

---

[151] Ibid.
[152] Ibid.
[153] Ibid.
[154] Ibid.
[155] Ibid.
[156] Turksen and others, 'D4.1 – Report on conviction rates in selected Member States' (EU PROTAX, 2020) 41.

taxes and, therefore, the difficulty in establishing strict criminal liability or culpability in many EU jurisdictions where these two legal tests do apply.[157]

Along with the difficulty above, an additional difficulty arises in prosecution when tax crimes have been systematically planned and executed 'over many years [compared with] tax crimes that have been committed in a single fraudulent transaction'.[158]

Generally, tax fraud and tax evasion are defining elements of any tax crime regime. Essentially, there are two key types of tax fraud and tax evasion that appear to be highly popular with tax criminals:

- underreporting of income using sales suppression; and
- over-reporting of deductions via false invoicing.

One of the reasons for the prominent use of these forms of tax crimes is that they are handy and easy to organise. These tax crimes can be further enabled by the landscape of the economy, such as cash economy and sharing economy. The nature of these crimes is such that they can be and are easily deployed in every jurisdiction, no matter the size. It is clear that the tax crime ecosystem also involves the following types of tax fraud and tax evasion:

- complete failure to report any income to tax authorities; and
- conduct of a similar nature which may be deemed to be intentional means to illegally avoid paying taxes due a taxpayer.[159]

It is clear that VAT fraud constitutes a significant part of tax fraud in the EU. Therefore, there is merited attention and priority given to the fight against VAT fraud in the EU.[160] VAT fraud generally refers to a phenomenon involving 'a fraudulent deduction/claim of input VAT and non-payment of output VAT'.[161]

The varied nature of the definitions of tax crimes across jurisdictions have a significant impact 'on the application of criminal law, the investigation and criminal proceedings'[162] as well as conviction and sentencing. For instance, the legal definitions and provisions underlying tax crimes can adversely affect LEAs during the prosecution procedures.[163]

There is a significant direct link between the differences in definition of tax crimes and cultural orientation differences across EU Member States. Empirical evidence from research projects does show the extent to which cultural elements such as perception of the public play a role in understanding and fighting tax crimes.

---

[157] Turksen and others, 'D1.2: Case Studies' 13.

[158] Ibid.

[159] Ibid.

[160] Regeringskansliet, 'Counteracting tax evasion, tax avoidance and money laundering', www.government.se/contentassets/099c10d6502745279ff7a8b11e379c9b/action-plan-counteracting-tax-evasion-tax-avoidance-and-money-laundering.pdf, accessed 16 March 2020.

[161] Fiscalis Tax Gap Project Group (FPG/041), 'The Concept of Tax Gaps Report on VAT Gap Estimations' (Brussels, European Commission, March 2016), https://ec.europa.eu/taxation_customs/sites/taxation/files/docs/body/tgpg_report_en.pdf, 20 March 2020.

[162] Turksen and others, 'D4.1 – Report on conviction rates' 41.

[163] Rasmouki and others, 'D2.3 Approaches to tax crimes'.

The varied definitions of tax crimes across jurisdictions do come with the need for clarity and adequacy in defining tax offences. When various tax crimes are precisely, clearly and adequately defined, it is 'possible to adapt the definition of the crimes, the sanctioning responses and often also the investigative powers to the concerned behaviours'.[164] This is a sort of tailored approach to the fight against tax crimes and conducive to legal certainty and predictability which can enhance tax compliance.

It is clear also that the excessive fragmentation of tax crime definitions can lead to greater difficulty for LEAs.

A general definition could be less precise, while providing a common approach for all tax-related crimes. This might make it simpler for LEAs to use but inadvertently increase the caseload for criminal investigations. Finding a clear and adequate definition for tax crimes is critical and must be achieved not only by each jurisdiction, but also with a view to how jurisdictional approaches resonate, in greater commonality, with the approaches of other jurisdictions especially in the EU. This is particularly so because countering transnational tax crimes – as evidenced by the PROTAX case studies – requires common approaches and legal definitions across jurisdictions. Therefore, no matter the details of a particular legal framework, it will be most effective if the law clearly defines the tax offences that are criminalised – a criminal sanction applies if the offence is proven by prosecutors.[165] At the same time, regardless of how tax crimes are defined and enforced, the OECD and EU underscore that tax crimes are grave and, therefore, are among their topmost priorities.

The next chapter critically examines the substantive principles of the TGPs in the light of the EU legal framework on countering tax crimes.

---

[164] Turksen and others, 'D4.1 – Report on conviction rates' 37–43.
[165] Ibid.

3

Substantive Principles

Introduction

The ambivalence surrounding the definition of tax crimes has significant implications for finding effective solutions to the problem of tax crimes. Member States of the EU and OECD are, however, united in their resolve to counter tax crimes in their respective jurisdictions – even though the levels of commitment in different jurisdictions, in this regard, are as varied as the definitions of tax crimes. The relevant legal frameworks and the policy imperatives of the EU and OECD provide a rallying point for synergy within and between the two organisations in matters concerning tax crimes.

In the European Union, the legal framework relating to financial accountability and integrity obliges EU Member States to counter financial crime, including tax crimes, money laundering, corruption, computer fraud, and the financing of terrorism. For instance, Article 325 of TFEU obliges EU Member States to effect measures against fraud and corruption so as to protect the financial interests of the Union.[1] Article 325, in part, states that:

> The Union and the Member States shall counter fraud and any other illegal activities affecting the financial interests of the Union through measures to be taken in accordance with this Article, which shall act as a deterrent and be such as to afford effective protection in the Member States, and in all the Union's institutions, bodies, offices and agencies.[2]

Article 325(1) above concerns unlawful activities that affect the Union's financial interests, as a whole, which must be countered together by all EU Member States and the Union body itself. Article 325(2) also obliges EU Member States to 'take the same measures to counter fraud affecting the financial interests of the Union as they take to counter fraud affecting their own financial interests'.[3] So the two provisions oblige EU Member States to join forces with the European Union in the fight against fraudulent activities such as tax crimes. In the same vein, the OECD urges Member States to work with the organisation to develop approaches to counter tax crimes in their respective jurisdictions. The TGPs, under the auspices of the OECD's Task Force on

---

[1] Consolidated Version of the Treaty on the Functioning of the European Union of 26 October 2012, JEU C 326/47, https://eur-lex.europa.eu/LexUriServ/LexUriServ.do?uri=CELEX:12012E/TXT:EN:PDF, accessed 23 March 2020.
[2] Ibid.
[3] Ibid.

Tax Crimes and Other Crimes (TFTC),[4] is one of the efforts by the OECD to counter tax crimes.

This chapter examines the extent to which the TGPs are aligned to the tax crime measures of the EU. It examines the TGPs, which can be classified as substantive principles. These principles are critical to the identification of tax crimes, prosecution of tax offenders as well as how to guarantee the protection of fundamental rights of taxpayers. This chapter, therefore, evaluates five of the TGPs: criminalisation of tax offences, tax crimes as a predicate offence for money laundering, adequacy of investigative powers, the effectiveness of powers to freeze, seize and confiscate assets, and taxpayers' rights and guarantees.

Box 4 The Encompassing Nature of Tax Crimes

> *Tax fraud and tax evasion, as tax crimes, come in many dimensions, forms and shapes – pervasive enough to touch numerous markets and sectors of every economy in the world – and posing inimical risks thereof. It is imperative to see tax crimes and approach tax crimes as an evasive virus – a Trojan horse that penetrates and infects any financial file at the least opportunity.*

TGP1: Ensure Criminalisation of Tax Offences[5]

This principle is the most germane in this book. The first of the TGPs is anchored on the recommended proposition by the OECD that every jurisdiction 'should have the legal framework in place to ensure that violations of tax law are included as a criminal offence [but not administrative or civil office], and that effective sanctions apply in practice'.[6] Figure 5 essentially captures a bird's eye-view of the first OECD global principle.

Justification for Criminalising Tax Offences

Why should tax offences be criminalised when the majority of taxpayers appear to be complying with their tax obligations? Can criminalising tax offences bring the minority of non-complying taxpayers back to compliance? To start with, the behaviour exhibited by tax criminals is not necessarily any different from the criminal behaviour shown

---

[4] The TFTC 'has a mandate to improve co-operation between tax and law enforcement agencies, including anti-corruption and anti-money laundering authorities, to counter financial crimes more effectively'. www.oecd.org/tax/crime/fighting-tax-crime-the-ten-global-principles.htm.

[5] Note that the numbering of the principles is for analytical purposes, not as they appear in the original document: see, OECD, *Fighting Tax Crime: The Ten Global Principles* (OECD Publishing, 2017) 13, www.oecd.org/tax/crime/fighting-tax-crime-the-ten-global-principles.htm, accessed 26 October 2019.

[6] Ibid, 13.

Figure 5 Key Highlights of TGP 1 – Criminalisation of Tax Offences[7]

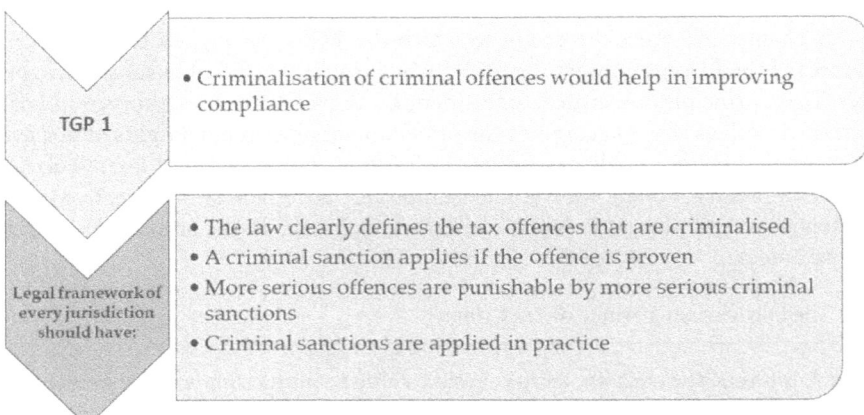

by criminals in other endeavours of life.[8] Therefore, criminal law theory regarding the behaviour of criminals and how that can be controlled applies also to the criminalisation domain of tax offences.

Although there is a recognition that the majority of taxable persons or taxpayers do voluntarily comply with their tax obligations as established in relevant tax laws, it has become clear, more than ever, that there are also taxable legal or natural persons who 'persevere in being non-compliant and use any means to evade their tax obligations'.[9] For such entities, it is not enough to improve their compliance with the tax laws using administrative monitoring and sanctions. The apparent reasonable alternative – perhaps, the more viable one in this regard – is to use criminal law to ensure compliance or to minimise non-compliance. The theory or the idea behind this is that criminal law and sanctions are likely to 'enhance the general preventive effect that criminal law enforcement can have and reduce noncompliance'.[10]

Lederman synthesises the literature on both deterrence and tax morale in tax compliance and argues that studies show that deterrence increases, not decreases, taxpaying and compliance (contrary to what some have argued).[11] Furthermore, by using the lens of accounting's 'fraud triangle', Lederman argues that deterrence and what are called 'positive motivational factors' can co-exist.[12]

Allingham and Sandmo have participated in many scholarly works that have exercised intellectual provenance in examining compliance behaviour of taxpayers who have the criminal proclivity to commit tax offences. They analysed 'individual taxpayers'

---

[7] Ibid, 14.

[8] See MS Moore, *Placing Blame: A Theory of the Criminal Law* (Oxford University Press, 2010); see S Shute and A Simester (eds), *Criminal Law Theory: Doctrines of the General Part* (Oxford Scholarship Online, 2010).

[9] OECD, *Fighting Tax Crime: The Ten Global Principles* 13.

[10] Ibid.

[11] L Lederman, 'Does Enforcement Reduce Voluntary Tax Compliance?' (2018) 395 *BYU L Rev* 627, https://papers.ssrn.com/sol3/papers.cfm?abstract_id=3222803, accessed 20 May 2020.

[12] L Lederman, 'The Fraud Triangle and Tax Evasion' (2019) 398 Research Paper, Working Paper, https://papers.ssrn.com/sol3/papers.cfm?abstract_id=3339558, accessed 20 May 2020.

decision on whether and to what extent to avoid taxes by deliberate underreporting'[13] – without considering over-reporting or failure to report tax returns at all (which are also essential criminal behaviours or actions of taxpayers). Allingham and Sandmo approached their study in relation to the works 'of economics of criminal activity'[14] such as provided in the publications of Becker,[15] and Tulkens and Jacquemin.[16] Allingham and Sandmo also analysed 'optimal portfolio and insurance policies in the economics of uncertainty' as provided in works such by Arrow,[17] and Mossin.[18] The landscape of the relevant criminal activities has been modified to a certain extent in terms of sophistication and approaches, given the globalised and technologically exposed disposition financial crimes have increasingly assumed. However, the fundamentals as provided in the days of old – carefully choreographed by the above authors and others at the time – have not significantly changed.

The work of Allingham and Sandmo on tax evasion or crime has been regarded as seminal. This work was carried out with a focus on personal income taxation. They presented a deterrent theoretical framework or model that essentially argued that the decision of taxpayers on the amount of tax to evade is similar to the choice they would make on 'the composition of a risky investment portfolio'.[19] This means that tax evasion decision-making by taxpayers is dependent upon the expected return they would generate from tax evasion and the kind of assessment they would make on the 'impact of the risk (ie risk-averse versus risk-neutral persons) on their welfare' when they evade taxes. With this deterrence model of tax evasion, the reasonable construction is that, if the penalty rate is higher or the tax audit probability is higher, the amount of tax evasion should be lower.[20]

Bonch-Osmolovskiy and others question the credibility of this model in respect of its 'predictions based on numbers or amounts in relation to tax evasion', arguing that tax evasion level as estimated by the model is rather very low and unconvincing. They, however, confirm the reasonableness of the 'marginal impact of tax evasion on the level of evasion' that has been articulated by Allingham and Sandmo. In effect, even without considering the amount of money involved, it is conclusive that the stricter or riskier the deterrent measures against tax evasion, the greater the likelihood of minimal or limited motives towards evading taxes.[21] Bonch-Osmolovskiy and others also counter

---

[13] MG Allingham and A Sandmo, 'Income tax evasion: A theoretical analysis (1972) 1 *Journal of Public Economics* 323, http://www3.nccu.edu.tw/~klueng/tax%20paper/1.pdf, accessed 11 November 2019.

[14] Ibid.

[15] See GS Becker, 'Crime and punishment: an economic approach' (1968) 76 *Journal of Political Economy* 169–217.

[16] See H Tulkens and A Jacquemin, 'The cost of delinquency: a problem of optimal allocation of private and public expenditure' (1971) 7133 CORE Discussion Paper.

[17] See KJ Arrow, *Essays in the theory of risk-bearing* (Markham Publishing Co, 1971).

[18] See J Mossin, 'Aspects of rational insurance purchasing' (1968) 76 *Journal of Political Economy* 553.

[19] M Bonch-Osmolovskiy, 'Study and Reports on the VAT Gap in the EU-28 Member States: 2018 Final Report' (Institute for Advanced Studies, IHS, TAXUD/2015/CC/131, 11 September 2018), https://ec.europa.eu/taxation_customs/sites/taxation/files/2018_vat_gap_report_en.pdf, accessed 16 December 2019; MG Allingham and A Sandmo, 'Income tax evasion: A theoretical analysis (1972) 1 *Journal of Public Economics* 323, http://www3.nccu.edu.tw/~klueng/tax%20paper/1.pdf, accessed 11 November 2019.

[20] M Bonch-Osmolovskiy, 'Study and Reports on the VAT Gap'.

[21] Ibid.

the homogenisation of taxpayers in the model by averring that, realistically, evasion of taxes differs across taxpayers such as self-employed taxpayers and employee taxpayers. Tax compliance will depend on how these groups are approached with the deterrence measures and the sense of civic duty taxpayers have appropriated 'to comply with their tax obligations, no matter the financial incentives available to them' since they, under this reasoning, are motivated intrinsically to obey the tax law.[22]

This thread of theoretical reasoning resonates with that of developments in the tax morale literature, as recently demonstrated by the survey results of Luttmer and Singhal.[23] Additionally, 'attitude of taxpayers towards tax authorities such as how legitimate they consider the tax authorities [to be]' also influences tax evasion.[24] This also appertains to a situation where the taxpayers have the notion that they are active participants in making tax decisions.[25]

Despite its limitations, Allingham and Sandmo's work on personal income has been so pervasive that a huge amount of tax evasion literature focuses on the taxation of personal or individual incomes. In recent times, however, with respect to taxes such as VAT, both corporations and individuals are considered, whereby corporations especially are becoming prominent in the evasion discourse. But the same models of tax evasion for individual taxpayers can be applied to corporations, given that natural persons such as the shareholders, directors and such beneficial owners of legal entities can still be targeted.[26] In effect, the deterrent model has significant merits for countering tax crimes. But this model, of course, has to be applied within the context of other countervailing issues which can influence the criminal behaviour of taxpayers, no matter how severe the criminal sanctions.

In practice, different jurisdictions tend to 'draw different conclusions as to precisely when the application of the criminal law is warranted' and how the law should be applied. The criminal legal provisions in every jurisdiction do however provide defining contours of the conduct of taxpayers that have been denoted as tax crimes, and the appropriate or applicable type of criminal sanctions. Because of the different conclusions drawn by jurisdictions, the 'defined actions and criminal sanctions' are expected to be and have been different across jurisdictions.

Box 5 Applying Criminal Sanctions to Tax Law, No Matter Jurisdictional Differences

> *Wherever dividing lines between non-compliant behaviour and criminal behaviour are drawn, it is important that jurisdictions have the possibility of applying criminal sanctions in respect of violations of the tax law.*[27]

---

[22] Ibid.

[23] EFP Luttmer and M Singhal, 'Tax Morale' (2014) 28 *Journal of Economic Perspectives* 149–68, https://pubs.aeaweb.org/doi/pdfplus/10.1257/jep.28.4.149, accessed 16 December 2019.

[24] RT Tyler, 'Psychological Perspectives on Legitimacy and Legitimation' (2006) 57 *Annual Review of Psychology* 375–400.

[25] J Alm, BR Jackson and M McKee, 'Fiscal exchange, collective decision institutions, and tax compliance' (1993) 22(3) *Journal of Economic Behavior & Organization* 285.

[26] M Bonch-Osmolovskiy, 'Study and Reports on the VAT Gap'.

[27] OECD, *Fighting Tax Crime* 14–15.

Application of criminal legal sanctions to the violations of tax law is important for a couple of reasons. From a preventative perspective, the following justifications exemplify such reasons: In the first place, it is most likely to create a critical platform that can 'send a message about the integrity, neutrality and fairness of the law'.[28] A sense of the rule of law at play will be signalled to the psyche and perception of the taxpaying public that anyone who disobeys tax law is not allowed to go scot-free. This is because the criminal law processes make provision for sanctions that are hardly forgettable as compared to the administrative law. It would, therefore, be taken by some taxpayers 'that nobody is above the law'.[29] However, if the intention is partly to action rule of law to achieve its intrinsic benefits, then it should be noted that mishandling the prosecution, conviction and sentencing of tax offenders who have been affected by the application of criminal law to tax law can cause a more damaging effect on the integrity of the legal framework governing tax crimes.

The second reason is grounded on the need for the law 'to act as a general deterrent for those people that could be tempted to evade their tax obligations if the opportunity arose, by providing serious reputational and punitive consequences of criminal activity'.[30]

The third reason relates to a specific deterrent measure. Thus, criminalising tax offences would serve 'as a specific deterrent for an individual that has been convicted and sanctioned in the past, so that they might be discouraged from doing so again'. Ensuring that penal provisions are actually enforced to punish offenders 'that have decided not to comply [with tax laws] is essential for both doing justice and strengthening the credibility of the penal provisions and the legal system itself'.[31]

The fourth reason can be attributed to creating an image of value and importance for tax and seriousness for tax offences. This reason can constitute part of the underlying forces of the first three reasons. But it is possible to distinguish it as a crucial rationale for the criminalisation of tax offences. Even though it can vary according to the cultural orientation of the jurisdiction, many taxpayers will obviously attach more seriousness to a tax offence that has been criminalised and which thus attracts criminal sanctions such as a prison sentence.

Additionally, criminalisation of tax offences can see to it that the needed investigative and enforcement powers under criminal law for unravelling the truth are achieved irrespective of the cooperation of the accused persons. As a result, some jurisdictions use this as an opportunity and/or a basis to engage in domestic cooperation of tax authorities with LEAs under criminal law and international cooperation under, for example, a Mutual Legal Assistance Treaty (MLAT).[32]

The case for criminalising tax offences is arguably as loaded and varied as the differences in legal frameworks and definitions of tax crimes across jurisdictions. However, it is clear that criminalising tax offences opens up the legal framework on tax administration and LEAs to rigorous legal scrutiny (given the real possibility of criminal sanctions

[28] Ibid.
[29] Ibid.
[30] Ibid.
[31] Ibid.
[32] Ibid.

such as a prison sentence), thereby enhancing the integrity of the legal system, tax administration, tax enforcement, asset recovery and governance. It also goes without saying that criminal justice[33] can complement administrative justice to deliver a holistic justice in tax governance. That is, criminalising tax offences does not mean that there cannot still be some tax offences that can be administratively handled. In tax matters, criminal law can act as a principal pillar upon which administrative/civil tax law builds complementary relationships for a robust tax system that benefits all.

The Pillars of Criminalisation of Tax Offences

As provided above, four pillars of criminalisation of tax offences are envisaged under TGP 1.

Pillar 1: *The Law Clearly Defines the Tax Offences that are Criminalised*

Two types of approach are envisaged under this pillar of clarity of definition of tax offences. The first approach is that criminal tax offences could 'be defined in a general manner to capture a wide range of activities such as criminal actions that intend to defraud the government'. The other approach is a situation 'where the law sets out the specific offences in more detail, each with individual requirements as to the precise actions that constitute a crime'.[34] These are the two 'different approaches' the TGPs have put out, based on what jurisdictions have been using. However, it is possible to synergise or consolidate these two approaches by both stating or defining the criminal offences 'in a general manner' and detailing specific tax offences. This way, the offences that may be stated in more detail can be captured by the law. This view is reinforced by PROTAX research that found that criminal tax law should be designed in such a way that the criminal offences are not only clearly defined, but are also adequate in terms of their efficacy in addressing different typologies of tax crimes.

Beyond the two approaches provided by the OECD and the synergistic approach drawn therefrom, the TGPs underscore that no matter the approach adopted by a jurisdiction in defining the criminal offences, jurisdictions may also take different approaches to the *threshold* at which an act is classified as a criminal offence.[35] Take for example the following approaches suggested by the TGPs:

i.   Jurisdictions may criminalise actions starting from simple non-compliance, such as any deliberate failure to correctly file a tax return.[36]

ii. Some other jurisdictions may apply the criminal law starting from a higher threshold, where the deliberate failure to comply with a tax obligation is accompanied by aggravating factors such as the amount of tax evaded exceeding a certain threshold,

---

[33] FD Greenberg, 'Justice and Criminal Justice' in FD Hawkins and others (eds), *Crime Control and Social Justice: The Delicate Balance* (Greenwood Press, 2003) 319–54.
[34] OECD, *Fighting Tax Crime: The Ten Global Principles* (OECD Publishing, 2017) 15.
[35] Ibid.
[36] Ibid.

the offence being committed repeatedly, taxable income being actively concealed, or records or evidence being deliberately falsified.[37]

iii. Alternatively, jurisdictions may have set a very high threshold to classify tax crime, such as organised crime for profit, or tax evasion accompanied by particularly aggravating circumstances.[38]

Obviously, the three alternatives have set out essential ingredients for tightening the noose on criminalising tax offences. But these approaches have merely brought out existing prominent practices without necessarily articulating the best practice which can be regarded as worth adopting by all countries, or which options should be considered by which categories of legal framework and culture. It is also not clear that while thresholds may be used to classify certain acts as a tax offence, this does not necessarily mean that these offences are treated as criminal acts which are subjected to criminal sanctions.

PROTAX research found that a low threshold regime for all legal systems is meritorious and commendable.[39] This appears to be in the right direction. It should be possible to keep the threshold regime as minimal as possible. It is even arguable if a threshold is needed at all. Regardless of a position taken, it is imperative that elements of crime that find their way into the tax system ought to be criminalised even if the sanctions that come with certain tax offences are minor due to a consideration of the degree of culpability. At the same time, LEAs and tax authorities must be conscious of costs and benefits of deploying criminal law provisions for all tax offences and review the effectiveness of criminal law on tax compliance regularly.

Some examples that are commonly found in respect of the jurisdictional approaches to tax crimes, as provided by the TGPs, include the following three categories in Table 7:

- non-compliance offences (may apply irrespective of intent or result);
- intentional tax offences; and
- specific offence categories.

Table 7 Categories and Examples of Tax Offences[40]

Classification	Common examples
Non-compliance offences (may apply irrespective of intent or result)	▪ Failure to provide required information, document or return ▪ Failure to register for tax purposes ▪ Failure to keep records ▪ Keeping incorrect records ▪ Making a false statement ▪ Non-payment of a tax liability

(continued)

---

[37] Ibid.
[38] Ibid.
[39] U Turksen and others, 'D1.2: Case Studies of Tax Crimes in the European Union' (EU PROTAX, 2018).
[40] OECD, *Fighting Tax Crime* 15.

Table 7 *(Continued)*

Intentional tax offences	▪ Destroying records
	▪ Deliberate failure to comply with tax law to obtain financial advantage
	▪ Evading tax or receiving refunds by fraud or illegal practices
	▪ Intentional reduction of tax using false documents, fictitious invoices
	▪ Counterfeit or forged documents to reduce tax
	▪ Intentionally or by gross negligence providing misleading information in a tax return to obtain tax advantage
	▪ Fraudulently obtaining refund/credit
	▪ Tax evasion in aggravated circumstances such as considerable financial benefit or conducted in a methodical manner
	▪ Theft from or defrauding the government
	▪ Obstructing an official of the tax authority
	▪ Accessory offences[41]
Specific offences	▪ Entering an arrangement that would make person unable to pay tax
	▪ Committing tax evasion as member of a gang
	▪ Commercial commission of tax evasion
	▪ Illegal use of zappers or sale suppression software
	▪ Identity theft[42]

Investigating selected legal cases representing typical and/or frequent tax crimes in EU Member States, creating substantial damage and involving corporate actors, it can be seen that there are different modi operandi of fraudulent activities to commit tax crimes, including the following: failing to file a tax return, deliberately under-reporting or omitting income, claiming false deductions, hiding or illegally transferring assets or income, overstating the amount of deductions, making false entries in records, failing to report income earned in the stock exchange, maintaining two sets of books, misusing trusts, abusing charitable deductions, and moving assets into secrecy jurisdictions.[43]

Table 7 (based on the OECD findings) lists detailed examples of tax offences (criminalised in varied degrees). However, there are methods, such as misusing trusts, abusing charitable deductions, and moving assets into secrecy jurisdictions, which have not been clearly captured by the list above. These three are candidates that can sometimes be dismissed or ignored by some jurisdictions, partly because of the unsettled and evasive nature of these methods and partly as a result of the powerful forces (MNCs and wealthy individuals behind them) which can influence law, as well as policy enforcement practices. In any case, tax crimes are very extensive and 'approaches to tax crimes in the European Union' and 'conviction rates in selected Member States' are

---

[41] Ibid.
[42] Ibid.
[43] R Kreissl and others, 'D1.1 – The Case Study Design: Guideline and template for case studies on tax crimes in Europe' (PROTAX, 2018).

varied. Furthermore, as established in chapter two of this book, the varied nature and volume of tax crimes makes the unification or harmonisation of definition of tax crimes complicated in the EU.

The EU has so far developed a reasonably comprehensive regulatory framework and legislation to counter VAT fraud in the EU.[44] In benchmarking this pillar of the TGP1 (ie, addressing clarity of defining tax offences) to the EU counter tax crime framework (especially in relation to financial fraud, including tax/VAT fraud), a number of EU tax measures can be found articulating and singing a similar hymn thereof – thus, ensuring a clear definition of tax offences.

The Convention that has been drawn up on the basis of Article K.3[45] of the Treaty on European Union, on the protection of the European Communities' financial interests of 26 July 1995,[46] including the Protocols thereto of 27 September 1996,[47] of 29 November 1996[48] and of 19 June 1997,[49] did establish the minimum rules on the definition of criminal offences and sanctions in the area of fraud affecting the Union's financial interests.[50] However, provisions in the AML framework have superseded and given more details of the offences relating to tax. These particularly include:

- Directive (EU) 2015/849 of the European Parliament and of the Council of 20 May 2015;[51]

- Directive (EU) 2018/843 of the European Parliament and of the Council of 30 May 2018 amending Directive (EU) 2015/849;[52]

- Directive (EU) 2017/1371 of the European Parliament and of the Council of 5 July 2017 on the fight against fraud to the Union's financial interests by means of criminal law;[53] and

---

[44] M Lamensch and E Ceci, 'VAT fraud: Economic impact, challenges and policy issues' (Study requested by the TAX3 Committee, PE 626.076, October 2018) 29.

[45] Particularly Art K.3(e) which states that, 'Common action on judicial cooperation in criminal matters shall include: … (e) progressively adopting measures establishing minimum rules relating to the constituent elements of criminal acts and to penalties in the fields of organised crime, terrorism and illicit drug trafficking'.

[46] Council Act of 26 July 1995 drawing up the Convention on the protection of the European Communities' financial interests (95/C 316/03) [1995] OJ C 316/48 (repealed on 6 July 2019).

[47] Council Act of 27 September 1996 drawing up a Protocol to the Convention on the protection of the European Communities' financial interests (96/C 313/01) [1996] OJ C 313/1.

[48] Council Act of 29 November 1996 drawing up, on the basis of Article K.3 of the Treaty on European Union, the Protocol on the interpretation, by way of preliminary rulings, by the Court of Justice of the European Communities of the Convention on the protection of the European Communities' financial interests (97/C 151/01) [1997] OJ C 151/1 (repealed on 6 July 2019).

[49] Council Act of 19 June 1997 drawing up the Second Protocol of the Convention on the protection of the European Communities' financial interests (97/C 221/02) [1997] OJ C 221/11.

[50] Directive (EU) 2017/1371 of the European Parliament and of the Council of 5 July 2017 on the fight against fraud to the Union's financial interests by means of criminal law [2017] OJ L 198/29–41.

[51] Directive (EU) 2015/849 of the European Parliament and of the Council of 20 May 2015 on the prevention of the use of the financial system for the purposes of money laundering or terrorist financing, amending Regulation (EU) No 648/2012 of the European Parliament and of the Council, and repealing Directive 2005/60/EC of the European Parliament and of the Council and Commission Directive 2006/70/EC [2015] OJ L 141/73.

[52] Directive (EU) 2018/843 of the European Parliament and of the Council of 30 May 2018 amending Directive (EU) 2015/849 on the prevention of the use of the financial system for the purposes of money laundering or terrorist financing, and amending Directives 2009/138/EC and 2013/36/EU, [2018] OJ L 156/43.

[53] Directive (EU) 2017/1371 of the European Parliament and of the Council of 5 July 2017 on the fight against fraud to the Union's financial interests by means of criminal law [2017] OJ L 198/29–41.

- Directive (EU) 2018/1673 of the European Parliament and of the Council of 23 October 2018 on combating money laundering by criminal law.[54]

With respect to the need to define tax offence, Recital 8 of Directive (EU) 2018/1673[55] provides that:

> Tax crimes relating to direct and indirect taxes should be covered by the definition of criminal activity, in line with the revised FATF Recommendations.[56] Given that different tax crimes in each Member State can constitute a criminal activity punishable by the sanctions referred to in this Directive, the definitions of tax crimes might diverge in national law. The aim of this Directive, however, is not to harmonise the definitions of tax crimes in national law.[57]

This effectively criminalises tax offences. However, the lingering question of harmonising the definitions of tax crimes has still been shelved and thrown out of scope of the Directive. This criminalisation imperative is confirmed in Article 3(1) of the Directive (EU) 2018/1673, especially in relation to fraudulent activity that is 'committed intentionally'.

The revised FATF Recommendations define criminal activity as:

> (a) all criminal acts that would constitute a predicate offence for money laundering in the country; or (b) at a minimum to those offences that would constitute a predicate offence as required by Recommendation 3.[58]

Recommendation 3 provides that jurisdictions are urged to 'criminalise money laundering on the basis of the Vienna Convention 1988[59] and the Palermo Convention 2000.[60] Countries should apply the crime of money laundering to all serious offences, with a view to including the widest range of predicate offences',[61] including tax offences. The Interpretive Note to Recommendation 3 (Money Laundering Offence) expatiates on details required of making and identifying tax offences as criminal activity and predicate offences of money laundering.[62]

In the same vein, criminal activity is defined by Directive (EU) 2018/1673 in Article 2(1)(q). The Directive deposits meaning and application of this provision in

---

[54] Directive (EU) 2018/1673 of the European Parliament and of the Council of 23 October 2018 on combating money laundering by criminal law, PE/30/2018/REV/1 [2018] OJ L 284/22.

[55] Ibid.

[56] See FATF, *International Standards on Combating Money Laundering and the Financing of Terrorism & Proliferation* (FATF 2012–2019) 115, www.fatf-gafi.org/recommendations.html, accessed 24 March 2020.

[57] Directive (EU) 2018/1673 of the European Parliament and of the Council of 23 October 2018 on combating money laundering by criminal law, PE/30/2018/REV/1 [2018] OJ L 284/22.

[58] See FATF, *International Standards on Combating Money Laundering and the Financing of Terrorism & Proliferation* (FATF 2012–2019) 115, www.fatf-gafi.org/recommendations.html, accessed 24 March 2020.

[59] United Nations Convention against Illicit Traffic in Narcotic Drugs and Psychotropic Substances [1988], www.unodc.org/pdf/convention_1988_en.pdf, accessed 24 March 2020.

[60] United Nations Convention against Transnational Organized Crime and the Protocols Thereto [2000], www.unodc.org/documents/middleeastandnorthafrica/organised-crime/UNITED_NATIONS_CONVEN-TION_AGAINST_TRANSNATIONAL_ORGANIZED_CRIME_AND_THE_PROTOCOLS_THERETO.pdf, accessed 24 March 2020.

[61] See FATF, *International Standards on Combating Money Laundering and the Financing of Terrorism & Proliferation* (FATF 2012–2019) 10.

[62] See FATF, *International Standards on Combating Money Laundering and the Financing of Terrorism & Proliferation* (FATF 2012–2019) 32.

national legal systems of EU Member States, encapsulating 'tax crimes relating to direct and indirect taxes, as laid down in national law'.[63] This deposition follows or build upon the definition of criminal activity in Recital 11 and Article 3(4)(f) of Directive (EU) 2015/849 of the European Parliament and of the Council of 20 May 2015,[64] which provides that criminal activity refers to 'any kind of criminal involvement in the commission of … all offences, including tax crimes relating to direct taxes and indirect taxes and as defined in the national law of the Member States' of the EU. These are in line with VAT fraud defined in Article 3 of Directive (EU) 2017/1371.

The criminal legal systems have some differences in EU Member States. The differences are, however, not significant relative to their functionality and impact. Therefore, as long as jurisdictions in the EU identify and classify tax offences as criminal activities, tax offences would have been effectively criminalised.

Pursuant to Article 83(1) of the TFEU,[65] Article 1(1) of Directive (EU) 2018/1673 'establishes minimum rules concerning the definition of criminal offences and sanctions in the area of money laundering'. Directive (EU) 2017/1371[66] further provides for the minimum requirements expected by Member States of the EU to define criminal offence in relation to tax offences and others affecting the financial interests of the EU. It states in Article 1 thereof, pursuant to Article 83(2) of TFEU,[67] that:

> This Directive establishes minimum rules concerning the definition of criminal offences and sanctions with regard to combatting fraud and other illegal activities affecting the Union's financial interests, with a view to strengthening protection against criminal offences which affect those financial interests, in line with the *acquis* of the Union in this field.[68]

According to Article 3(2) of Directive (EU) 2017/1371,[69] fraudulent conduct has been particularised. This has been examined in chapter two. Essentially, constituents of tax fraud as they affect the interests of the EU have been provided, much in the similar

---

[63] Directive (EU) 2018/1673 of the European Parliament and of the Council of 23 October 2018 on combating money laundering by criminal law, PE/30/2018/REV/1 [2018] OJ L 284/22.

[64] Directive (EU) 2015/849 of the European Parliament and of the Council of 20 May 2015 on the prevention of the use of the financial system for the purposes of money laundering or terrorist financing, amending Regulation (EU) No 648/2012 of the European Parliament and of the Council, and repealing Directive 2005/60/EC of the European Parliament and of the Council and Commission Directive 2006/70/EC [2015] OJ L 141/73.

[65] TFEU (2012), Art 83(1) states: '1. The European Parliament and the Council may, by means of directives adopted in accordance with the ordinary legislative procedure, *establish minimum rules concerning the definition of criminal offences and sanctions in the areas of particularly serious crime with a cross-border dimension resulting from the nature or impact of such offences or from a special need to combat them on a common basis*. These areas of crime are the following: terrorism, trafficking in human beings and sexual exploitation of women and children, illicit drug trafficking, illicit arms trafficking, *money laundering, corruption, counterfeiting of means of payment, computer crime and organised crime …*'.

[66] Directive (EU) 2017/1371 of the European Parliament and of the Council of 5 July 2017 on the fight against fraud to the Union's financial interests by means of criminal law [2017] OJ L 198/29–41.

[67] TFEU (2012), Art 83(2) states: 'If the approximation of criminal laws and regulations of the Member States proves essential to ensure the effective implementation of a Union policy in an area which has been subject to harmonisation measures, *directives may establish minimum rules with regard to the definition of criminal offences and sanctions in the area concerned*. Such directives shall be adopted by the same ordinary or special legislative procedure as was followed for the adoption of the harmonisation measures in question, without prejudice to Article 76.'

[68] Directive (EU) 2017/1371 of the European Parliament and of the Council of 5 July 2017 on the fight against fraud to the Union's financial interests by means of criminal law [2017] OJ L 198/29.

[69] Ibid.

shape and fashion shown in the Pillar 1 of TGP1. With these particulars, Directive (EU) 2017/1371[70] has provided specific elements of financial fraud, and particularly tax/VAT fraud. However, the Directive focuses on VAT fraud – understandably because of the serious nature and high volume of VAT fraud in the EU. In any case, both direct and indirect tax offences have been criminalised by Recital 8 and Article 2(1)(q) of Directive (EU) 2018/1673 as well as Recital 11 and Article 3(4)(f) of Directive (EU) 2015/849.

Criminal Liability for Accessories (Particularly Professional Enablers)

A feather in the cap of defining tax offences under Pillar 1 of the TGP1 is that jurisdictions are also required or expected to ensure that they 'criminalise the act of aiding, abetting, facilitating or enabling the commission of a tax offence by others, or conspiracy to commit a tax offence, ("accessories"), such as actions taken by professional enablers'. This requirement is practiced in many jurisdictions. Before establishing this requirement, OECD survey data from 22 jurisdictions evinced that 'accessories, including professional enablers, are criminally responsible, and in most cases can be held liable for the same offence and the same criminal sanction'. Thus, accessories are also held criminally liable for tax crimes committed. There are some instances where the accessories 'can be liable for an increased penalty, such as where they are tax professionals and their facilitation of the offence is considered to be an aggravating factor'. The data from the OECD survey also showed that three jurisdictions 'apply significant civil penalties for professional enablers or promoters'. Thus, some countries that do not hold accessories criminally accountable employ appreciable civil law remedies to hold accessories liable and penalise them in significant ways. Demonstrably, majority of the 31 countries do hold accessories such as professional enablers (including accountants, lawyers and related consultants) criminally liable for tax offences.

In the case studies conducted by PROTAX, however, it is intriguing to find that in most of these cases that had professional enablers, the prosecutors were more interested in the main culprits than the enablers who had enabled the criminal scheme to be materialised. In Spain, for instance, several consultants and related intermediaries were found to be at the centre of aiding Lionel Messi and his father, Jorge Messi, to defraud 'the public treasury of three years' tax debt' between 2007, 2008 and 2009. They were convicted, on appeal, at Spain's Supreme Court in 2017,[71] having had initial or earlier judgment by the Provincial Court of Barcelona (Audiencia Provincial de Barcelona) on 5 July 2016. Yet, despite the involvement of professional enablers, the prosecutors were mainly focused on pursuing Messi and his father for tax fraud. A novel finding by PROTAX in the case studies relating to professional enablers was that:

> The role of enablers has two sides to the story. On one hand, they are there to assist their clients, and on the other hand authorities depend on the evidence (a requirement in criminal prosecutions) obtained from enablers to counter tax evasion. They are usually the key actors in many trials [but are hardly themselves ever prosecuted].[72]

---

[70] Ibid.
[71] See Tribunal Supremo Sala de lo Penal Sentencia núm. 374/2017 Roj: STS 1885/2017 – ECLI: ES:TS: 2017:1885.
[72] Turksen and others, 'D1.2: Case Studies' 311.

This dual role played by professional enablers was also highlighted in the 2019 focus group discussions of PROTAX. The foundation of the duality problem of professional enablers was found to have a number of building blocks. The corner stone, as it came out from the focus group's report on approaches to tackling tax crimes, is founded on understanding and defining the limits of enablers, recognition of some of the enablers' role as crime fighters in national legal frameworks, unpicking the difficulty in differentiating the legal role and the illegal role of enablers, as well as addressing cross-border jurisdictional issues in holding liable professional enablers who assist tax offender to commit tax crimes. For instance, part of the issue is that the enablers cover a wide range of professions reaching beyond the realm of traditional financial sector institutions including, as FATF recommendations on AML/TF have it, 'casinos, real estate agents, dealers in precious metals and precious stones, lawyers, notaries, other legal professions and accountants, trust and company service providers'.[73] Additionally, the lack of clarity in the toolkits provided for addressing untoward behaviour of professional enablers presents a lingering dilemma for LEAs. The PROTAX focus group report, for example, noted that:

> The complex practices and solutions worked out by or involving the different kinds of enablers are rarely straightforward illegal acts of tax crime. Not only are there grey areas in written law that allow for wide discretion and competing interpretations, but [also] the complex division of labour in tax-related financial flows, involving different professionals and stretching across multiple jurisdictions often makes it difficult to apply *mens rea* or principles of strict legal liability.[74]

Similar sentiments were highlighted at the PROTAX conference at which experts shared perspectives on countering tax crimes in the light of the findings from the focus groups on approaches to tackling tax crimes in the EU. In particular, the following narrative in the PROTAX conference report is instructive as it emphasises the need for special consideration to be given to law in books and law in reality or in action with respect to the dual role of enablers:

> Kreissl outlined two primary points most relevant for the role enablers play in the context of tax crimes. Firstly, they have a dual role in reporting tax crime and defending client interests. Secondly, they play a role in influencing policy. Enablers have a role in providing advice to clients, and navigating complex tax law on behalf of corporations, or whatever that specific role is. However, they have also been 'responsibilised' by authorities, a role that should in fact be an LEA role. The focus groups showed an understanding of the conflicts between enablers, LEAs and authorities that took on very different forms. This conflict is demonstrated by information sharing. Enablers must balance their role in informing authorities with another question: what does this mean for the privacy and data protection of my clients? The second key point about this dual role is the influence over the policy framework. There is usually a strong representation by enablers – for example, the big four accountancy firms. However, very rarely if at all is there representation from NGOs, which produces a bias in the policy process.[75]

---

[73] Rasmouki and others, 'D2.3 Approaches to tax crimes in the European Union' (EU PROTAX, 2019) 83.

[74] Ibid.

[75] M Hall and others, 'D2.4 – Conference Report summarising and documenting contributions from T2.7' (EU PROTAX, 2020) 7.

Liability for Legal Persons

Apart from liability of enablers in the counter tax crime ecosystem, Pillar 1 of TGP1 underscores that corporate liability must also be placed on the criminalisation radar. This TGP establishes the need for legal persons and legal arrangements to also be prosecuted and held criminally liable for tax crimes. It should be possible to prosecute companies for tax crimes, hold them criminally liable and impose sanctions on key company representatives 'such as directors, officers, agents or key employees of the legal person/arrangement'.[76] The OECD survey data on these aspects found the following as demonstrating the ability of jurisdictions to hold entities criminally responsible or liable: a majority of the 31 respondents (71 per cent) responded in the affirmative to the question 'Is it possible to hold legal entities criminally liable for tax offences?' The balance of the survey respondents responded in the negative. See Table 8 for a list of jurisdictions in the respective categories of whether or not the jurisdiction holds corporate entities criminally liable.

Table 8 Criminal Liability for Tax Offences in Selected Jurisdictions across the World[77]

Are legal persons held criminally liable for tax offences?		Total
Yes	*No*	
Respondents from jurisdictions in the majority	*Respondents from jurisdictions in the minority*	
Australia	Brazil	
Austria	El Salvador	
Canada	Finland	
Czech Republic	Georgia	
Denmark	Germany	
France	Greece	
Iceland	Indonesia	
Japan	Italy	
Lithuania	Sweden	
Luxembourg		
Malaysia		
Netherlands		
New Zealand		
Norway		
Singapore		
Slovak Republic		
Slovenia		

(continued)

[76] OECD, *Fighting Tax Crime* 16.
[77] Ibid.

Table 8 *(Continued)*

Are legal persons held criminally liable for tax offences?		Total
Yes	*No*	
Respondents from jurisdictions in the majority	*Respondents from jurisdictions in the minority*	
South Africa		
Spain		
Switzerland		
United States		
United Kingdom		
22	9	31

PROTAX case studies also found that Ireland (not featured among the 31 countries listed) also holds corporate entities criminally liable for tax offences.

Box 6 Corporate Tax Law in Ireland

> *In Ireland, companies are considered legal persons and are liable for prosecution for criminal offences committed on their behalf, if it can be shown that the company management were aware of the crime. Officers of companies may be held directly responsible for offences committed by the company or committed with their consent and/or connivance.*[78]

One of the intriguing features from the PROTAX case studies came from Italy which, at that time, did not have corporate liability for tax offences whereby case law (the court) attempted to provide a bridge between the lack of corporate criminal liability for tax offences in statutes and the evolving need to hold legal persons liable. More recently, however Italy introduced corporate criminal liability for tax offences on the back of the EU PFI Directive at the end of 2019 under Law Decree No 124 of 26 October 2019.

Furthermore, as in most civil law jurisdictions, in Germany the legal concept of corporate liability does not exist. In the German legal framework, the principle of *Societas delinquere non potest*[79] is applied, which is based on the strictly personal character of criminal sanctions which therefore may only be imposed on natural persons and not on companies. The prevailing opinion in Germany is that a company cannot be criminally liable. However, companies can be recipients of criminal legal consequences or administrative sanctions. One example is the seizure of assets under section 74 ff StGB (German Criminal Code, *Strafgesetzbuch* 1998), 22ff OWiG (Administrative Offences Act 1968).[80] The most important administrative sanction is a financial penalty

---

[78] Turksen and others, 'D1.2: Case Studies' 237.
[79] 'Society cannot be wrong'.
[80] Turksen and others, 'D1.2: Case Studies' 259–60; see Administrative Offences Act (OWiG) 1968, www.gesetze-im-internet.de/owig_1968/BJNR004810968.html, accessed 26 March 2020.

under section 30 OWiG which enables the state to impose a financial penalty on a legal person if it committed a crime or an administrative offence.[81]

Another PROTAX case study, also not featured in the OECD's 31 countries above, is Malta. Malta was found not to have criminal liability for tax offences committed by legal persons – the concept of corporate liability does not exist. However, one of the general principles of criminal law in Malta is that a body corporate is represented by its directors, and the representatives of a body corporate are answerable to the offences committed by such an entity.[82] Thus the individuals behind the company (its directors) are criminally responsible where a tax crime is carried out by a corporation.

In some of the 22 countries listed above that reported criminal liability for tax crimes, a number of challenges await investigators and prosecutors – a point of highlighting the dichotomy between law in books and law in action or in reality. A good example of this is the United Kingdom where the concept of corporate liability for criminal offences, including tax offences, exists. However, there are a number of difficulties in attributing liability to corporate offenders. The Ministry of Justice has highlighted these difficulties in a recent call for evidence on corporate liability for economic crime.[83] In the United Kingdom, to attribute liability to a corporate offender, it must be shown that the 'directing mind and will' of the corporation (such as the board of directors, the managing directors and perhaps other superior officers of the company)[84] possessed the requisite *mens rea* of the offence.[85] This is not an easy task and demonstrates the challenges in attributing liability to corporate offenders especially with respect to the requirement of the guilty mind of the 'directed mind and will' of the corporation. The PROTAX UK case study provided a reasoning that also shows that 'if senior officers of a company obscure their involvement in financial crimes, a company cannot be held responsible'. This was the basis for establishing a new corporate offence of failure to prevent the facilitation of UK and foreign tax evasion in the United Kingdom, a unique feature which has been added to the list of strict liability offences in the United Kingdom.

In Spain and Austria there seem to be no significant legal hurdles in holding corporations criminally liable.

Corporate liability exists in Spain. Article 31(1) *bis* of the Spanish Criminal Code provides that 'legal entities shall be criminally liable for offences committed in their name or on their behalf, and for their benefit, by their legal representatives and administrators, whether *de facto* or *de jure*'. Article 31 *bis* (2) provides enforceability of criminal liability of legal entities. If any entity is not captured by Article 31 *bis* with respect to felonies due to lack of legal personality thereof, Article 126 would be applied by the judge, who could use their own discretion as to the determination of criminal liability and enforceability thereof. Articles 250, 251 and 251 *bis* (in particular) provide

---

[81] Turksen and others, 'D1.2: Case Studies' 259–60.

[82] Ibid, 269.

[83] Ministry of Justice, 'Corporate liability for economic crime: call for evidence' (Consultation, 31 January 2018), www.gov.uk/government/consultations/corporate-liability-for-economic-crime-call-for-evidence, accessed 26 July 2018.

[84] *Tesco Supermarkets Ltd v Nattrass* [1972] AC 153, 171, HL.

[85] *Lennard's Carrying Co Ltd v Asiatic Petroleum Co Ltd* [1915] AC 705, 713, HL.

penalties thereof. Articles 290 to 294 of the Criminal Code set out corporate offences, providing for their prosecution and the imprisonment of offenders. Article 328 also provides for penalties for criminal liabilities established under Article 31 *bis*. Article 66 sets out rules and guidelines for judges to determine offences and punishment or mitigation thereof.[86]

In Austria, even though it is clear that the legal persons and their officials are, by law, held accountable for tax crimes, it is not clear whether the law in the books effectively translates into law in action. Legal entities are subjects to criminal liability according to the Legal Entities Liability Act (LELA) BGBl[87] I No 151/2005, amended by Federal Act BGBl I No 26/2016. The LELA has been implemented into the Fiscal Penal Code (FPC) by Federal Act BGBl I No 161/2005 and entered into force on 1 January 2006. Legal entities (as described in section 1 LELA) are criminally liable for tax offences committed by their decision-makers or employees (section 2 LELA). This liability neither excludes the perpetrator from prosecution, nor does conviction of the perpetrator exclude the liability of the legal entity.[88] Criminal liability must be proven in a regular criminal procedure. Therefore, legal entities and their legal representatives are treated like accused persons and have the same procedural rights (section 17 LELA; section 56 para 5 FPC).

However, criminal corporate liability for tax offences is being established in all EU countries. On liability of legal persons, Directive (EU) 2018/1673 provides in Article 7 that:

> Member States shall take the necessary measures to ensure that legal persons can be held liable for any of the offences referred to in Article 3(1)[89] and (5)[90] and Article 4[91] committed for their benefit by any person, acting either individually or as part of an organ of the legal person and having a leading position within the legal person, based on any of the following: (a) a power of representation of the legal person; (b) an authority to take decisions on behalf of the legal person; or (c) an authority to exercise control within the legal person.[92]

---

[86] Turksen and others, 'D1.2: Case Studies' 145.

[87] BGBl is the abbreviation for *Bundesgesetzblatt* (Official Gazette for the publication of Austrian federal legislation).

[88] Turksen and others, 'D1.2: Case Studies' 190–91.

[89] Art 3(1) of the Directive states: 'Member States shall take the necessary measures to ensure that the following conduct, when committed intentionally, is punishable as a criminal offence: (a) the conversion or transfer of property, knowing that such property is derived from criminal activity, for the purpose of concealing or disguising the illicit origin of the property or of assisting any person who is involved in the commission of such an activity to evade the legal consequences of that person's action; (b) the concealment or disguise of the true nature, source, location, disposition, movement, rights with respect to, or ownership of, property, knowing that such property is derived from criminal activity; (c) the acquisition, possession or use of property, knowing, at the time of receipt, that such property was derived from criminal activity.'

[90] Art 5 of the Directive states: '1. Member States shall take the necessary measures to ensure that the offences referred to in Articles 3 and 4 are punishable by effective, proportionate and dissuasive criminal penalties. 2. Member States shall take the necessary measures to ensure that the offences referred to in Article 3(1) and (5) are punishable by a maximum term of imprisonment of at least four years. 3. Member States shall also take the necessary measures to ensure that natural persons who have committed the offences referred to in Articles 3 and 4 are, where necessary, subject to additional sanctions or measures.'

[91] Art 4 of the Directive provides: 'Member States shall take the necessary measures to ensure that aiding and abetting, inciting and attempting an offence referred to in Article 3(1) and (5) is punishable as a criminal offence.'

[92] Directive (EU) 2018/1673 of the European Parliament and of the Council of 23 October 2018 on combating money laundering by criminal law, PE/30/2018/REV/1 OJ L 284/22.

This imperative provision highlights the difficulty in establishing both the guilty act and the guilty mind of senior officials of a corporation in order to hold the corporation legally accountable for criminal offences.[93]

Article 7(2) of Directive (EU) 2018/1673 reinforces the criminal liability of a legal person for tax offences. Article 7(3) thereof also holds criminally liable 'natural persons who are perpetrators, inciters or accessories in any of the offences referred to in Article 3(1) and (5) and Article 4' of the Directive (EU) 2018/1673. It is worth noting that the conduct of tax crimes is, to some extent, described in the money laundering offences and offences relating to aiding and abetting, inciting and attempting. But there is some clarification of the tax crime offences in Articles 3, 4, 5, and 6 of Directive (EU) 2017/1371 (albeit not as detailed as exemplified in the requirements of the Pillar 1 of the TGP1) – a directive which was required to be transposed[94] into national laws by 6 July 2019.

With the AML legal framework of the EU, in effect, money laundering and related financial crimes such as tax crimes as well as the act of aiding and abetting, inciting and attempting to commit a criminal offence such as tax offences are required to be integrated into national laws of the EU Member States as criminal offences against corporate entities by 3 December 2020.[95] When EU Member States succeed in transposing the above provisions into their national laws by that date, the 27 EU Member States will have in place relevant legal provisions for holding both corporations and natural persons criminally liable for laundering the proceeds from tax offences. The challenge, however, is that even the preceding directives[96] (except Directive (EU) 2015/849, whose measures have been somewhat substantially transposed by all EU jurisdictions) have not been effectively transposed into national laws of the EU Member States. Essentially, there is a slow pace in transposing the tax crime-related directives. A number of countries usually miss the deadline for transposing the relevant directives into national law. It does appear that there is a culture of lingering transposition of EU directives, partly due to structural difficulties and partly as a result of political commitment. In order to articulate the deserving prominence of tax crimes, it would be more effective to have a provision that clearly provides for extensive details of instances for holding corporations criminally liable for tax offences (such as tax fraud) which are then defined with common features across all EU Member States.

Hosting Legal Frames

The criminalised offences, whether for legal or natural persons, can be hosted or harboured by the following legislative domains.

- statute, legislation or code that covers 'all criminal activities';
- general tax act or code;

---

[93] Turksen and others, 'D1.2: Case Studies'.
[94] Directive (EU) 2017/1371, Art 17.
[95] Directive (EU) 2018/1673, Art 13.
[96] Directive (EU) 2015/849 (transposition deadline: 26 June 2017); Directive (EU) 2018/843 (transposition deadline: 10 January 2020); Directive (EU) 2017/1371 (transposition deadline: 6 July 2019).

- income tax or VAT statutes; or
- specific statutes.[97]

Regardless of the approaches to defining and hosting tax offences, TGP1 suggests that 'the legal provisions should state the elements that constitute the crime'. This should include clear presentation or definition of 'the specific conduct or activity that constitutes the criminal act, as well as the required mental state of the person in committing the activity (such as intention, recklessness or gross negligence)'.[98]

The parameters provided by EU tax and criminal law, as established in the foregoing provisions and other regulatory instruments with similar effects that have not been considered, show that the EU counter tax crime regulatory framework clearly provides for the definition of certain tax offences and tax crimes (eg, VAT fraud), generally. The lesson that the EU can learn from the TGP1 in relation to Pillar 1 of criminalising tax crimes is that, in future, an extensive list and definitions of different tax offences should be provided to its Member States. A useful lesson the OECD TGP1 can also learn from the EU legal framework in defining tax crimes is that the VAT framework and the proposed definitive VAT system[99] is an exemplary step, although it is not without some limitations such as a tension that can arise between EU Member States in the implementation of the 'one stop shop'.[100] A fundamental weakness with both OECD and EU tax crime countering regimes in clearly defining tax crimes is that they do not make a clear attempt to harmonise the definitions of tax crimes.

In effect, as noted in chapter two, the definitions of tax crimes in the EU and OECD have significant clarity, but not the needed adequacy. Taken together, clarity and adequacy of definitions of tax crimes are moderate. This evaluation came out during PROTAX focus group discussions in 2019. Figure 6 characterises the opinions of the focus group discussants.

Therefore, in spite of some commonalities among the EU Member States established through the EU legal framework, there are clear variations in how criminalising of tax offences and their violations are defined and applied in EU countries. The EU's legal framework on tax crimes provides no settled or clearly articulated definition of tax crimes and how Member States should clearly counter it, either. Consequently, tax crime counter-measures suffer from a lack of clear definitional jurisdiction.

What the foregoing perspectives suggest is that there is room for improvement in tax crime definitions in both EU and OECD rulebooks. They also emphasise the need to harmonise the frameworks of tax crime definitions not just within the EU but also in the OECD and globally, so that it would be easier to exchange relevant information on tax crimes and to effectively enforce tax laws. There is clearly room to argue that tax crimes are universal crimes with multiple victims. Without clear and adequate definitions of tax crimes which are based on significant notions of harmony, it does not only affect information exchange and interpretation among the LEAs but also affects other features

---

[97] OECD, *Fighting Tax Crime: The Ten Global Principles* 15.
[98] Ibid.
[99] European Commission, 'Single VAT Area', https://ec.europa.eu/taxation_customs/business/vat/action-plan-vat/single-vat-area_en#heading_3, accessed 13 April 2020.
[100] M Lamensch and E Ceci, 'VAT fraud: Economic impact, challenges and policy issues' (Study requested by the TAX3 Committee, PE 626.076, October 2018).

Figure 6 Clarity and Adequacy of Tax Crime Definitions in EU

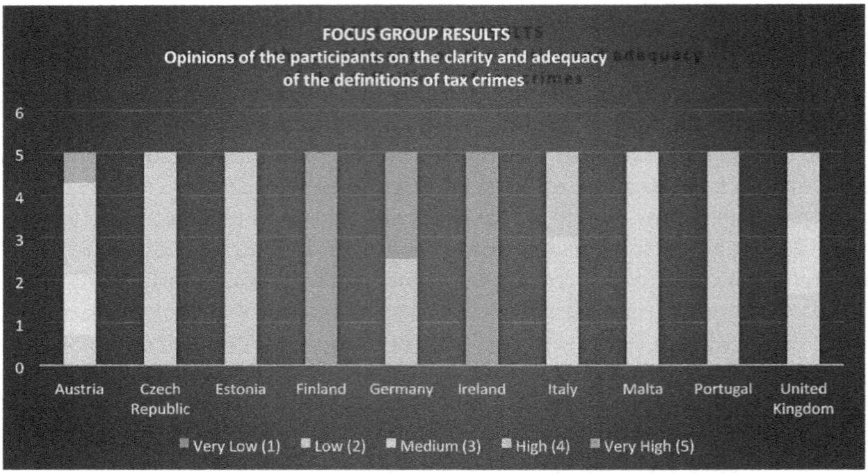

in the tax ecosystem such as investigation, prosecution and sanctions. The second pillar of criminalisation of tax crimes is, therefore, the need to apply appropriate sanctions to criminalised tax offences.

Pillar 2: A Criminal Sanction Applies if the Offence is Proven

Sanctions are among the core elements of any criminal law. The nature of the quality and quantity of sanctions in a given society reflect the disposition or character of social solidarity[101] and the sense of justice in that society. Simple and complex societies have different levels of conformity, which require different levels of stringent measures to draw people into the solidarity frame. Whereas simple societies have high degrees of willingness to conform to the social order or norms, complex societies have lower levels of conformity to the societal rulebook.[102]

Consequently, with simple societies, 'normative sanctions tend to be informal in nature, substantive in application, and limited in use'.[103] In complex societies, however, normative sanctions tend 'to be formal in nature, procedural in application, and frequent in use'.[104] Without the need to delve much into development of sanctions and in light of the limited space available in this book, it is worth noting only that societies today are becoming more complex by the day and, therefore, the need for formalised sanctions and applications thereof has become apparent. Take the supranational nature of EU and the international DNA of OECD, liberalisation of international trade and globalisation

---

[101] E Durkheim, *The Division of Labour in Society* (Free Press, 1964); D Black, *The Behaviour of Law* (Academic Press, 1976).

[102] P Cordella, 'Criminal Sanctions' (Cengage, Encyclopedia.com, updated 3 May 2020), www.encyclope-dia.com/social-sciences/encyclopedias-almanacs-transcripts-and-maps/criminal-sanctions, accessed 7 May 2020.

[103] Ibid.

[104] R Michalowski, *Order, Law and Crime* (Random House, 1985).

footprints everywhere, for instance; such developments have made determination of the contours of social solidarity and conformity to the societal rulebook more complicated. Indeed, the increasing stratification, morphology, and bureaucracy of modern society give rise to certain complexities in criminal law and criminal sanctions.[105]

As a result, the landscape of criminal conduct has been transmuted from an offence by an individual or group of individuals against another individual or group of individuals in community context, to an offence that is committed by an individual or group of individuals against the whole of society or entire jurisdiction.[106] An offence is a behaviour or conduct that is contrary to the social solidarity and/or the dictates of the law.

Behaviours that have usually been considered as 'harmful to the moral, political, economic, or social well-being of society',[107] or to social solidarity, are normally defined as criminal behaviours which are deemed to deserve formal sanctions of the state.[108] This means that behaviours considered as criminal consist of 'transgressions of both the prohibitions and obligations that define a particular society'.[109] In fact, deviant behaviours are defined or identified as crimes through the process of criminalisation, which includes the calculation of necessary and proportional sanctions for each crime.[110] In fact, central to the study of crime and law has been the view that 'behaviours become defined as criminal and deemed worthy of punitive sanctions' in the course of time.[111] This imperative is synchronised with the functionalist perspective of criminal law, which argues that criminalising a behaviour results from 'a consensus among members of a society'.[112] From the viewpoint of the consensus, the underpinning imperative is that criminal law encapsulates the set of behaviours or conduct that is deemed 'to be most threatening to the social [solidarity or] structure of society and the well-being of its members'.[113]

Sanctions against criminal behaviour are diverse across different jurisdictions, depending upon the frontiers of social solidarity and how seriously undermining that solidarity is taken. These sanctions against crimes can consist of 'capital punishment, imprisonment, corporal punishment, banishment, house arrest, community supervision, fines, restitution, and community service'.[114] So, they can take the form of confinement in prison and/or fines where payment of a monetary sanction by the culprit is required. The sanctions may demonstrate the anger of society against deviants who want to vitiate or pull down the building blocks of social solidarity. In doing so, sanctions become the face of limiting culprits' fundamental liberties and rights, which are ordinarily accorded to everyone within the frame of the social order. The EU provides that sanctions are intended to serve as a strong deterrent for potential offenders.[115]

---

[105] D Black, *The Behaviour of Law*.

[106] P Cordella, 'Criminal Sanctions'; N Christie, 'Conflicts as Property' (1977) 17 *British Journal of Criminology* 1.

[107] Ibid.

[108] N Walker, *Punishment, Danger and Stigma: The Morality of Criminal Justice* (Blackwell, 1980).

[109] Cordella, 'Criminal Sanctions'.

[110] Ibid.

[111] Ibid.

[112] E Durkheim, *The Division of Labor in Society* (Free Press, 1964); Cordella, 'Criminal Sanctions'.

[113] JQ Wilson, *Thinking about Crime* (Basic Books, 1979)

[114] Cordella, 'Criminal Sanctions'.

[115] Directive (EU) 2017/1371, recital 18.

The nature of criminal sanctions must be prescribed by criminal law.[116] The type and severity of the sanctions must be clear, predictable and consistent. In the field of taxation, it is possible to also find criminal sanctions against tax offences. The extent to which an offence is perceived by society as a serious one, 'and the underlying philosophy of punishment',[117] dictate to the authorities the quality and quantity of criminal sanctions they will develop and apply to any culprit of the offence. The question that arises, therefore, concerns whether offences against tax laws are perceived as serious and what underlying philosophy will predicate quality and quantity of sanctions? In terms of the underlying philosophy of applicable sanctions, the argument has traditionally been along consequential and non-consequential or categorical lines.[118]

In terms of consequential grounds for sanctions, proponents argue that punishment or sanctions serve as a preventative measure against committing crimes in the future. The consequentialist argument is also utilitarian in that, among other things, it advocates for society to 'inflict harm' on or seriously penalise those that also inflict harm or disobey (offend) the social order or solidarity. This, it is believed, will help in the prevention of 'greater harms that would be caused by future crimes'.[119]

However, the utilitarian approach further posits that no criminal sanctions should be used to punish behaviour or conduct which has been assessed as not harming the society. The philosophy is, therefore, provided as self-limiting. This philosophy adds that 'the severity of the penalty should only slightly outweigh the benefit derived from the criminal behaviour'.[120] Furthermore, if there are alternatives to punishment, at any point, these should be employed whenever they are proven to be as effective as punishment.[121] By so doing, both the happiness and wellbeing of society is maximised. There are other consequentialist grounds apart from utilitarianism. Essentially, the penalising philosophy of consequentialism is anchored on the imperative that the consequences (or harm) of an offence should form the basis of reaching judgement as to the rightfulness or wrongfulness of the offence and appropriate punishment or reward (if any) that is commensurate with the conduct.

With respect to the non-consequentialism, punishment of a culprit of criminal offence is justified 'as an intrinsically appropriate response to crime'.[122] The retributive approach is typical of non-consequentialist theory. It, besides other things, provides for or advocates punishment to be used as a means by which the advantage that is originally gained by a criminal behaviour is eliminated. The argument goes that punishment can alternatively be used as a means by which 'moral balance that was lost as a result of a crime' is restored.[123] The retributivist approach sees a criminal conduct as a behaviour that isolates the offender or culprit from the community or social solidarity framework. With this separation, it is incumbent upon society to bring the offender back to the

---

[116] Walker, *Punishment, Danger and Stigma*.

[117] Cordella, 'Criminal Sanctions'.

[118] Ibid.

[119] Ibid; C Beccaria, *On Crimes and Punishment* (Bobbs-Merrill, 1980).

[120] Cordella, 'Criminal Sanctions'.

[121] J Bentham, 'Punishment and Utility' in J Murphy (ed), *Punishment and Rehabilitation* (Wadsworth, 1995).

[122] A Duff and D Garland, 'Introduction: Thinking about Punishment' in RA Duff and D Garland (eds), *A Reader on Punishment* (Oxford University Press, 1994); Cordella, 'Criminal Sanctions'.

[123] Cordella, 'Criminal Sanctions'.

community. To this end, penalising the offender is the only means by which the culprit can be restored to the society or the separation can be repaired.

The utilitarian and retributivist philosophical orientations have played a dominant role in providing basis or justification for sanctions to be imposed. However, other justifications have recently provided a basis for punishments, including incapacitation[124] and rehabilitation.[125] Recent developments have nonetheless been captured within the framework of either consequentialism or non-consequentialism.

There have been criticisms of these philosophical approaches to criminalisation of behaviours from functional and conflict theory perspectives. The functional perspective essentially argues that by the very nature of social solidary and how harmful behaviours are defined, it is always possible for some behaviours to fall outside the perimeters of acceptable conduct at any point in time. Why punish such behaviours then? For instance, a behaviour might be criminalised today but then decriminalised tomorrow, in the same way as an acceptable conduct today can be deemed to be unacceptable and need to be criminalised in future. This pendulum of unsettled direction of swinging other than what may be regarded as a social consensus on what is right or wrong, may only provide a platform for injustice to be done to others who do not fall in line. This argument flies in the face of the idea of collective good and the need to regulate behaviours to achieve social good and maintain the balance of society. After all, it is worth remembering that social solidarity is not confined to a society and population in a given country but also includes communities of states such as the European Union (a regional international community)[126] as well as those under the umbrella of the OECD (a larger intercontinental community).

On the other hand, the conflict perspective sees criminalisation and penalisation of certain behaviours as simply an effort of powerful people or those clothed with power in society to remain in control – criminalising and punishing behaviours that mainly affect the less powerful in society. Thus, 'behaviours more likely to be committed by the less powerful are defined as criminal while behaviours more likely committed by the powerful are not defined as criminal'.[127] The conflict perspective has been developed into different formulations. The key ones include conflict theories that identify a conflict of:

- cultural groups;[128]
- norms;[129]
- socioeconomic interests;[130] and
- bureaucratic interests.[131]

---

[124] N Morris, '"Dangerousness and Incapacitation", Record of the Association of the Bar in the City of New York' in A Duff and D Garland (eds), *A Reader on Punishment* (Oxford University Press, 1994).

[125] E Rotman, *Beyond Punishment: A New View of the Rehabilitation of Offenders* (Greenwood Press, 1990); also see Cordella, 'Criminal Sanctions'.

[126] For legal and philosophical foundations of the principle of solidarity in the EU see U Turksen, *EU Energy Relations with Russia – Solidarity and the Rule of Law* (Routledge, 2018).

[127] T Bernard, *The Consensus – Conflict Debate: Form and Content in Social Theories* (University Press, 1983); J Reiman, *The Rich Get Richer and the Poor Get Prison* (Wiley, 1998); Cordella, 'Criminal Sanctions'.

[128] See T Sellen, *Culture, Conflict and Crime* (Social Science Research Council, 1938).

[129] See G Vold, *Theoretical Criminology* (Oxford University Press, 1958).

[130] See K Marx, 'Theories of Surplus Value' in TB Bottomore and M Rubel (eds), *Karl Marx: Selected Writings in Sociology and Social Philosophy* (McGraw-Hill, 1964).

[131] See A Turk, *Criminality and Legal Order* (Rand McNally, 1969); see also Cordella, 'Criminal Sanctions'.

These conflict theories share common grounds regarding the understanding 'that criminal law and criminal sanctions are utilised to support the average best interest of those with power'.[132] In this regard, the conflict theories are settled in their assumption that the state does 'apply criminal sanctions in such a manner that they are not perceived as overly coercive while at the same time preserving the existing power arrangements thereby maintaining the legitimacy of criminal law'.[133]

The argument in the context of power imbalance in employing criminal sanctions is not entirely accurate because some criminal behaviours such as robbery and murder (and tax fraud for that matter) can be seen exhibited by both the powerful and less powerful in the society. Nonetheless, a little look below the surface would reveal some amount of underlying truth in the settled position taken by the conflict theories. For instance, with those conflict theories from the socioeconomic perspective,[134] an immediate example can be cited of just how and why it has taken too long for tax avoidance schemes of MNCs to be criminalised when the resulting effect of what they do is similar to tax fraud and tax evasion practices committed by relatively less powerful or less organised structure of the global society. Here, it would depend then upon who the powerful in society are. The defining limits of who the powerful people in society are remain uncharted.

These critiques appear to have a low level of patronage in current criminological or penological[135] discourse. They, nevertheless, serve as an awakening call to ensure that the criminalisation process is continually assessed to improve its structures, objectives, functionality and impact. The issue raised about the tax avoidance of MNCs, for instance, appears to be a very valid concern to consider and address by the solidarity structures of the global society. In effect, the consequentialism and non-consequentialist theoretical persuasions continue to provide credible underlying philosophies for criminalisation and penalisation of certain behaviours such as intentional failure to pay required taxes by both natural and legal persons.

Although these philosophical justifications can be seen as idealistic,[136] they have always provided grounds upon which these ideals are translated into action, in terms of formulating and enacting the criminal law provisions on sanctions. Reconnecting law in books with law in action comes into play. Thus, whatever the underlying philosophical foundations of criminal sanctions on tax offences, it should and must be possible to maximise the translation of the legal provisions drawn from philosophical persuasions to real time compliance, enforcement and sanctioning regimes. In the same vein, whatever trajectory a jurisdiction navigates, the need to ensure compliance with the rules of social solidarity or the laws of the society has always been a centripetal force.

To this end, therefore, Pillar 2 of the criminalisation principle (TGP1) provides that:

> The legal provision should include a penalty if the elements of the crime are proven. Penalties should be designed to encourage compliance and prevent non-compliance by providing

---

[132] Ibid.

[133] Ibid.

[134] See Marx, 'Theories of Surplus Value'.

[135] A Duff and D Garland, 'Introduction: Thinking about Punishment' in RA Duff and D Garland (eds), *A Reader on Punishment* (Oxford University Press, 1994).

[136] Cordella, 'Criminal Sanctions'.

a credible threat. Any statute of limitations on imposing a criminal penalty should reflect the seriousness of the crime and the prescribed punishment.[137]

Three key considerations can be harvested from the above proposition of the sanctions pillar, or Pillar 2 of TGP1.

i.   To define the legal imposition of a sanction, elements of crime must be clearly defined in such a way that these elements can be proven.[138]

ii. The primary purpose of sanctions is to engender compliance and prevent non-compliant behaviour.[139] This requires that jurisdictions should strive to institute maximum sentences – particularly prison sentences – for those found guilty. An OECD survey of 31 countries for the TGPs showed that South Africa had the topmost maximum sentences, followed by Greece, Slovak Republic and Slovenia. These were then followed by six jurisdictions that had the same ranking of maximum prison sentences (United States, Japan, Germany, Czech Republic, Australia, and Austria). Malaysia had the lowest maximum prison sentence, followed ascendingly by Finland. See Figure 7 for a diagram demonstrating the full picture of the prison sentences of 31 jurisdictions across the world as of 2017.[140]

Figure 7   OECD Survey Responses on Maximum Prison Sentence in 31 Countries[141]

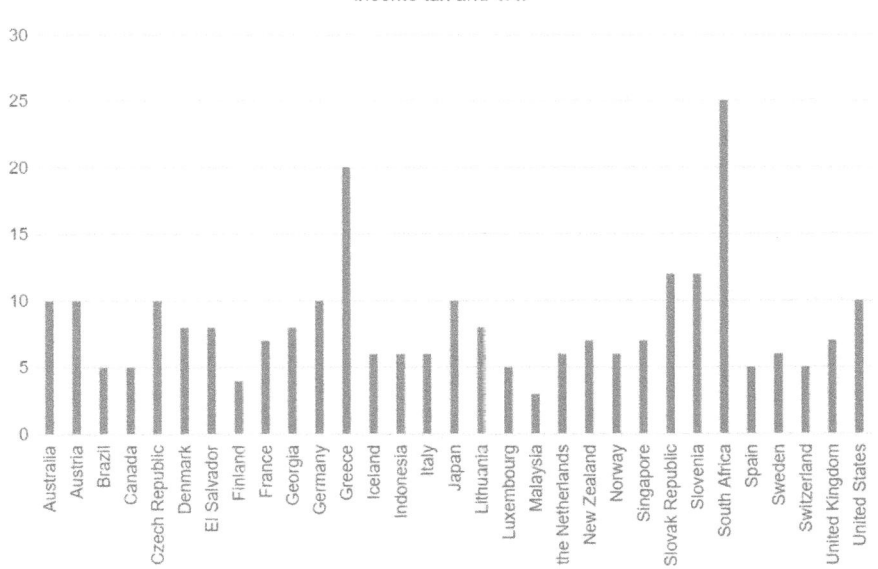

Maximum prison sentence for a tax offence (years) – income tax and VAT

---

[137] OECD, *Fighting Tax Crime* 15.

[138] Ibid.

[139] Ibid.

[140] Note that these data are subject to change since legal frameworks of jurisdictions continue to adapt to the proposals being made by international institutions such as OECD and EU as well as their own national priorities and research outputs.

[141] OECD, *Fighting Tax Crime* 15.

iii. The statute of limitations is expected to correspond to the level of seriousness of the tax crime. The statute of limitations should be sufficiently long for serious crimes. This 'allows agencies with sufficient time to identify and prosecute criminal acts'. A long statute of limitations is particularly relevant with regards to 'complex cases which can take a long time to successfully investigate and prosecute'.[142]

Maximum Sanctions

In the EU legislative framework, sanctions have been provided for both legal and natural persons. These can be found in instruments such as Directive (EU) 2017/1371 and Directive (EU) 2018/1673 as well as Directive (EU) 2015/849[143] and its amending legislation, Directive (EU) 2018/843 (particularly, Article 1). Directive (EU) 2017/1371 provides minimum rules for sanctions in relation to tax crime definitions.[144] This imperative is affirmed in Directive (EU) 2018/1673. In terms of maximum sanctions, Recital 18 of Directive (EU) 2017/1371 establishes that:

> Where a Member State's law does not provide for an explicit threshold for considerable damage or advantage as a basis for a maximum penalty, the Member State should ensure that the amount of damage or advantage is taken into account by its courts in the determination of sanctions for fraud and other criminal offences affecting the Union's financial interests ... for offences against the common VAT system, the threshold as of which the damage or advantage should be presumed to be considerable is, in conformity with this Directive, EUR 10 000 000. The introduction of minimum levels of maximum imprisonment sanctions is necessary in order to ensure equivalent protection of the Union's financial interests throughout the Union.[145]

The above provision of Directive (EU) 2017/1371 emphasises the relationship that needs to be established between the level of harm or damage of offences such as tax crimes and that of the maximum sanctions which are commensurate with the level of harm. The obligation of EU Members 'to provide for sanctions of imprisonment for the commission of criminal offences' is only limited to criminal offences that are of a serious nature'.[146] But the directive does not preclude Member States of the EU from instituting prison sanctions to non-serious criminal offences, except that EU Member States are obliged to ensure that 'levels of sanctions [do] not go beyond what is proportionate for the offences'.[147]

At the same time, the provision above echoes the need for uniformity of sanctions in the EU by requiring EU Member States to establish minimum threshold for maximum sanctions. Apart from the incentives the uniformity of rules removes, uniformity of tax rules makes cooperation between LEAs' Member States easier. There are other benefits for setting a baseline upon which punishment for criminal offences with

---

[142] Ibid.
[143] Directive (EU) 2015/849, Art. 58–60.
[144] Ibid, Art 1.
[145] Directive (EU) 2017/1371, recital 18.
[146] Ibid, recital 12.
[147] Ibid, recital 15.

similar elements is carried out in the EU. Beyond the damaging scenarios provided by the above provision of Directive (EU) 2017/1371, it also articulates that Member States are not precluded from assessing to discover other damaging scenarios of crimes that can be appropriately penalised. Thus, the directive 'does not prevent Member States from providing for other elements which would indicate the serious nature of a criminal offence, for instance when the damage or advantage is potential, but of very consider-able nature'.[148]

Article 7 of Directive (EU) 2017/1371 re-emphasises cardinal principles in sanctioning natural persons – sanctions on criminal offences such as tax crimes should be 'effective, proportionate and dissuasive criminal sanctions'.[149] Article 5(1) of Directive (EU) 2018/1673 affirms these principles of imposing penalties against natural persons.

These principles are also applicable to legal persons as enshrined in Article 9 of Directive (EU) 2017/1371. Article 58(1) of Directive (EU) 2015/849 lays down these principles from the administrative sanctions' standpoint. EU Member States are required to ensure that these principles are integrated in the national sanctions regime. The principles do not, however, prejudice 'the exercise of disciplinary powers by the competent authorities against public officials'.[150]

At the same time, Article 7 of Directive (EU) 2017/1371 provides that tax crimes and other criminal offences, as provided 'in points (a),[151] (b)[152] and (c)[153] of Article 3(2) and in Article 4',[154] committed by natural persons must be 'punishable by a maximum penalty which provides for imprisonment',[155] whereby 'a maximum penalty of at least four years of imprisonment [is imposed] when they involve considerable damage or advantage'[156] involving more than €100,000. Directive (EU) 2018/1673 affirms a 'maximum term of

---

[148] Ibid, recital 18.

[149] Ibid, Art 7(1).

[150] Ibid, Art 7(5).

[151] Ibid, Art 3(2)(a) provides: 'in respect of non-procurement-related expenditure, any act or omission relating to: (i) the use or presentation of false, incorrect or incomplete statements or documents, which has as its effect the misappropriation or wrongful retention of funds or assets from the Union budget or budgets managed by the Union, or on its behalf; (ii) non-disclosure of information in violation of a specific obligation, with the same effect; or (iii) the misapplication of such funds or assets for purposes other than those for which they were originally granted.'

[152] Ibid, Art 3(2)(b) provides: 'in respect of procurement-related expenditure, at least when committed in order to make an unlawful gain for the perpetrator or another by causing a loss to the Union's financial interests, any act or omission relating to: (i) the use or presentation of false, incorrect or incomplete statements or documents, which has as its effect the misappropriation or wrongful retention of funds or assets from the Union budget or budgets managed by the Union, or on its behalf (ii) non-disclosure of information in violation of a specific obligation, with the same effect; or (iii) the misapplication of such funds or assets for purposes other than those for which they were originally granted, which damages the Union's financial interests.'

[153] Ibid, Art 3(2)(c) provides: 'in respect of revenue other than revenue arising from VAT own resources referred to in point (d), any act or omission relating to: (i) the use or presentation of false, incorrect or incomplete statements or documents, which has as its effect the illegal diminution of the resources of the Union budget or budgets managed by the Union, or on its behalf (ii) non-disclosure of information in violation of a specific obligation, with the same effect; or (iii) misapplication of a legally obtained benefit, with the same effect.'

[154] Ibid, Art 4 regarding other criminal offences affecting the Union's financial interests including corruption, misappropriation, and money laundering.

[155] Ibid, Art 7(2).

[156] Ibid, Art 7(3).

imprisonment of at least four years,'[157] but in this case, for money laundering offences (which are connected to tax crimes).

Article 5(3) of Directive (EU) 2018/1673 elevates the status of money laundering offences by providing that: 'Member States shall also take the necessary measures to ensure that natural persons who have committed [money laundering offences] are, where necessary, subject to *additional sanctions* or *measures*'. Although tax crimes and money laundering appear interconnected, they sometimes have some distinct silos in counter measures. Therefore, there has to be some emphasis also placed on providing additional measures or sanctions against tax criminals beyond the sanctions stipulated in Article 7 of Directive (EU) 2017/1371 subject to points (a), (b) and (c) of Article 3(2) and in Article 4 thereof.

However, 'the damage or advantage resulting from the criminal offences referred to in point (d)[158] of Article 3(2) and subject to Article 2(2)[159] shall always be presumed to be considerable'.[160] Reading point (d) of Article 3(2) and Article 2(2) of Directive (EU) 2017/1371 together, intentional act or omission involving cross-border offence on VAT own resources attracts a (rather high) minimum threshold of €10,000,000 to be qualified as a serious offence. VAT own resource defines the percentage drawn from the harmonised VAT base of each EU Member State.[161] VAT own resource is illustrated as follows:

> VAT own resource accrues from the application for the period 2014–2020 of a uniform call rate to the national VAT base, determined in accordance with rules that are common to all Member States. The uniform VAT assessment base is established following the provisions of the VAT Directive[162] and the Council Regulation 1553/89[163] on the definitive uniform arrangements for the collection of own resources accruing from VAT.[164]

The call rate is currently 0.30 per cent for all Member States with the exception of 'Germany, the Netherlands and Sweden that benefit from a reduced call rate of 0.15%'

---

[157] Ibid, Art. 5(2) and 7.

[158] Ibid, Art 3(2) provides: 'that in respect of revenue arising from VAT own resources, any act or omission committed in cross-border fraudulent schemes in relation to: (i) the use or presentation of false, incorrect or incomplete VAT-related statements or documents, which has as an effect the diminution of the resources of the Union budget; (ii) non-disclosure of VAT-related information in violation of a specific obligation, with the same effect; or (iii) the presentation of correct VAT-related statements for the purposes of fraudulently disguising the non-payment or wrongful creation of rights to VAT refunds'.

[159] Ibid, Art 2(2) states that: 'In respect of revenue arising from VAT own resources, this Directive shall apply only in cases of serious offences against the common VAT system. For the purposes of this Directive, offences against the common VAT system shall be considered to be serious where the intentional acts or omissions defined in point (d) of Article 3(2) are connected with the territory of two or more Member States of the Union and involve a total damage of at least EUR 10 000 000'.

[160] Ibid, Art 7(3).

[161] European Commission, 'Value added tax-based own resource', https://ec.europa.eu/info/strategy/eu-budget/revenue/own-resources/value-added-tax_en, accessed 19 April 2020.

[162] Council Directive 2006/112/EC of 28 November 2006 on the common system of value added tax, [2006] OJ L 347/1.

[163] Council Regulation (EEC, Euratom) No 1553/89 of 29 May 1989 on the definitive uniform arrangements for the collection of own resources accruing from value added tax [1989] OJ L 155/9.

[164] European Commission, 'Value added tax-based own resource', https://ec.europa.eu/info/strategy/eu-budget/revenue/own-resources/value-added-tax_en, accessed 19 April 2020; see also Council Regulation (EEC, Euratom) No 1553/89 of 29 May 1989 on the definitive uniform arrangements for the collection of own resources accruing from value added tax, [1989] OJ L 155/9, Art 4(4), Art 6(4) and title iv.

in this period. Using the capping[165] mechanism, 'the national VAT base to which the call rate is applied cannot exceed 50 per cent of the gross national income (GNI) of the Member State'.[166] The peculiar huge minimum threshold for qualification as serious offence in Article 3(2)(d) and Article 2(2) regarding VAT own resources also attracts a minimum maximum imprisonment of four years.

As intimated earlier, the threshold for criminalisation of tax crimes is better lower than higher in order to show the level of seriousness attached to these offences and to make them unattractive. The €100,000 threshold for criminal offences other than VAT own resources and the €10,000,000 minimum threshold for VAT own resources appear to be a high threshold for natural persons committing tax crimes in the way established in Articles 3 and 4 of Directive (EU) 2017/1371 on criminal offences against the financial system of the EU.

Reading 7(4) of Directive (EU) 2017/1371 closely, suggests however that EU Member States are free to impose criminal sanctions on tax crimes (other than VAT) with a damage or advantage threshold of €10,000. This provision provides that with criminal offences such as tax crimes involving 'damage of less than EUR 10 000 or an advantage of less than EUR 10 000, Member States may provide for sanctions other than criminal sanctions'.[167] Thus, non-criminal sanctions such as non-custodial sentences are advised to be imposed when the damage or advantage threshold is not up to €10,000 – beyond which criminal sanctions such as maximum imprisonment and severe fines may be applied by the EU Member States.

However, understandably, instead of maximum imprisonment imposed on natural persons, the sanctions for legal persons:

> shall include criminal or non-criminal fines and may include other sanctions, such as:
> (a) exclusion from entitlement to public benefits or aid (b) temporary or permanent exclusion from public tender procedures; (c) temporary or permanent disqualification from the practice of commercial activities; (d) placing under judicial supervision; (e) judicial winding-up; (f) temporary or permanent closure of establishments which have been used for committing the criminal offence.[168]

The above sanctions for legal persons under Article 9 of Directive (EU) 2017/1371 appear to provide substantial deterrent force against companies intending to commit tax crimes in the EU.

Related to the sanctions for legal persons (who are involved in money laundering offences) are administrative sanctions against obliged entities under Article 58 of Directive (EU) 2015/849. Article 59 gives a picture as to who are affected by the sanctions in the directive and against whom the sanctions are imposed. Obliged entities

---

[165] Capping of VAT bases was initiated in order to ensure that the burden of the VAT-based own resource is shared 'more fairly among EU Member States'; see European Commission, 'Value added tax-based own resource', https://ec.europa.eu/info/strategy/eu-budget/revenue/own-resources/value-added-tax_en, accessed 19 April 2020.

[166] European Commission, 'Value added tax-based own resource', https://ec.europa.eu/info/strategy/eu-budget/revenue/own-resources/value-added-tax_en, accessed 19 April 2020; see also Council Regulation (EEC, Euratom) No 1553/89 of 29 May 1989 on the definitive uniform arrangements for the collection of own resources accruing from value added tax, [1989] OJ L 155/9, Art 4(4), Art 6(4) and title iv.

[167] Art 7(4).

[168] Directive (EU) 2017/1371, Art 9.

(enablers) are the focus of this legislation.[169] The directive outlines obliged entities as including the following:

- credit institutions;[170]

- financial institutions;[171]

- natural or legal persons acting in the exercise of their professional activities including (i) auditors, external accountants and tax advisors; (ii) notaries and other independent legal professionals; (iii) trust or company service providers not already covered by (i) and (ii) above; (iv) estate agents; (v) other persons trading in goods amounting to €10,000 or more; and (vi) providers of gambling services.[172]

With respect to obliged entities and the required rules on administrative sanctions, Article 58 of Directive (EU) 2015/849 provides that:

> Member States shall ensure that obliged entities can be held liable for breaches of national provisions transposing this Directive in accordance with this Article and Articles 59 to 61.[173] [And that] … Member States shall lay down rules on administrative sanctions and measures[174] and ensure that their competent authorities may impose such sanctions and measures with respect to breaches of the national provisions transposing this Directive, and shall ensure that they are applied.[175]

Essentially, Article 58 provides for administrative sanctions against obliged entities, the need for establishing governing rules for application by competent authorities, and eventual enforcement of the sanctions arising therefrom.

In the event that Member States decide not to implement rules for administrative sanctions or measures for breaches, as found in Article 58(1), which are subject to criminal sanctions in their national law – which they may do – it shall be incumbent upon Member States to communicate to the European Commission about the relevant criminal law provisions in their jurisdictions. Furthermore, additional provision has been inserted in Article 58(2)[176] by the amending legislation, Directive (EU) 2018/843, that: it is the obligation of Member States to 'ensure that where their competent authorities identify breaches which are subject to criminal sanctions, they inform the law enforcement authorities in a timely manner.'[177] Here, the provision emphasises the need for collaboration between competent authorities and LEAs in a timeous manner.

Directive (EU) 2015/849 gives a minimum threshold of an offence to be a misconduct that is 'serious, repeated, systematic, or a combination thereof'[178] which offends requirements of customer due diligence,[179] suspicious transaction reporting,[180]

---

[169] Directive (EU) 2015/849, Art 59(1).
[170] Ibid, Art 2(1)(1).
[171] Ibid, Art 2(1), (2).
[172] Ibid, Art 2(1), (3).
[173] Ibid, Art 58(1).
[174] This is without prejudice to the right of EU Member States to impose criminal sanctions; see Directive (EU) 2015/849, Art 58(2).
[175] Art 58(2).
[176] Directive (EU) 2015/849.
[177] Directive (EU) 2018/843, Art 1(38).
[178] Directive (EU) 2015/849, Art 59(1).
[179] Ibid, Art 59(1) (a), from Art. 10 to 24 thereof.
[180] Ibid, Art 59(1) (b), from Art. 33 to 35 thereof.

record-keeping[181] and internal controls.[182] The repeated and systematic elements are tests that, of course, appear reasonable but they can make proving of the offence committed by the obliged entities a bit complex or, at the minimum, it makes the threshold of the offence less strong or solid. This is so because instead of determining only the serious nature of a tax crime that, for instance, has been committed by a professional enabler, a prosecutor will have to establish proof of the repeated and systematised nature of the offence. The resultant effect is that a number of offenders can get off the hook, especially where there is inadequate competence amongst prosecutors and judges – which, by the way, was reported by a number of participants of the PROTAX focus groups particularly with respect to some judges' lack of expertise in fiscal matters, tax crimes and money laundering offences deriving from them.

Article 59(2) provides for five different administrative sanctions that can, at least, be applied to obliged entities:

Table 9 Administrative Sanctions for Obliged Entities

▪ **A public statement which identifies the natural or legal person and the nature of the breach**[183] **– this is akin to naming and shaming, and all the more a minor punishment, to some extent.**
▪ **An order requiring the natural or legal person to cease the conduct and to desist from repetition of that conduct**[184] **– this amounts to reprimand and good behaviour and could just be a minor punishment.**
▪ **Where an obliged entity is subject to an authorisation, withdrawal or suspension of the authorisation**[185] **– a withdrawal would amount to severe punishment since they can lose their source of livelihood but only if there is additional restriction not to authorise such persons to operate again.**
▪ **A temporary ban against any person discharging managerial responsibilities in an obliged entity, or any other natural person, held responsible for the breach, from exercising managerial functions in obliged entities**[186] **– this amounts to a nature of suspension that is minor at the very least.**
▪ **Maximum administrative pecuniary sanctions of at least twice the amount of the benefit derived from the breach where that benefit can be determined, or at least €1,000,000**[187] **– this administrative sanction appears punitive if the least threshold of €1,000,000 is only applied to small or medium-sized entities or low-worth individuals. Large-scale entities and high-worth natural persons with high income levels should be given a higher threshold of minimum punishment.**

It can be gleaned from Table 9 that only the punishment that has to do with the 'withdrawal' and/or the €1,000,000 minimum threshold penalty are deterring. The rest of the administrative sanctions therein are basically minor. However, as a derogation of

---

[181] Ibid, Art 59(1) (c), at Art 40 thereof.
[182] Ibid, Art 59(1) (d), from Art. 45 to 46 thereof.
[183] Ibid, Art 59(2)(a).
[184] Ibid, Art 59(2)(b).
[185] Ibid, Art 59(2)(c).
[186] Ibid, Art 59(2)(d).
[187] Ibid, Art 59(2)(e).

the €1,000,000 least pecuniary sanction for both legal and natural persons, provision is available under Article 59(3)(b) for the maximum pecuniary sanction of, at least, 'EUR 5 000 000 or 10% of the total annual turnover according to the latest available accounts approved by the management body for legal persons',[188] and, least, €5,000,000 for natural persons. These appear to be adequate.[189] A curious element, however, is that the introduction to this provision states that it applies 'when the obliged entity concerned is a *credit institution or financial institution*'.[190] One wonders how this remit captures natural persons rather than only institutions as stipulated. Article 59(3)(b) of Directive (EU) 2015/849 needs introspection, if not amendment. It appears that the drafter's intention is about natural persons associated with credit and financial institutions. Article 58(3), however, appears to give a rendition that cures this conflictual understanding. The provision states that EU Member States are obliged to:

> [E]nsure that where obligations apply to legal persons in the event of a breach of national provisions transposing this Directive, sanctions and measures can be applied to the members of the management body and to other natural persons who under national law are responsible for the breach.[191]

What this provision implies is that sanctions for legal persons can be applicable to natural persons principally associated with the legal persons under the regime of obliged entities. Article 58(3) appears to provide flexible attraction of sanctions for legal persons, on the surface, since the focus appears to be on management body and related natural persons responsible for any breech but not necessarily on the legal person itself. However, a little look down below the surface shows that Article 59 of Directive (EU) 2015/849 provides a remedy.[192] A careful look at these provisions of this directive[193] would conclude that there is inadequate clarity of thought in Articles 58(3) concerning liability of legal persons and 59(3)(b) relating to sanctions for natural persons in respect of credit and financial institutions.

It is instructive to note that EU Member States are entitled 'to empower competent authorities to impose additional types of administrative sanctions' in addition to the above administrative sanctions.[194] Furthermore, EU Member States are granted the discretion to impose criminal sanctions that could strengthen the provisions in Articles 58 and 59 of Directive (EU) 2015/849. Thus, the administrative sanctions for obliged entities are not necessarily mutually exclusive from criminal sanctions. Ironically, though, they can be complementary but can also be contradicting or overloading the sanctions scale if care is not taken by the relevant authorities. In any case, Article 9 of Directive (EU) 2017/1371 is a subsequent legal provision that provides augmentation and support for the measures provided in Articles 58 and 59 of Directive (EU) 2015/849.

---

[188] Ibid, Art 59(3)(a).
[189] Ibid, Art 59(3)(b).
[190] Ibid, Art 59(3)(b).
[191] Ibid, Art 58(3).
[192] Directive (EU) 2015/849.
[193] Ibid.
[194] Ibid, Art 58(4).

It does appear that Directive (EU) 2015/849 provides, as it was set out to do, the sanctions and measures that are sufficiently broad for allowing EU 'Member States and competent authorities to take account of the differences between obliged entities, [particularly] between credit institutions and financial institutions and other obliged entities, [regarding] their size, characteristics and the nature of the business'.[195] It may be said that Articles 58 to 62 of Directive (EU) 2015/849 provide significant pillars upon which administrative sanctions can be raised for obliged entities due to their cross-cutting nature, but clarity of purpose, thought and action is always the best and are required in some instances of the provisions so aforementioned.

There is also the issue of double sanction regimes. Double- or two-sanction regimes can be found in a number of – if not all – EU jurisdictions. That is, the jurisdictions diversely apply both administrative and criminal sanctions to natural and legal persons alike. The following outputs from PROTAX focus groups exemplify the double-sanction regimes in EU Member States.

Table 10 PROTAX Focus Groups – Views on Double-Sanction System

Estonia – Focus Group:	The fact that the legal system in Estonia allows for parallel criminal and administrative procedures can lead to overlaps in some cases.
Finland – Focus Group:	The problem in Finland, as in many other countries in the EU, is in respect of the rulings of the European Court of Human Rights on the *ne bis in idem* principle. This has forced Finland to change its legislation on procedures concerning levying of penal tax and sentencing of criminal penalties to avoid double jeopardy.
Italy – Focus Group:	Italy adopts a 'double-track' system of enforcement to deal with tax offences. Some offences are administrative offences, penalised through administrative law and the sanctions therein. Others are criminal offences thus are penalised and /or punished through criminal sanctions. According to the participants, it would not make sense to criminalise acts which are already effectively penalised with administrative sanctions. Thresholds also respond to the need not to overwhelm the judicial system with prosecutions of minor offences that can be dealt with as administrative offences.

Although both administrative and criminal sanctions may be imposed by jurisdictions, it is imperative to respect the *ne bis in idem* principle. Countries that adopt a double-sanction regime must not be engaged in double jeopardy. In this regard, just as is founded in the EU case law, recital 59 particularly posits that:

> In transposing this Directive,[196] Member States should ensure that the imposition of administrative sanctions and measures in accordance with this Directive, and of criminal sanctions in accordance with national law, does not breach the principle of *ne bis in idem*.

The *ne bis in idem* principle is also highlighted in recitals 17, 21 and 28 of Directive (EU) 2017/1371 and in *Åklagaren v Hans Åkerberg Fransson*[197] in which the principle was

---

[195] Ibid, recital 59.
[196] Directive (EU) 2015/849.
[197] C-617/10, *Åklagaren v Hans Åkerberg Fransson* (Judgment of the Court (Grand Chamber) 26 February 2013).

maintained but clarified that although this principle has been successfully laid down in Article 50 of the Charter of Fundamental Rights of the European Union:[198]

> [it] does not preclude a Member State from imposing successively, for the same acts of non-compliance with declaration obligations in the field of VAT, a tax penalty and a criminal penalty in so far as the first penalty is not criminal in nature, a matter which is for the national court to determine.[199]

It could be argued that, the maximum sentences stipulated in law and applied in practice do generally present a picture of leniency for tax criminals (natural persons) in most EU jurisdictions as exemplified in the sampled study by PROTAX on approaches to countering tax crimes across the EU. The general consensus was that the sanctions regime for tax crimes in the EU, particularly in their backyards, is not effective enough. For instance, participants in the Germany Focus Group highlighted 'the ineffectiveness of the sanctions for tax crimes [in Germany]. The threshold that can lead to a jail sentence is €1 Million [a very high threshold]. Compared to other countries, failing to comply with tax law is not punished severely.'[200]

Reasons for Lenient Maximum Sanctions

A number of reasons account for the predominance of the leniency regime in the EU. The first reason is lack of, limited or weak sentencing guidelines for judges when they are presented with tax offences. Indeed, the lack of these guidelines for judges does lead 'to inconsistent sentencing'[201] whereby judges may exercise judicial discretion or activism, as the case may be. One of the countries that, however, presents an exception is Finland, where there is 'a sentencing method that is a documented best practice without being a codified law'[202] or guidelines. It must be noted that although judicial discretion can be and has always been variedly exercised, the nature of variation depends on the judicial culture of the jurisdiction. The issue of leniency of sanctions, in this regard, is embedded both in the lack of, limited or weak guidelines that advise on the seriousness of tax offences and judicial culture towards tax crimes in the jurisdictions.

The second reason that accounts for leniency in maximum imprisonment sentencing relates to the authorities' prioritisation of 'recovery of criminal assets along with the prevention of tax crime as opposed to punishment through maximum jail sentences'.[203] This scenario is exemplified in Estonia, Germany, the United Kingdom and Italy. Thus, the objective of sanctions come to play. If the key objective of the government or authorities is to maximise revenue from tax offences, it may sometimes not see imprisonment as a viable tool to realising this objective. In Germany, for example, assets acquired through crime and forfeiture of illegal capital gain 'can be transferred to the State'.[204] Interestingly, however, stiffer punishments can also serve as a preventive tool which

---

[198] Charter of Fundamental Rights of the European Union [2012] OJ C 326/391.
[199] C-617/10, *Åklagaren v Hans Åkerberg Fransson* (Judgment of the Court (Grand Chamber) 26 February 2013), para 37.
[200] Rasmouki and others, 'D2.3 Approaches to tax crimes' 33.
[201] Ibid.
[202] Ibid.
[203] Ibid.
[204] s73 ff, 29a OWiG.

revenue-focused approach goes along with. Because of the complications in the matrix of the exact policy and legislative path to take, it is important that all of these measures – prevention, imprisonment and assets recovery – are prioritised without one considered a priority over the other. The simple notion is that they are not mutually exclusive and, therefore, are connected to each other in the counter tax crime ecosystem.

The third reason behind the lenient maximum imprisonment regime for tax crimes in many EU jurisdictions is that cost and benefit approach is sometimes applied. Judges use a cost-benefit approach 'because if they issue high jail sentences, the offenders would represent a cost to the taxpayer'.[205] This would be at the heart of the harmonious interaction between judicial discretion and state policy on tax crimes.

The fourth reason concerns the low level of competence of some judges in fiscal matters. Indeed, there are some judges that just lack the needed expertise in fiscal matters such as in tax crimes, to the extent that they are not able to fully comprehend the complete textual relevance and philosophical underpinnings of legislative instruments in tax matters. Some countries have, therefore, made provision for availing fiscal experts to judges who may not fully understand fiscal matters. But this sometimes hits roadblocks. For instance, in Portugal, 'judges and prosecutors can use experts in fiscal matters. But the lack of financial means hinders this in practice as no remuneration is offered to the experts'.[205]

The fifth reason for the lenient sanctions regime in the EU jurisdictions is that plea-bargaining is used in a number of these jurisdictions. They use guilty pleas as a prosecution strategy. Guilty pleas strategy, when not abused and the defendant is legally protected, is required 'to serve justice in any trial'[207] for tax crimes. In Ireland, for example, 'the fact that 90 percent of suspects plead guilty constitutes a significant mitigation factor for lenient sentencing'.[208]

Apart from the above five reasons, there is also the issue of discriminatory sentencing according to social status such as the 'differences in sentencing suspects belonging to different socio-economic backgrounds'.[209] In this, 'the less educated and less well-off [an accused is], the more [the accused is] required to prove lack of criminal intent and subsequently the more likely [the accused is] to receive a harsh sentence. Participants from the Finland focus group [were of the belief] that this behaviour displayed by some judges can be attributed to "unconscious prejudice"'.[210]

It does appear, however, that although the focus that drew out these responses from the PROTAX focus groups was on tax crimes, the deficits relating to maximum imprisonment sentence are not only limited to tax crimes but also stretch 'to all aspects of economic crime'.[211] In fact, economic crime is often treated by some jurisdictions as lesser crime compared to other types of crime. But there appears to be a changing trajectory towards taking economic crimes, including tax crimes, more seriously. The mind-set of tax, judicial authorities and other LEAs is critical and appears to be changing.

---

[205] Rasmouki and others, 'D2.3 Approaches to tax crimes'.
[206] Ibid, 53.
[207] Turksen and others, 'D1.2: Case Studies' 143.
[208] Ibid, 53.
[209] Ibid.
[210] Ibid.
[211] Ibid.

In the Czech Republic, for instance, a PROTAX focus group participant posited that the mind-set of police officers and prosecutors in this regard is changing and tax crime is no longer seen as a victimless crime. The change in mind-set for judges proves more challenging. Some countries such as the United States, however, apply stiffer penalties to economic criminals.[212]

Statute of Limitations

Directive (EU) 2017/1371 also recognises the statute of limitations suggested in the above Pillar 2's three considerations of dealing with sanctions of proven criminal offences. But it is arguable whether the five-year period suggested as a minimum for a statute of limitation in Directive (EU) 2017/1371 is long enough. Historically, a minimum of five years has been a period usually assigned to statute of limitations in a number of countries, particularly from Classical Athens in which limitation period covered all cases, apart from prosecution of homicide cases which did not have limitation period and prosecution of non-constitutional laws.[213] The Directive (EU) 2017/1371 provides as follows:

> Member States should lay down rules concerning limitation periods necessary in order to enable them to counter illegal activities at the expense of the Union's financial interests. In cases of criminal offences punishable by a maximum sanction of at least four years of imprisonment, the limitation period should be at least five years from the time when the criminal offence was committed. This should be without prejudice to those Member States which do not set limitation periods for investigation, prosecution and enforcement.[214]

Further particulars of limitation periods for criminal offences affecting the Union's financial interests are featured in Article 12. It carries the same import as above, except that there are further imperatives such as a right to derogate from the minimum limitation of five years to three years 'provided that the period may be interrupted or suspended in the event of specified acts'.[215] Statutes of limitation are essentially provided in legislation in order to serve as a safeguard for protecting parties, particularly defendants.[216] In this regard, a number of reasons are provided for statutes of limitation, three of which are that:

- Defendants might no longer have the evidence necessary to disprove or refute a claim that is stale.[217]

- Plaintiffs or applicants that have valid or good causes of action, and have the ability to enforce such causes of action, should pursue them with reasonable diligence.[218]

- There would otherwise be the possibility of litigating long-dormant claims, to lead to cruelty rather than justice.[219]

---

[212] ACCA, 'Economic crime in a digital age' (January 2020), www.accaglobal.com/content/dam/ACCA_Global/professional-insights/EconomicCrime/JasonPiper.EconomicCrime.pdf, accessed 18 April 2020.

[213] DS Allen, *The World of Prometheus: The Politics of Punishing in Democratic Athens* (Princeton University Press, 2003).

[214] Directive (EU) 2017/1371, recital 22.

[215] Ibid, Art 12(3).

[216] S Hetherington, *Halsbury's Laws of England centenary essays* (LexisNexis Butterworths, 2007).

[217] *Jones v Bellgrove Properties Ltd* [1949] 2 KB 700; *Donovan v Gwentoys Ltd* [1990] 1 All ER 1018.

[218] *Cayzer, Irvine & Co v Board of Trade* [1927] AC 610.

[219] *A'Court v Cross* [1825] 3 Bing 329; *Lloyd's v Butler* [1949] 2 All ER 226.

These differing reasons find expression in case law, as referenced above. They also have a basis in literature. Allen has, for instance, provided illustrations as to how efforts to prevent 'sycophants' from using the lapse of time to dubiously accuse other people were behind the institution of limitation periods in ancient Greece.[220]

Pillar 2 of TGP1, 'criminal sanction applies if proven', effectively resonates with the provisions provided in the AML regime of the EU.[221] Indeed, with respect to the EU sanction measures in relation to proven criminal tax offences, the relevant EU legislative framework provides a comprehensive picture. But as it would appear, the sanctions are spread across a couple of legal instruments in a manner that can be described as needing some coherence and consolidation. These instruments in the EU AML legal framework also capture Pillars 3 and 4 of the requirements of the TGP1.

Pillar 3: More Serious Offences are Punishable by More Serious Criminal Sanctions

The third pillar of the TGP1 or criminalisation of tax crimes is related to the second pillar thereof. It provides that the more serious tax offences are, the more serious or severe the criminal sanctions should be.[222]

Figure 8   Appropriate Measure of Punishment for More Serious Tax Offences

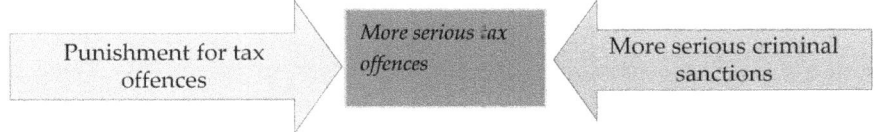

This pillar of TGP1 recognises that a range of behaviour constitutes tax crime. It posits that the objectives of criminalising tax offences can be achieved if the position of the law is that 'more serious behaviour or crimes committed in graver circumstances should be punishable by more serious criminal sanctions, proportionate to the nature of the offence'.[223] Aggravating circumstance falls into the more serious tax offences. In the EU, aggravating circumstance is when criminal offences such as tax crimes are 'committed within a criminal organisation in the sense of Framework Decision 2008/841/JHA'.[224]

No matter the criminalisation approaches jurisdictions have developed or adopted to categorise types of tax offences and their level of seriousness, it is crucial for each jurisdiction to ensure that 'the seriousness of the offence … [does] correspond to the seriousness of the consequences for the offender'.[225] These have been provided in EU law as discussed above.

---

[220] Allen, *The World of Prometheus*.
[221] Including also, Directive (EU) 2015/849; Directive (EU) 2017/1371; Directive (EU) 2018/849; Directive (EU) 2018/1673.
[222] OECD, *Fighting Tax Crime: The Ten Global Principles* (OECD Publishing, 2017).
[223] Ibid.
[224] Directive (EU) 2017/1371, Art 8.
[225] OECD, *Fighting Tax Crime* 17.

Pillar 4: Criminal Sanctions are Applied in Practice

The fourth pillar of the TGP1 relates to Pillars 2 and 3 thereof. Its focus is on going beyond the law in the books to the law in practice in relation to sanctions. Thus, it provides that criminalised tax laws that are not enforced or enforceable are almost next to nothing. Therefore, jurisdictions must ensure that laws that criminalise tax offences are duly enforced.

In this regard:

> Where the offence is proven in a court proceeding, the criminal sanction that is most likely to be effective and is appropriate to the facts and circumstances should be applied. Penalties should be applied fairly and consistently.[226]

Three key legal principles are embedded in the above proposition of Principle 4 of the TGP1:

   i.   Prosecution must be in a position to prove culpability of the accused – this is the duty of the prosecutors.

  ii.   Successful prosecution must correspond with the application of relevant criminal sanctions – this is the duty of the judge.

 iii.   Sanctions must comply with the rule of law tenets of fairness and consistency whereby there is certainty and predictability in the penalties as they are applied to future cases with similar facts, circumstances and scale or severity – this is the duty of the judge.

The onus rests on prosecutors and judges to, therefore, ensure that culprits are processed and appropriately penalised.

Empirical data drawn from PROTAX focus groups provide interesting insights into not just the law in statute books of selected European jurisdictions but also the law in action regarding maximum prison sentences in courts as they apply to tax crimes. Focus group participants had been asked whether tax offenders ever receive a maximum sentence in their jurisdiction, not in terms of a fine but a fine combined with imprisonment. The motivation behind this question was triggered 'in light of prominent cases across the EU where despite successful investigation and prosecution procedures, the judiciary pronounced lenient sentences which do not reflect the severity of the offences'. An interesting observation which directed research focus on maximum prison sentence was that:

> [S]entences in the form of punitive fines bring back criminal [proceeds] into the coffers of governments, [but such proceeds] do not represent as much of a deterrent as incarceration. This is particularly relevant in the case of large scale and sophisticated tax crimes, where offenders are not burdened by the payment of a fine. Furthermore, a sentence in the form of a fine does not send a strong signal to the public as to the seriousness of the offence. Ultimately, this type of sentences does not only affect the perception of the public of this type of crime but can also cause a mistrust in the ability of the state institutions to bring about justice when dealing with powerful corporations, or individuals.[227]

---

[226] Ibid.
[227] Rasmouki and others, 'D2.3 Approaches to tax crimes' 52.

As can be seen in Table 11, focus group responses from these jurisdictions indicate that despite the fact that all of them have varied maximum imprisonment sentences in statutes, the majority of them ironically do not get to apply the sentences by the courts. A possible explanation has been highlighted just above regarding the appetite of courts to impose fines as sanctions for tax crimes instead of incarceration. However, the PROTAX case studies also reveal that in spite of the pervasive nature of low sanctioning regime in the European jurisdictions in which case studies were conducted, 'some jurisdictions (such as Portugal) [in the EU] impose heavy criminal sanctions for tax crimes with little consideration given to so-called "sweetheart deals"'.[228]

Table 11 Focus Group Information on Maximum Imprisonment for Tax Crimes in EU[229]

European countries	*Maximum imprisonment sentence*[230]	*Has it been applied?*	*Examples of sentences applied or witnessed by participants*[231]
Austria	5 years	N/A[232]	N/A
Czech Republic	10 years	No	A one-year prison period is an example of a prominent case. And seven years for the officials who were facilitating the crime.
Estonia	7 years	No	The prosecutor considers mitigating circumstances after setting four years as a sentence.
Finland	4 years	Yes	Proportional to damage in the case of tax and drug crimes. So, crimes involving bigger amounts will receive an upper quartile sentence.
Germany	10 years	No	A public policy expert shared a statistic published by the criminal court: In 2018 there were 1,580 years of imprisonment judgments out of 20,000 tax crime cases. But there are no details as to whether these years of imprisonment will be effectively served.
Ireland	5 years	No	Punitive fee following a guilty plea (90 per cent of suspects plead guilty). A suspended sentence.
Italy	6 years	Yes	Pecuniary measures.
Malta	6 months	No	Administrative fees. If any criminal prosecutions were to be carried out, the participants see such a scenario as unlikely.

(continued)

---

[228] Turksen and others, 'D1.2: Case Studies' 14.
[229] Rasmouki and others, 'D2.3 Approaches to tax crimes' 52–53.
[230] Maximum imprisonment sentence means, in context, sentence for aggravated forms of tax crimes.
[231] It is worth noting that these examples are, at best, anecdotal and mainly based on the memory of the discussants within the time of the focus group discussions. They are to highlight expert opinions of the participants to have a real feel of the practitioners' observations of the law.
[232] Non-applicable due to lack of information from the focus group discussants in a particular area.

Table 11 *(Continued)*

European countries	Maximum imprisonment sentence[230]	Has it been applied?	Examples of sentences applied or witnessed by participants[231]
Portugal	8 years	No	The participants stated that the maximum they have witnessed is six years.
UK	10 years[233]	N/A	N/A

Although no information about application of the five years' imprisonment maximum sentence and examples thereof were provided during the focus groups in Austria, during the PROTAX case studies, some insights were gained into the sanctions regime in Austria. It was found that 'penalties for legal entities are the same as provided for natural persons. If imprisonment is the main sanction provided for a specific offence, fines have to be imposed instead (eg, tax fraud [Art 39 para 3 FPC])'.

Interestingly, in Table 11, Finland has the lowest maximum sentence, of four years, but the country gets to apply it, unlike Germany and Czech Republic, which have highest maximum imprisonment sentence of 10 years but are said not to apply them – per the understanding of the focus group participants.

Data gathered by the OECD to illustrate the nature of tax penalties applied in practice in various jurisdictions did evince that it may be appropriate to impose monetary penalties. This would depend on the case. An instance is that most of the surveyed jurisdictions with data availability indicated that 'fines were imposed by the competent authorities in respect of violations of the tax law'[234] – a clear demonstration of minimal utilisation of maximum prison sentence.[235]

Table 12 Survey Responses: Fines Imposed for Criminal Violations of Tax Law[236]

Jurisdiction[237]	Imposed fines in 2015 and 2016 (€ million equivalent)	
	2015	**2016**
Australia[238]	13.3	10.9
Austria[239]	132.7	23.2
Canada	2.8	6.8
Czech Republic[240]	0.9	0.9
Denmark	N/A	46.8[241]

[233] Conspiracy to defraud is punishable with the imprisonment for a term not exceeding 10 years or a fine or both, while for the offence of cheating the Public Revenue the maximum sentence is potentially life imprisonment, or an unlimited fine.

[234] OECD, *Fighting Tax Crime* 17.

[235] Ibid.

[236] Ibid.

[237] Income tax, in the context of this OECD survey, means 'direct taxes imposed on the income of individuals and the income/profits of entities such as corporate tax'; see ibid.

[238] 'Figures for Australia represent fines and reparations imposed through both CDPP and ATP Prosecutions'; see ibid.

[239] Figures for Austria represent fines imposed following criminal court convictions.

[240] Figures for Czech Republic represent individuals and entities; see ibid.

[241] OECD, *Fighting Tax Crime* 17.

Table 12 shows that Austria achieved the highest amount from the imposition of fines in 2015 (though data for Denmark were not found). For this period, Australia achieved the second highest amount of imposed fines. The lowest achieved amount was for the Czech Republic – the country maintained the same position in 2016. In 2015, however, Denmark topped the list of achievers in fine imposition, followed respectively by Austria and Australia. Canada was last but one in this enterprise for both 2015 and 2016 although more than doubling the amount achieved in 2015 for the subsequent year.

Table 13 Fines Imposed for Criminal Violations of Tax Law (In Millions And Euro Equivalent)[242]

Jurisdiction	Imposed fines in 2015 and 2016 (€ million equivalent)	
	2015	2016
France	22.9	N/A
Germany[243]	126.6	189.9
Iceland	14.3	6.2
Japan	16.2	12.4
Lithuania	1.2	1.0
Malaysia	0.07	0.06
Singapore[244]	0.7	0.3
South Africa	0.7	0.6
Spain	496.8	1,065.2
Switzerland	17.3	12.4
United Kingdom	0.8	1.7
United States	Over 2,077	Over 18.6
Total	**Over 2 924**	**1 397**[245]

Tables 12 and 13 reveal a number of things:

- No data were provided for 2015 by Denmark and for 2016 by France – they are, therefore, excluded from any trend analysis.

- Apart from Canada, Germany, Spain and the United Kingdom, there was largely a decline in the amount of fines imposed from 2015 to 2016. Interest of jurisdictions in imposition of fines may be dwindling in these affected jurisdictions to occasion this downward shift. It is also possible that the more criminalising regime of tax offences being advocated for by the TGP1 and the TGPs generally, may be gaining significant grounds leading to other available options more attractive than the fines.

---

[242] Ibid.
[243] Figures for Germany include the total fines determined, total monetary amounts assessed pursuant to s 153a of the Code of Criminal Procedure and total penalties that became legally binding; see ibid.
[244] Figures for Singapore represent fines to court and penalties to court; see ibid.
[245] OECD, *Fighting Tax Crime* 17.

- All the countries show that they apply, to some extent, their tax offence legal provisions relating to fines.

- The decline of fine imposition in Austria was phenomenal (more than five times in decline) while that of the United States was phenomenal (more than 111 times in decline) – a likely loss of interest in fines.

- The increment of fine imposition in Spain was more than double the preceding year, just as that of Canada and the United Kingdom.

Pillar 4 of TGP1 has suggested the appropriateness for jurisdictions to apply 'alternative types of criminal sanctions … depending on the relevant case'.[246] The alternative types of criminal sanctions can include the following:

- community service;
- naming and shaming offenders or enablers;
- disqualification from holding certain offices;
- suspension of licence or other privileges;
- specific orders to forfeit or return assets; or
- a combination of the above.[247]

Indeed, OECD found that of the 31 jurisdictions surveyed, 16 (namely: Australia, Canada, Czech Republic, Denmark, France, Greece, Lithuania, Malaysia, New Zealand, the Netherlands, Singapore, Slovak Republic, South Africa, Sweden, United Kingdom, United States)[248] did respond that 'they have used sanctions other than imprisonment or a fine in 7,239 cases in total in 2015 and 2016'.[249] The 7,239 cases for this period included cases on the following six areas:

- financial sanction (eg, non-fine monetary payment, compensation, asset forfeiture) – 1,125 cases;
- community service – 435 cases;
- restriction on employment/services/profession/holding office – 688 cases;
- naming and shaming in media/publication – 142 cases;
- personal restriction (eg, travel, driving, home/community detention, suspended sentence) – 980 cases;
- other (good behaviour, probation, public work) – 3,869 cases.[250]

Of these, 'other (good behaviour, probation, public work)' constituted the majority with 3,869 cases (53.45 per cent). This was followed by 'financial sanction' with 1,125 cases (15.54 per cent). The penal area that received the least cases is 'naming and shaming', with 142 cases (2.0 per cent). It stands to reason that jurisdictions may not fancy or appreciate the effectiveness of the 'naming and shaming' in the enterprise of tax crime

---

[246] Ibid, 18.
[247] Ibid.
[248] Ibid.
[249] Ibid.
[250] Ibid.

counter-measures. One of the things that could account for this situation is a possible dwindling of cultural values, where reputational damage does not matter to some people as long as they would be strong enough to ignore the scandal for a few weeks. Such stories eventually fizzle out with time, society may not fully come back to it and life goes on as normal again. It is revealing and maybe rather curious that the majority of the cases use 'good behaviour, probation, public work' as a potent penalising tool for tax offences. This is interesting on two grounds. It wakes us up to the alternative reality, instead of confinement at the expense of the state, of utilising or transforming the energies of offenders in productive enterprises that put the offenders outside their comfort zones, which may significantly benefit the society that has been harmed by the misconduct of the offender. The other ground is that public work as a penalty could be a more painful way of 'naming and shaming' tax offenders when packaged well along with community service (which rather received a low patronage by the cases).

Benchmarking TGP1 – Criminalisation of Tax Offences

All of these alternative criminal sanctions are provided by the legislative instruments of the EU. And for Pillar 4 of TGP1, it is reasonable to conclude that the requirement that jurisdictions should apply their criminal sanctions in practice has not been substantially met by most EU jurisdictions. A lot more has to be done to encourage EU jurisdictions and others alike to apply stiffer sanctions to tax crimes in practice.

The PROTAX study found that even though the selected 11 European jurisdictions have operational legal frameworks that counter tax crime, many of those legal frameworks are not highly effective in criminalising tax offences. This claim supports the conclusion of the European Parliamentary Research Service in 2017, which revealed that those EU countries that responded to the survey 'had a functioning legal framework to fight tax avoidance, tax evasion and money laundering'. This included:

- The national legal provisions for countering tax avoidance and tax evasion vary significantly from each other. They have differing legal mechanisms which have 'a mix of administrative and criminal offences and sanctions, differences in relation to natural/legal persons, different ways of tackling tax avoidance' and tax evasion.[251]

- Implementation of the legal framework of the EU such as on AML and related crimes like tax crimes had been anticipated by some countries and included in their national legal frameworks. However, other EU Member States neither anticipated nor implemented the relevant provisions on time. EU jurisdictions such Germany, the Netherlands, Slovenia, Croatia and Latvia had, for instance, anticipated the adoption of the EU legal framework on AML including Directive (EU) 2015/849 (or the fourth AML Directive) and responded appropriately. To date, most of the EU Member States have significantly transposed the fourth AML Directive but the

---

[251] E Thirion and A Scherrer, 'Member States' capacity to fight tax crimes: Ex-post impact assessment' (European Parliamentary Research Service (EPRS), EU Parliament, 2017) 7, www.europarl.europa.eu/RegData/etudes/STUD/2017/603257/EPRS_STU(2017)603257_EN.pdf, accessed 9 October 2019.

implementation of the subsequent instruments in the EU legal framework on financial crime has still not received significant patronage by the Member States.[252]

- Most EU Members participate 'in international action such as the FATF, or the Warsaw Convention'.[253] However, some EU Member States have not ratified the Warsaw Convention.[254]

At the same time, although varying, EU Member States have established 'a wide range of preventive measures, sanctions and investigative and prosecuting instruments'.[255] Further, recent media leaks such as the Panama Papers have served as a wake-up call for many countries across the world.[256] Thirion and Scherrer found, for example, that almost all the participating EU Member States in their study mentioned the practical action they have taken in reaction to the Panama Papers. Apart from some EU Members identifying over 3,000 EU-based eligible taxpaying individuals and companies that were associated with the Panama Papers, some concerned EU Member States also collectively launched at least 1300 inquiries, audits and investigations into Panama Papers revelations.[257] This shows the extent to which piercing the veils of tax evasion schemes can go a long way to pressuring authorities to act with a sense of urgency.

However, the principle of criminalising violations of tax laws is still some distance away from appreciation when it comes to EU anti-tax evasion and fraud laws. This claim is particularly undergirded by the lack of harmony of national laws on the definition of tax crimes. While requiring that tax crimes are predicate offences for the purposes of money laundering, Directive (EU) 2018/1673 (the sixth AMLD) has not addressed the lack of harmony in the definition of tax crimes in national laws. Critically, since large-scale tax crimes are international in nature and require cross-border collaboration in order to effectively counter them, this lack of definitional harmony on tax crimes could still pose a significant bottleneck to the identification of what really constitute tax crimes that can be readily investigated and produced relevant results to which these penalties and sanctions can be effectively applied.

It would, however, be sufficient to observe that this principle of criminalisation of tax crimes has a reasonable showing in EU legal instruments such as Council Framework Decision 2001/500/JHA of 26 June 2001 on money laundering, the identification, tracing, freezing, seizing and confiscation of instrumentalities and the proceeds of crime;[258] Directive 2014/42/EU of the European Parliament and of the Council of 3 April 2014 on the freezing and confiscation of instrumentalities and proceeds of crime in the European Union;[259] Directive (EU) 2017/1371 of the European Parliament and

---

[252] Ibid.

[253] Council of Europe Convention on Laundering, Search, Seizure and Confiscation of the Proceeds from Crime and on the Financing of Terrorism 2005, www.coe.int/en/web/conventions/full-list/-/conventions/treaty/198, accessed 12 February 2020.

[254] E Thirion and A Scherrer, 'Member States' capacity to fight tax crimes: Ex-post impact assessment' (European Parliamentary Research Service (EPRS), EU Parliament, 2017) 7.

[255] Ibid.

[256] Ibid.

[257] Ibid.

[258] Council Framework Decision 2001/500/JHA of 26 June 2001 on money laundering, the identification, tracing, freezing, seizing and confiscation of instrumentalities and the proceeds of crime ([2001] OJ L 182/1–2).

[259] [2014] OJ L 127/39–50.

of the Council of 5 July 2017 on the fight against fraud to the Union's financial interests by means of criminal law;[260] Directive (EU) 2018/843 of the European Parliament and of the Council of 30 May 2018 amending Directive (EU) 2015/849;[261] and Directive (EU) 2018/1673 of the European Parliament and of the Council of 23 October 2018 on combating money laundering by criminal law.[262]

However, these principal legal instruments for fighting tax crimes in the EU appear to be insufficient to effectively criminalise tax offences at the Union level and, to some extent, in their respective jurisdictions.[263] These instruments are primarily focused on AML imperatives but extend their coverage to tax crimes and other financial crimes because of their relationship with each other. Indeed, tax crimes are recognised as predicate offences for money laundering in the EU. The next TGP, therefore, considers these relationships.

TGP2: Tax Crimes as a Predicate Offence for Money Laundering

Understanding Predicate Offences

There is usually an intrinsic linkage between tax offences and other financial crimes such as money laundering, since 'criminals fail to report their income from illicit activities for tax purposes'.[264] It is also usually likely for 'criminals to over-report' their income, which would have attracted taxes, 'in an attempt to launder the proceeds of crime'.[265] These form the bedrock for opening the understanding of the TGP2.

This TGP is centred on the proposition that jurisdictions should endeavour to 'designate tax crimes as one of the predicate offences for money laundering'.[266] Designating tax crimes as predicate offences implies that culprits thereof 'can be charged with the offence of money laundering as well as with the [underlying] predicate offence itself'.[267] The TGP2 draws much of its inspiration from FATF Recommendation 3, which provides that:

> Countries should criminalise money laundering on the basis of the Vienna Convention and the Palermo Convention. Countries should apply the crime of money laundering to all serious offences, with a view to including the widest range of predicate offences.[268]

---

[260] Directive (EU) 2017/1371 of the European Parliament and of the Council of 5 July 2017 on the fight against fraud to the Union's financial interests by means of criminal law ([2017] OJ L 198/29–41).

[261] [2018] OJ L 156/43–74.

[262] [2018] OJ L 284/22–30.

[263] It should be noted that enforcement mechanisms and human factors which impede them need remedies and development also.

[264] Ibid.

[265] OECD, *Effective Inter-Agency Co-operation in Fighting Tax Crimes and Other Financial Crimes*, 3rd edn (OECD Publishing, 2017) 5, www.oecd.org/tax/crime/effective-inter-agency-co-operation-in-fighting-tax-crimes-and-other-financial-crimes.htm, accessed 12 March 2020.

[266] OECD, *Fighting Tax Crime* 54.

[267] OECD, *Fighting Tax Crime* 54.

[268] See FATF, *International Standards on Combating Money Laundering and the Financing of Terrorism & Proliferation* (FATF, 2012–19), www.fatf-gafi.org/recommendations.html, accessed 24 March 2020.

The TGP describes predicate offences as the 'specified types of criminal activity that give rise to funds or assets'.[269] Criminals may launder such funds or assets in order to obscure the illegal sources from which they are drawn.

> [Predicate offences such as] drug trafficking[270] can generate revenue, and through one of the basic steps of placement, layering and integration, conceal the illegal source of the funds, allowing the drug trafficker to use the funds without generating suspicion of criminal activity.[271]

Tax crimes as predicate offences also behave in a similar manner as that of drug trafficking illustrated above, albeit evaded tax may come from a legal (and illegal) activity such as the sale of day-to-day items or income from services provided. Proceeds generated by tax fraud are by definition illegal funds which would need to be hidden, placed out of the reach of the authorities, moved and integrated back into the economy without raising any suspicion. In the FATF Recommendations, 'tax crimes (related to direct and indirect taxes)'[272] were determined as predicate offences for money laundering.[273] These also apply to other economic crimes such as 'illicit trafficking in stolen and other goods; corruption and bribery; fraud; counterfeiting currency; [and] counterfeiting'.[274] Such predicate offences involve the use of close layers of trusted associates who apply surreptitious procedures to get their transactions through. Complex systems and methods are, therefore, used by launderers to be able to escape being caught by authorities – a clear reason for applying robust mechanisms to countering them.

Approaches for Predicate Offences

PROTAX notes that one of the essential strategies for countering 'tax crimes is to prevent and punish the laundering of proceeds from tax offences'.[275] A number of approaches can be used to designate tax crimes as predicate offence for money laundering. The TGP2 identifies three key approaches as follows: inclusive approach, threshold approach and the list approach.[276]

---

[269] OECD, *Fighting Tax Crime* 54.

[270] To fully understand the ecosystem of predicate offences for money laundering, see the full list as provided by the FATF Recommendations: 'participation in an organised criminal group and racketeering; terrorism, including terrorist financing; trafficking in human beings and migrant smuggling; sexual exploitation, including sexual exploitation of children; illicit trafficking in narcotic drugs and psychotropic substances; illicit arms trafficking; *illicit trafficking in stolen and other goods; corruption and bribery; fraud; counterfeiting currency; counterfeiting* and piracy of products; environmental crime; murder, grievous bodily injury; kidnapping, illegal restraint and hostage-taking; robbery or theft; smuggling (including in relation to customs and excise duties and taxes); *tax crimes (related to direct taxes and indirect taxes)*; extortion; forgery; piracy; and insider trading and market manipulation'; see FATF, *International Standards on Combating Money Laundering*; OECD, *Fighting Tax Crime*.

[271] OECD, *Money Laundering Awareness Handbook for Tax Examiners and Tax Auditors* (OECD Publishing, 2009), www.oecd.org/ctp/crime/money-laundering-awareness-handbook-for-tax-examiners-and-tax-auditors.pdf, accessed 9 October 2020; OECD, *Fighting Tax Crime* 54.

[272] FATF, *International Standards on Combating Money Laundering*.

[273] OECD, *Fighting Tax Crime* 54.

[274] FATF, *International Standards on Combating Money Laundering* 116.

[275] Rasmouki and others, 'D2.3 Approaches to tax crimes' 34.

[276] OECD, *Fighting Tax Crime* 54.

Figure 9 Approaches to Designating Tax Crimes as Predicate Offences for Money Laundering

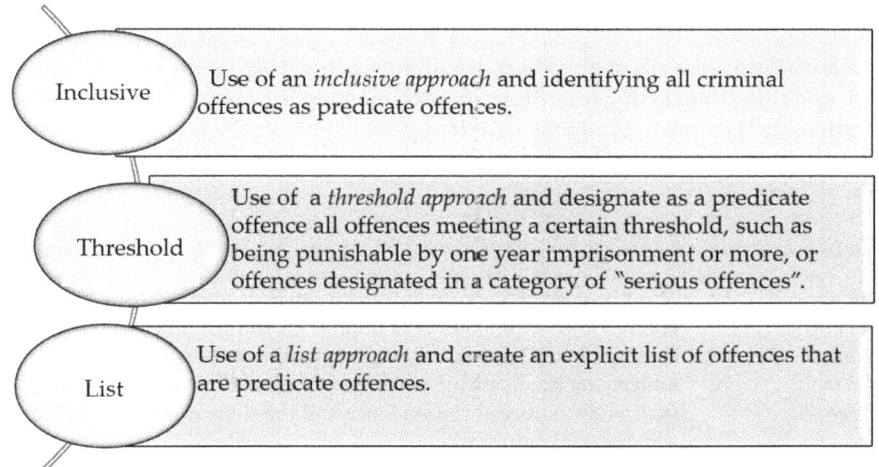

The above approaches are used by various countries in different ways. TGP2 has not recommended any approach except to put them out. Of course, the choice of an appropriate and suitable approach will again depend on the nature of the jurisdiction concerned and its legal infrastructure. However, a careful look at them would reveal some interesting perspectives that may make one approach preferable to the others. Based on the survey data, the OECD found the overwhelming majority of the countries (which responded to the survey) used the inclusive approach. The threshold approach was the least used by jurisdictions while the combination of the list and threshold received the same patronage as the patronage given to list alone. The list approach is second to the inclusive approach. One of the dangers of the list approach is that the law may fall behind the pace at which criminal conduct mutates and that this would be dependent political dictates at one point or another. The process of inclusion may become a political football for political actors depending on the personalities and political ideologies at play. Two main reasons can be adduced for this popularity.

The first is that it makes it easier for LEAs because they would be relieved of the burden of trying to allocate a given criminal behaviour as a predicate offence using the criteria provided in law. The second is that it widens the counter crime net to rope in many criminals into prosecution. This can help increase the number of convictions, thus giving out a deterrent message and possibly reducing crime. However, the inclusive approach may sometimes overwhelm investigators and prosecutors as well as the courts with criminal cases in a particular area of trial – say money laundering. There is strong reasonable cause for jurisdictions to choose the inclusive approach if they can construct the needed infrastructure and resources to implement it.

Reasons for Designating Predicate Offences

There are a couple of reasons for designating tax offences as predicate offences for money laundering. Essentially, designating tax crimes as predicate offences for money laundering provides a basis on which to build the necessary infrastructure to prosecute tax crimes. This will facilitate effective investigation and prosecution of both money laundering and the underlying tax offences. It tends to close the escape route straddling between the mutual walls of tax crimes and money laundering. In the end, it is possible to use one stone to kill two birds. Thus, in implementing legal strategies for countering tax crimes as they relate to money laundering, evidence can be found to successfully prosecute both of the offences. See some of the key reasons expatiated by TGP2 are given in Table 14.

Table 14 Key Reasons for Designating Tax Crimes as Predicate Offences for Money Laundering

Making underlying predicate offence chargeable	▪ **This gives opportunity to authorities to have greater scope 'to secure a conviction and/or to impose greater penalties'. In practice, however, investigation and/or prosecution of the offence and underlying predicate offence depends upon 'the case and factors such as the nature of the evidence and the elements of the offence which must be proven'.[277]**
Filing of STRs	▪ 'Financial institutions and other designated professionals and reporting entities are required to file STRs, which report suspicions that a client's funds are the proceeds of a criminal activity, including money laundering as well as predicate offences. As such, STRs can include suspicions of where a client's funds are the proceeds of tax crimes. This can provide greater intelligence from the private sector to the government authorities. In order for this to be more effective, awareness of the risks and indicators is needed amongst the relevant reporting entities of funds being the proceeds of tax crimes. These reports are filed with the FIU.'[278]
Sharing STRs including predicate offences with FIUs	▪ 'STRs are analysed by the FIU and where relevant intelligence is disseminated to the domestic competent authorities responsible for investigating and/or prosecuting the relevant predicate offence. As such, it is possible for STRs to be shared by the FIU with the authority responsible for investigating and/or prosecuting tax crimes.'[279]
Expansion of platform of international cooperation to include tax crime authorities	▪ 'The mechanisms for international co-operation under the FATF Recommendations apply as between authorities that have responsibility for investigating and/or prosecuting money laundering and predicate offences. Where tax crimes are included as predicate offences, those avenues for international co-operation are expanded to include authorities responsible for investigating and/or prosecuting tax crimes. This includes direct exchange of information and mutual legal assistance, both between tax investigatory and/or prosecution authorities and between tax and non-tax investigatory/prosecution authorities.'[280]

---

[277] OECD, *Fighting Tax Crime* 54.
[278] Ibid.
[279] See also TGP9 in ch 4 below.
[280] See also TGP10 in ch 4 below; see also OECD, *Fighting Tax Crime* 55.

Impact

With respect to the impact of including tax crimes as predicate offence for money laundering, an OECD survey to assist the formation of TGP2 revealed that this activity 'has had a practical and positive impact' on the work of jurisdictions surveyed. These impacts include:

- 'better inter-agency co-operation' – the inclusion engenders cordial relations between agencies from different areas of the counter crime ecosystem;[281]
- 'having better access to information (particularly from the FIU and increased STRs)' – the inclusion does facilitate information exchange between intelligence agencies, FIUs and related LEAs;[282]
- easier investigations and increased prosecutions – the inclusion facilitates the work of investigators and prosecutors and more possibly the judges;[283]
- 'deterrent effect on would-be offenders' – the inclusion acts as a preventative tool through the deterrence it provides;[284] and
- 'international cooperation' – this was not clearly mentioned amongst survey participants, but in responding to whether they included tax offences committed in a foreign land or outside their jurisdictions, 19 out of 31, or about 61.3 per cent, said they, indeed, extend predicate offences to tax crimes committed in such other jurisdictions in line with the FATF Recommendations.[285] By this, jurisdictions can only succeed in prosecuting such crimes when they cooperate internationally among themselves.

The above impacts are not mutually exclusive – they are interrelated. However, achieving 'better inter-agency co-operation' was 'the most reported impact of tax crimes' designated as a predicate offence. Jurisdictions were reported to have included in the 'better inter-agency cooperation' the following elements:

- more awareness amongst other law enforcement, intelligence agencies and amongst the private sector of the possibility of tax crimes occurring;[286]
- better avenues for communication with other agencies;[287] and
- increased ability to work with other agencies on particular cases and more generally on strategic and policy matters.[288]

The PROTAX focus group in Malta revealed that differences in designating tax crimes as a predicate offence 'are sometimes an issue since they affect the kind of information that is collected from or channelled to other FIUs'.[289] This implies that agencies in

---

[281] OECD, *Fighting Tax Crime* 55.
[282] Ibid.
[283] Ibid.
[284] Ibid.
[285] Ibid, 56.
[286] Ibid.
[287] Ibid, 55.
[288] Ibid.
[289] Rasmouki and others, 'D2 3 Approaches to tax crimes' 80.

different jurisdictions would have to be united in designating and enforcing tax crimes as a predicate offence. This is more of both inter-agency and international cooperation necessities. In the area of tax crimes, therefore, better inter-agency cooperation eventually improves harmony and the drive towards achieving the collective purpose of countering the crimes.

Both PROTAX focus groups and the OECD survey results on the impact of predicate offences have demonstrated the overarching and cross-cutting nature of the benefits of including tax crimes in the list of predicate offences for money laundering.

Benchmarking TGP2 – The General AML Framework in the EU

Both recital 14 of Directive (EU) 2015/849 (fourth AMLD) and recital 18 of Directive (EU) 2018/843 (fifth AMLD)[290] recognise tax crimes as predicate offences for money laundering, in the similar way as done by recitals 5, 8 and 9 of Directive (EU) 2018/1673 (sixth AMLD)[291] and the definition of criminal activity by the revised FATF Recommendations. In addition, Directive (EU) 2017/1371[292] contributes to the AML framework in the EU, which provides the general infrastructure for tax crimes as predicate offence for money laundering to be effectuated. But four legal instruments in the EU AML framework just mentioned above, and provided in Figure 10, provide the general AML framework. Figure 10 shows a layout providing more salient provisions of predicate offences for money laundering in the EU legal framework. EU directives that also contribute to the EU AML legal framework include the following:

- Directive 2009/138/EC, on insurance and reinsurance.[293]

- Directive 2013/36/EU,[294] regarding access to the activity of credit institutions and the prudential supervision of credit institutions and investment.

- Directive 2014/17/EU regarding credit agreements for consumers relating to residential immovable property.[295]

- Directive 2014/59/EU on framework for the recovery and resolution of credit institutions and investment firms.[296]

---

[290] Directive (EU) 2018/843 of the European Parliament and of the Council of 30 May 2018 amending Directive (EU) 2015/849 on the prevention of the use of the financial system for the purposes of money laundering or terrorist financing and amending Directives 2009/138/EC and 2013/36/EU, PE/72/2017/REV/1, [2018] OJ L 156/43.

[291] Directive (EU) 2018/1673 of the European Parliament and of the Council of 23 October 2018 on combating money laundering by criminal law, PE/30/2018/REV/1 [2018] OJ L 284/22.

[292] Recital 7, Art 4(1).

[293] Directive 2009/138/EC of the European Parliament and of the Council of 25 November 2009 on the taking-up and pursuit of the business of Insurance and Reinsurance (Solvency II), [2009] OJ L 335/1.

[294] Directive 2013/36/EU of the European Parliament and of the Council of 26 June 2013 on access to the activity of credit institutions and the prudential supervision of credit institutions and investment firms, amending Directive 2002/87/EC and repealing Directives 2006/48/EC and 2006/49/EC, [2013] OJ L 176/338.

[295] Directive 2014/17/EU of the European Parliament and of the Council of 4 February 2014 on credit agreements for consumers relating to residential immovable property and amending Directives 2008/48/EC and 2013/36/EU and Regulation (EU) No 1093/2010, [2014] OJ L 60/34.

[296] Directive 2014/59/EU of the European Parliament and of the Council of 15 May 2014 establishing a framework for the recovery and resolution of credit institutions and investment firms and amending Council

Figure 10 Layout of Relevant Provisions of Predicate Offences in EU Law

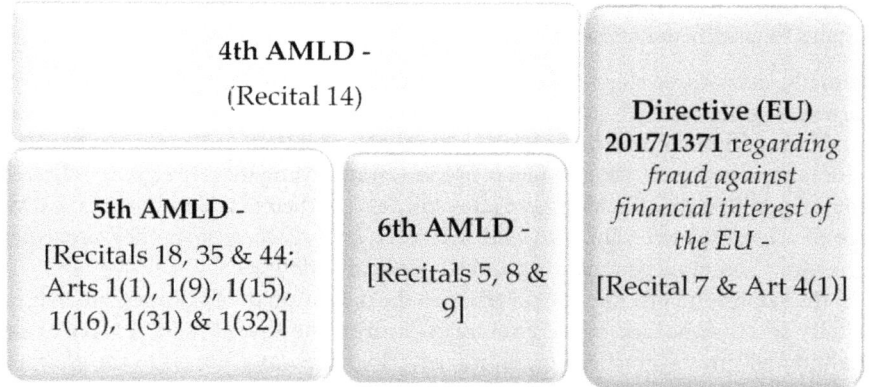

The provisions above have established strong pillars for the predicate offences of tax evasion and tax fraud in the AML regime of the EU. In recital 5 of the sixth AMLD, for instance, it is provided that:

- There should be a sufficiently uniform definition of predicate offences for money laundering in the EU.[297]

- All criminal offences in the sixth AMLD that are punishable by imprisonment should be taken as predicate offences for money laundering.[298]

- If the application of penalty thresholds does not already make offences that attract imprisonment for predicate offences for money laundering, EU Member States are required to 'include a range of offences within each of the categories of offences listed in' in the sixth AMLD. In this regard, EU 'Member States should be able to decide how to delimit the range of offences within each category'.[299] Broadening the list of offences in the categories for predicate offences is critical, in this regard.

- In a situation 'where a category of offences, such as terrorism or environmental offences, includes offences set out in legal acts of the Union', the sixth AMLD should make reference to those legal acts. EU Member States should consider any offence provided in 'those legal acts as constituting a predicate offence for money laundering'.[300]

- At the same time, 'any kind of punishable involvement in the commission of a predicate offence as criminalised in accordance with national law should also be considered as a criminal activity for the purposes of' the sixth AMLD.[301]

Directive 82/891/EEC, and Directives 2001/24/EC, 2002/47/EC, 2004/25/EC, 2005/56/EC, 2007/36/EC, 2011/35/EU, 2012/30/EU and 2013/36/EU, and Regulations (EU) No 1093/2010 and (EU) No 648/2012, of the European Parliament and of the Council, [2014] OJ L 173/190.

[297] Directive (EU) 2018/1673, recital 5.
[298] Ibid.
[299] Ibid.
[300] Ibid.
[301] Ibid.

- Where the Union law grants permission to EU 'Member States to provide for sanctions other than criminal sanctions', the sixth AMLD 'should not require Member States to classify the offences in those cases as predicate offences'.[302]

Essentially, using these elements of AML framework to counter money laundering and its predicate offences such as tax crimes 'should result in Member States laying down *effective, proportionate and dissuasive* administrative sanctions and measures in national law for failure to respect the national provisions transposing this Directive'.[303] There has been a recognition that EU Member States still have, in their legal frameworks, 'a diverse range of administrative sanctions and measures for breaches of the key preventative provisions'[304] on money laundering and its predicate offences.

In the same vein, just like the diversity in the definition of tax crimes which creates difficulty in cross-border crime counter-measures, the diversity in respect of sanctions and measures against money laundering does present a danger to the efforts that have been 'made in combating money laundering'.[305] As a result, the response of the Union has been 'at risk of being fragmented'. It is difficult to conclude if the fourth AMLD succeeded in presenting a unifying front or force for sanctions and measures on money laundering and its predicate offences across the EU Member States. This is because the range of options given to Member States are still wide and imbued with national discretions that can all the more vitiate the unification of sanctions and other measures. Neither the fifth nor the sixth AMLD has effectively remedied this situation.

The fourth AMLD has so far provided 'for a range of administrative sanctions and measures by Member States at least for *serious, repeated or systematic breaches* of the requirements relating to customer due diligence measures, record-keeping, reporting of suspicious transactions and internal controls of obliged entities'.[306] As analysed in the previous section of this book, the threshold qualification in the form of *serious, repeated or systematic breaches of the requirements* does pose a burden on prosecutors in terms of elements required to prove an offence. It also adds series of provisions in which discretions can be exploited to benefit diversity at the expense of unified sanctions and measures.

Whatever variations that may come by, tax crimes have now been well established as predicate offences for money laundering by international institutions such as the EU, OECD and FATF along with most of their compliant Member States transposing such criminal offences into their national laws.[307] The FATF, particularly in its 2012 Recommendations,[308] has clearly 'recognised the linkages between tax crimes and money laundering by adding tax crimes to the list of designated predicate offences for money laundering purposes'.[309] Indeed, the EU and OECD AML frameworks on predicate

---

[302] Ibid.
[303] Directive (EU) 2015/849, recital 59.
[304] Ibid.
[305] Ibid.
[306] Ibid.
[307] OECD, *Fighting Tax Crime*.
[308] FATF, *International Standards on Combating Money Laundering* 116.
[309] OECD, *Effective Inter-Agency Co-operation*.

offences such as tax crimes are largely inspired by or drawn from the prescriptions of the FATF. This is one of the best contributions so far regarding the criminalisation of tax crimes, as established in the TGP1.

In fact, the European Parliament, in a 2019 resolution, underscored the significant steps the fourth and fifth AMLDs have taken 'in improving the effectiveness of the Union's efforts to combat the laundering of money from criminal activities' and its predicate offences.[310] An important score-line drawn by the 2019 resolution of European Parliament is also that the EU 'AML framework chiefly relies on a preventive approach to money laundering, with a focus on the detection and the reporting of suspicious transactions'.[311] In support of this position, it can be observed that the AML directives of the EU do 'strengthen the fight against money laundering with reference to tax crimes by way of an integrated strategy'[312] in the preventative pathways.

Indeed, making tax offences part of predicate offences for money laundering has been partly inspired by this imperative of preventative measures. In the same spirit, the fourth and fifth AMLDs have highlighted measures such as exposing the identity of ultimate beneficial owners (UBO) particularly through the central beneficial ownership registers required to be established and operationalised by the EU Member States.[313] The old saying that 'prevention is better than cure' could not be more accurate, in this regard.

Having benchmarked TGP1 and TGP2 respectively relating to criminalisation of tax offences and making tax offences a predicate offence for money laundering (which altogether has characterised the core of the criminal law framework), it is imperative to see how EU tax crime counter-measures are benchmarked with the OECD global principle regarding the need to grant investigators adequate powers to be able to effectively investigate tax crimes – this is TGP3, which follows.

TGP3: Need to have Adequate Investigative Powers

The central point around which the TGP3 navigates is the relevance and necessity of empowering investigators with the needed mandate to have the capabilities to conduct effective and efficient investigations into tax crimes. This principle essentially provides that jurisdictions must ensure that their laws provide relevant investigative authorities with the 'appropriate investigative powers to successfully investigate tax crimes'.[314]

It is a cardinal imperative in any criminal investigation, including tax crimes, that the investigation is set out to ensure that the needed truth about the commission of a

---

[310] Report on financial crimes, tax evasion and tax avoidance: European Parliament resolution of 26 March 2019 on financial crimes, tax evasion and tax avoidance (2018/2121(INI)), www.europarl.europa.eu/doceo/document/TA-8-2019-0240_EN.html, accessed 10 February 2020.
[311] Report on financial crimes, tax evasion and tax avoidance.
[312] Rasmouki and others, 'D2.3 Approaches to tax crimes' 34.
[313] Directive (EU) 2015/849, Art. 30 and 31, particularly; Directive (EU) 2018/843, Art. 1(15) and 1(17), particularly.
[314] OECD, *Fighting Tax Crime* 25.

crime is found for use in the prosecution of or redressing the balance with the offender. In order to do this, criminal investigators investigate the 'alleged criminal (tax) behaviour' or conduct.

> [Therefore, in investigating an alleged criminal conduct] criminal investigators will generally seek to find and analyse information for the purposes of determining whether or not a crime has been committed. Investigations can result in finding both incriminating ('inculpatory') evidence and evidence that confirms innocence ('exculpatory evidence'). This is used [by] prosecution authorities to decide whether or not to prosecute the accused.[315]

Without appropriate tools and authority to investigate, it is inescapable that shoddy or defective investigations may be conducted whereby culprits or offenders easily get away with their criminal conduct, while the innocent may suffer the inconveniences of investigations and prosecution and possible conviction for crimes not committed if factors such as the following hold sway:

- the prosecutor is smarter or is more resourceful;
- an innocent defendant has poor defence; and/or
- the judge lacks the necessary competence, for instance, in fiscal matters or cross-border tax crimes.

As in many fields, in the landscape of tax crimes, criminals are always changing their strategies in complexity and scope. Aware that LEAs are out there to fish them out and hold them to account, criminals devise every available strategy and method to 'hide the criminal nature of their conduct' and evade being detected and/or caught.[316] This presents a great challenge to LEAs.

It is, therefore, critical that LEAs responsible for tax crimes are provided with the 'appropriate range of investigative powers in order to [detect and] obtain the necessary information'[317] on the criminal behaviour of taxpayers. Investigation of tax crimes requires the effectiveness of tracking 'the source and movement of financial assets' as well as the array of individuals that may be involved. Capability to procure this effectiveness thereof is a valuable ingredient for establishing the commission of tax fraud (such as VAT carousel fraud) 'and to identify the role of an intermediary or accessory [such as professional enablers], even where the assets themselves have been moved'[318] as one of the key elements of an effective enforcement regime is the recovery of the proceeds of the crime in question.

However, empowering investigative agencies[319] with the needed capabilities can be tailored rather than omnibus. Different investigative authorities can have different sets of responsibilities, and powers granted to them should be consistent with the investigative body's mandate and responsibilities. Of course, some general empowerment can be done for all manner of investigators. But there also has to be some

---

[315] Ibid, 25.
[316] Ibid, 26.
[317] Ibid.
[318] Ibid.
[319] OECD, *Effective Inter-Agency Co-operation in Fighting Tax Crimes.*

particularisation of granting powers to investigators. Therefore, the TGP3 suggests, the nature and extent of investigatory powers in a given agency may vary dependent upon which agency has responsibility for investigating tax crimes in a particular jurisdiction.[320]

There are a number of key levels of strategies used to counter financial crimes such as tax crimes. These fundamentally include:

- the prevention of offence;
- the detection of offence;
- the investigation of offence;
- the prosecution of offence;
- conviction and sentencing of offender; and
- the recovery of the proceeds of crime from the criminal.[321]

Each of the above strategic stages of counter tax crime has some form of investigative mechanism embedded therein. Based on the circumstances surrounding an offence and the counter tax crime ecosystem, the above strategic levels are open for use or participation by different agencies of the government, such as:

- the tax administration;
- the customs administration;
- the AML authorities (including FIUs);
- the police and specialised LEAs (including authorities in charge of the investigation of corruption offences);
- the public prosecutor's office; and
- the financial regulators; as well as
- the magistrates, judges or justices.[322]

Each of these agencies must conduct some form of investigation within their remit in order to arrive at conclusions about the case and alleged offence/s in question. While some of them have their preoccupation mandate as investigators, such as the police, all the above are clothed with one form of investigative power or another with the exception of, arguably, the magistrates/judges that rarely have the responsibility to conduct investigations. However, magistrates/judges would also sometimes have to conduct some form of preliminary investigation to gain a full picture of a case or ascertain if there is probable cause to reach a conclusion that the accused is really guilty as charged. Indeed, in Spain for example, an examining judge can and does direct investigations into tax offence cases.

---

[320] OECD, *Fighting Tax Crime* 26.
[321] Ibid.
[322] OECD, *Effective Inter-Agency Co-operation in Fighting Tax Crimes* 26.

Models for Investigative Competences of Agencies

There is a range of organisational models for structuring each of the above agencies and how to allocate competences to each of them in order to perform at the various stages of strategies to counter crime, outlined above. Studying models applied across a number of countries, the OECD developed the following four models for allocating competence to an investigative agency for carrying out criminal tax investigations.[323]

Table 15 Investigation Models Applied by Selected Jurisdictions[324]

Models used by different jurisdictions	Investigation competence for agencies
Model I[325]	▪ Tax administration is charged with the responsibility to direct and conduct investigations into offences.
Model II[326]	▪ Tax administration is mandated to carry out investigations under the direction of the public prosecutors.
Model III[327]	▪ Specialist tax agency outside tax administration is clothed with the responsibility to conduct tax offence investigations, which may involve public prosecutors. It is typically carried out but not always under the Ministry of Finance.
Model IV[328]	▪ Police or public prosecutor is granted the responsibility to carry out tax offence investigations.[329]

In Model I, tax administration may not possess:

> [I]nvestigative powers, expertise or resources, such as the ability to search and seize, intercept communications and demand production of documents. [in the event that] the tax administration is responsible for conducting criminal tax investigations but does not have the full range of investigative powers itself, these powers should still be available indirectly where needed, such as through the ability to call on the police or another agency to provide investigatory services.[330]

---

[323] Ibid.
[324] Ibid.
[325] Jurisdictions that have applied the Model I, as found by OECD research are: Australia, Canada, Germany, Greece, India, Ireland, Israel, Japan, Korea, Malaysia, New Zealand, Singapore, South Africa, Switzerland, Uganda, the United Kingdom and the United States; see OECD, *Effective Inter-Agency Co-operation in Fighting Tax Crimes* 11.
[326] Jurisdictions that have applied the Model II, as found by OECD research are: Austria, Azerbaijan, El Salvador, Estonia, Germany, Hungary, Latvia, the Netherlands, Portugal, Serbia, Sweden, Spain and the United States. In Spain investigations are currently directed by an examining judge; see OECD, *Effective Inter-Agency Co-operation in Fighting Tax Crimes* 12.
[327] Jurisdictions that have applied the Model III, as found by OECD research are: Georgia, Ghana, Greece, Iceland and Turkey; see OECD, *Effective Inter-Agency Co-operation in Fighting Tax Crimes* 12.
[328] Jurisdictions that have applied the Model IV, as found by OECD research are: Belgium, Brazil, Burkina Faso, Chile, Colombia, Costa Rica, the Czech Republic, Denmark, Ecuador, Finland, France, Greece, Iceland, Lithuania, Luxembourg, Mexico, Norway, Peru, the Slovak Republic, Slovenia, Spain and Sweden; see OECD, *Effective Inter-Agency Co-operation in Fighting Tax Crimes* 12.
[329] OECD, *Effective Inter-Agency Co-operation in Fighting Tax Crimes* 11; OECD, *Fighting Tax Crime* 26.
[330] OECD, *Fighting Tax Crime* 26.

What this suggests is that cooperation with other agencies in the ecosystem is an empowering proposition for tax administration charged with the responsibility to investigate tax crimes. This does not appear to be enough, although it can help if cooperation is highly effective. As long as an agency has the responsibility to investigate tax crimes, the agency should be granted all the more with full investigative powers within the contextual remit.

In Model II, 'the investigative powers [of the tax administration] most likely are similar to the investigative powers of the police conducting other financial investigations'. This is because the police or public prosecutor is responsible for conducting and/or directing investigations. Disposition of Model II is similar to Model IV except that in the latter the police are more directly or solely responsible for criminal tax investigations with possible support given by the tax administration.[331]

With respect to Model III, 'an agency separate to the tax administration is responsible for investigating tax crime cases, and the investigative powers are also most likely similar to the investigative powers of the police'.[332] In this regard, the tax administration does not have investigative powers as such. The tax administration could only support the agency with such investigative competence to conduct investigations. But because the agency with the relevant competence here is a specialist tax agency, cooperation between it and the tax administration could be more naturally cohesive. Of course, although this arrangement can ensure that different institutions are not involved in double investigations (leading to waste of state resources), if tax administration has full investigative powers and another agency, say, the police also has such competence, there would not be a clash or double activity if the two agencies cooperate effectively to ensure that the agency that first initiates the process of investigation is allowed to solely continue the investigation and with cooperation between other relevant agencies all the way to the conclusion of investigations on a particular offence.

A possible Model V, which could be leveraged, is that the public prosecutor, police and the tax administration could conduct joint investigations under the needs assessment of the public prosecutor who eventually ends up in court to prosecute the offence. This model could leverage the structure and functionality of the Joint Investigation Teams (JIT) for national criminal investigations. Inspired by the model JIT agreement,[333] the JIT has been aptly described by Europol as 'an established efficient and effective cooperation tool amongst national investigative agencies when tackling cross-border crime. They facilitate the coordination of investigations and prosecutions conducted in parallel across several States.'[334]

The proposed Model V could effectively be built upon the logic and principles anchoring the JIT at the national level. The UK's Joint Money Laundering Intelligence

---

[331] OECD, *Fighting Tax Crime* 26.

[332] Ibid.

[333] Council Resolution on a Model Agreement for Setting up a Joint Investigation Team (JIT) (2017/C 18/01), [2017] OJ C18/1.

[334] Europol, 'Joint Investigation Teams – JITs: Numerous successes across the board', www.europol.europa. eu/activities-services/joint-investigation-teams, accessed 21 April 2020.

Taskforce (JMLIT) is more specific on money laundering and modelled along the lines of the JIT on intelligence-gathering between the private sectors and public sectors including exchanges between LEAs and financial institutions.

The JMLIT is a wing of the United Kingdom's National Economic Crime Centre. It is a public-private partnership platform on which law enforcement and the financial sector foster relations 'to exchange and analyse information relating to money laundering and wider economic threats'. JMLIT is made up of more than 40 financial institutions, the Financial Conduct Authority, Cifas,[335] and five LEAs, thus the NCA,[336] HMRC, the SFO,[337] the City of London Police, and the Metropolitan Police Service.[338] The JMLIT is presented as 'an innovative model for public/private information sharing that has generated very positive results since its inception in 2015, and is considered internationally to be an example of best practice'.[339] Indeed, the JMLIT even appears to provide an exemplary model worth emulating at the EU level, since it makes provision for unique close private participation in cooperation on intelligence-gathering. However, the Network of National Experts on Joint Investigation Teams (JITs Network)'s collaboration with Eurojust[340] and Europol[341] enables an emerging form of investigative cooperation at the EU level, which appears promising. JITs Network, on the backing of the Council of the European Union, is defined as follows:

> A [JIT] is an international cooperation tool based on an agreement between competent authorities – both judicial (judges, prosecutors, investigative judges …) and law enforcement – of two or more States, established for a limited duration and for a specific purpose, to carry out criminal investigations in one or more of the involved States.[342]

On matters concerning tax, the JITs Network ought to also effectuate collaboration with Eurofisc[343] and OLAF.[344] The JIT is, thus, a mobilisation tool for ad hoc investigators to conduct a specific investigation in a defined time. It should be possible for an architecture that networks – not on ad hoc basis – all relevant agencies with investigative powers on a common platform where parallel, simultaneous and joint investigations can be carried out on tax crimes in a harmonised manner.

While some of the models provided by TGP3 are deemed to be 'long-standing and were established as a country's framework for law enforcement was developed', there are

---

[335] Credit Industry Fraud Avoidance System, www.cifas.org.uk/.

[336] National Crime Agency, www.nationalcrimeagency.gov.uk.

[337] Serious Fraud Office, www.sfo.gov.uk.

[338] NCA, 'National Economic Crime Centre: Joint Money Laundering Intelligence Taskforce', www.nationalcrimeagency.gov.uk/what-we-do/national-economic-crime-centre, accessed 11 April 2020.

[339] Ibid.

[340] European Union Agency for Criminal Justice Cooperation.

[341] The European Union Agency for Law Enforcement Cooperation is an agency of the European Union responsible for helping Member States of the EU to counter serious international crimes and terrorism.

[342] JITs Network, 'Joint Investigation Teams Practical Guide' (Council of the European Union, 14 February 2017).

[343] Eurofisc fosters administrative cooperation in countering tax crimes, particularly VAT fraud; see Regulation on administrative cooperation and combating VAT fraud (Council Regulation 904/2010, OJ L268/1).

[344] Detects, investigates and stops fraud with EU funds.

other models that 'reflect more recent policy decisions'.[345] A consideration of the fifth model being suggested above could reflect innovative policy decisions.

The TGP3 posits that no matter what the organisational model that is applied by a jurisdiction, it is imperative that the agencies in charge of investigation of tax offences 'should have the investigative powers that it considers are necessary and effective in the context of its own mandate, and taking into account the ability to work with other [LEAs] which may have additional powers'.[346] TGP3 further provides that the investigative powers granted to agencies 'should allow accessing information and evidence in the digital world in addition to the more traditional sources of information'.[347]

There has been no precision regarding 'circumstances and legal procedures that need to be followed' so as to apply investigative powers. TGP3 points out that while jurisdictions have been represented to possess 'direct powers', it is not intended 'to reflect that the power can be used in all investigations of a tax offence, but that the agency [can] exercise the powers itself in the authorised circumstances (including where a warrant or court authorisation is granted to the agency)'.[348] At the same time, reference made to indirect powers of agencies through another agency in jurisdictions does reflect 'an arrangement where the power would be exercised by a different agency outside the criminal tax investigation agency, such as by the police'.[349]

Therefore, whereas the direct powers are limitless or not absolute but are reasonably carried out in context and authorisation, the indirect powers are performed by an agency on behalf of other agencies charged with criminal investigation. Within reasonable limits, therefore, direct and indirect powers should be granted to agencies responsible for criminal tax investigations.

Pillars of Adequate Investigative Powers

Essentially, the TGP3 has provided the following eight investigation powers as pillars upon which agencies are appropriately allocated competences for. These are illustrated in Figure 11.

Legal Investigative Powers

In practice, the OECD's research found the distributions regarding allocation of direct and indirect powers of investigative powers across 30 countries shown in the following tables.[350]

---

[345] OECD, *Effective Inter-Agency Co-operation in Fighting Tax Crimes* 11.
[346] OECD, *Fighting Tax Crime* 27.
[347] Ibid.
[348] Ibid.
[349] Ibid.
[350] The situation has not changed dramatically since the report of the research was launched in 2017.

Figure 11 Pillars of Having Adequate Investigative Powers

1. *Powers to obtain third party documentary information*	•Including subpoena, production order,or such other powers that can demand or compel third parties to hand over documentary information.
2. *Search powers*	•Search property, enter property, seize physical evidence (e.g. books, other records).
3. *Power to intercept mail and telecommunications*	•Power to conduct reviews on someone's communications particularly sent electronically.
4. *Power to search and seize computer hardware, software, phones and digital media*	•Search and seize physical evidence, secure digital evidence.
5. *Powers to interview*	•Initiate interview and, if provided in law, compel respondents to give information.
6. *Power to conduct covert surveillance*	•Monitoring of movements, conversations and other activities covertly.
7. *Power to conduct undercover operations*	•Taking a different identity to obtain information and evidence.
8. *Power to arrest a person*	•Stop, restrain and put someone in custody to be charged and/or further interviewed if permitted by law.

Table 16a Legal Investigative Powers in Jurisdictions

Legal powers	*Full direct powers* Agency responsible for tax crime investigation can be authorised to exercise the power itself	*Indirect powers via another agency* Agency responsible for tax crime investigation can seek assistance of another agency to exercise the power on its behalf	**Not available**

(continued)

Table 16a *(Continued)*

Powers to obtain third party documentary information	Australia, Austria, Canada, Czech Republic, Finland, France, Georgia, Germany, Greece, Iceland, Indonesia, Italy, Japan, Lithuania, Luxembourg, Malaysia, the Netherlands, New Zealand, Norway, Singapore, Slovak Republic, Slovenia, South Africa, Spain, Sweden, Switzerland, United States, United Kingdom.	Australia, Brazil, El Salvador, Sweden.	N/A
Search powers	Australia, Austria, Canada, Czech Republic, Finland, France, Georgia, Germany, Greece, Iceland, Indonesia, Italy, Japan, Lithuania, Luxembourg, Malaysia, the Netherlands, New Zealand, Norway, Singapore, Slovak Republic, Slovenia, South Africa, Spain, Sweden, Switzerland, United Kingdom, United States.	Australia, Brazil, El Salvador, Italy, Sweden.	Switzerland

As shown in Table 16a, the majority of the countries have direct rather than indirect powers to obtain third party documentary information and search powers. Only Australia, Brazil, El Salvador, Italy, and Sweden granted indirect powers to search in their legal frameworks. Intriguingly, Australia, Italy, and Sweden granted both direct and indirect powers to conduct searches. Also, in the OECD survey, only Switzerland was said to have granted no powers to tax crime agencies or associates to conduct searches.

Table 16b Legal Investigative Powers in Jurisdictions

Legal powers	*Full direct powers* Agency responsible for tax crime investigation can be authorised to exercise the power itself	*Indirect powers via another agency* Agency responsible for tax crime investigation can seek assistance of another agency to exercise the power on its behalf	Not available
Power to intercept mail and telecommunications	Australia, Austria, Brazil, Czech Republic, Finland, France, Germany, Greece, Italy, Lithuania, Luxembourg, the Netherlands, Norway, Slovak Republic, Slovenia, United Kingdom.	Iceland, Italy, South Africa, Spain.	Canada, Japan, El Salvador, Indonesia, Malaysia, New Zealand, Singapore, Slovenia, Sweden, Switzerland, United States.

(continued)

Table 16b *(Continued)*

Power to search and seize computer hardware, software, cell phones and digital media	Australia, Austria, Canada, Czech Republic, Finland, France, Georgia, Germany, Greece, Iceland, Indonesia, Italy,	Australia, Brazil, Czech Republic, El Salvador, Italy, Sweden, Switzerland.	N/A
	Japan, Lithuania, Luxembourg, Malaysia, the Netherlands, New Zealand, Norway, Singapore, Slovak Republic, Slovenia, South Africa, Spain, Sweden, Switzerland, United Kingdom, United States.		

In Table 16b, it can be seen that a significant number of countries do not allow agencies to intercept mail and telecommunications. Only a few jurisdictions grant indirect powers for the interception. However, majority of jurisdictions still granted such powers. Meanwhile, a majority of the jurisdictions surveyed have had the power to search and seize computer hardware, software, mobile phones and digital media. Countries such as Australia, Czech Republic, Italy, Sweden, and Switzerland were said to grant both direct and indirect powers to tax crime agencies to search and seize computer hardware, software, mobile phones and digital media. Brazil and El Salvador also granted indirect powers, in this regard.

Table 16c Legal Investigative Powers in Jurisdictions

Legal powers	*Full direct powers* **Agency responsible for tax crime investigation can be authorised to exercise the power itself**	*Indirect powers via another agency* **Agency responsible for tax crime investigation can seek assistance of another agency to exercise the power on its behalf**	Not available
Powers to interview	Australia, Austria, Canada, Czech Republic, Finland, Georgia, Germany, Greece, Iceland, Indonesia, Italy, Japan, Lithuania, Luxembourg, Malaysia, the Netherlands, New Zealand, Norway, Singapore, Slovak Republic, Slovenia, South Africa, Spain, Sweden, Switzerland, United Kingdom, United States.	Australia, Brazil, Greece.	N/A

(continued)

Table 16c *(Continued)*

Power to conduct covert surveillance	Australia, Austria, Brazil, Canada, Czech Republic, Finland, France, Georgia, Greece, Italy, Japan, Lithuania, Luxembourg, the Netherlands, New Zealand, Norway, Singapore, Slovak Republic, Slovenia, Spain, Sweden, United Kingdom, United States.	Australia, Czech Republic, El Salvador, Iceland.	Germany, Indonesia, Malaysia, South Africa, Switzerland
Power to conduct undercover operations	Australia, Austria, Finland, France, Georgia, Germany, Greece, Japan, Lithuania, Luxembourg, the Netherlands, New Zealand, Norway, Slovak Republic, Slovenia, Sweden, United Kingdom, United States.	Australia, Brazil, Canada, Czech Republic, El Salvador, Iceland, Spain.	Indonesia, Italy, Malaysia Singapore, South Africa, Switzerland.

From Table 16c, while the majority of countries granted direct powers to interview, power to conduct covert surveillance and power to conduct undercover operations, with few such indirect powers granted, Germany, Indonesia, Malaysia, South Africa and Switzerland granted no power to conduct covert surveillance. In the same vein, the OECD survey found that Indonesia, Italy, Malaysia Singapore, South Africa, and Switzerland granted no power to tax crime agencies to conduct undercover operations.

Table 16d Legal Investigative Powers in Jurisdictions

Legal powers	*Full direct powers* Agency responsible for tax crime investigation can be authorised to exercise the power itself	*Indirect powers via another agency* Agency responsible for tax crime investigation can seek assistance of another agency to exercise the power on its behalf	Not available
Power to arrest a person	Australia, Austria, Denmark, Finland, France, Georgia, Greece, Lithuania, Luxembourg, Slovak Republic, Sweden, the Netherlands, Norway, Slovenia, United Kingdom United States.	Brazil, Canada, Czech Republic, Iceland, Indonesia, Italy, Japan, Spain, Switzerland.	Australia, El Salvador, Germany, Greece, Malaysia, New Zealand, Singapore, South Africa, Sweden, Switzerland.

Table 16d reveals that a significant number of jurisdictions came out in the OECD survey as having indirect power to arrest a person just like the number of jurisdictions that granted neither direct nor indict power to arrest a person. A majority of the 30 countries (16) were however said to grant such arrest powers. Ironically, Australia,[351]

---

[351] No powers granted to the Australian Taxation Office (ATO).

Greece[352] and Sweden[353] were said to grant direct arresting powers while, at the same time, not granting such powers to tax crime agencies. Switzerland also appeared to have allocation for both indirect powers[354] and not making such arrest powers available to tax crime agencies such as the cantonal tax authorities.

In effect, the trend from the foregoing analysis on the eight investigative powers include the following:

- Across all the eight powers, a significant majority of jurisdictions granted only direct competence to tax crime agencies.
- There are only a few countries that jointly granted both direct and indirect powers.
- Few countries granted only indirect powers.
- A significant number of countries were said to have no availability of powers to search (only Switzerland), intercept mail and telecommunications, conduct covert surveillance, conduct undercover operations, and arrest.
- Very few countries granted powers and also made such powers unavailable in certain circumstance – mainly due to the agencies such powers were granted to.
- Most jurisdictions appear to have reasonable degree of powers granted to tax crime agencies.
- EU Member States such as Austria, Czech Republic, Denmark, Finland, France, Germany, Greece, Italy, Lithuania, Luxembourg, Slovak Republic, Slovenia, Spain, Sweden and the Netherlands that were featured in the OECD survey have had one form of direct investigative powers granted to tax crime agencies.
- Austria, Greece, Finland, Lithuania, Luxembourg, Slovak Republic and Slovenia are EU Member States that have had direct investigative powers granted to tax crime agencies for all the eight power formations above.
- More than half of the EU Member States that did not feature in all the eight power formations granted one form of investigative powers or another to tax crime agencies.
- An unsettled trend exists in the kind of investigative powers legally granted to tax crime agencies and/or associates across jurisdictions.

Benchmarking TGP3 – Agencies Having Adequate Investigative Powers

The foregoing distribution of jurisdictions across the domains of indirect and direct powers in granting competence or responsibility to tax crime agencies and their associates were corroborated by the PROTAX focus groups. And, these interactive activities revealed also the differentiated nature of how each country chooses to allocate

---

[352] No available powers granted to the Financial Intelligence Unit (FIU). In Greece, the FIU is in charge of collecting, investigating and analysing STRs from both natural and legal persons 'under special obligation, as well as every other information that is related to the crimes of money laundering and terrorist financing and the source of funds investigation'; see OECD, *Fighting Tax Crime: The Ten Global Principles* (OECD Publishing 2017)75.

[353] No available powers for the Tax Fraud Investigation Unit (TFIU) within the Swedish Tax Agency (STA).

[354] Indirect powers granted to the Federal tax administration or a public prosecutor.

responsibility to different agencies in their respective tax ecosystems. The PROTAX focus groups closely gauged the adequacy of legal powers granted to the LEAs, with particular reference to investigations and prosecutions. It turned out that majority of the participants rated the adequacy of the legal powers granted to them to fulfil their role as reasonably good. The rating was based on the following options: very good (level 5), good (level 4), medium (level 3), poor (level 2) and very poor (level 1).

Figure 12 shows a graph that was generated[355] to choreograph the range of responses or opinions of the focus group discussants on this.

Figure 12 Adequacy of Legal Powers[356]

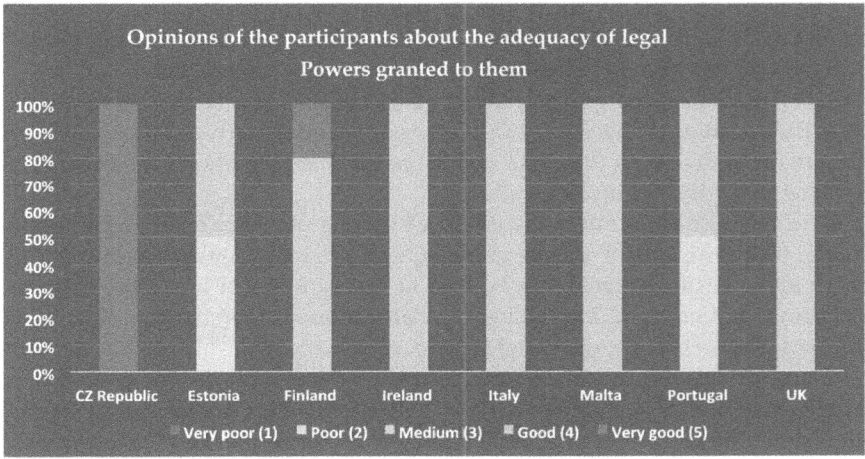

Although the above results from PROTAX focus groups were not clearly delineated as to the adequacy of legal powers (investigation or prosecution or both), it was observed that beyond the general level of contentment with legal powers that was expressed, participants did evoke aspects that required improvements, including the following.

The focus group in Finland emphasised the need for more investigation powers in aspects, such as: investigators' requirement to inform suspects when searching for electronic evidence, which might cause the suspects to delete the evidence if they are informed about the investigation – therefore, this requirement should be waived or abolished; the undercover legislation being rather complex and needing simplification; the investigative power granted to the tax administration not being enough and therefore needs to be granted more investigative powers.[357] These can significantly affect prosecution success in Finland, if not checked.

In Portugal, the focus group established that there was a need to provide direct access for the PJ[358] investigators to fiscal and tax information, since lack of such access

---

[355] Rasmouki and others, 'D2.3 Approaches to tax crimes' 58.
[356] Ibid.
[357] Ibid.
[358] *Polícia Judiciária* – Judicial Police, the national criminal investigation police agency in Portugal.

was impeding their ability to conduct investigations; the FIU was also said to have no 'legal power to suspend and freeze bank accounts' – this needs to change.[359]

In Ireland the focus group underscored that 'for any economic crime [the *Garda*,[360] for instance] can arrest someone for interrogation for 24 hours … [but although] there [can be] strong evidence, there is not enough time to go through this evidence'[361] – thus the duration for interrogation could extend beyond 24 hours to allow for thorough examination of evidence (this might have to be cautiously permitted since some investigators could use longer time to frustrate the suspects and thereby abuse their fundamental rights).

The UK focus group brought up an exemplified understanding that 'tax inspectors … have the legal power to investigate cases going back to 20 years but lack the necessary resources to do so'[362] – thus a problem connecting how extensive investigative power can all too well be vitiated by inadequate resources for the investigators.

In the Estonian focus group, although the ETCB[363] is a tax crime investigation agency, it was said not to have surveillance authority and powers, and thus 'has to cooperate with the police' to get this done – which needs changing since it can frustrate and/or prolong the process of investigation.

Tax secrecy also came out in the PROTAX focus groups as a hurdle to information exchange by investigators. For instance, the Czech Republic focus group intimated that how tax secrecy is interpreted 'has evolved in such a way that it is a big obstacle for information exchange and international collaboration' in investigation. This requires going 'back to the roots (ie, the initial purpose of tax secrecy)' which is that 'tax secrecy in … many jurisdictions was meant as a formal way to protect the books and business information of companies thus preventing a situation where a state agent leaks information about the company to the competitors'.[364] It was not meant to be interpreted as preventing the exchange of information with LEAs. Also, in the Austrian focus group, it was articulated that because of tax secrecy, data are difficult to come by in certain areas and the data that are collected are not utilised due to 'stonewalling'. For instance, in an audit of a supermarket chain, data were 'collected from supplying farmers who were not flat-rate farmers as stated. However, due to tax secrecy, this data was not used further' because of 'stonewalling'.[365]

Additionally, in the PROTAX case studies (D1.2), the Italian case study pointed out that the analysis of the large number of documents usually entailed in the investigation of tax crimes cannot be conducted directly by investigators, due to their complexity. Thus, in Italy external accountants are involved to conduct the analysis for the prosecution of tax crimes.

At the same time, LEAs face practical issues in investigation and prosecution procedures in order to use their legal powers. These include 'not having direct access to information related to suspects, short periods of interrogations and asset freezing, inability to use collected records for criminal investigation'. Another hurdle relates to

---

[359] Rasmouki and others, 'D2.3 Approaches to tax crimes' 59.
[360] *An Garda Síochána* is the Ireland's National Police and Security Service.
[361] Rasmouki and others, 'D2.3 Approaches to tax crimes' 59.
[362] Ibid.
[363] Estonian Tax and Customs Board.
[364] Rasmouki and others, 'D2.3 Approaches to tax crimes' 30.
[365] Ibid.

the limited ability of investigators 'to deploy the necessary resources in order to use the legal powers in practice'.[366] To address this challenge, Recital 19 of Directive (EU) 2018/1673 urges Member States of the EU to make available to investigators 'sufficient personnel and targeted training, resources and up-to-date technological capacity'.[367]

These perspectives and sentiments were largely shared, in varied forms, by other countries that hosted the PROTAX focus groups. In all these countries, although focus group discussants opined that the legal powers granted them was reasonably adequate (from medium to very high level), there were significant underlying issues that still needed remedying.

Table 17 sets out the key legal instruments that affect investigative powers in the EU.

Table 17 Key EU Legal Investigative Instruments

Legislation	Key relevant provisions
Directive (EU) 2017/1371	Articles 12 & 15(1); Recitals 20 & 23.
Directive (EU) 2015/849	Articles 40, 41(4) & 58(4).
Directive (EU) 2018/843	Articles 1(30), 1(37), 1(15), 1(16), 1(37), 1(41); & Recitals 4 & 50.
Directive (EU) 2018/1673	Article 11; Recitals 17 & 19.

For instance, according to Article 11 of Directive (EU) 2018/1673 in relation to investigative tools:

> Member States shall take the necessary measures to ensure that effective investigative tools, such as those used in combating organised crime or other serious crimes are available to the persons, units or services responsible for investigating or prosecuting the offences referred to in Article 3(1) and (5) and Article 4 [of Directive (EU) 2018/1673].[368]

This provision essentially provides for containment of all the eight powers of TGP3 to be granted to investigators in the EU Member States. It also reinforces Article 58(4) of Directive (EU) 2015/849, which obliges Member States of the EU to grant competent authorities with 'all the supervisory and investigatory powers that are necessary for the exercise of their functions'.[369]

With these foregoing legal instruments and relevant provisions, TGP3 is appropriately recognised and put in motion by the EU.[370] The powers granted by these EU legal instruments are, to some extent, effective. However, effective implementation across all the EU Member States are still being challenged, given the diversity of legal systems, cultural and political orientation, resource inadequacy and such other peculiarities which could be faced differently by different EU Member States. Indeed, the sufficiency of the powers that have been granted to investigators can still be said to be either relative or limited. There is so much focus on competent authorities to the neglect of other investigators who may not be assigned the status of competent authority.

---

[366] Ibid, 59.

[367] This obligation relates to TGP7 (availability of adequate resources for tax investigation), which is expatiated in the relevant section below.

[368] Directive (EU) 2018/1673 of the European Parliament and of the Council of 23 October 2018 on combating money laundering by criminal law ([2018] OJ L 284/22–30), Art 11.

[369] Directive (EU) 2015/849, Art 58.

[370] Directive (EU) 2018/1673.

TGP4: Need to have Effective Powers
to Freeze, Seize and Confiscate Assets

One of the issues that stand in the way of LEAs is inadequate powers to freeze, seize and confiscate assets of suspected tax criminals. TGP4 is one of the OECD's 10 global principles that are of substantive nature. This principle implores jurisdictions to 'have the ability to freeze/seize assets in the course of a tax crime investigation, and the ability to confiscate assets'.[371]

The UNODC generally defines freezing or seizing of assets as a temporary prohibition of 'the transfer, conversion, disposition or movement of property or temporarily assuming custody or control of property on the basis of an order issued by a court or other competent authority'.[372] With this definition, freezing and seizing are interrelated concepts but they can have slightly different meanings. Particularly, while freezing refers to 'an action that temporarily suspends rights over the asset, and for example may apply to bank accounts which are fungible', seizure characterises 'an action to temporarily restrain an asset or put it into the custody of the government, and for example may apply to physical assets such as a vehicle'.[373]

In the EU legal framework, freezing is defined as 'the temporary prohibition of the transfer, destruction, conversion, disposal or movement of property or temporarily assuming custody or control of property'.[374] In this definition provided by the EU, an element of prohibition of destruction is also highlighted. Thus, an opportunity is not given to the suspected criminal to destroy the property. This appears to close up the lacuna and tighten up the noose on the layers of defining freezing and seizing of assets. At the same time, this definition combines freezing and seizing, since property against which the measures are taken is considered to consist of physical (tangible) and non-physical (intangible) assets.[375] In general, the two concepts (freezing and seizing) are actioned 'to temporarily prevent the movement of assets pending the outcome of a case'.[376]

On the other hand, the United Nations Convention against Transnational Organized Crime 2000[377] defines asset confiscation (including forfeiture where applicable) as 'the permanent deprivation of property by order of a court or other competent authority'.[378]

Directive 2014/42/EU[379] underscores that freezing and confiscation are autonomous concepts.[380] Thus, while freezing is actioned during investigations and prosecution up until conviction, confiscation is usually carried out upon or after conviction. In general

---

[371] OECD, *Fighting Tax Crime* 37.
[372] United Nations Convention against Transnational Organized Crime and the Protocols thereto [2000], Art 2(f).
[373] OECD, *Fighting Tax Crime* 38.
[374] Directive 2014/42/EU, Art 2(5).
[375] Ibid, recital 12.
[376] OECD, *Fighting Tax Crime* 38.
[377] Art 2(g).
[378] Ibid.
[379] Recital 13.
[380] See G Letsas, 'Autonomous Concepts, Conventionalism, and Judicial Discretion' in *A Theory of Interpretation of the European Convention on Human Rights* (Oxford University Press, 2007) 2.

terms, the application of confiscation (which may include forfeiture) comes 'after the final outcome of a case, as it is a final measure that stops criminals from accessing assets obtained from a crime'.[381] Each of the two concepts is, thus usually, independent of the other.

However, in non-conviction-based confiscations, it is possible that freezing and confiscation can flow into each other or be interconnected.[382] Thus, a frozen property can be confiscated by the authorities without necessarily de-freezing the asset (so that the suspected criminal may, for instance, regain access to the property). Moreover, confiscation does lead 'to the final deprivation of property' of the criminal, while property preservation or freezing 'can be a prerequisite to confiscation and can be of importance for the enforcement of a confiscation order'.[383]

Directive 2014/42/EU[384] further provides that the generally autonomous nature of these two concepts 'should not prevent Member States from implementing [the] Directive using instruments which, in accordance with national law, would be considered as sanctions or other types of measures'.[385] The vagueness of the layers of autonomy between these concepts and how differently they can be approached by EU Member States do complicate the common conceptualisation of freezing and confiscation in the EU. This situation can impede cross-border cooperation on issues concerning these concepts and subsequently investigation and prosecution of tax crimes.

It is imperative that confiscation is carried out in accord with national law, and also that it should not violate international law,[386] in particular international human rights law. The onus on jurisdictions is not only to carry out confiscations according to any national law but to also to ensure that national law relating to freezing/seizing and confiscation is aligned with the principle of proportionality and best practice.[387]

The TGP4 posits that for a successful criminal investigation,

> [T]he assets that gave rise to or are the product of tax crime are adequately secured throughout the investigations, it is important that the investigation agencies can freeze/seize such assets for the duration of the investigation and the criminal procedure.[388]

This proposition is critical because when investigating tax offences, the ability to interrupt the movement of financial assets can be essential in identifying or preventing an offence or tracing the source and beneficial ownership of assets and entities involved in the case. At the same time, it should be possible for agencies to 'have the authority to confiscate assets that gave rise to or are the product of tax crimes'. Such a power or authority is significantly important in the fight against tax crimes because 'financial assets are easily removed from one jurisdiction to another and cause financial damage for governments'.[389] These assets need to be made inaccessible to the suspect during

---

[381] OECD, *Fighting Tax Crime* 38.
[382] See Directive 2014/42/EU, recital 27.
[383] Ibid, recital 26.
[384] Ibid, recital 13.
[385] Ibid, recital 13.
[386] OECD, *Fighting Tax Crime* 38.
[387] Ibid.
[388] Ibid.
[389] Ibid.

investigations to facilitate investigations and to deter the suspect from disposing of or enjoying the assets before investigations and prosecutions are completed. After prosecution, the assets need to be taken away if they are found to be drawn from criminal proceeds.

To make the prevention of and fight against organised crime such as tax crimes effective, proceeds of such crimes should be neutralised 'and should be extended, in certain cases, to any property deriving from activities of a criminal nature'.[390] In fact, beyond provision of 'severe legal consequences for committing such crime', one of the most effective measures used to counter serious crimes such as tax crimes is for jurisdictions to ensure that there is 'effective detection and the freezing and confiscation of the instrumentalities and proceeds of crime'.[391]

TGP4, therefore, entreats jurisdictions to endeavour to make freezing/seizing and confiscation of assets a possibility 'for both domestic and foreign tax investigations and judgments'.[392] In this regard, the proposition is that domestic law should provide the legal power to make freezing/seizing and confiscation a possibility, especially for the national cases. For the international cases, such an endeavour 'may be undertaken in response to a request for mutual legal assistance in accordance with international agreements such as an MLAT',[393] which is featured in the TGP10 regarding international cooperation.

The OECD survey indicates that 'respondents have [varied] legal ability to apply seizing and confiscation powers in respect of foreign tax investigations and foreign court judgments (eg, following an MLAT request)'.[394] It does show that many jurisdictions in the OECD have granted investigators, prosecutors and the court the legal power to seize and confiscate assets – albeit in varying degrees.

In effect, the necessity of freezing, seizing and confiscation of assets tends to be huge and compelling. Such powers particularly help in preventing the disposal of proceeds of crime and ensuring that a suspect is unable to enjoy the criminal proceeds, or for preservation of physical evidence of a particular crime. By the nature of confiscation of assets, it usually amounts to a sanction or penalty in certain jurisdictions. Even if a jurisdiction does not assign confiscation as a sanction in national law, it can still be classified as sanction within the scope of analysis. Some jurisdictions also use confiscation as 'a way to ensure pecuniary fines are paid'.[395]

Essentially, what freezing/seizing and confiscation altogether does is that, it gets criminal activities disrupted through inhibition of

> access to assets that would have been beneficial to the individual or organisation committing the crime or can prevent the criminal assets from being employed to commit further crimes. The freezing / seizing and confiscating of criminal assets is also a deterrent measure as it can reduce the profitability of committing tax crimes.[396]

---

[390] Directive 2014/42/EU, recital 1.
[391] Ibid, recital 3.
[392] OECD, *Fighting Tax Crime* 38.
[393] Ibid.
[394] Ibid, 40.
[395] Ibid, 38.
[396] Ibid.

TGP4 has, as can be seen in Figure 13, five key mechanisms across two parameters – freezing/seizing and confiscation. The five mechanisms are discussed in turn below.

Figure 13 Mechanisms for Freezing and Confiscation of Assets

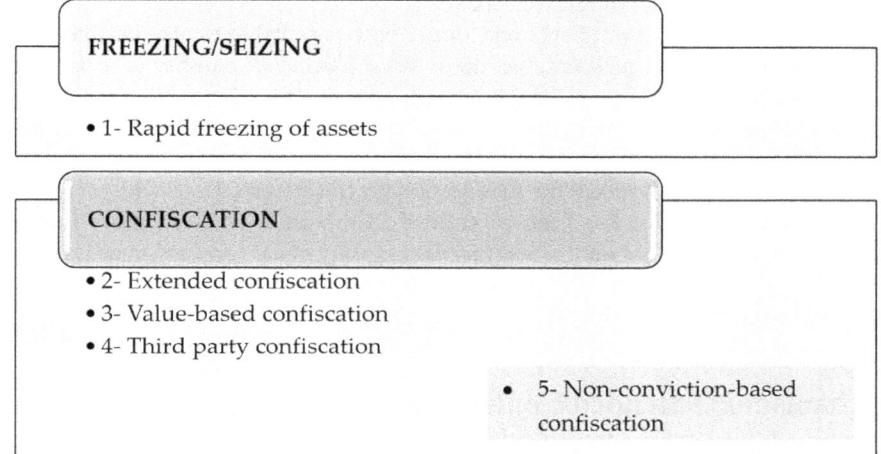

Mechanism 1: Rapid Freezing/Seizing of Assets

Since criminals have sophisticated and interconnected channels to quickly move their assets across different jurisdictions in order to hide and/or dissipate them, freezing/seizing of the assets has to be deliberate and should come with equal measures of rapidity and interconnectedness. In freezing/seizing assets, speed matters hugely if the appropriate objectives are to be achieved. This is driven by the fact that 'criminals can quickly transfer funds out of the [reach of relevant] agencies or dispose of property if [the criminals] become aware that the criminal investigation agencies are investigating them'.[397] In that case, the relevance of the legal authority and operational capacity to rapidly freeze/seize assets in urgent cases is huge where, for instance, there is imminent loss of the property under investigation.[398]

TGP4, therefore, urges relevant agencies in every jurisdiction to generally have the ability to rapidly execute freezing orders within 24 and 48 hours. In the EU, Directive 2014/42/EU provides that for dissipation of property to be prevented 'before a freezing order can be issued', EU Member States should empower their competent authorities 'to take immediate action in order to secure such property'.[399] The power to freeze was found to be available in a majority (18 jurisdictions) of the 29 countries surveyed by the OECD regarding its use in tax crime investigations.[400] Of the 18 jurisdictions, 11 were EU countries.

---

[397] Ibid, 39.
[398] Ibid.
[399] Directive 2014/42/EU, recital 26.
[400] OECD, *Fighting Tax Crime* 40.

There were, however, eight countries that had no such power, while three countries had indirect power to freeze/seize assets exercised through an agency other than the relevant tax crime agency.[401] Of the eight that had no availability of such power, three were from the EU, while Italy was the only EU country that featured among those with indirect powers to rapidly freeze/seize assets.

While most of the respondents had direct power available to rapidly freeze/seize assets in their respective jurisdictions, there was a significant number of jurisdictions that had a challenge with the availability of such powers. This suggests that more should be done by many jurisdictions in order to achieve the objective served by the availability of the power to freeze/seize assets under investigation in criminal tax offences.

However, care must be taken not to sensationally freeze/seize assets without concrete evidence that a tax crime has been committed. Although it is a temporary measure, exercising this power still requires reasonableness, duty of care and safeguards (such as oversight by the courts), since if it is capriciously exercised, the harm incurred could be huge to the suspected tax criminal.

Mechanism 2: Extended Confiscation

This is a confiscation mechanism that entails both confiscation of property that is linked to a specific crime, and the confiscation of 'additional property which the court determines constitutes the proceeds of other crimes'. Thus, the extended nature of this confiscation is that it targets other criminal assets of the criminal who has been charged with tax crime. So, if a legal or natural person is charged with tax evasion and there is a realisation that the offender has been involved in other tax crimes or any other crimes such as money laundering, corruption, financing of terrorism, the court can be granted the power of extended confiscation to confiscate assets which could reasonably have been drawn from proceeds of these other crimes.

TGP4 reasons that this mechanism could be useful to effectively tackle organised criminal activities to not only confiscate property associated with a specific crime, but also additional property which the court deems to be the proceeds of other crimes.[402] Jurisdictions are, therefore, advised to let this power find expression in their legal frameworks and practice.

The OECD survey of 28 jurisdictions found that an overwhelming majority of them (20 jurisdictions) had this extended power directly available to relevant agencies relating to tax matters. Of the 20 jurisdictions, 12 were EU Member States,[403] constituting a majority of 60 per cent.[404] Only four did not have this power, while four other jurisdictions having indirect power of this mechanism exercised it through another agency. Greece and Italy respectively were the EU countries that featured under the non-availability of extended confiscation power and having indirect power of confiscation.

---

[401] OECD, *Fighting Tax Crime* 40.

[402] Ibid.

[403] Austria, Czech Republic, Finland, France, Germany, Lithuania, Luxembourg, Slovenia, Spain, Sweden and the Netherlands, as well as the United Kingdom.

[404] This will be 55 per cent if the United Kingdom is excluded from the EU data when it leaves the EU at the end of December 2020.

Thus, this power was found to be popular amongst the respondents. It stands to reason that most jurisdictions would find this power a useful tool for countering tax crimes.

The legal imperative that undergirds this mechanism is that the criminal ought to be dispossessed of all ill-gotten wealth, to serve as a severe deterrent to interconnected crimes such as organised crime and to serve a warning that a criminal will not be allowed to enjoy other criminal wealth that may not necessarily be connected to a specific tax crime in contention. This is supported by provisions such as Article 12 of the UN Convention against Transnational Organized Crime 2000.

A challenge, however, arises as to the proportionality and legitimacy of such an extended action, since the assets of the specific criminal offence being prosecuted should ordinarily be the focus other than other assets of crimes which may not necessarily be receiving rigorous legal procedures and attention as compared to the present specific criminal offence. In fact, the other 'potential' crimes for which the proceeds might be confiscated may already have been effectively prosecuted and relevant sanctions applied in the past. Therefore, extending confiscatory power to cover such already prosecuted offence may not only share sensitive borders with double jeopardy but also it may amount to abuse of the right to property of the criminals.

Although this extended confiscation power allows for a holistic approach to addressing confiscation of criminal assets, the extension of such power needs to be more reasonably and delicately exercised by the courts. The exercise of this power should not be decided by mere suspicion but informed by reasonable grounds and evidence. It should be that a supposed criminal proceed that is not currently prosecuted effectively must be thoroughly assessed to ensure that the criminal offence that might have produced such an asset must also be rigorously pursued to avoid possible double jeopardy and abuse of fundamental rights of the tax criminal.

Mechanism 3: Value-Based Confiscations

Value-based confiscation is a confiscation mechanism that grants power to 'a court to impose a pecuniary liability equivalent to the amount of the criminal proceeds'.[405] The application of this mechanism is carried out when the court has determined the amount of the benefit accruing directly or indirectly to an individual from criminal conduct, and the order is executable against any asset of the individual.[406] So once a case on tax fraud is successfully prosecuted, for instance, and a sanction is of pecuniary nature, inability of the offender to settle the pecuniary penalty would attract a determination of the court to attach any of the available assets of the offender to the value of the pecuniary liability imposed. With the value-based confiscation, therefore, the issue of confiscation is not necessarily imposed on assets drawn from proceeds of crime. Instead, the confiscation is carried out against any assets of the offender.

The OECD survey of 29 jurisdictions had a majority of the respondents (20 jurisdictions) indicating that their jurisdictions had powers granted to relevant tax

---

[405] OECD, *Fighting Tax Crime* 40.
[406] Ibid.

crime-related agencies to exercise value-based confiscations. Of the 20 jurisdictions, 12 were EU Member States[407] (a majority of 60 per cent), while eight jurisdictions were not. Six jurisdictions had no such powers available to relevant agencies at all. Greece was the only EU country that was featured under this category of non-availability of value-based confiscation powers. Three jurisdictions had indirect powers to exercise value-based confiscations through another agency other than the relevant tax crime related agency. Italy on the other hand was the only EU country that was featured under this category of indirect powers. Therefore, this mechanism appears to also be significantly popular in a number of jurisdictions, a possible indication of the usefulness of applying this power to counter tax crimes.

Mechanism 4: Third Party Confiscations

With respect to confiscation power on a third party, the confiscation seeks 'to deprive someone other than the offender – the third party – of criminal property. This applies where that third party is in possession of assets which are knowingly transferred to him/ her by the offender to frustrate confiscation'.[408] Indeed, just like the extended confiscations, except that this is more extended, it is feasible to use this mechanism to confiscate criminal assets from organised crime. With this mechanism, the focus of confiscation is extended beyond the primary criminal offender to include a secondary person who will have received the property and/or benefited therefrom. More often than not, the third party is primarily a receiver of the property transferred by the offender in order for the receiver to pose as a ruse so as to escape detection and confiscation of the criminal property by authorities.

According to TGP4, this mechanism of third-party confiscation has the capacity to 'alleviate the risk that an agency could be frustrated by the suspect transferring criminal property to a third party to avoid confiscation'. The OECD survey of 28 jurisdictions found that a simple majority of the respondents (15 jurisdictions) indicated availability of the power of third-party confiscation granted to relevant tax crime agencies. Of the 15 jurisdictions, 10 were EU Member States,[409] constituting a majority of about 66.7 per cent in this category of available powers for third party confiscations. Nine jurisdictions (with three EU countries[410]) did not have any availability of third-party confiscation power granted to relevant agencies while only four jurisdictions (with one EU country)[411] had indirect availability of this power granted through another agency other than the responsible tax crime related agency.[412]

Although a simple majority, this measure does not appear more popular in many jurisdictions compared to the preceding mechanisms. It is not clear as to what may have

---

[407] Austria, Czech Republic, Finland, France, Germany, Lithuania, Luxembourg, Slovenia, Spain, Sweden, the Netherlands and the United Kingdom.
[408] OECD, *Fighting Tax Crime* 41.
[409] Austria, Czech Republic, Finland, France, Germany, Lithuania, Luxembourg, the Netherlands, Slovenia and Spain.
[410] Greece, Sweden and the United Kingdom (though this country is almost out of the EU).
[411] Italy.
[412] Ibid.

accounted for the relatively low popularity of this measure, since it is a crucial measure to make confiscation of criminal assets more effective. It is trite knowledge that as soon as a criminal is being pursued, the immediate logical step taken by the criminal is to hide assets from the authorities – and one viable path is to find a strategy of moving the criminal assets in ways that make it difficult for LEAs to identify and link such assets to the criminal being convicted. It therefore stands to reason that all jurisdictions will have this third-party confiscation power expressly established in their legal framework and judicial practice in ways that empower LEAs to be able to effectively confiscate criminal assets. This power should, thus, be adopted by all jurisdictions in accord with the rule of law and fundamental rights.[413]

Mechanism 5: Non-Conviction-Based Confiscation

The three conviction mechanisms discussed above are conviction-based powers granted to relevant tax crime agencies to exercise. Thus, they are exercised when prosecution is successful and conviction obtained. However, there are also occasions whereby a non-conviction-based confiscation mechanism is required by the relevant agencies. It means that power is granted to relevant agencies 'to seize assets without a criminal trial and conviction'.[414] According to TGP4, this mechanism of non-conviction-based confiscation is characteristic of

> … an enforcement action taken against the asset itself and not the individual. It is a separate action from any criminal proceeding and requires proof that the property is the proceeds or an instrumentality of crime. In some jurisdictions, the criminal conduct must be established using a standard of proof of the balance of probabilities, which reduces the burden for the agency and means that it may be possible to obtain the assets even where there is insufficient evidence to support a criminal conviction.[415]

Transparency International avers that non-conviction-based confiscation has different models, including the following:

- preventative procedure – as in Italy;[416]
- administrative procedure – as in Switzerland;[417] or
- civil procedure – as in the United Kingdom and other common law countries.[418]

As the model names of this confiscation type suggest, they do not apply criminal execution procedures. Additionally, this type of confiscation can be conducted *in personam*[419]

---

[413] OECD, *Fighting Tax Crime* 41; see UN Convention Against Transnational Organized Crime 2000, Art 12(8).
[414] OECD, *Fighting Tax Crime* 41.
[415] Ibid.
[416] M Perdriel-Vaissière, L Brillaud and C Portela, 'Into the void: The EU's struggle to recover the proceeds of grand corruption' (Transparency International EU, 2019) 29, http://transparency.eu/wp-content/uploads/2019/09/Asset_recovery_report.pdf, accessed 20 April 2020.
[417] Ibid.
[418] Ibid.
[419] Imposition of a personal liability against an offender.

or *in rem*.[420] *In personam* or *in rem* non-conviction-based confiscation depends 'on whether the legal action is targeted against the person or the property'. This procedure is based on circumstances[421] of each case involved.

By the nature of its arrangement, non-conviction-based confiscation is akin to a double-edged sword. Although the focus is often on pursuing, freezing and confiscating criminal assets, the nature of a tax crime could also influence prosecutor's decision to pursue criminal charges against the offender in court. Both of these actions can be concomitantly pursued within the boundaries of reasonableness. For instance, in Portugal, the PROTAX focus group found the dual approach is used whereby asset recovery is carried out in parallel with criminal investigation/conviction. Some of the focus groups interestingly acknowledged 'that the non-conviction based confiscation using the civil order applied in the UK would be a good practice to adopt'.[422] Even though the property confiscation must meet the test that 'the property is the proceeds or an instrumentality of crime',[423] it is vulnerable to abuse by LEAs, since it does not face the rigorous criminal trial process in court[424] and with the oversight of the judiciary. Even those that undergo rigorous criminal conviction procedures sometimes tend to be susceptible to undesirable consequences.

Considering the impact of asset recovery on suspects, actual criminals and their family members, Fletcher critiques how the confiscation regime is conducted (eg, calculations or the miscalculations of criminal assets subject to freeze, recovery, etc) and whether the current post-conviction confiscation regime under POCA[425] is excessive or disproportionate. What is most revealing and interesting are the facts (based on Bullock's empirical work in 2014[426]) of how the solicitors misinformed their clients when it comes to 'benefit figure' and the subsequent financial (eg, accruing interest) and socio-economic consequences, which hinder rehabilitation and re-entry into the labour market. These have negative impact on mental health and family (such as relationship breakdowns, depression and recidivism).[427] The combination of these factors, it is argued, inflicts 'iatrogenic harm'[428] to people who are subject to confiscation orders. Such an oppressive regime disregards proportionality and is not conducive to human rights and legitimacy of state punishment.[429]

In order to prevent the victimisation of their partners and/or dependants by confiscating authorities, offenders that participated in Fletcher's research brought up insights that could inspire a rethink of the way non-conviction-based confiscations,

---

[420] Imposition of a general liability against an offender and others who may be associated with a property in contention.

[421] Perdriel-Vaissière, *et al*, 'Into the void' 29.

[422] Rasmouki and others, 'D2.3 Approaches to tax crimes' 90.

[423] OECD, *Fighting Tax Crime* 41.

[424] Perdriel-Vaissière, *et al*, 'Into the void' 31.

[425] Proceeds of Crime Act 2002 of the United Kingdom.

[426] K Bullock, 'Criminal benefit, the confiscation order and the post-conviction confiscation regime' (2014) 62 Crime, Law and Social Change 45, in C Fletcher, 'Social value or social harm? The impact of the Proceeds of Crime Act 2002 upon the defendant and their families' in K Benson, C King and C Walker (eds), *Assets, Crimes and the State: Innovation in 21st Century Legal Responses* (Routledge, 2020) 79, 91.

[427] C Fletcher, 'Social value or social harm? The impact of the Proceeds of Crime Act 2002 upon the defendant and their families' in K Benson, C King and C Walker (eds), *Assets, Crimes and the State: Innovation in 21st Century Legal Responses* (Routledge, 2020) 79, 91.

[428] The harm that usually relates to illness that is caused or induced by a particular treatment – in this case, sickness caused by the nature of how the offenders are handled by those in charge of confiscation.

[429] Fletcher, 'Social value or social harm?' 93.

as well as third-party and extended confiscations are particularly carried out. The participants observed that the way their 'partner's legitimately acquired assets' were subjected to confiscation and recovery is problematic. The following remark by one of the research participants is particularly instructive and presents just how the approach and impact of confiscation in the United Kingdom has been perceived by some people to be wrong:

> That's fucking wrong innit? That's not confiscating money from crime. She's legit, her assets are legit and she wasn't even with me when I committed the offences. That's theft, not confiscation.[430]

In the light of this understanding, some research participants explained that they felt they had no choice but to 'detach' themselves from their families 'on paper'.[431] In redressing the balance, the empirical narratives presented by Fletcher do highlight a number of imperatives, including the following six key propositions:

i.   The principle of proportionality must be seen to be effectively enforced by confiscating authorities.
ii. Fundamental human rights should by no means be derogated by the need to impose punitive measures on criminals, and therefore these rights must be safeguarded, in practice, at all material times during confiscation.
iii. There must be a better understanding of the effects of confiscation of assets in order to enhance the efficiency, effectiveness and impact of recovery of assets.
iv. Personnel involved in confiscation must highly competent, disciplined and well-resourced in order to more fairly carry out recovery of assets.
v.   Solicitors representing clients subject to confiscation could be regularly given capacity building in matters concerning confiscation and recovery of assets.
vi. There is the need for robust remedial mechanisms in legal and institutional frameworks on confiscation and recovery of assets.

Directive (EU) 2018/1673 recommends non-conviction-based confiscation, but under qualified circumstances. This EU Directive urges EU Member States to 'strongly consider enabling confiscation in all cases where it is *not possible to initiate or conclude criminal proceedings*, including in cases where the offender has died'.[432]

The OECD survey of 29 jurisdictions found that majority (13 jurisdictions) did not confer this power of non-conviction-based confiscation to the relevant tax crime agency. Of the 13 jurisdictions, eight were EU Member States[433] while the remaining five countries[434] were not. Of the 11 jurisdictions that indicated the availability of such a power in their jurisdictions, six[435] were EU Member States (forming a majority of about 54.5 per cent in this category of available powers). Of the five jurisdictions that had indirect powers availed through another agency than the relevant tax crime related agency, Italy was the only EU country that featured.[436] Apparently, this mechanism

---

[430] Ibid, 79–90.
[431] Ibid.
[432] Directive (EU) 2018/1673, recital 16.
[433] Finland, France, Greece, Lithuania, Slovak Republic, Spain, Sweden, and The Netherlands.
[434] Canada, Switzerland, Georgia, South Africa and Indonesia.
[435] Austria, Czech Republic, Germany, Luxembourg, Slovenia, and United Kingdom (if UK is excluded from the EU as it is exiting, the percentage in this category will be about 45.5 per cent).
[436] OECD, *Fighting Tax Crime: The Ten Global Principles* (OECD Publishing 2017) 41.

is the least popular in many jurisdictions relative to the other confiscation measures. TGP4, however, provides that for effective recovery of criminal assets, jurisdictions are expected to ensure that the six requirements listed in Table 18 are met.

Table 18 Requirements of Effective Criminal Asset Recovery

Governance framework	■ **Having the necessary governance framework to ensure criminal law enforcement agencies operate transparently and are adequately supervised in connection with the handling of assets to ensure integrity.**[437]
Necessary expertise	■ Having the necessary investigative, legal and operational expertise.[438]
Organisational structure	■ Putting in place a clear organisational structure to manage asset cases. Given that these cases can require specialised investigative and legal expertise which may be located across different agencies, it can be efficient to put in place a specialised multi-agency unit with trained practitioners and adequate resources focussing on asset recovery.[439]
Protection of rights	■ Ensuring that the rights of suspects are protected during an asset recovery process.[440]
Effective process	■ Having a process to safely manage the assets.[441]
International cooperation	■ Efficiently using international cooperation, given that asset recovery cases can be complex and involve criminal assets located in foreign jurisdictions.[442]

Apart from the six requirements provided by TGP4, it can be added that in conducting non-conviction-based confiscations, it is imperative to utilise efficient and effective inter-agency collaboration so as to have all the needed information and exercise of interconnected duties from all relevant agencies. These requirements serve as essential safeguards to ensure that the process of confiscating assets without conviction is properly managed to protect the legitimate interests of all parties. One of the key merits of this mechanism is that LEAs are not expected to go through a long court process to confiscate criminal assets, so that criminal assets would be confiscated in time and prosecution resources might be saved if further criminal proceedings are not to be pursued.

Just like the preceding principles that have been benchmarked, the application of TGP4 across jurisdictions is not consistent. This principle, therefore, notes 'that the precise circumstances and legal procedures that need to be followed in order to use freezing/seizing or confiscations measures vary' across jurisdictions. In fact, availability of a given mechanism in a jurisdiction can also vary in its application in investigations of a tax offence within that jurisdiction.

It is possible for all the mechanisms to be available in a jurisdiction or in a given agency. It is also possible to have varying degrees of the availability of these mechanisms

---

[437] Ibid. 41.
[438] Ibid.
[439] Ibid.
[440] Ibid.
[441] Ibid.
[442] Ibid.

in a particular jurisdiction or across all jurisdictions. There is also the possibility of having some of the mechanisms in a jurisdiction or across agencies therein. Determination of the availability of all these mechanisms in a particular jurisdiction or in an agency is dependent upon several factors, including the organisational structure for investigating tax offences; the law enforcement agency responsible for tax offences; the nature (type and value) of the tax offences; and the particular legal system which may not permit certain mechanisms that do not confer powers to confiscate of assets or the granting of permission of necessary legal and procedural authorisations[443] for a given investigation into a particular tax case.

In effect, although the mechanisms for the freezing/seizing and confiscating assets do vary across jurisdictions, there are five key mechanisms that have been availed for consideration: rapid freezing/seizing of assets, extended confiscation, value-based confiscations, third-party confiscations, and non-conviction-based confiscation.[444] TGP4 does provide infrastructure to help eliminate incentives associated with committing tax crime, since assets acquired therefrom could be completely dispossessed by competent authorities when the tax criminals are caught.

As it were, with TGP4, just like most of the other TGPs, the experiences of various countries on freezing/seizing and confiscation of assets are mobilised without clear indication of a superior alternative action for jurisdictions. It appears appealing to deploy all of these mechanisms in every jurisdiction based on freezing/seizing and confiscation objective and strategy in the light of best international legal practices that have appropriate synchrony with national legal framework and comply with safeguards availed by fundamental human rights and procedural rights.

Benchmarking TGP4 – Agencies Having Freezing/Seizing and Confiscation Powers

To benchmark these tenets of TGP4, one can quickly remark that the EU legal framework, to some extent, provides for all the requirements of TGP4. At the same time, PROTAX research has found that most EU jurisdictions have varying degrees of significant freezing/seizing and confiscation powers granted to relevant agencies.

Table 19 sets out a categorisation of recent EU legal instruments and provisions that demonstrate compliance, reinforcement and enhancement of TGP4.

Table 19 EU Legal Instruments and Provisions for TGP4

Corresponding EU legal instruments	*Key applicable provisions*				
Directive (EU) 2017/1371	Article 10				
Directive 2014/42/EU	Recitals 1, 2, 3, 4, 5, 6, 7, 12, 13, 26 & 27	Articles 3 & 4	Articles 5, 6 & 7	Article 8 & 9	Article 10 &11

(continued)

---

[443] OECD, *Fighting Tax Crime* 38.
[444] Ibid.

Table 19 *(Continued)*

Corresponding EU legal instruments	Key applicable provisions		
Directive (EU) 2018/843	Recital 44	Article 1(13)	Article 1(16)
Directive (EU) 2018/1673	Recitals 3 & 16	Article 9	

The relevant EU legal instruments which provide foundational infrastructure for the above recent key legal instruments include:

- Council Framework Decision 2001/500/JHA;[445]
- Council Framework Decision 2005/212/JHA;[446]
- Council Framework Decision 2003/577/JHA;[447] and
- Council Framework Decision 2006/783/JHA.[448]

While the first two foundational instruments have had some amendments by the recent key legal instruments in Table 19,[449] the last two instruments have been replaced. Article 39[450] provides that, as from 19 December 2020, Council Framework Decision 2003/577/JHA[451] and Council Framework Decision 2006/783/JHA shall be effectively replaced by the Regulation (EU) 2018/1805 regarding mutual recognition of freezing and confiscation orders.[452]

Regulation (EU) 2018/1805 is the latest EU legal instrument on freezing and confiscation that complements Directive 2014/42/EU in asset recovery. This Regulation seeks 'to facilitate cross-border asset recovery and make the freezing and confiscation of criminal assets across the EU quicker and simpler'.[453] Its application affects every 'freezing and confiscation orders issued within the framework of proceedings in criminal matters, thus including conviction and non-conviction based confiscation'.[454]

---

[445] Council Framework Decision 2001/500/JHA of 26 June 2001 on money laundering, the identification, tracing, freezing, seizing and confiscation of instrumentalities and the proceeds of crime, [2001] OJ L 182/1.

[446] Council Framework Decision 2005/212/JHA of 24 February 2005 on confiscation of crime-related proceeds, instrumentalities and property, [2005] OJ L 68/49.

[447] Council Framework Decision 2003/577/JHA of 22 July 2003 on the execution in the European Union of orders freezing property or evidence, [2003] OJ L 196/45.

[448] Council Framework Decision 2006/783/JHA of 6 October 2006 on the application of the principle of mutual recognition to confiscation orders, [2006] OJ L 328/59.

[449] The two framework decisions particularly amended by Art 14 of Directive 2014/42/EU.

[450] Regulation (EU) 2018/1805 of the European Parliament and of the Council of 14 November 2018 on the mutual recognition of freezing orders and confiscation orders, [2018] OJ L 303/1.

[451] Provisions of Council Framework Decision 2003/577/JHA had been replaced by Directive 2014/41/EU of the European Parliament and of the Council of 3 April 2014 regarding the European Investigation Order in criminal matters, [2014] OJ L 130/1, per Art 34(2) thereof.

[452] Regulation (EU) 2018/1805 of the European Parliament and of the Council of 14 November 2018 on the mutual recognition of freezing orders and confiscation orders, [2018] OJ L 303/1.

[453] European Commission, 'Commission adopts the report "Asset recovery and confiscation: Ensuring that crime does not pay"' (Migration and Home Affairs, 2 June 2020), https://ec.europa.eu/home-affairs/news/20200602_commission-adopts-report-asset-recovery-confiscation-ensuring-crime-does-not-pay_en, accessed 16 June 2020.

[454] Ibid.

Although Regulation (EU) 2018/1805 will enhance cross-border cooperation and is a milestone in this direction together with Directive 2014/42/EU and supporting legal instruments, there is more room for improvement since the confiscation rate in the EU has been estimated to be just 1 per cent. This is obviously too low, which gives chance or opportunity for criminals (particularly, organised crime groups) 'to invest in the expansion of their criminal activities and to infiltrate the legal economy'.[455]

Directive 2014/42/EU[456] has many relevant provisions and stands as a principal legal instrument for freezing and confiscating assets in the EU.[457] Most of the other legal provisions on freezing and confiscation in the EU complement Directive 2014/42/EU[458] which has been able to harmonise, at least by providing the minimum legal standards and rules on the freezing, management and confiscation of criminal assets in the EU.[459]

In order to defeat the motive of tax crimes (which is predominantly financial gain), Recital 1 of Directive 2014/42/EU requires EU Member States to grant competent authorities the needed instruments or power 'to trace, freeze, manage and confiscate the proceeds of crime'.[460] With particular focus on money laundering, the Council Framework Decision 2001/500/JHA of 26 June 2001[461] provides complementary provisions for using freezing and confiscation to counter financial crimes.[462]

Directive (EU) 2018/1673, the sixth and most recent EU AMLD, recognises the minimum rules laid down in Directive 2014/42/EU regarding 'freezing and confiscation of the instrumentalities and proceeds of crime in criminal matters'.[463] It is required that EU Member States, 'as a minimum, ensure the freezing and confiscation of the instrumentalities and proceeds of crime in all cases provided for in Directive 2014/42/EU'.[464] Recital 5 of Directive 2014/42/EU provides that the minimum rules adopted 'will approximate the Member States' freezing and confiscation regimes, thus facilitating mutual trust and effective cross-border cooperation'.[465] An opportunity is given to Member States to propose further common rules in confiscation. This, therefore, recognises that the EU does not have exclusive competence or impose limitations over these rules which are, thus, applied based on the subsidiarity principle.

More revealingly, Article 1 of Directive 2014/42/EU provides that while the Directive has established 'minimum rules on the freezing of property with a view to possible

---

[455] Ibid.
[456] Member States were to transpose provisions of Directive 2014/42/EU into national law by 4 October 2016.
[457] Directive 2014/42/EU of the European Parliament and of the Council of 3 April 2014 on the freezing and confiscation of instrumentalities and proceeds of crime in the European Union, [2014] OJ L 127/39.
[458] European Commission, 'Confiscation and freezing of assets', https://ec.europa.eu/info/law/cross-border-cases/judicial-cooperation/types-judicial-cooperation/confiscation-and-freezing-assets_en, accessed 25 April 2020.
[459] European Commission, 'Commission adopts the report "Asset recovery and confiscation: Ensuring that crime does not pay"' (Migration and Home Affairs, 2 June 2020), https://ec.europa.eu/home-affairs/news/20200602_commission-adopts-report-asset-recovery-confiscation-ensuring-crime-does-not-pay_en, accessed 16 June 2020.
[460] Directive 2014/42/EU, recital 1.
[461] Council Framework Decision 2001/500/JHA of 26 June 2001 on money laundering, the identification, tracing, freezing, seizing and confiscation of instrumentalities and the proceeds of crime, [2001] OJ L 182/1.
[462] Directive 2014/42/EU, Art 3(d).
[463] Directive (EU) 2018/1673, recital 16.
[464] Ibid.
[465] Directive 2014/42/EU; see also ibid, recital 27.

subsequent confiscation and on the confiscation of property in criminal matters', it does this 'without prejudice to the procedures that Member States may use to confiscate the property in question'.[466] The rules grant competence to the EU Member States while obliging the Member States to comply with the minimum common rules for effective collaborative efforts towards freezing and confiscating properties of criminals.[467] The Directive 2014/42/EU essentially provides for provisions on:

- non-conviction-based confiscation (at least if the accused or suspected person absconds or is ill);[468]
- extended confiscation for a specific list of criminal offences;
- third-party confiscation;[469]
- management of frozen and confiscated property;[470]
- clarifications regarding freezing of property with a view to subsequent confiscation, including 'urgent' freezing;[471]
- strict safeguards, ensuring that the rights of parties, affected by freezing or confiscation proceedings are upheld;[472] and
- obligation of Member States to collect and maintain comprehensive statistics on freezing and confiscation.[473]

With respect to freezing, EU Member States are obliged, per Article 7, to:

> take the necessary measures to enable the freezing of property with a view to possible subsequent confiscation. Those measures, which shall be ordered by a competent authority, shall include urgent action to be taken when necessary in order to preserve property.[474]

The tenets in Article 7(1) effectively measure up to the Mechanism 1 of TGP4 regarding 'rapid freezing/seizing of assets'.[475] Freezing of third party possessions articulated by the TGP4 is also in tandem with Article 7(2) which states that a 'property in the possession of a third party, as referred to under Article 6[476] [of the Directive] can be subject to freezing measures for the purposes of possible subsequent confiscation'.[477] However, the

---

[466] Ibid, Art 1.
[467] Directive (EU) 2018/1673, recital 16.
[468] European Commission, 'Confiscation & asset recovery', https://ec.europa.eu/home-affairs/what-we-do/policies/organized-crime-and-human-trafficking/confiscation-and-asset-recovery_en, accessed 16 June 2020.
[469] Ibid.
[470] Ibid.
[471] Ibid.
[472] Ibid.
[473] Ibid.
[474] Directive 2014/42/EU, Art 7(1).
[475] Ibid, Art 7.
[476] Without prejudicing bona fide third parties, Art 6 of Directive 2014/42/EU states that EU 'Member States shall take the necessary measures to enable the confiscation of proceeds, or other property the value of which corresponds to proceeds, which, directly or indirectly, were transferred by a suspected or accused person to third parties, or which were acquired by third parties from a suspected or accused person, at least if those third parties knew or ought to have known that the purpose of the transfer or acquisition was to avoid confiscation, on the basis of concrete facts and circumstances, including that the transfer or acquisition was carried out free of charge or in exchange for an amount significantly lower than the market value.'
[477] Directive 2014/42/EU, Art 7.

language used in TGP4 is third-party confiscation not third-party freezing albeit freezing measures could lead to confiscation. So, effectively the general contours of TGP4 and Article 7(2) are aligned with each other. Furthermore, for effective confiscation and recovery, the EU obliges its Member States to

> … take the necessary measures to enable the detection and tracing of property to be frozen and confiscated even after a final conviction for a criminal offence or following proceedings in application of Article 4(2)[478] and to ensure the effective execution of a confiscation order, if such an order has already been issued.[479]

The provision in Article 9 of Directive 2014/42/EU essentially requires powers, structures and instruments to be availed to relevant authorities in order to effectively freeze and confiscate assets of criminal association. The confiscation power granted to relevant authorities is also highlighted in Article 4 of Directive 2014/42/EU and Article 9 of Directive (EU) 2018/1673. Article 4(1) makes provision for value-based convictions established in Mechanism 3 of the TGP4. In the same vein, Article 4(2) makes provision for non-conviction-based confiscations as provided in Mechanism 5 of the TGP4. Extended powers are provided in Article 5[480] whereby EU Member States are obliged to empower relevant authorities to confiscate criminal assets and reasonably related assets of the convicted person. This provision effectively aligns with Mechanism 2 of TGP4. For crimes against the financial interest of the Union, Article 10 of Directive (EU) 2017/1371 echoes the obligation of EU Member States to 'take the necessary measures to enable the freezing and confiscation of' criminal assets and the obligation of Member States bound by Directive 2014/42/EU to continue to comply with that Directive.[481]

Furthermore, Directive (EU) 2018/843 provides that Member States of the EU should ensure that AML rules are not only properly implemented by obliged entities but also that they should strengthen the role of public authorities acting as competent authorities such as authorities that have the function of freezing and confiscating criminal assets. Member States are urged 'to strengthen the role of other relevant authorities including anti-corruption authorities and tax authorities'.[482] Directive (EU) 2018/843 also grants power to competent authorities to have access to beneficial ownership information of suspected or convicted criminals. It provides that:

> Member States shall ensure that competent authorities and FIUs have timely and unrestricted access to all information held in the central register [which hosts beneficial ownership information] … without alerting the entity concerned. [Competent authorities, in this regard, are the public authorities that include] tax authorities, supervisors of obliged entities and authorities that have the function of … tracing and seizing or freezing and confiscating criminal assets.[483]

---

[478] Ibid, Art 4(2) provides that, 'Where confiscation on the basis of paragraph 1 is not possible, at least where such impossibility is the result of illness or absconding of the suspected or accused person, Member States shall take the necessary measures to enable the confiscation of instrumentalities and proceeds in cases where criminal proceedings have been initiated regarding a criminal offence which is liable to give rise, directly or indirectly, to economic benefit, and such proceedings could have led to a criminal conviction if the suspected or accused person had been able to stand trial.'
[479] Ibid, Art 9.
[480] Ibid.
[481] Directive (EU) 2017/1371, Art 10.
[482] Directive (EU) 2018/843, recital 44.
[483] Ibid, Art 1(13)(e).

Article 1(16)(d) of the Directive (EU) 2018/843 further provides for access to beneficial ownership information. Here, there is an obligation on the EU Member States to
endeavour to make accessible, information on the beneficial ownership of a trust or
a similar legal arrangement, to entities such as competent authorities as identified in
Article 1(13)(e) above.[484] Empowering relevant authorities to have access to beneficial
ownership information is a huge step, since no freezing or confiscation exercise can be
reasonably successful if information on those who matter the most are not meaning-
fully available and accessible to the relevant authorities. The power generated from this
imperative deepens the scope of the requirements put out by TGP4.

Article 9 of Directive (EU) 2018/1673[485] obliges EU Member States to ensure
'that their competent authorities freeze or confiscate, in accordance with Directive
2014/42/EU'[486] on freezing and confiscation of assets. In a survey, the OECD found
that all the 11 EU Member States[487] of the 26 jurisdictions that were featured in the
survey did grant their competent tax authorities powers to seize and confiscate assets of
tax criminals in respect of foreign tax matters.[488] Of the 23 participating countries that
had availability of such powers granted to relevant authorities, about 47.8 per cent[489] of
them were EU Member States, namely Austria, Czech Republic, Finland, France, Italy,
Luxembourg, the Netherlands, Slovenia, Spain, Sweden and the United Kingdom.[490]
Indeed, of the 26 participating countries, only three (Germany, Brazil and Indonesia)
did not have such powers available to competent tax authorities. This implies that over
50 per cent of EU Member States may not have all the relevant powers granted to their
competent tax authorities to effectively carry out the freezing, seizing and confiscation
of assets of tax criminals.

The PROTAX focus groups examined the dynamics in which the power to freeze
and confiscate is granted and exercised. In general terms, the findings thereof reflected
the survey results of the OECD under TGP4. Thus, a majority of discussants observed
that they have relevant powers to freeze and confiscate. For instance, in the Malta focus
group, it was reported that the police have the power to freeze assets but 'have to ask the
office of the attorney general to request the judge to freeze the assets'. Thus, the police
liaise with the office of attorney general to get through the judge before an asset can be
frozen. This safeguarding measure is likely to ensure that attorney general office is in a
better position to determine any rights, procedures, possible outcomes and implications
of a case being investigated. However, if care is not taken, a prolonged process of going
through the bureaucracies could give a fertile opportunity for the suspected criminal to
move his/her assets before the court orders a freeze.

---

[484] Ibid, Art 1(16)(d).

[485] Directive (EU) 2018/1673 of the European Parliament and of the Council of 23 October 2018 on combating money laundering by criminal law, PE/30/2018/REV/1 [2018] OJ L 284/22.

[486] Directive 2014/42/EU of the European Parliament and of the Council of 3 April 2014 on the freezing and
confiscation of instrumentalities and proceeds of crime in the European Union, [2014] OJ L 127/39.

[487] The participating EU Member States with available freezing powers will number 10 in the survey when
the United Kingdom exits the EU.

[488] OECD, *Fighting Tax Crime*.

[489] Or 38.5 per cent if the UnitedKingdom (now exiting EU) is excluded from the list of EU countries with
available freezing and confiscation powers.

[490] OECD, *Fighting Tax Crime*.

In the Czech Republic focus group, however, discussants 'cited positive elements in the Czech anti-tax crime eco-system such as the ability to freeze assets for three days by the FIU and for an unlimited period by the police; and obtain necessary information from financial institutions'. According to the participants, a good practice is that the FIU can 'obtain relevant information even in cases where financial institutions attempt to hinder the process'. However, there are instances where banks connive with customers to move money around.

> [In this regard, there are some banks that assist their clients to shift funds to another bank and thus escape the system by suspending the transaction subject to the FIU request and exploiting the suspension time to ask the client information before rejecting the transaction, hence offering the client the possibility to transfer the funds elsewhere.

This is deviant behaviour, which is intrinsic in such an environment unless the loopholes are closed. Assets can easily be moved around to escape the long arm of the law. Thus, even though the FIU can freeze suspected criminal assets, it does not appear that the process is rapid enough, although appears to move relatively faster than in Malta.

The dispensation in Estonia was presented such that, with 'freezing orders, the FIU can freeze the whole account leaving only a minimum amount for the suspect's living costs, while the prosecutor is only entitled to freeze the amount tied to the damage'.[491] The principle of proportionality appears to be evidently demonstrated by the prosecutor, in this regard. Though it is not clear how rapid this process of freezing is, it emerged that 'while legal time limit for freezing orders is 30 days, it can be extended for a year following a court order' upwards to a 'limitless' duration. This suggests that significant investigative powers are available to the Estonian LEAs.

These are illustrations to explain that while only a few countries do not have legal powers to freeze suspected criminal assets, the majority of them have such powers except that these powers are either not fully granted or are constrained. It is, therefore, imperative that EU Member States effectively grant the needed 'powers to seize, confiscate and recover the proceeds of crime'[492] as established by the EU legal instruments such as Directive 2014/42/EU and Directive (EU) 2018/1673.

With the sixth AMLD,[493] which requires EU Member States to transpose its provisions into national law by 3 December 2020,[494] it is expected that the Directive 2014/42/EU and the fifth AMLD[495] will be further enhanced. One of the more pertinent provisions of Directive (EU) 2018/1673 is also that the EU and its Members have been urged to, when taking measures in matters such as appertaining to freezing and confiscation of assets, consider the 'FATF Recommendations and instruments of other international organisations and bodies active in the fight against money laundering and

[491] Rasmouki and others, 'D2.3 Approaches to tax crimes' 29.

[492] Ibid, 94.

[493] Directive (EU) 2018/1673.

[494] Ibid Art 13.

[495] Directive (EU) 2018/843 of the European Parliament and of the Council of 30 May 2018 amending Directive (EU) 2015/849 on the prevention of the use of the financial system for the purposes of money laundering or terrorist financing and amending Directives 2009/138/EC and 2013/36/EU, PE/72/2017/REV/1 [2018] OJ L 156/43.

terrorist financing.[496] Additionally, relevant Union legal acts are expected to be appropriately aligned with the 'revised FATF Recommendations'.[497]

Another strong expectation, in this direction, is that the EU will transpose the requirements of the Council of Europe Convention on Laundering, Search, Seizure and Confiscation of the Proceeds from Crime and on the Financing of Terrorism into the EU's legal order. In fact, this is an obligation because the EU is a signatory to this convention.[498] The recognition by the EU of the Stockholm Programme[499] and the Justice and Home Affairs Council Conclusions on confiscation and asset recovery[500] adopted in June 2010' is also a step in the right direction.[501] This arguably provides 'a more effective identification, confiscation and re-use of criminal assets'.[502] It is hoped that, where there are differences between the EU legal order and these international regimes which have a bearing on the efforts to win the fight on freezing and confiscating of assets, the EU will make it reasonably flexible for its Member States to comply with any additional provisions in the frameworks of other relevant international institutions not found in the EU counter measures.

Owing to the fact that there have been limitations to the availability of statistics on amounts recovered from confiscations, and the underutilised nature of confiscation procedures,[503] Article 11 of Directive 2014/42/EU requires measures to be put in place to keep records up to date on different layers of confiscations, which could also evidence the extent to which confiscation procedures are applied by the EU Member States.[504] Reliable statistics on confiscation of assets associated with judicial decisions on criminal tax offences are a good instrument for helping relevant agencies in the tax crime countering ecosystem to take effective and efficient decisions and assess their performance.

In order to facilitate access to financial information on financial assets, Directive (EU) 2019/1153[505] has provided essential pillars upon which competent authorities, LEAs and relevant financial institutions can cooperate with each other in order to freeze and confiscate suspected criminal assets. Thus, this Directive does grant institutions such as the LEAs and National Asset Recovery Offices[506] with the 'direct access to bank account information for the purposes of fighting serious crime'. This seeks to help

---

[496] Directive (EU) 2018/1673, recital 3.

[497] Ibid.

[498] Ibid.

[499] 'The Stockholm Programme – An open and secure Europe serving and protecting the citizens' (Council document 17024/09, adopted by the European Council on 10/11 December 2009).

[500] Justice and Home Affairs Council Conclusions on confiscation and asset recovery of June 2010 (Council document 7769/3/10).

[501] Directive 2014/42/EU, recital 16.

[502] Ibid.

[503] Ibid, recital 4.

[504] Ibid, Art 11.

[505] Directive (EU) 2019/1153 of the European Parliament and of the Council of 20 June 2019 laying down rules facilitating the use of financial and other information for the prevention, detection, investigation or prosecution of certain criminal offences, and repealing Council Decision 2000/642/JHA PE/64/2019/REV/1 [2019] OJ L 186/122.

[506] For details about the current EU regime designed for Asset Recovery offices, see Council Decision 2007/845/JHA of 6 December 2007 concerning cooperation between Asset Recovery Offices of the Member States in the field of tracing and identification of proceeds from, or other property related to, crime, [2007] OJ L 332/103.

in improving the cooperation between LEAs and FIUs while facilitating information exchange between the FIUs as well.[507]

The Commission implementation reports on Framework Decisions 2003/577/JHA, 2005/212/JHA and 2006/783/JHA had shown that the regimes that then existed to ensure extended confiscation and mutual recognition of freezing and confiscation orders were not completely effective. A key hindrance that was highlighted by these reports had to do with the differences between EU Member States with respect to their relevant laws on this matter.[508] Although the liberty and discretion available to EU Member States to establish their own additional measures do present a source for differences and tensions between laws of EU Member States, the minimum rules advocated for in Directive 2014/42/EU, if they were to be fully implemented and enforced, would have mitigated this problem, to a great extent.

However, even with the reinforcement of these minimum rules in subsequent legal instruments such as Directive (EU) 2018/1673, it is intriguing to note that the position regarding the challenges posed by these differences in laws on freezing and confiscating of assets have not greatly shifted. In effect, the challenge found in implementation reports on Framework Decisions 2003/577/JHA, 2005/212/JHA and 2006/783/JHA does appear to linger on. It needs to be countered as a priority.

It suffices to note that at the EU level, substantial minimum measures to freeze and confiscate criminal assets that align with the TGP4 have been legislatively provided and substantively operationalised in most Member States of the EU. Thus, even though, in practice, some Member States of EU have not yet fully implemented certain provisions in the foregoing legal instruments, in theory, as the legal order in this field has shown, EU criminal law has demonstrably adopted significant measures that should enable competent authorities to freeze and confiscate proceeds of crime. When effectively deployed, these instruments, to some extent, will eliminate 'the financial incentives which drive crime'.[509]

In a recent EU report on recovery and confiscation of assets,[510] a number of important points were highlighted as follows:

- The need for swift access by Asset Recovery Offices to a minimum set of data, held in national registries and databases.[511]

- The need to exchange information via SIENA[512] to enable the swift and secure communication of crime-related information.[513]

---

[507] European Commission, 'Confiscation & asset recovery', https://ec.europa.eu/home-affairs/what-we-do/policies/organized-crime-and-human-trafficking/confiscation-and-asset-recovery_en, accessed 16 June 2020.

[508] Directive 2014/42/EU, recital 8.

[509] Directive (EU) 2018/1673, recital 16.

[510] European Commission, 'Report from the commission to the European Parliament and the Council: Asset recovery and confiscation: Ensuring that crime does not pay' (COM (2020) 217 final, 2 June 2020), https://ec.europa.eu/home-affairs/sites/homeaffairs/files/what-we-do/policies/european-agenda-security/20200602_com-2020-217-commission-report_en.pdf, accessed 16 June 2020.

[511] Ibid.

[512] Secure Information Exchange Network Application (SIENA), which ensures 'the secure exchange of sensitive and restricted information' in the EU.

[513] European Commission, 'Report from the commission to the European Parliament and the Council: Asset recovery and confiscation: Ensuring that crime does not pay' (COM (2020) 217 final, 2 June 2020).

- The need to enhance the Asset Recovery Offices' powers (for example, urgent freezing powers and the ability to trace assets following a final criminal conviction).[514]
- The need to set fixed and strict time limits within which an Asset Recovery Office must respond to a request by a counterpart.[515]

These imperatives have the active potential to 'further strengthen the capacity of the Asset Recovery Offices to trace and identify criminal assets'[516] in the EU. The EU has demonstrably utilised and escalated, in its legal framework, the principle to grant needed power to relevant authorities to freeze/seize and confiscate assets. However, some EU Member States are still struggling to fully translate the EU legal instruments into more concrete deliverables.[517] Another issue that often comes up in some of these jurisdictions is not related to adequacy or efficacy of powers but to the concerns pertaining to fundamental rights of suspected and convicted tax criminals and/or their family members and dependants.

One would have, in fact, noticed that TGP1 to TGP4 involve processes that require reasonable care by authorities in order not to trample upon the fundamental rights of suspected tax criminals. The next TGP takes a look at the extent to which the TGPs above and the other TGPs (TGP6 to TGP10) can serve as a harvesting forum for engendering fundamental rights in tax crime measures in the EU.

TGP5: Protection of Taxpayers' Rights

Protection of human dignity at all material times is a necessary duty for those that have been mandated to exercise regulatory authority over the conduct or behaviour of the people. Everyone, no matter who they are and what they have done or what they have not done, is entitled to be guaranteed fundamental rights. The rights of a suspected tax criminal, therefore, need to be protected. TGP5 underscores that anyone that is 'subject to a criminal tax investigation should be able to rely on certain procedural and fundamental rights, which are afforded to everyone suspected or accused of a criminal act, including tax crimes'.[518]

TGP5 aims at protecting the rights of suspected tax offenders. Thus, taxpayers that have been 'suspected or accused of committing a tax crime must be able to rely on basic procedural and fundamental rights'[519] in contesting the claims or accusations by authorities. This imperative is protected, at least in theory, by the constructional and legislative arrangements of all the EU Member States and all OECD countries. The courts in these

---

[514] Ibid.
[515] Ibid.
[516] Ibid.
[517] As of June 2020, Bulgaria, Luxembourg and Romania were yet to implement Directive 2014/42. European Commission, Report from the Commission to the European Parliament and the Council – Asset recovery and confiscation: Ensuring that crime does not pay, 02.06.2020, COM(2020) 217 final, 5, https://ec.europa.eu/home-affairs/sites/homeaffairs/files/what-we-do/policies/european-agenda-security/20200602_com-2020-217-commission-report_en.pdf, accessed 24 July 2020.
[518] OECD, *Fighting Tax Crime* 68.
[519] Ibid, 67.

jurisdictions also consistently favour the protection and promotion of this principle. At the same time, there are several respected international legal instruments that safeguard and promote the protection of fundamental and procedural rights of all.

For instance, the United Nations' Universal Declaration of Human Rights (UDHR) 1948, International Covenant on Civil and Political Rights 1966 (ICCPR) and International Covenant on Economic, Social and Cultural Rights 1966 (ICESCR) establish fundamental human rights which command universal respect especially with regards to the UDHR from which subsequent international human rights instruments were drawn. The rights therein are 'to be universally protected'.[520]

Another set of examples which safeguard and promote these rights can be found in the European Convention on Human Rights 1950 (ECHR), Charter of the Fundamental Rights of the European Union 2012,[521] and the African Charter on Human and Peoples' Rights 1981 (ACHPR), and the Principles and Guidelines on the Right to a Fair Trial and Legal Assistance in Africa 2003.

Key Fundamental Rights

These instruments provide for the protection of several rights. Nine fundamental rights have particularly been promoted by TGP5. These are the right to:

1. presumption of innocence;
2. be advised of suspected taxpayers' rights;
3. be advised of the particulars of what taxpayers are accused of;
4. remain silent;
5. access and consult a lawyer and entitlement to free legal advice;
6. interpretation and translation;
7. access documents and case material (also referred to as right to full disclosure);
8. a speedy trial;
9. protection from *ne bis in idem* (ie, double jeopardy).[522]

These and related rights can be relied upon by the suspected or accused tax offender to safeguard their human dignity. They are rights that, for TGP5, 'may be given effect in domestic law by being enshrined in a jurisdiction's constitution or bill of rights, or within criminal procedure law'.[523] In fact, in the most part, these rights find expression in domestic legal instruments except that enforcement has been a challenge for some jurisdictions.[524]

---

[520] Ibid, 68.

[521] Charter of Fundamental Rights of the European Union [2012] OJ C 326/391.

[522] OECD, *Fighting Tax Crime* 68.

[523] Ibid.

[524] There is wealth of literature containing rigorous critques and comparative analysis of enforcement of fundamental human rights across the globe. See eg, A Medecigo, *Rule of Law and Fundamental Rights: Critical Comparative Analysis of Constitutional Review in the United States, Germany and Mexico* (Springer, 2016) and F Fabbrini, *Fundamental rights in Europe: Challenges and transformations in comparative perspective* (Oxford University Press, 2014).

It is imperative that criminal tax investigation agencies are aware of these fundamental rights. This is because if they fail to be abreast of these rights, it may have an adverse effect on an investigation and prosecution of a tax crime, for example, where evidence obtained becomes inadmissible or the accused is acquitted if the individual's rights were violated.[525]

As the ecosystem of the criminal measures to counter tax offences can be vulnerable to abuse of rights of suspects, TGP5 advocates that:

> [In situations] where a criminal investigation may have originated as an ordinary civil examination or audit procedure, jurisdictions should have safeguards to ensure that the rights of an accused are protected when there is a change from administrative to criminal law. For example, in a civil examination, the taxpayer has an obligation to provide information to the tax administration; however, in a criminal investigation, the suspect may have the right to remain silent.[526]

The significance of this conflict of jurisdictions between civil and criminal law to tax administrations is phenomenal. This is as a result of the fact that tax administrations that direct and conduct investigations are confronted with both administrative/civil and criminal issues on which appropriate decisions would have to be made about which line of action to take. Indeed, there is a blurry line between a civil tax matter and a criminal tax matter, in cases where the law does not clearly define conduct and respective roles of agencies. This correspondingly 'can require judgement and may be unclear'.[527]

In practice, it appears that in most jurisdictions 'a civil investigation becomes a criminal investigation when there is a reasonable suspicion that a crime had been committed, or where the facts indicate that a crime may have been committed'. There are, however, other jurisdictions that apply 'an objective marker to determine when a civil matter becomes a criminal investigation, and which is based on a threshold of the amount of tax evaded'.[528] While some jurisdictions concurrently conduct civil and criminal investigations, others do not see it as the right course of action.

There are fertile grounds for double jeopardy if reasonable care is not taken by authorities. The OECD survey, however, interestingly had many of the respondents stating that 'there are safeguards to ensure that the rights of an accused are protected when there is a parallel civil and criminal investigation, such as ensuring the investigations are run independently'.[529] This is appealing to hear but conscious efforts must always be made to tread cautiously when applying both civil and criminal measures at the same time.

Benchmarking TGP5 – Protection of Fundamental Rights

An observation from the PROTAX report provides a useful insight into the outlook of the issue from the perspective of the courts:

> The European Court of Human Rights (ECtHR) and the Court of Justice of the European Union (CJEU) have elaborated an 'autonomous' notion of criminal offence. Based on that

---

[525] OECD, *Fighting Tax Crime* 68.
[526] Ibid, 68.
[527] Ibid, 69.
[528] Ibid.
[529] Ibid.

concept, an administrative offence may be considered criminal under human rights laws. Administrative and civil offences for tax violations may fall within the broader definition of 'crime' elaborated by [the jurisprudence of European courts]. Therefore, the principles of legality, fair trial, *ne bis in idem* and proportionality envisaged by the Charter of the Fundamental Rights of the European Union also apply to administrative sanctions.[530]

This notion is drawn from the position of the CJEU in *Åklagaren v Åkerberg Fransson* that the relevant criteria for assessing whether tax penalties are criminal in nature are categorised into three:

- the legal classification of the offence under national law;
- the very nature of the offence; and
- the nature and degree of severity of the penalty that the person concerned is liable to incur.[531]

EU Member States have substantive laws that are generally in line with international and regional human rights instruments that require investigators and LEAs to respect the basic procedural and fundamental rights of citizens. As exemplified above, the Charter of Fundamental Rights of the EU 2000[532] and the European Convention of Human Rights 1950 guarantee the respect of fundamental human rights of EU citizens. These human rights instruments have more protective provisions than the rights mentioned in the TGP5. For instance, right to privacy is a guaranteed provision in ECHR Article 8, which is hard to find in the TGPs. However, as highlighted by a number of scholars, tax laws in the EU do not always and substantially integrate such tenets to sufficiently protect the rights of suspected tax law offenders.[533]

For example, it is an outstanding issue regarding the double jeopardy sanctioning regime in some Member States of the EU where offenders are susceptible to both administrative and criminal sanctions, at the same time, with unrealistic optimism to secure taxpayers' rights in such a process. This, obviously, is a challenge and a risk for the protection of fundamental rights even though they are clearly provided for by the ECHRs.

It is worth noting that although the preamble of DAC 1[534] imposes on Member States of EU to do more to ensure protection of fundamental rights and that recital 19 of DAC 1 actually asserts that the directive respects fundamental rights, it is difficult to fully appreciate how really human rights such as the right to privacy can be adequately and reasonably protected in the era of automatic exchange of information to as many agencies and countries as possible.[535] Other EU legal instruments significantly provide

---

[530] Rasmouki and others, 'D2.3 Approaches to tax crimes' 1.

[531] C-617/10, *Åklagaren v Åkerberg Fransson* [EUCJ] [GC], 26 February 2013, para 35.

[532] Charter of Fundamental Rights of the EU, [18 December 2000]; Charter of Fundamental Rights of the European Union, [2012] OJ C 326/391.

[533] V Mitsilegas and N Vavoula, 'The Evolving EU Anti-Money Laundering Regime: Challenges for Fundamental Rights and the Rule of Law' (2016) 23(2) *MJ* 261; X Oberson, *International exchange of information in tax matters: towards global transparency* (Edward Elgar Publishing, 2015); C Endresen, 'Taxation and the European Convention for the Protection of Human Rights: Substantive Issues' ((2017) 45 (8/9) *Intertax* 508.

[534] Directive on Administrative Cooperation (DAC) (2011/16/EU).

[535] Oberson, *International exchange of information.*

support for the protection of taxpayers' rights. For instance, Directive (EU) 2017/1371 regarding fraud against EU financial interest, provides that:

> The intended dissuasive effect of the application of criminal law sanctions requires particular caution with regard to fundamental rights. This Directive respects fundamental rights and observes the principles recognised in particular by the Charter of Fundamental Rights of the European Union (the 'Charter').[536]

These rights include:

- liberty and security;
- the protection of personal data;
- the freedom to choose an occupation and right to engage in work;
- the freedom to conduct a business;
- property;
- an effective remedy and to a fair trial;
- the presumption of innocence and the right of defence;
- the principles of the legality and proportionality of criminal offences and sanctions; and
- the principle of *ne bis in idem*.[537]

The Directive commits EU Member States to fully respect and implement the above rights and principles.[538] This recital is quite telling, as it particularises the rights that must be respected by the EU Member States.

In the same vein, Directive (EU) 2018/1673, particularly recital 21 and Article 14 thereof, give recognition and reporting mechanism on enforcement impacts of the sixth AMLD. Article 8 of Directive 2014/42/EU also provides safeguards for protection of fundamental rights such as fair trial, right to property and right to a lawyer.[539] However, more sophisticated as they continue to become, tax criminals can easily exploit the guarantees granted to them by these legal instruments. During the PROTAX focus groups, one of the issues raised was how suspected tax criminals use the human rights protections to frustrate tax enforcement (investigation and prosecution). Statute of limitations or time limitations for criminal cases can be indicated as one of these strategies which criminals exploit.[540] This, therefore, requires a delicate balancing act within the limits of reasonableness to both protect the rights of suspected taxpayers and the duty to hold tax offenders accountable.

The foregoing legal instruments of the EU present clear picture that the tenets that undergird the TGP5 are effectively provided, and even more, by the numerous human rights provisions in the EU legal framework, some of which have not been articulated in this book because they are basically reinforcing provisions of the ones articulated here. It stands to reason, therefore, that although sufficient protection may not be given

---

[536] Directive (EU) 2017/1371, recital 28.
[537] Ibid.
[538] Ibid.
[539] Directive 2014/42/EU, Art 8.
[540] Rasmouki and others, 'D2.3 Approaches to tax crimes' 1.

to suspects of tax crimes in the EU, their rights are reasonably protected according to, amongst others, the dictates of the sixth AMLD and recitals 16, 24, 31, 33, 38, 39, and 40, as well as Articles 6 and 8 of Directive 2014/42/EU. There are also substantive *locus standi* rights in the EU which enable natural and legal persons to invoke their rights against the state (and state agencies, such LEAs).[541]

Conclusion

This chapter has examined five TGPs (namely: criminalisation of tax offences, tax offence as predicate offence for money laundering, investigative powers for authorities, power to freeze/seize and confiscate assets, and protection of suspects' rights) in relation to EU tax crime measures and the compatibilities thereof. The five TGPs have been evaluated in relation to EU tax crime measures such as such as Directive (EU) 2017/1371, Directive 2014/42/EU, Directive (EU) 2018/1673, Directive (EU) 2018/843, and Directive (EU) 2015/849.

It is evident that legal systems across the world differ – some marginally and others substantially. The differences in legal systems of jurisdictions tend to reflect and interact 'with the particular culture, policy and legislative environment' of those jurisdictions. However, the OECD has noted that, regardless of the particularities of any legal framework, tax enforcement in that regime would be most effective if countries collectively ensure that their respective legal regimes satisfy the following requirements: 'The law clearly defines the tax offences that are criminalised; A criminal sanction applies if the offence is proven; More serious offences are punishable by more serious criminal sanctions; and Criminal sanctions are applied in practice.'[542] These were the elements that dictated the pace for TGP1.

Although EU Directive (EU) 2017/1371 provides clear definitions of and sanctions for VAT offences against the Union, the overall clarity about the definition of tax offences (and the relevant thresholds for these offences) across EU Member States are varied. With Directive (EU) 2017/1371, a number of points would stand out in respect of criminalisation of tax offences in the EU legal framework, including:

- Tax offences are criminalised and defined (albeit not quite clearly or in harmony).
- The scope of the Directive is limited to the most serious forms of VAT fraud, particularly 'VAT fraud through missing traders, and VAT fraud committed within a criminal organisation, which create "serious" threats to the common VAT system and thus to the Union budget'.[543]
- The threshold for determining seriousness of VAT fraud (€10,000,000) is too high.

---

[541] European Court of Human Rights, Practical Guide on Admissibility Criteria, 31 August 2019, www.echr.coe.int/Documents/Admissibility_guide_ENG.pdf; and European Parliament, DG for Internal Policies, Citizens' Rights and Constitutional Affairs, Standing up for your rights – *Locus Standi*, 2012, www.europarl.europa.eu/RegData/etudes/etudes/join/2012/462478/IPOL-JURI_ET(2012)462478_EN.pdf, accessed 24 July 2020.

[542] OECD, *Fighting Tax Crime* 14.

[543] M Lamensch and E Ceci, 'VAT fraud: Economic impact, challenges and policy issues' (Study requested by the TAX3 Committee, PE 626.076, October 2018) 32; Directive (EU) 2017/1371.

- Fraud that is committed within a criminal organisation pursuant to Framework Decision 2008/841/JHA117 is regarded as an aggravating circumstance.[544]
- Legal and natural persons are both held liable.[545]

At the heart of criminalisation of tax offences is fraud. Tax fraud is an intentional and wilful falsification of information by a person or persons and/or failing to submit/report to tax authorities the information regarding tax liability, with the aim of limiting or reducing their tax liability. Simply put, it is a conduct in which someone constructs a process to deceive the state (therefore the public at large) so as to reduce or eliminate the payment of a given tax with the aim of unfair and illicit gain. Fiscalis notes that tax fraud can also be seen as 'criminal attacks aimed at fraudulently generating repayments of tax'.[546] Tax evasion often entails intentional under-declaration of taxable income or transactions. However, tax evasion also captures non-declaration of taxable income or transactions.[547]

The sixth AMLD of the EU has enhanced the level of stringent measures reasonable enough to deter tax crimes and for which all Member States must adopt. Article 8 of the sixth AMLD deals with liability of legal persons and essentially provides that legal persons must be sanctioned effectively, proportionately and dissuasively with criminal and non-criminal penalties. Additionally, it gives jurisdiction to judges to impose any additional punitive measures they deem fit, including fines; excluding tax offenders from having entitlement and access to public services support and funding, including access to tender procedures; permanently banning tax offenders from engaging in commercial business; judicially winding up the company and to completely shut down businesses that have been employed by the taxpayer to commit the tax offence.[548]

Article 5 of the sixth AMLD also provides for effective, dissuasive and proportionate criminal penalties on offences under Articles 3 and 4 thereof. Penalties range from 'a maximum term of imprisonment of at least four years' to 'where necessary ... additional sanctions or measures'. These sanctions for legal and natural persons appear extensive and exacting or substantially punitive since, on one hand, a business entity that is found culpable of tax crimes can be made to suffer severe consequences, including closure of the company. And on the other hand, natural persons now attract a minimum of four years' imprisonment, in addition to other sanctions deemed fit. These are significant improvements in the sanctioning regime.[549]

The maximum sanctions provided for natural persons in breach of Directive (EU) 2017/1371 is at least four years' imprisonment. Cases in the directive that qualify for this sanction 'should include at least those involving considerable damage done or advantage gained whereby the damage or advantage should be presumed to be considerable

---

[544] Directive (EU) 2017/1371, Art 8.
[545] Lamensch and Ceci, 'VAT fraud' 32; Directive (EU) 2017/1371.
[546] Fiscalis Tax Gap Project Group (FPG/041), 'The Concept of Tax Gaps Report on VAT Gap Estimations' (European Commission, March 2016), https://ec.europa.eu/taxation_customs/sites/taxation/files/docs/body/tgpg_report_en.pdf, 20 March 2020.
[547] Ibid.
[548] Directive (EU) 2018/1673 of the European Parliament and of the Council of 23 October 2018 on combating money laundering by criminal law, PE/30/2018/REV/1 [2018] OJ L 284/22.
[549] Ibid.

when it involves more than EUR 100 000'.[55C] The damage or advantage should have resulted 'from the criminal offences referred to in points (a), (b) and (c) of Article 3(2) and in Article 4' to qualify for the test of considerable damage. However, 'the damage or advantage resulting from the criminal offences referred to in point (d) of Article 3(2)[551] and subject to Article 2(2)[552] shall always be presumed to be considerable'.[553]

The defining characteristics of getting to effectively and efficiently investigate, prosecute and convict tax criminals are all the more still enmeshed in unchartered trajectories. This observation could not be more right, especially so, because neither the criminal nor the administrative legal instruments, presently in force, have effectively addressed the tax loopholes.

Having analysed the TGP1 to TGP5, which are essentially the substantive principles of the TGPs, the next set of TGPs to look at are labelled as structural/procedural principles.

---

[550] Directive (EU) 2017/1371, Art 7(3).

[551] Ibid, Art 3(2) provides: 'that in respect of revenue arising from VAT own resources, any act or omission committed in cross-border fraudulent schemes in relation to: (i) the use or presentation of false, incorrect or incomplete VAT-related statements or documents, which has as an effect the diminution of the resources of the Union budget; (ii) non-disclosure of VAT-related information in violation of a specific obligation, with the same effect; or (iii) the presentation of correct VAT-related statements for the purposes of fraudulently disguising the non-payment or wrongful creation of rights to VAT refunds.'

[552] Ibid, Art 2(2) states that: 'In respect of revenue arising from VAT own resources, this Directive shall apply only in cases of serious offences against the common VAT system. For the purposes of this Directive, offences against the common VAT system shall be considered to be serious where the intentional acts or omissions defined in point (d) of Article 3(2) are connected with the territory of two or more Member States of the Union and involve a total damage of at least EUR 10 000 000.'

[553] Ibid, Art 7(3).

4

Structural/Procedural Principles

Introduction

This chapter continues with the analysis of the TGPs in relation to applicable EU tax measures. It takes a critical look at the TGPs which are structurally and procedurally inclined. Five of the TGPs are considered in the following sections.

TGP6: Devising Effective Strategy for Countering Tax Crimes

Strategy characterises a unique approach that presents clear pathways and activities through which defined needs of a person or group of persons (legal or natural) and/or sovereign states and international organisations (as the case is here) can be satisfied or met. In relation to tax crimes, TGP6 describes an overall strategy as 'a document which states the objective of the tax authorities, identifies the relevant risks of non-compliance with the tax law, and sets out the plan for addressing those risks'.[1]

Strategy is one of the most important instruments for countering tax crimes. For strategy to adequately and satisfactorily serve the needs of persons or organisations, it needs to be effective. In order to ensure that tax crimes are most effectively countered, tax authorities are required not only to devise 'a range of strategies for encouraging compliance, to respond to the different attitudes of taxpayers to complying with their obligations',[2] but also should ensure that these strategies are effective.

TGP6 essentially avers that 'to ensure the effectiveness of the law on tax crimes, jurisdictions should have a strategy for addressing tax crimes. The strategy should be regularly reviewed and monitored'.[3]

Strategies in enacting tax criminal laws and that of enforcing these laws must both be effective. In particular, for effective enforcement of tax criminal laws, in practice, it is important that jurisdictions devise 'a coherent strategy for enforcing the law'.[4] The overall strategy should be able to have acceptance or 'buy-in from senior officials' that are responsible for implementing this strategy.

---

[1] OECD, *Fighting Tax Crime: The Ten Global Principles* (OECD Publishing, 2017) 20.
[2] Ibid, 14.
[3] Ibid, 19.
[4] Ibid. 20.

Compliance Behaviour and Measures

TGP6 posits that, in general terms, every jurisdiction is required to have an overall tax compliance strategy (ideally designed in light of its specific tax ecosystem needs) which should encapsulate 'the full range of compliance'.[5] This includes:

- encouraging voluntary compliance – efforts should be made to ensure that taxpayers would be willing to voluntarily pay their tax debts timeously or report themselves to settle their tax debts or related liabilities which have been in default;

- addressing inadvertent or unintentional non-compliance with tax laws – providing mechanisms that frontally tackle unintentional non-compliance and stimulate cooperation with taxpayers involved in unintentional non-compliance with the tax laws or related laws;

- confronting tax avoidance – effectively tackling legal but unacceptable schemes to dodge the payment of taxes;

- countering tax evasion and serious crime – effectively tackling criminal schemes to circumvent the obligation to pay taxes.[6]

Based on the components of the overall compliance strategy above, there are a range of behaviours and measures which can be used by every jurisdiction to stimulate compliance by taxpayers. Table 20 exemplifies these behaviours and measures to enhance compliance.

Table 20 Behaviours and Measures for Enhancing Compliance with Tax Law[7]

	Tax issue	*Approach to counter fraud*	*Examples of counter measures*
Anti-fraud measures	*Tax fraud (serious organised crime)*	*Combatting and preventing fraud*	▪ *Tax investigation audits* ▪ *Prosecution and penalties* ▪ *Elimination from legal financial sectors* ▪ *Cooperation with the judiciary and LEAs* ▪ *Threat analysis* ▪ *Asset recovery* ▪ *Ensuring transparency*
	Tax evasion (shadow economy, income underreporting, illegal employment	*Controls and sanctions*	▪ *Preventive controls,* ▪ *Tax investigations* ▪ *Tax audits (risk analysis)* ▪ *Prosecution and penalties* ▪ *Cooperation between LEAs and partners* ▪ *Tax collection* ▪ *Asset recovery*

(continued)

[5] Ibid.
[6] Ibid.
[7] Ibid.

Table 20 *(Continued)*

	Tax issue	Approach to counter fraud	Examples of counter measures
	Tax avoidance (aggressive tax planning, avoidance models)	Monitoring and cooperation	▪ Risk management ▪ Office and field staff controls ▪ Official first visits ▪ Tax collection ▪ Information exchange
Other counter fraud mechanisms	Tax compliance (voluntary disclosure, fulfilment of tax obligations)	Support and simplification	▪ Information and forms ▪ Cooperation with interest groups ▪ Horizontal monitoring ▪ Advance rulings ▪ Application of technology

The behaviours and measures in Table 20 are not exhaustive, as the range of measures to stimulate compliance with tax laws can be very wide due to the evolving and complicated nature of the behaviours of taxpayers and their criminal machinations.

Threat Assessment

One of the elements that enable the formulation of a most effective strategy is to first conduct 'a threat assessment' in order to identify the risks, gaps and threats. This is an essential exercise because when relevant gaps and threats are known, it will ensure that the response can be tailored, prioritised and targeted to address those threats. There should not be many risks that spring surprises on LEAs without prior detection. If this happens, it can easily pose a danger to resources and effectiveness in counter-measures. However, threat assessment should not be done anyhow because this can also pose significant danger to the available resources.

It is recognised that no jurisdiction or tax authority has infinite resources. Resources 'must be allocated efficiently on the basis of priorities'. In this regard, tax authorities should be able to establish a process that identifies the threats 'posed to the enforcement of the tax laws, and how serious these are'. The assessment of threats should ideally include 'current, emerging and future risks'[8] ideally based on or against a set of objective benchmarks with the involvement of all key stakeholders as well as external qualified stakeholders who would have no conflict of interest in such an assessment. In conducting a threat assessment, a jurisdiction should be able to identify 'the specific risks of tax crimes' prevailing in that jurisdiction. In doing so, consideration should be given to:

- the particular context or environment (cultural, political, legal, economic and technological); and

---

[8] Ibid.

- draw on the insights of other agencies responsible for fighting financial crimes (if there is the need to do so).

In order to assess threats effectively, it is important to ensure that the threats are prioritised based on the likelihood that they will occur and whether it portends a serious impact if such threats do occur.[9] Threat assessment results are important because they may help in the identification of specific needs, including:

- establishing a cross-agency task force to address a particular risk;
- launching a public awareness campaign;
- building technical capacity in a particular area;
- engaging with the private sector; or
- informing the need to make changes to the law.[10]

Identifying Key Elements of an Overall Strategy

Strategy is a broad concept and, therefore, designing it can take diverse forms. In recognition of this understanding, TGP6 provides an approach for preparing a strategy to counter tax crimes:

- Identification of risks – establish possible current, emerging and future risks.
- Assessment and prioritisation of risks – thus, considering which risks pose more danger and deserve critical attention.
- Monitoring of performance against plan – close observation that takes stock of progress towards achievement of objectives, activities and timelines in the overall plan.
- Evaluation of compliance outcomes – careful assessment of the objectives against the results or outcomes drawn from the compliance measures.
- Analysing compliance behaviour (causes and options for treatment) – critical review of how taxpayers behave towards tax measures including what induces particular compliance behaviours and how to address such behaviours.
- Determining treatment strategies – finding out the strategies that can be used to address the problem.
- Planning and implementation of strategies – deciding on clearly thought out plan or plans to implement the strategies.

Figure 14 adaptively illustrates the approach outlined above in the preparation of a strategy for countering tax crimes.[11]

---

[9] Ibid, 21.
[10] Ibid, 19.
[11] Ibid.

Figure 14 Key Elements for Preparing an Overall Strategy against Tax Crimes[12]

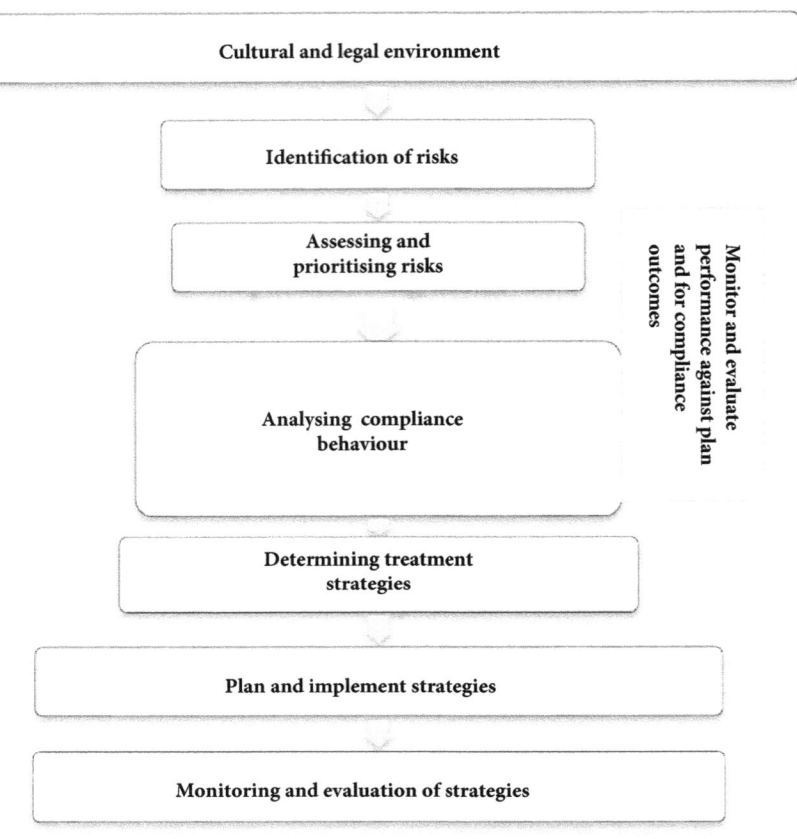

Having carried out the threat assessment and with this approach in mind, jurisdictions can then prepare an effective strategy. This would entail key elements such as:

- Defining the objectives/performance indicators/outputs. These could focus on achieving prevention, detection and enforcement goals.

- Articulating the resources available to address these risks. This includes legal powers, funding, personnel, expertise, stakeholders in other government agencies, sources of intelligence, investigation and enforcement tools including domestic and international cooperation.

- Identifying the challenges for the tax authority in being able to address the risks and how those challenges can be mitigated.

- Devising an operational plan for achieving the objectives for the identified risks. This is conducted through the usage of the available resources and tools and including criminal law enforcement.

---

[12] Ibid.

- Preparing a communications strategy. This is significant because it will shape public perceptions and behaviour. It can also help in educating the public, and building public confidence in the fair enforcement of tax laws.
- A plan for periodically reviewing performance and measuring the effectiveness and currency of the compliance strategy.

The above, as presented by TGP6, thus involves assessment of strategic objectives, risks, resources, and plan of action to communication, and monitoring/evaluation.

This process has to be participatory. In fact, the importance of participatory and integrated strategy in countering tax crimes cannot be overemphasised. Relevant stakeholders, including policy makers, investigators, enforcement and prosecution officials and other agencies such as AML authorities, are supposed to be widely consulted. The consultative exercise should be carried out in accord with legal system, policy and legislative environment and general structure of law enforcement of every jurisdiction. It is particularly the case that serious tax crimes likely raise other matters of criminal law including money laundering and corruption. This signifies the need for every jurisdiction to include tax crimes in an overall serious crime strategy, or a strategy specifically for addressing financial crimes.

Cases in point that have been illustrated to support these data points include Finland which has formulated a national strategy for countering the shadow economy and economic crime; Austria, which has formulated a specific Tax and Customs Compliance strategy [along with] annual Internal Security Strategies with broad focus on economic crime and money laundering; and the United Kingdom where the tax authority (HMRC) contributes to the National Strategic Assessment for Serious and Organised Crime. An OECD survey found that many jurisdictions prepare their strategies in coordination with other agencies, such as anti-corruption, economic crime units, police, the prosecutor, financial intelligence unit, customs, securities regulators and the ministry of justice. Thus, they utilise the principle of inter-agency domestic cooperation, as established in TGP9 below.

Interdisciplinary cooperation in strategy formulation and implementation is as important as inter-agency collaboration. It is, thus, imperative that tax crime strategies include a mechanism for criminal and non-criminal tax officials to share expertise, processes and intelligence. Doing this is critical because there is supposed to be a symbiotic relationship between officials in charge of criminal and non-criminal tax matters. Turksen and Abukari note that the difference between criminal and non-criminal jurisdictions of tax offences can be blurry at times.[13] Therefore, the functions to counter these offences can be interconnected. An instance can be associated with a scenario where:

> [T]he non-criminal function will have relevant intelligence for investigating tax crimes, both on specific cases as well as general trends. Likewise, the criminal function will also have information relevant for civil tax compliance, including on cases where it was not possible to

---

[13] U Turksen and A Abukari, 'OECD's global principles and EU's tax crime measures' [2020] *Journal of Financial Crime*, www.emerald.com/insight/content/doi/10.1108/JFC-09-2019-0118/full/html, accessed 26 June 2020.

pursue a criminal conviction but a civil audit may be appropriate, or to inform of a criminal conviction.[14]

The underlying imperative set out above necessitates strategic coordination between the criminal and non-criminal tax officials, as it will contribute to ensuring a coherent use of resources, efficient prioritisation of cases and avoidance of duplication of efforts by both the tax administration and criminal law enforcement officials. At the same time, consultation exercises (in policy and regulatory-related aspects in particular) with the public or key sectors would enhance societal ownership and acceptance thus can contribute not only to transparency and accountability but also to better tax compliance overall. Public participation and consultation will also serve as a source of deterrence, with the knowledge of the public that there is effective cooperation between the criminal and non-criminal functions across the society. Perception of fairness for the compliant taxpayer will be enhanced. In rolling out these cooperative mechanisms, however, consideration must be given to fundamental human rights of accused persons especially when it concerns criminal matters.

In respect of the kind of interdisciplinary cooperation as established above, the OECD survey found that almost every jurisdiction that participated in the survey had a process for civil tax officials to refer suspicions of tax crimes to the relevant authority, and in many of these cases there was a legal obligation to do so. The features that were considered as being instrumental in ensuring effectiveness of the collaboration in strategy implementation were, among others, as follows:

- giving training to civil tax officials for them to identify indicators of a crime;
- putting in place a clearly identified and central contact point for sending referrals;
- the use of a standard form made it possible for all relevant data to be gathered for use by the criminal investigation authority; and
- holding meetings to generate relevant feedback between the civil and criminal investigators including during the process for deciding how to proceed with the individual referrals.

Strategic Principles

There have to be certain essential principles in every tax crime countering strategy. TGP6 noted the United Kingdom's 2013[15] Serious and Organised Crime Strategy as having such features.[16] This strategy focuses 'more broadly on serious crimes (including financial and organised crime)', rather than specifically on tax crimes. However, it does exemplify key elements to formulating an overall counter tax crime strategy.

---

[14] OECD, *Fighting Tax Crime* 25.

[15] As updated in 2018 up until April 2019. (Note that the principles in the 2013 version have not changed except that further details of rigour and approach were added) – see HM Government, *Serious and Organised Crime Strategy* (Collection, last updated 25 April 2019), www.gov.uk/government/collections/serious-and-organised-crime-strategy, accessed 17 April 2020.

[16] HM Government, *Serious and Organised Crime Strategy* (October 2013), https://assets.publishing.service.gov.uk/government/uploads/system/uploads/attachment_data/file/248645/Serious_and_Organised_Crime_Strategy.pdf, accessed 17 April 2020.

The strategy is undergirded by four key principles: Pursue (prosecuting and disrupting serious and organised crime), Prevent (preventing people from engaging in serious and organised crime), Protect (increasing protection against serious and organised crime), and Prepare (reducing the impact of serious and organised crime).[17] These are illustrated in Figure 15.

Figure 15 Principles Underpinning Strategy for Countering Tax Crimes

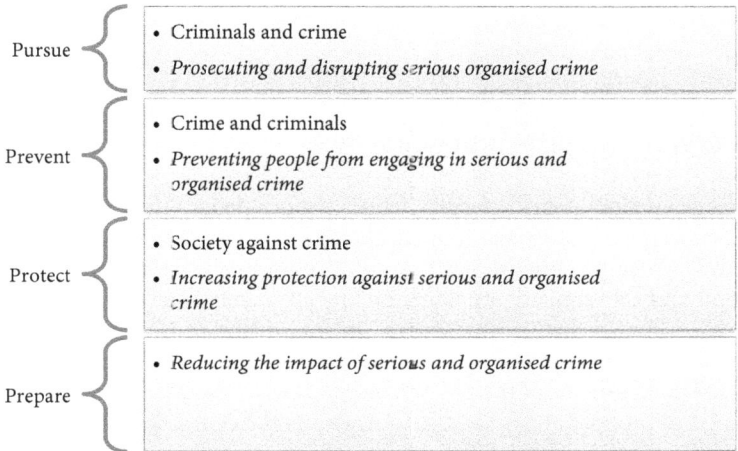

As usual, TGP6 leaves adoption of an overall strategy to the domestic legal dictates. Thus, the specific strategy to adopt is dependent upon the 'legal system, policy, legislative environment and general structure of law enforcement'[18] of each jurisdiction. As intimated under TGP3 concerning the need to grant adequate investigative powers to investigative agencies, a number of key levels[19] of strategies are used to counter tax crimes, including:

- prevention of offences;
- detection of offences;
- investigation of offences;
- prosecution of offences;
- conviction and sentencing of offenders;
- the recovery of the proceeds of crime from criminals.

All the above strategic levels do provide significant elements to be embedded in the strategies required to yield better results and outcomes. Jurisdictions should take into consideration the above strategic levels when formulating their counter tax crime strategies.

---

[17] Ibid.
[18] Ibid.
[19] OECD, *Effective Inter-Agency Co-operation in Fighting Tax Crimes and Other Financial Crimes*, 3rd edn (OECD Publishing, 2017) 11; OECD, *Fighting Tax Crime* 26.

Benchmarking the Strategic Framework – Effective Strategy for Countering Tax Crimes

By way of benchmarking the EU strategies, at the EU level, the legal framework has a number of provisions that require EU Member States to develop strategies to counter tax crimes in their various jurisdictions. At the same time, a major strategic framework for countering tax crimes in the EU straddles across a number of strategic pillars. It is worth underscoring that strategy and its development in the EU amount to a complex framework – if not an untidy one.

EU General Strategic Framework

The EU has general strategic priorities which are decided by the political institutions of the Union (eg, the European Council, the Council of Ministers and the European Parliament)[20] which are then drafted as a policy and/or legal documents by the EU Commission and subsequently implemented by all stakeholders concerned (including inevitably the Member States and citizens). In regards to taxation, tax compliance and enforcement, as established earlier, the competence to raise taxes and set tax rates rests with national governments of the EU. What the EU essentially does, in accordance with the principles of proportionality and subsidiarity, is the coordination of 'some national tax rules and tax rates, where differences might discourage people from buying and selling in other EU countries'. At the same time, the EU engages in the promotion of 'cooperation between its member countries for tackling tax avoidance and tax evasion, eliminating discrimination cases, and reducing compliance burdens'.[21]

In effect, tax collection and countering tax crimes 'are competences of EU Member States'. But because of the globalising nature of the world, the EU makes available 'a framework and offers instruments to effectively handle cross-border tax issues'.[22] How effective these instruments are can be a subject of debate. So, although it is the competence of the EU Member States, the development of a strategy to counter tax crimes mutually rests collectively with the EU and its Member States.

Generally, the strategy of the EU is developed and translated into policies by the European Commission.[23] The EU level strategy and policies are drawn down to sectoral and national level strategies and policies. For instance, the Lisbon Strategy[24] which presented a 10-year economic and social strategy seeking to reposition 'the EU within

---

[20] See eg, the European Council, 'A New Strategic Agenda for the EU 2019–2024', www.consilium.europa.eu/en/eu-strategic-agenda-2019-2024/,; and European Parliament, 'The Secretary General, Strategic Planning', 2016, www.europarl.europa.eu/RegData/publications/2016/0002/P8_PUB%282016%290002_XL.pdf, accessed 24 July 2020.

[21] European Commission, 'Policy: Taxation', https://ec.europa.eu/info/policies/taxation_en, accessed 18 April 2020.

[22] European Commission, 'Role of the EU: An action plan to combat tax fraud and evasion', https://ec.europa.eu/taxation_customs/fight-against-tax-fraud-tax-evasion/role-eu_en, accessed 14 March 2020.

[23] European Commission, 'Policy: Taxation'. The initiation of such strategic work may stem from the Council of Ministers, the European Parliament and/or the EU Commission itself.

[24] European Parliament, 'Lisbon European Council 23 and 24 March 2000: Presidency Conclusions', www.europarl.europa.eu/summits/lis1_en.htm, accessed 18 April 2020.

the changed context of worldwide competition and the paradigm shift to a knowledge economy and an innovation-based model of growth',[25] was an EU-level strategy with economic prominence which was supposed to be translated into national level strategic frameworks. However, the Lisbon Strategy was deemed to be a failure by some – which gained a lot of traction in news and speeches of some of the leaders of EU Member States.[26]

One of those who did not mince words on this failure was the then Prime Minister of Spain, Rodríguez Zapatero, who averred that the Lisbon Strategy failed partly because of its non-binding nature – thus, the next strategy of the EU, the Europe 2020 strategy, needed to be binding.[27] While it was argued that this failure was typically influenced by the lack of binding nature of the strategy, it sounds bewildering that the Europe 2020 Strategy which has succeeded the Lisbon Strategy has not been made effectively binding in order to avoid the pitfalls related to implementation deficits.[28]

The current general EU strategy is the Europe 2020 Strategy,[29] which was launched in 2010. This strategy is the agenda of the EU to ensure 'growth and jobs for the current decade'. Its objective puts emphasis on 'smart, sustainable and inclusive growth in order to improve Europe's competitiveness and productivity and underpin a sustainable social market economy'.[30] In order to realise this objective by 2020, key targets have been adopted by the EU in five areas: employment,[31] research and development,[32] climate change and energy,[33] education,[34] and poverty and social exclusion.[35] Targets at the EU level are 'translated into national targets[36] in each EU Member State, reflecting different situations and circumstances'.[37]

---

[25] A Bongardt and F Torres, 'Lisbon Strategy' in E Jones, A Menon and S Weatherill (eds), *The Oxford Handbook of the European Union* (Oxford University Press, 2012).

[26] C Wyplosz, 'The failure of the Lisbon strategy' (VOX, 12 January 2010), https://voxeu.org/article/failure-lisbon-strategy, accessed 18 April 2020; Charlemagne, 'Do Europeans want a dynamic economy?' *The Economist* (European politics, 8 January 2010), www.economist.com/charlemagne/2010/01/08/do-europeans-want-a-dynamic-economy, accessed 18 April 2020; see also DW, 'Spain calls for binding EU economic goals – and penalties' (*Business*, 8 January 2010), www.dw.com/en/spain-calls-for-binding-eu-economic-goals-and-penalties/a-5098907, accessed 18 April 2020.

[27] DW, 'Spain calls for binding EU economic goals'; see P Copeland and D Papadimitriou (eds), *The EU's Lisbon Strategy: evaluating success, understanding failure* (Palgrave Macmillan, 2012).

[28] Bongardt and Torres, 'Lisbon Strategy'.

[29] European Commission, 'Europe 2020: A strategy for smart, sustainable and inclusive growth' (Communication from the Commission, COM (2010) 2020 final, 3 March 2010), https://eur-lex.europa.eu/LexUriServ/LexUriServ.do?uri=COM:2010:2020:FIN:EN:PDF, accessed 18 April 2020.

[30] Eurostat, 'Europe 2020 – Overview', https://ec.europa.eu/eurostat/web/europe-2020-indicators#:~:text=The%20Europe%202020%20strategy%20is%20the%20EU%27s%20agenda,areas%3A%20Employment%3B%20Research%20%26%20Development%3B%20Climate%20change%20, accessed 19 April 2020.

[31] Headline target: '75% of the population aged 20 to 64 years to be employed'.

[32] Headline target: '3% of GDP to be invested in the R&D sector'.

[33] Headline targets: 'Greenhouse gas emissions to be reduced by 20% compared to 1990; share of renewable energy sources in final energy consumption to be increased to 20%; and energy efficiency to be improved by 20%'.

[34] Headline targets: 'Share of early school leavers to be reduced under 10%; and at least 40% of 30 to 34 years old to have completed tertiary or equivalent education'.

[35] Headline target: 'At least 20 million people fewer at risk of poverty or social exclusion'; see Eurostat, 'Europe 2020 – Overview'.

[36] See Eurostat, 'Europe 2020 Targets' (Updated 7 March 2017), https://ec.europa.eu/eurostat/documents/4411192/4411431/Europe_2020_Targets.pdf, accessed 19 April 2020.

[37] Eurostat, 'Europe 2020 – Overview'.

In essence, the Europe 2020 Strategy has 'three priorities (smart growth, sustainable growth, and inclusive growth); five headline targets,[38] and seven flagship initiatives'[39] including 'resource efficient Europe' which entails six political priorities for 2019–24.[40] The 2020 Strategy was drawn out based on the fact that the development and translation of EU Strategy into policies and initiatives are pillared on two main aspects from which the six priorities of the 'resource efficient Europe flagship' initiative are generated:

i.   Planning, implementing, and reporting – part of the key elements covered are:

   - Strategic planning – consisting of Commission work programme, strategic plans and management plans. The strategic plans are particularly germane in strategising tax crime measures. This was especially so with respect to the strategic plan 2016–20.[41]

   - The six EU priority areas – namely, a European Green Deal (striving to be the first climate-neutral continent); a Europe fit for the digital age (empowering people with a new generation of technologies); an economy that works for people (working for social fairness and prosperity); a stronger Europe in the world (Europe to strive for more by strengthening its unique brand of responsible global leadership); promoting a European way of life (building a Union of equality in which all have the same access to opportunities); and a new push for European democracy (nurturing, protecting and strengthening democracy).[42] Of these, an economy that works for people is particularly germane in strategising to counter tax crimes.

ii. Policies based on particular topics – three of the numerous policy areas covered are:

   - Economy, finance and the euro[43] (this has six policy areas[44] including EU economic situation[45] and EU economic governance[46] which feature tax issues).

[38] These are: 'the employment rate of the population aged 20–64 should increase to 75 per cent; three per cent of the EU's GDP should be invested in research and development; the "20/20/20" climate/energy targets should be met (including an increase to 30 per cent of emissions reduction if the conditions are right); the share of early school leavers should be under 10 per cent and at least 40 per cent of the younger generation should have a tertiary degree; 20m fewer people should be at risk of poverty'; see Department of Finance, 'The Europe 2020 strategy' (Gov.UK), www.finance-ni.gov.uk/articles/europe-2020-strategy#toc-1, accessed 18 April 2020.

[39] These initiatives are: 'Innovation union, Youth on the move, Digital agenda for Europe, Resource efficient Europe, An industrial policy, An agenda for new skills and jobs, European platform against poverty'; see Department of Finance, 'The Europe 2020 strategy' (Gov.UK), www.finance-ni.gov.uk/articles/europe-2020-strategy#toc-1, accessed 18 April 2020.

[40] See European Commission, '6 Commission priorities for 2019-24' (Priorities), https://ec.europa.eu/info/strategy/priorities-2019-2024, accessed 18 April 2020.

[41] European Commission, 'Strategic plan 2016-2020 – Economic and Financial Affairs' (Planning and Management Document), https://ec.europa.eu/info/publications/strategic-plan-2016-2020-economic-and-financial-affairs_en accessed 19 April 2020.

[42] European Commission, '6 Commission priorities for 2019-24'.

[43] European Commission, 'Economy, finance and the euro: Policies' (Policy), https://ec.europa.eu/info/strategy/economy-finance-and-euro_en, accessed 19 April 2020.

[44] The rest of the six policy areas are 'EU as a borrower, financial assistance to EU countries, structural reforms, and international economic issues'; see ibid.

[45] European Commission, 'EU Economic governance: monitoring, prevention, correction', https://ec.europa.eu/info/business-economy-euro/economic-and-fiscal-policy-coordination/eu-economic-governance-monitoring-prevention-correction_en, accessed 19 April 2020.

[46] Ibid.

- Fraud prevention (which provides two policies: 'Fighting fraud relating to EU expenditure, revenue or staff'; and 'Tax fraud and tax evasion' which leads to the taxation policy topic in the next point).[47]

- Taxation[48] (this features tax issues including providing a framework for EU Member States to counter cross-border 'tax fraud and tax evasion in a coordinated way').[49]

From the first aspect (i) above, the priority – an economy that works for people – has been highlighted because of its immediate relevance.[50] 'An economy that works for people' consists of five key policy areas:

- a deeper and fairer economic and monetary union;[51]

- jobs, growth and investment;[52]

- boosting jobs;[53]

- European semester;[54] and

- the internal market[55] of the EU.[56]

The last two policy areas are more germane in the context of analysis of strategy here. Indeed, the last two policy areas form a framework that can influence the first three policy areas for the 'economy that works for people' priority. The 'internal market' has key policies such as 'single market strategy,[57] capital markets union, labour mobility, and action plan for fairer corporate taxation.'[58] The 'single market strategy' and 'action plan for fairer corporate taxation'[59] are closer to issues concerning countering of tax crimes, with the latter particularly seeking to tackle tax abuse, ensure sustainable revenues and support a better business environment in the 'single market'. They are prominent

---

[47] European Commission, 'Fraud prevention: Policies' (Policy), https://ec.europa.eu/info/strategy/fraud-prevention_en, accessed 19 April 2020.

[48] European Commission, 'The fight against tax fraud and tax evasion'.

[49] European Commission, 'Taxation: Policies' (Policy), https://ec.europa.eu/info/policies/taxation_en, accessed 19 April 2020.

[50] European Commission, 'An economy that works for people: Working for social fairness and prosperity' (Priority), https://ec.europa.eu/info/strategy/priorities-2019-2024/economy-works-people_en, accessed 18 April 2020.

[51] European Commission, 'A deeper and fairer economic and monetary union: Policies areas', https://ec.europa.eu/info/strategy/priorities-2019-2024/economy-works-people/deeper-and-fairer-economic-and-monetary-union_en, accessed 19 April 2020.

[52] European Commission, 'Jobs, growth and investment: Policies', https://ec.europa.eu/info/strategy/priorities-2019-2024/economy-works-people/jobs-growth-and-investment_en, accessed 19 April 2020.

[53] European Commission, 'Boosting jobs', https //ec.europa.eu/info/strategy/priorities-2019-2024/economy-works-people/jobs-growth-and-investment/boosting-jobs_en, accessed 19 April 2020.

[54] See European Commission, 'The European Semester', https://ec.europa.eu/info/business-economy-euro/economic-and-fiscal-policy-coordination/eu-economic-governance-monitoring-prevention-correction/european-semester_en, accessed 24 April 2020.

[55] European Commission, 'Internal Market', https //ec.europa.eu/info/strategy/priorities-2019-2024/economy-works-people/internal-market_en, accessed 18 April 2020.

[56] Department of Finance, 'The Europe 2020 strategy'.

[57] See European Commission, 'The Single Market Strategy', https://ec.europa.eu/growth/single-market/strategy_en, accessed 18 April 2020; European Commission, 'Single Market initiatives overview', https://ec.europa.eu/commission/publications/single-market-initiatives-overview_en, accessed 18 April 2020.

[58] European Commission, 'Internal Market'.

[59] European Commission, 'Action Plan on Corporate Taxation' (June 2015), https://ec.europa.eu/taxation_customs/business/company-tax/action-plan-corporate-taxation_en, accessed 18 April 2020.

policies, in the context of this book, drawn from one of the seven flagship initiatives of the Europe 2020 Strategy. They involve countering of tax crimes in the EU.

In another breath, European Semester seeks to achieve four main goals for EU Member States:

- to secure sound public finances – thus, excessive government debt will be avoided;
- to prevent excessive macroeconomic imbalances in the EU;
- to embark on structural reforms, towards creation of more jobs and growth; and
- to take steps in 'boosting investment' across the EU.[60]

The European Semester, therefore, provides a framework for the assessment of compliance of EU Member States with the EU's economic rules, coordination of 'economic policies across EU countries in an annual cycle'[61] and addressing the EU's economic challenges.[62] The European Semester was introduced in 2010, which gives an opportunity to EU Member States to undertake discussions on 'their economic and budget plans and monitor progress at specific times throughout the year'. The United Kingdom will no longer participate in the European Semester analysis after 31 December 2020, in the light of 'the provision of the withdrawal agreement on the transition period' for Brexit.[63]

The EU Commission and Council as well as the EU Member States have roles to play in the Semester. Whereas the EU Commission carries out an annual detailed analysis of plans for budget, macroeconomic and structural reforms for each EU Member State, after which country-specific recommendations for the next 12–18 months are made for the governments of the EU Member States, the EU Council plays the role of endorsing and adopting the proposals made by the EU Commission. The EU governments are then charged with the responsibility to make 'policy decisions in response to the country-specific recommendations'[64] in accordance with a suitable course of action for each Member State.[65]

Thematic factsheets[66] are key features of implementing each Semester cycle. They are provided within the 'core policy areas of the European Semester'. The factsheets 'provide cross-country information on economic or social challenges, useful policies

---

[60] European Commission, 'The European Semester: why and how'.

[61] European Commission, 'An economy that works for people: Working for social fairness and prosperity' (Priority), https://ec.europa.eu/info/strategy/priorities-2019-2024/economy-works-people_en, accessed 18 April 2020.

[62] European Commission, 'The European Semester'.

[63] Ibid.

[64] See European Commission, 'EU country-specific recommendations', https://ec.europa.eu/info/business-economy-euro/economic-and-fiscal-policy-coordination/eu-economic-governance-monitoring-prevention-correction/european-semester/european-semester-timeline/eu-country-specific-recommendations_en, accessed 19 April 2020.

[65] European Commission, 'The European Semester: why and how'.

[66] European Commission, 'Thematic factsheets', https://ec.europa.eu/info/business-economy-euro/economic-and-fiscal-policy-coordination/eu-economic-governance-monitoring-prevention-correction/european-semester/thematic-factsheets_en, accessed 19 April 2020.

to address them, and examples of good practice'. Two of the core policy areas in which countering of tax crimes is featured are:

- fiscal stability – which features assessment on curbing aggressive tax planning; and
- public administration – which features assessment on curbing aggressive tax,[67] tackling corruption,[68] and taxation[69] generally.

With respect to policies based on particular topics as provided in (ii) above, particularly in taxation focusing on tax fraud and tax evasion, the policy of the EU is on the provision of a framework for EU Member States to counter 'cross-border tax fraud and tax evasion[70] in a coordinated way'.[71] A related EU policy on taxation is the policy on tax cooperation and control whereby the EU 'provides a legal framework for cooperation, information exchange and mutual assistance between EU tax authorities'[72] – the aim being to increase transparency and information access on some aspects of criminal matters in EU Member States.[73]

It should be noted that the policies and initiatives underpinning the Europe 2020 Strategy are interconnected – and at best convoluted. Therefore, although some are specifically directed towards tax crimes, the achievement of the other policies and initiatives will all the more support the achievement of the tax related efforts.

As it were, the current EU strategy is just about six months to the end of its life cycle. An assessment[74] by Eurostat provides that, since its launch, this strategy has made 'an important contribution to the socio-economic development' of the EU, including high record of employment, meeting of the 'greenhouse gas emissions ... and the higher education targets', as well as putting Europe 'on track with the renewable energy and energy efficiency targets'.[75] Recognisably, there are still significant outstanding issues

---

[67] See European Commission, 'European Semester Thematic Factsheet: Curbing Aggressive Tax Planning', https://ec.europa.eu/info/sites/info/files/file_import/european-semester_thematic-factsheet_curbing-agressive-tax-planning_en_0.pdf, accessed 19 April 2020.

[68] See European Commission, 'European Semester Thematic Factsheet: Fight against Corruption', https://ec.europa.eu/info/sites/info/files/file_import/european-semester_thematic-factsheet_fight-against-corruption_en_0.pdf, accessed 19 April 2020.

[69] See European Commission, 'European Semester Thematic Factsheet: Taxation', https://ec.europa.eu/info/sites/info/files/file_import/european-semester_thematic-factsheet_taxation_en_1.pdf, accessed 19 April 2020.

[70] The policy on tax fraud and tax evasion has been expatiated at: European Commission, 'The fight against tax fraud and tax evasion'.

[71] European Commission, 'Policy: Taxation', https://ec.europa.eu/info/policies/taxation_en, accessed 18 April 2020.

[72] The policy on tax cooperation and control has the following components: tax administrations and tax compliance; cooperation between tax administrations and businesses; enhanced administrative cooperation in the field of (direct) taxation; commission expert group on automatic exchange of financial account information; VAT and administrative co-operation; excise taxation; tax identification numbers (TIN); and tax recovery as well as the Fiscalis Programme; and Guidelines for a Model for a European Taxpayers' Code; see European Commission, 'Tax Co-operation and control', https://ec.europa.eu/taxation_customs/business/tax-cooperation-control_en, accessed 19 April 2020.

[73] European Commission, 'Policy: Taxation'.

[74] See further details in 2019 Report: Eurostat, 'Smarter, greener, more inclusive? Indicators to support the Europe 2020 Strategy' https://ec.europa.eu/eurostat/documents/3217494/10155585/KS-04-19-559-EN-N.pdf/b8528d01-4f4f-9c1e-4cd4-86c2328559de.

[75] Eurostat, 'Europe 2020 – Overview'.

that need to be addressed in order to stimulate more investment in research and innovation and for fighting poverty and social exclusion.[76] One of the key specific areas that require serious attention is countering tax crimes, otherwise revenue targets, socioeconomic development and integrity of the strategic efforts may be compromised.

Pursuant to Article 317 of TFEU and Article 36 of Regulation (EU, Euratom) 2018/1046,[77] the European Commission is mandated to implement, in cooperation with its Member States,[78] 'the EU budget, complying with sound financial management principles and applying effective and efficient internal control, which includes preventing, detecting, correcting and following-up on fraud and other irregularities'. In this regard, and pursuant to Article 325(1) of TFEU, the EU and the Member States are required to counter fraud and any other illegal activities that affect EU's financial interests. The tax crime and fraud strategies and action plans of the EU are part of the fraud counter-measures.

The 2012 Action Plan, 2016 VAT Plan and Commission Anti-Fraud Strategy (CAFS) of 2019[79] and its accompanying 2019 Action Plan[80] are typical strategic plans to consider in this discourse.

EU Tax Fraud and Evasion Initiatives

Based on its current competences, EU develops the instruments that allow 'for co-operation and exchange of information among its Member States on all sorts of taxes, particularly savings taxation and VAT. EU legislation enables collaboration between national tax authorities in various ways.'[81]

The Fiscalis Programme[82] is one of the platforms that encourage collaboration between tax authorities. It particularly facilitates working visits by tax officials to other

---

[76] Ibid.

[77] Regulation (EU, Euratom) 2018/1046 of the European Parliament and of the Council of 18 July 2018 on the financial rules applicable to the general budget of the Union, amending Regulations (EU) No 1296/2013, (EU) No 1301/2013, (EU) No 1303/2013, (EU) No 1304/2013, (EU) No 1309/2013, (EU) No 1316/2013, (EU) No 223/2014, (EU) No 283/2014, and Decision No 541/2014/EU and repealing Regulation (EU, Euratom) No 966/2012, OJ L 193/1.

[78] Note that the EU budget is of interest to its Member States especially so that the latter 'collect and spend up to 80% of the EU budget'; COM (2019) 196 final (CAFS, 29 April 2019) 5.

[79] European Commission, 'Commission Anti-Fraud Strategy: enhanced action to protect the EU budget' (Communication From The Commission to the European Parliament, The Council, The European Economic and Social Committee, The Committee of the Regions and the Court Of Auditors, COM(2019) 196 final, 29 April 2019), https://ec.europa.eu/anti-fraud/sites/antifraud/files/2019_commission_anti_fraud_strategy_en.pdf, accessed 23 January 2020.

[80] European Commission, 'Commission Staff Working Document – Action Plan accompanying the document Commission Anti-Fraud Strategy: enhanced action to protect the EU budget' – Communication From the Commission to the European Parliament, the Council, the European Economic and Social Committee, The Committee of the Regions and the Court of Auditors, COM(2019) 196 final' (SWD(2019) 170 final 29 April 2019), https://ec.europa.eu/anti-fraud/sites/antifraud/files/2019_commission_anti_fraud_strategy_action_plan_en.pdf, accessed 23 January 2020.

[81] European Commission, 'Role of the EU: An action plan to combat tax fraud and evasion', https://ec.europa.eu/taxation_customs/fight-against-tax-fraud-tax-evasion/role-eu_en, accessed 14 March 2020.

[82] See European Commission, 'The Fiscalis 2020 Programme', https://ec.europa.eu/taxation_customs/fiscalis-programme_en, accessed 3 May 2020.

Member States as well as joint actions.[83] Furthermore, expert groups are created to support the framework of countering tax crimes in the EU. These expert groups include:

- Code of Conduct on Business Taxation group[84] – this is at the Council of Ministers level, where EU Member States 'assess each other's tax regimes to identify harmful tax measures'. The group gets to enforce EU Member States' commitment to abolish existing harmful measures and refrain from introducing new ones.[85]

- The Tax Policy Group[86] – at which 'personal representatives of EU finance ministers [meet to] discuss issues such as double taxation and tax avoidance'.[87]

- Other groups such as national tax authorities, VAT Committee, VAT forum, VAT expert group, and Group on the future of VAT.[88] These groups 'bring the EU, Member States and/or representatives of business together to discuss how to improve the operation of tax systems in practice'.[89]

Looking into the future, based on experience, the competences of the EU, legal and technical set-ups currently being implemented have to be improved and reinforced. To this end, monitoring and improvement of EU efforts to counter tax crimes have been a continuing process and should continue unabated. These formed the basis for EU Commission to adopt 'an Action Plan' in 2012 – 'an Action Plan to strengthen the fight against tax fraud and tax evasion' (2012 Action Plan).[90]

The 2012 Action Plan

The 2012 Action Plan presents 34 key action points to counter tax crimes now and in the future. It has set out clear steps to enhance administrative cooperation and to support the development of the existing good governance policy, the wider issues of interaction with tax havens and of tackling aggressive tax planning and other aspects, including tax-related crimes[91] and unfair competition.[92] It is interesting and reassuring to note that the negative impact of tax crimes on competition are seemingly acknowledged here. However, the criminal legal provisions and subsequent sanctions imposed on tax criminals across the EU do not incorporate this element when assessing the negative impact and damage that a specific tax offence inflicts on competition and intra-community trade.

---

[83] European Commission, 'Role of the EU: An action plan to combat tax fraud and evasion'.
[84] Council Conclusions of 9 March 1998 concerning the establishment of the Code of Conduct Group (business taxation) (98/C 99/01), https://eur-lex.europa.eu/legal-content/EN/TXT/PDF/?uri=CELEX:31998Y0401(01)&from=EN, accessed 4 May 2020; see also Council of the European Union, 'Code of Conduct Group (Business Taxation)', https://www.consilium.europa.eu/en/council-eu/preparatory-bodies/code-conduct-group/, accessed 4 May 2020.
[85] European Commission, 'Role of the EU: An action plan to combat tax fraud and evasion'.
[86] See European Commission, 'Commissioner Šemeta launches Tax Policy Group to push forward fundamental issues in taxation (P/10/1312, 12 October 2010), https://ec.europa.eu/commission/presscorner/detail/en/IP_10_1312, accessed 4 May 2020.
[87] European Commission, 'Role of the EU: An action plan to combat tax fraud and evasion'.
[88] Ibid.
[89] Ibid.
[90] European Commission, 'An Action Plan to strengthen the fight against tax fraud and tax evasion', 6.
[91] Ibid.
[92] European Commission, 'Role of the EU: An action plan to combat tax fraud and evasion'.

The 2012 Action Plan has four phases of initiatives to counter tax crimes:

- the initiatives the EU Commission has already taken;
- new initiatives that can be progressed this year;
- initiatives planned for next year; and
- initiatives that require a longer timeframe.

These initiatives were sequenced on the backdrop of 'the need not to overload Member States and to take account of their capacity to take the necessary actions'. Thus, the EU was neither overambitious nor made any attempt to overburden EU Member States to implement these initiatives. But in trying to be realistic and reasonable, there is the risk of underestimating the scale of tax crimes in Member States. Perhaps, in designing the initiatives, reasonable and realistic though the EU Commission could have been, the serious scale and volume of tax crimes in the EU should have been the driving force behind the implementation of this EU anti-fraud action plan.

The analysis below consists of series of tables that feature all the 34 anti-fraud and anti-tax-evasion measures with brief comments regarding the implementation.[93] The tables are categorised into three thematic areas:

- better use of existing instruments and commission initiatives to be progressed;
- new commission initiatives; and
- future initiatives and actions to be developed.

With respect to better use of existing instruments and the Commission's initiatives expected to be progressed against tax fraud and evasion, the analysis set out in Tables 21a–m was conducted.

Table 21a Existing Tax Fraud and Evasion Instruments

Actions	*Comments*
1. New framework for administrative cooperation	This is implemented through DAC amendments[94] which are in the process of being codified.
2. Closing savings taxation loopholes	Savings Directive repealed to close the loopholes by Council Directive (EU) 2015/2060.[95]
3. Draft anti-fraud and tax cooperation agreement	An agreement with applicable provisions is in force.[96]

---

[93] H Zourek, 'Fighting tax fraud and evasion' (European Commission, https://ec.europa.eu/taxation_customs/sites/taxation/files/resources/documents/taxation/tax_fraud_evasion/2013-12-05_press-briefing.pdf, accessed 22 January 2020.

[94] See European Commission, 'New framework in the EU for Administrative Cooperation', https://ec.europa.eu/taxation_customs/sites/taxation/files/docs/body/administrative_coop.pdf, accessed 23 April 2020; see also European Commission, 'Administrative cooperation in (direct) taxation in the EU', accessed 23 April 2020.

[95] Council Directive (EU) 2015/2060 of 10 November 2015 repealing Directive 2003/48/EC on taxation of savings income in the form of interest payments, [2015] OJ L 301/ 1; see also Council Directive 2014/107/EU of 9 December 2014 amending Directive 2011/16/EU as regards mandatory automatic exchange of information in the field of taxation, [2014] OJ L 359/ 1.

[96] See Agreement between the European Union and the Principality of Liechtenstein on supplementary rules in relation to the instrument for financial support for external borders and visa, as part of the Internal Security Fund for the period 2014 to 2020, OJ L 7/4.

The above three strategic actions address administrative cooperation, savings taxation and cooperation agreement. These have been implemented. The three actions relating to better use of existing instruments (4, 5 and 6) below have also been implemented.

Table 21b Existing Tax Fraud and Evasion Instruments

Actions	*Comments*
4. Quick Reaction Mechanism against VAT fraud	The proposed Directive in this regard was adopted on 15 November 2012.[97]
5. Optional application of the VAT reverse charge mechanism	The full Directive has been adopted and is being applied.[98]
6. EU VAT forum	The VAT forum mandate[99] has been reviewed[100] and participation of Members[101] in the forum has been encouraging.[102]

As part of this plan, seven new measures or initiatives were introduced by the EU Commission to counter tax crimes. They are briefly explored in turn from action 7 to action 13 below:

Action 7 recommends that third party countries should be encouraged to apply minimum standards. This action has been executed.

Table 21c Existing Tax Fraud and Evasion Instruments

Actions	*Comments*
7. Recommendation regarding measures intended to encourage third countries to apply minimum standards of good governance in tax matters	Re-evaluation of the Commission's Recommendations[103] within three years after adoption and thereafter have shown that there were and are still challenges related to the third-party tax governance mechanisms. Strict measures are being introduced by the EU, in this regard, which Panayi aptly describes as 'hardening of soft law' in this area.[104]

---

[97] European Economic and Social Committee, 'VAT fraud – Quick reaction mechanism', www.eesc.europa.eu/en/our-work/opinions-information-reports/opinions/vat-fraud-quick-reaction-mechanism, accessed 23 April 2020; See European Commission, 'Proposal for a COUNCIL DIRECTIVE amending Directive 2006/112/EC on the common system of value added tax as regards a quick reaction mechanism against VAT fraud' (31 July 2012 COM (2012) 428 final, 2012/0205 (CNS), https://eur-lex.europa.eu/LexUriServ/LexUriServ.do?uri=COM%3A2012%3A0428%3AFIN%3AEN%3APDF, accessed 23 April 2020.

[98] Council Directive (EU) 2018/1695 of 6 November 2018 amending Directive 2006/112/EC on the common system of value added tax as regards the period of application of the optional reverse charge mechanism in relation to supplies of certain goods and services susceptible to fraud and of the Quick Reaction Mechanism against VAT fraud, ST/12033/2018/REV/1 OJ L 282/5; for an assessment of how far it has been applied by EU Member States see: European Commission, 'Assessment of the application and impact of the optional 'Reverse Charge Mechanism' within the EU VAT system' (EY Final Report November 2014), https://ec.europa.eu/taxation_customs/sites/taxation/files/docs/body/kp_07_14_050_en.pdf, accessed 23 April 2020.

[99] Commission Decision (2012/C198/05) of 3 July 2012 on setting up the EU VAT forum.

[100] Commission Decision of 16.7.2018 renewing the mandate of the EU VAT Forum, C(2018) 4422 final, https://ec.europa.eu/taxation_customs/sites/taxation/files/c-2018-4422-renewal-eu-vat-forum_en.pdf, accessed 23 April 2020.

[101] European Commission, 'List of the organisations appointed as members of the EU VAT Forum, (2018-2022)', https://ec.europa.eu/taxation_customs/sites/taxation/files/resources/documents/taxation/vat/key_documents/eu_vat_forum/vat-forum_membres_en.pdf, accessed 23 April 2020.

[102] See further details at: 'EU VAT Forum', https://ec.europa.eu/taxation_customs/business/vat/eu-vat-forum_en, accessed 23 April 2020.

As can be seen below on aggressive tax planning and platform for tax good governance, regarding the new initiatives (8 and 9), the former has been implemented requiring more tightening of measures while the latter has been appreciably implemented.

Table 21d Existing Tax Fraud and Evasion Instruments

Actions	Comments
8. Recommendation on aggressive tax planning	Although 'a vague legal and an operative tool',[105] aggressive tax planning endangers fight against tax crimes. The EU is contributing to international fora such as OECD global tax transparency.[106] The e-commerce package has also been adopted to improve standards in e-commerce. The recommendations[107] have been largely pursued but still have a long way to go.
9. Creation of a Platform for Tax Good Governance	This is established with participation from 'the tax authorities of all Member States and 15 organisations representing business, civil society and tax practitioners'. OECD is allowed to observe.[108] The EU has established a good footprint in providing measures for tax good governance internally and externally.[109]

In addition, with respect to the EU Commission's new initiatives (10 and 11) below regarding harmful business taxation and the TIN, significant achievements have been made *albeit* requiring further improvements.

Table 21e Existing Tax Fraud and Evasion Instruments

Actions	Comments
10. Improvements in the area of harmful business taxation and related areas	Some improvements[110] have been made especially in mitigating harmful tax competition.[111] However, there is still much to be done to ensure harmonisation, consolidation and compliance of tax rules.

(continued)

---

[103] Commission Recommendation of 6.12.2012 regarding measures intended to encourage third countries to apply minimum standards of good governance in tax matters Brussels, 6.12.2012 C (2012) 8805 final, https://ec.europa.eu/taxation_customs/sites/taxation/files/docs/body/c_2012_8805_en.pdf, accessed 23 April 2020.

[104] CHJI Panayi, W Haslehner and E Traversa (eds), *Research Handbook on European Union Taxation Law* (Edward Elgar, 2020) 139.

[105] Ibid.

[106] See OECD, 'Global Forum on Transparency and Exchange of Information for Tax Purposes: Putting an end to offshore tax evasion', www.oecd.org/tax/transparency/, accessed 23 April 2020; see particularly OECD, 'Global Forum members', www.oecd.org/tax/transparency/who-we-are/members/, accessed 23 April 2020.

[107] 2012/772/EU: Commission Recommendation of 6 December 2012 on aggressive tax planning, [2012] OJ L 338/41.

[108] European Commission, 'Platform for Tax Good Governance', https://ec.europa.eu/taxation_customs/business/company-tax/tax-good-governance/platform-tax-good-governance_en#:~:text=The%20Platform%20for%20Tax%20Good,identify%20and%20address%20double%20taxation, accessed 23 April 2020.

[109] Panayi et al (eds), *Research Handbook on European Union Taxation Law* 34.

[110] See European Commission, 'Action Plan on Corporate Taxation' (June 2015), https://ec.europa.eu/taxation_customs/business/company-tax/action-plan-corporate-taxation_en, accessed 23 April 2020.

[111] See European Commission, 'Harmful Tax Competition', https://ec.europa.eu/taxation_customs/business/company-tax/harmful-tax-competition_en, accessed 23 April 2020.

Table 21e *(Continued)*

Actions	Comments
11. 'TIN on EUROPA' portal	Taxpayer Identification Number on Europa is an information exchange tool being used.[112] But the effectiveness of this tool requires thorough evaluation.

The Commission's new initiatives 12 and 13 on exchange of information and Euro denaturant have made huge strides except that the latter requires further improvement.

Table 21f Existing Tax Fraud and Evasion Instruments

Actions	Comments
12. Standard forms for exchange of information in the field of taxation	The information exchange mechanism in Council Directive 2011/16/EU[113] has been amended a number of times (DAC1–DAC6) to accommodate the necessity to make information exchange more effective.[114] But this regime still needs further improvement in the kinds of data exchanged.
13. A Euro denaturant for completely and partly denatured alcohol	This initiative has been rolled out by Commission Implementing Regulation (EU) 2017/2236.[115]

Although not all the timeframes were effectively met, the translation of most of them into strategic legal frames has been encouraging especially when they are considered together.[116] However, more efforts should be garnered towards getting all EU Member States to fully embrace and implement these as minimum actions while leveraging that to escalate the present strategies into concrete and more elaborate future actions. In Table 21, a brief commentary on each of the future measures envisaged by the 2012 Action Plan is provided. These measures contain 21 actions or initiatives by the EU Commission. With respect to the then future actions to be undertaken in the short term (in 2013), seven actionable initiatives were provided. Two of these (14 and 15) regarding the resolve to tackle mismatches and strengthen anti-abuse provisions have been achieved.

---

[112] EU Open Data Portal, 'Taxpayer Identification Number (TIN)', https://data.europa.eu/euodp/en/data/dataset/taxpayer-identification-number-tin, accessed 23 April 2020.

[113] Council Directive 2011/16/EU of 15 February 2011 on administrative cooperation in the field of taxation and repealing Directive 77/799/EEC OJ L 64/1 – also known as DAC1.

[114] European Commission, 'Administrative cooperation in (direct) taxation in the EU', https://ec.europa.eu/taxation_customs/business/tax-cooperation-control/administrative-cooperation/enhanced-administrative-cooperation-field-direct-taxation_en, accessed 23 April 2020.

[115] See Commission Implementing Regulation (EU) 2017/2236 of 5 December 2017 amending Regulation (EC) No 3199/93 on the mutual recognition of procedures for the complete denaturing of alcohol for the purposes of exemption from excise duty, C/2017/7995 OJ L 320/6.

[116] L Cerioni, *The European Union and Direct Taxation: A Solution for a Difficult Relationship* (Routledge, 2015).

Table 21g Existing Tax Fraud and Evasion Instruments

Actions	Comments
14. A revision of the Parent-Subsidiary Directive (2011/96/EU)	Directive 2011/96/EU revised by Directive (EU) 2015/121.[117]
15. A review of anti-abuse provision in EU legislation	Parent-Subsidiary Directive[118] has been reviewed to prominently feature prohibition of abuse.[119] The Merger and Interest Directives have since not been reviewed. Article 5 of the Interest Directive[120] however frontally counters fraud and abuse. The Mergers Directive appears not to feature issues of abuse.[121]

At the same time, the then future actions to be undertaken in the short term (in 2013) (16, 17 and 18), regarding enhancing tax compliance has been achieved while promotion of EU 'standards, instruments and tools', and enhancing tax governance still require further improvements.

Table 21h Existing Tax Fraud and Evasion Instruments

Actions		Comments
Promote EU standards, instruments and tools	16. Promote the standard of automatic exchange of information in international fora and the EU IT tools	Being implemented. It is a continuing process.
Enhance tax compliance	17. A European taxpayer's code	Code guidelines[122] developed and relevant consultations conducted.[123]
Enhance tax governance	18. Reinforced cooperation with other law enforcement bodies	Implemented through the fourth, fifth and sixth AMLDs. Needs further reinforcement.

Still on actions to be undertaken in the short term (in 2013) below, while actionable initiative 19 has been significantly implemented, albeit requiring further improvements, that of initiative 20 has been achieved.

---

[117] Council Directive (EU) 2015/121 of 27 January 2015 amending Directive 2011/96/EU on the common system of taxation applicable in the case of parent companies and subsidiaries of different Member States [2015] OJ L 21/1.

[118] Directive 2011/96/EU.

[119] Council Directive (EU) 2015/121.

[120] Consolidated text: Council Directive 2003/49/EC of 3 June 2003 on a common system of taxation applicable to interest and royalty payments made between associated companies of different Member States, https://eur-lex.europa.eu/legal-content/EN/TXT/?uri=CELEX:02003L0049-20130701, accessed 25 April 2020.

[121] See Council Directive 2009/133/EC of 19 October 2009 on the common system of taxation applicable to mergers, divisions, partial divisions, transfers of assets and exchanges of shares concerning companies of different Member States and to the transfer of the registered office of an SE or SCE between Member States, [2009] OJ L 310/4.

[122] European Commission, 'Guidelines for a Model for A European Taxpayers' Code' (Reference Ares (2016) 6598744–24/11/2016, European Union, 2016), https://ec.europa.eu/taxation_customs/business/tax-cooperation-control/guidelines-model-european-taxpayers-code_en#:~:text=The%20European%20Taxpayers'%20Code%20is%20a%20model%20of%20behaviour%20for,is%20a%20non%2Dbinding%20instrument, accessed 25 April 2020.

[123] Ibid.

Table 21i Existing Tax Fraud and Evasion Instruments

Actions		Comments
Enhance administrative cooperation	19. Promote the use of simultaneous controls and the presence of foreign officials for audits	Implemented to some extent.[124]
Action regarding third countries	20. Obtain an authorisation from Council to start negotiations with third countries for bilateral agreements on administrative cooperation in the field of VAT	This authorisation has been obtained and agreements have been reached with third countries including Norway.[125] Even UK has already been considered as a third country and EU Council has already taken a decision for negotiations therewith.[126]

The future anti-fraud and evasion measures continue to be examined regarding actions to be undertaken in the medium term (by 2014). These constitute 11 actionable initiatives. Regarding the need to enhance exchange of information (21, 22 and 23), implementation is still underway.

Table 21j Existing Tax Fraud and Evasion Instruments

Actions	Comments
21. Develop computerised format for automatic exchange of information (AEOI)	Directive 2011/16/EU on exchange of information has been amended to accommodate new measures of AEOI.[127] Requires further improvement.
22. Use of an EU Tax Identification Number (TIN)	Most of EU Members currently use TIN.[128]
23. Rationalise IT instruments	Being implemented.[129]

Still on actions to be undertaken in the medium term (by 2014), the following observations have been made on tackling trends and schemes of tax fraud and tax evasion (24, 25 and 26).

---

[124] See M Lang and others (eds), *Introduction to European Tax Law on Direct Taxation*, 5th edn (Linde, 2018) 281.

[125] See Council of the European Union, 'Agreement between the European Union and the kingdom of Norway on administrative cooperation, combating fraud and recovery of claims in the field of value added tax' (28 November 2017), http://data.consilium.europa.eu/doc/document/ST-14390-2017-INIT/en/pdf, accessed 20 February 2020.

[126] European Commission, 'Recommendation for a Council Decision authorising the opening of negotiations for a new partnership with the United Kingdom of Great Britain and Northern Ireland (3 February 2020, COM(2020) 35 final), https://ec.europa.eu/info/sites/info/files/communication-annex-negotiating-directives.pdf, accessed 25 April 2020.

[127] Council Directive 2014/107/EU of 9 December 2014 amending Directive 2011/16/EU as regards mandatory automatic exchange of information in the field of taxation OJ L 359/1.

[128] See European Commission, 'TIN – Taxpayer Identification Number', https://ec.europa.eu/taxation_customs/business/tax-cooperation-control/administrative-cooperation/tax-identification-numbers-tin_en#:~:text=Most%20EU%20countries%20use%20Tax,such%20as%20name%20and%20address, accessed 25 April 2020.

[129] See Directive 2014/55/EU of the European Parliament and of the Council of 16 April 2014 on electronic invoicing in public procurement Text with EEA relevance [2014] OJ L 133/1; see also Eli Hadzhieva, 'Impact

Table 21k Existing Tax Fraud and Evasion Instruments

Actions	Comments
24. Guidelines for tracing money flows	Implemented. Requires further improvement.
25. Enhance risk management techniques and in particular compliance risk management	Implemented. Requires further improvement.
26. Extend EUROFISC to direct taxation	This is yet to be effectively expressed in the governing regulations.[130]

On the last set of actions which were to be undertaken in the medium term (by 2014) in the light of future initiatives and actions to be developed, the following observations are provided for the need to enhance tax compliance (27, 28, 29, 30 and 31) in the EU.

Table 21l Existing Tax Fraud and Evasion Instruments

Actions	Comments
27. Create a one stop shop approach in all Member States	Implemented. Requires further improvement.
28. Develop motivational incentives including voluntary disclosure programmes	Implemented.[131] Requires further improvement.
29. Develop a tax web portal	Implemented.[132]
30. Propose an alignment of administrative and criminal sanctions	The proposal[133] has been translated into Directive (EU) 2017/1371.[134] Yet, this alignment appears not to be effective enough.[135] The frontier between the two regimes is still blurry. Requires further improvement.
31. Develop an EU Standard Audit File for Tax (SAF-T)	Implemented.[136]

of Digitalisation on International Tax Matters: Challenges and Remedies' (Study Requested by the TAX3 Committee, European Parliament, PE 626.078 – February 2019).

[130] See Consolidated text: Council Regulation (EU) No 904/2010 of 7 October 2010, https://eur-lex.europa.eu/legal-content/GA/TXT/?uri=CELEX:02010R0904-20200101, accessed 25 April 2020; See also Council Regulation (EU) 2018/1909 of 4 December 2018 amending Regulation (EU) No 904/2010 as regards the exchange of information for the purpose of monitoring the correct application of call-off stock arrangements ST/12850/2018/INIT OJ L 311/1.

[131] See European Commission, 'EU VAT forum voluntary disclosure and related issues' (26 May 2015), https://ec.europa.eu/taxation_customs/sites/taxation/files/resources/documents/taxation/vat/key_documents/eu_vat_forum/voluntary_disclosure.pdf, accessed 25 April 2020; see also CC Williams, 'Elements of a preventative approach towards undeclared work: an evaluation of service vouchers and awareness raising campaigns' (European Platform Undeclared Work, May 2018).

[132] See European Commission, 'Online services and databases for Taxation', https://ec.europa.eu/taxation_customs/online-services-and-databases-taxation_en, accessed 25 April 2020.

[133] European Commission, 'Proposal for a Directive of the European Parliament and of the Council on the fight against fraud to the Union's financial interests by means of criminal law' (COM (2012) 363/2, 11 July 2012).

[134] Directive (EU) 2017/1371 of the European Parliament and of the Council of 5 July 2017 on the fight against fraud to the Union's financial interests by means of criminal law, OJ L 198/29.

[135] See K Ligeti, S Tosza (eds), *White Collar Crime: A Comparative Perspective* (Hart Publishing, 2018).

[136] See Global indirect tax management, 'Standard Audit File for Tax Purposes (SAF-T)' (Tax assurance research, 23 May 2015), https://globalindirecttaxmanagement.com/thought-leadership-publications/

On actions to be undertaken in the longer term (beyond 2014) in the light of future initiatives and actions to be developed against tax fraud and evasion measures, the following analysis has been done on enhancing further close cooperation (32, 33 and 34) in the EU.

Table 21m   Existing Tax Fraud and Evasion Instruments

Actions	*Comments*
32. A methodology for joint audits by dedicated teams of trained auditors	Multilateral control under the framework of Fiscalis Programme in Regulation (EU) No 1286/2013,[137] as well as Art. 11 and 12 of Directive 2011/16/EU[138] and Regulation (EU) No 904/2010[139] provide arrangement, process and legal foundation for this action to be carried out. Yet, it does appear there is no clear methodology designed for dedicated trained auditors.[140]
33. Develop mutual direct access to national databases	A central depository administered by the EU Commission allows direct access by EU Members to databases mutually connected to this central unit. These central databases include 'Taxes in Europe' database,[141] Taxpayer Identification Number,[142] SEED (System for Exchange of Excise Data),[143] and VAT Information Exchange System[144] that provides evidence of development of this mutual direct access.[145] Largely, direct database access still depends on the scope of access granted to other Member States by another EU Member State.

(continued)

building-blocks-of-a-vat-control-framework/elements-of-gst-control-framework-singapore/28-phenix-consulting/179-standard-audit-file-for-tax-purposes-saf-t html, accessed 25 April 2020.

[137] Regulation (EU) No 1286/2013 of the European Parliament and of the Council of 11 December 2013 establishing an action programme to improve the operation of taxation systems in the European Union for the period 2014-2020 (Fiscalis 2020) and repealing Decision No 1482/2007/EC OJ L 347/25.

[138] Art 11 has not been uniformly implemented by EU Member States while Art 12 has been 'either initiated or taken part in simultaneous controls since the entry into force of the Directive by almost all Member States'; see European Commission, 'Commission Staff Working Document on the application of Council Directive (EU) no 2011/16/EU on administrative cooperation in the field of direct taxation – Accompanying the document – Report from the Commission to the European Parliament and the Council on the application of Council Directive (EU) no 2011/16/EU on administrative cooperation in the field of direct taxation' (SWD(2017) 462 final, 18 December 2017), https://eur-lex.europa.eu/legal-content/EN/TXT/HTML/?uri=SWD:2017:462:FIN&from=EN, accessed 25 April 2020.

[139] Council Regulation (EU) No 904/2010 of 7 October 2010 on administrative cooperation and combating fraud in the field of value added tax (recast), https://eur-lex.europa.eu/legal-content/EN/TXT/?uri=CELEX:02010R0904-20200101> accessed 26 April 2020.

[140] See European Commission, 'EU joint transfer pricing forum: a coordinated approach to transfer pricing Controls within the EU' (Taxud/D2, October 2018), https://ec.europa.eu/taxation_customs/sites/taxation/files/jtpf_report_on_a_coordinated_approach_to_transfer_pricing_controls_within_the_eu_en.pdf, accessed 26 April 2020.

[141] European Commission, 'TEDB – "Taxes in Europe" database', https://ec.europa.eu/taxation_customs/economic-analysis-taxation/taxes-europe-database-tedb_en, accessed 26 April 2020.

[142] European Commission, 'TIN – Taxpayer Identification Number', https://ec.europa.eu/taxation_customs/business/tax-cooperation-control/administrative-cooperation/tax-identification-numbers-tin_en, accessed 26 April 2020.

[143] European Commission, 'SEED on Europa', https //ec.europa.eu/taxation_customs/dds2/seed/seed_home.jsp?Lang=en, accessed 26 April 2020.

[144] European Commission, 'VIES VAT number validation', https://ec.europa.eu/taxation_customs/vies/vieshome.do?locale=en, accessed 26 April 2020.

[145] European Commission, 'Online services and databases for Taxation', https://ec.europa.eu/taxation_customs/online-services-and-databases-taxation_en, accessed 26 April 2020.

Table 21m *(Continued)*

Actions	Comments
34. Elaborate a single legal instrument for administrative cooperation for all taxes	Being implemented. Consolidation of two[146] of the key four[147] foundational legal instruments for direct and indirect taxes on administrative cooperation in EU has been individually done except Regulation No 389/2012/EU[148] and Directive 2010/24/EU.[149] However, a single legal instrument for administrative cooperation for all taxes is yet to be developed or elaborated. The EU should work towards this goal by developing proposals that can be gradually observed and considered by Member States to appreciate the appropriate time for implementation by Member States. Alternatively, the regulation/directive can be enacted on a single legal instrument which should have a longer term of transposition to allow for national legislative adjustments.

One of the key highlights is the need to reduce costs and complexities in the tax crime countering ecosystem. The 2012 Action Plan provides that the necessity to ensure reduction of 'costs and complexity of tax systems for both the taxpayers and the tax administrations' will provide a significant guide for future work on the strategic actions. The need for and the impact of a user-friendly tax compliance system and processes were also identified as key factors in optimising tax revenues during the PROTAX focus groups and during its conference in 2019.[150] In respect of taxpayers, reduction in 'costs and complexity would encourage better tax compliance'.[151] Regarding tax administration, cost and complexity reduction through 'the development and full use of automated

---

[146] Eur-lex, 'Consolidated text: Council Regulation (EU) No 904/2010 of 7 October 2010' (1 January 2020), https://eur-lex.europa.eu/legal-content/GA/TXT/?uri=CELEX:02010R0904-20200101, accessed 26 April 2020; Eur-lex, 'Consolidated text: Council Directive 2011/16/EU of 15 February 2011 on administrative cooperation in the field of taxation and repealing Directive 77/799/EEC' (1 January 2018), https://eur-lex.europa.eu/legal-content/EN/TXT/?uri=celex:02011L0016-20180101, accessed 26 April 2020.

[147] Council Directive 2010/24/EU of 16 March concerning mutual assistance for the recovery of claims relating to taxes, duties and other measures, [2010] OJ L 84/1; Council Regulation No 904/2010/EU of 7 October 2010 on administrative cooperation and combating fraud in the field of value added tax, [2010] OJ L 268/1; Council Directive 2011/16/EU of 15 February 2011 on administrative cooperation in the field of taxation and repealing Directive 77/799/EEC OJ L 64/1; Council Regulation No 389/2012/EU of 2 May 2012 on administrative cooperation in the field of excise duties and repealing Regulation (EC) No 2073/2004 [2012] OJ L 121/1.

[148] Council Regulation No 389/2012/EU of 2 May 2012 on administrative cooperation in the field of excise duties and repealing Regulation (EC) No 2073/2004 [2012] OJ L 121/1 (for proposed amendment, see Eur-lex, 'Proposal for a Council Regulation amending Regulation (EU) No 389/2012 on administrative cooperation in the field of excise duties as regards the content of electronic register COM/2018/349 final' – 25 May 2018; for related legal instruments supporting cooperation in relation to electronic register, see Council Directive (EU) 2020/262 of 19 December 2019 laying down general excise duty arrangements (recast) ST/14107/2019/INIT [2019] OJ L 58/42; and Decision (EU) 2020/263 of the European Parliament and of the Council of 15 January 2020 on the computerization of movement and surveillance of excise goods (recast) PE/37/2019/REV/2 OJ L 58/43).

[149] Council Directive 2010/24/EU of 16 March concerning mutual assistance for the recovery of claims relating to taxes, duties and other measures, [2010] OJ L 84/1.

[150] M Hall et al, 'D2.4 Conference Report summarising and documenting contributions from T2.7' (EU PROTAX, 2020).

[151] European Commission, 'An Action Plan to strengthen the fight against tax fraud and tax evasion', 6.

tools and risk management techniques', for example, should be able to 'release human and budgetary resources to concentrate on achieving targeted objectives',[152] especially on countering tax crimes.

The foregoing constitutes an array of action points that characterise the strategic pillars outlined by TGP6, including the operational context, risk/threat assessment, analysis of compliance behaviour, monitoring and evaluation, as well as planning and implementation. However, the strategic pillars presented by TGP6 are not clearly articulated with imbued strategic principles that is coded in a consolidated strategic document for all EU Member States to pursue. A couple of specific deficits include the fact that the 2012 Action Plan has been unable to effectively:

- Articulate country-by-country reporting by MNCs as a key transparency initiative to counter aggressive tax planning. Nonetheless this has been addressed by subsequent EU counter-measures, especially emanating from the Anti-Tax Avoidance Package[153] (ATAP).

- Feature the CCCTB[154] as a tool for countering aggressive tax planning.[155] This has been catered for in the 2015 Tax Transparency Package.[156]

- Address the impact of the FATCA[157] on Member States of the EU, such as making it possible for EU Member States to be given similar treatments in the FATCA.[158]

Although some outstanding issues remain unaddressed, there has been significant feat made towards the execution of the 2012 Action Plan. The opportunities provided by the 2012 Action Plan are many. These include measures:

- concerning EU definition of tax havens;

- concerning AEOI and closer cooperation to counter tax evasion and elusion or aggressive tax planning;

- on EU taxpayers' charter and revision of the Parent-Subsidiary Directive which has the potential to create new opportunities for countering tax evasion;

- relating to tax crimes might being made a predicate offence of money laundering;

---

[152] Ibid.

[153] European Commission, 'Anti-Tax Avoidance Package' https://ec.europa.eu/taxation_customs/business/company-tax/anti-tax-avoidance-package_en, accessed 10 February 2020.

[154] Common Consolidated Corporate Tax Base.

[155] European Commission, 'Common Consolidated Corporate Tax Base (CCCTB)', https://ec.europa.eu/taxation_customs/business/company-tax/common-consolidated-corporate-tax-base-ccctb_en, accessed 10 February 2020.

[156] European Commission, 'Tax Transparency Package' (March 2015), https://ec.europa.eu/taxation_customs/business/company-tax/tax-transparency-package_en, accessed 10 February 2020.

[157] The US Foreign Account Tax Compliance Act 2010 (FATCA) 'generally requires that foreign financial Institutions and certain other non-financial foreign entities report on the foreign assets held by their U.S. account holders or be subject to withholding on withholdable payments', www.irs.gov/businesses/corporations/foreign-account-tax-compliance-act-fatca, accessed 24 July 2020.

[158] Eurodad et al, 'Analysis: EU Action plan to strengthen the fight against tax fraud and tax evasion' (December 2012), https://eurodad.org/files/integration/2012/12/EC-Action-Plan-analysis2.pdf, accessed 18 April 2020.

- concerning criminalisation of money laundering;
- relating to the need for enhanced due diligence by relevant professionals;
- on the need for greater international cooperation between tax authorities and other law enforcement; and
- on the need for greater transparency in beneficial ownership regime.[159]

All the above opportunities have been tapped into and exploited by the EU in its continued measures to counter tax crimes.

After more than seven years of implementation of the 2012 action plan, the EU's current priority areas for its Member States, as of 2020, have essentially been to:

- make the necessary improvements to their national tax administrations and systems;[160]
- make full use of the existing European toolbox;[161] and
- agree on new rules and instruments where relevant.[162]

These three pillars have been the spirit driving the 2012 Action Plan – and have been re-emphasised, going forward. The European Commission, with the 2012 Action Plan, is tasked to ensure that all the actions thereof are consistently and compatibly implemented with the Multiannual Financial Framework for 2007–13[163] and the Multiannual Financial Framework[164] for 2014-20.[165]

It is obvious that with the ravaging impact of Covid-19,[166] the provisions made for the last three quarters of 2020 would be derailed from its timeline. The European

---

[159] Ibid.
[160] European Commission, 'Role of the EU: An action plan to combat tax fraud and evasion'.
[161] Ibid.
[162] Ibid.
[163] See Multiannual financial framework for 2007–2013: European Parliament resolution of 22 September 2010 on the proposal for a Council regulation laying down the multiannual financial framework for the years 2007–2013 (COM (2010)0072–2010/0048(APP)) (2012/C 50 E/12), https://eur-lex.europa.eu/LexUriServ/LexUriServ.do?uri=OJ:C:2012:050E:0064:0067:EN:PDF, accessed 22 April 2020; see also the amended version at: Communication from the Commission to the European Parliament and the Council concerning the revision of the multiannual financial framework (2007-2013) COM/2007/0549 final, https://eur-lex.europa.eu/legal-content/en/ALL/?uri=CELEX:52007DC0549, accessed 22 April 2020.
[164] See Council Regulation (EU, Euratom) No 1311/2013 of 2 December 2013 laying down the multiannual financial framework for the years 2014–2020, OJ L 347/884, https://eur-lex.europa.eu/legal-content/en/TXT/?uri=CELEX:32013R1311, accessed 22 April 2020; see also the amended version at: European Commission, 'Multiannual financial framework 2014-2020', https://ec.europa.eu/info/strategy/eu-budget/documents/multiannual-financial-framework/2014-2020_en, accessed 22 April 2020.
[165] For negotiations and proposals towards the 2021–2027 Multiannual Financial Framework, see European Commission, 'Multiannual financial framework 2021–2027', https://ec.europa.eu/info/strategy/eu-budget/documents/multiannual-financial-framework/2021-2027_en, accessed 12 May 2020; European Commission, 'MFF Legislation' (First published, May 2020), https://ec.europa.eu/info/publications/mff-legislation_en, accessed 7 June 2020.
[166] OECD, *Coronavirus: The World Economy at risk* (OECD Interim Economic Assessment 2 March 2020); Douglas A Rediker and Giovanna De Maio, 'Order from chaos: Europe and the existential challenge of post-COVID recovery' (Brookings, 20 April 2020), www.brookings.edu/blog/order-from-chaos/2020/04/20/europe-and-the-existential-challenge-of-post-covid-recovery/, accessed 26 April 2020; European Commission, 'The impact of the Covid-19 pandemic on global and EU trade' (Chief Economist Team, DG Trade, European Commission, 17 April 2020), https://trade.ec.europa.eu/doclib/docs/2020/april/tradoc_158713.pdf, accessed 26 April 2020; also see the World Bank, 'Global Economic Prospects: Europe and Central Asia'

Commission has stepped in with an adjustment plan[167] to cater for these imbalances – including responses[168] to tax instruments in the EU. Due to the uncertainties surrounding the duration and impact of Covid-19, it makes sense to continue to give allowance for amendments to the frameworks in order to continually redress the balance.

While the 2012 Action Plan was being implemented, other action plans and strategic initiatives were developed to complement the 2012 Plan. These principally include the 'Commission Anti-Fraud Strategy: enhanced action to protect the EU budget' along with its Action Plan[169] (ie, 2019 Action Plan)[170] and the Action Plan on VAT towards a single EU VAT area (ie, 2016 VAT Plan).

The 2016 VAT Plan

Directive (EU) 2017/1371[171] provides that the most serious forms of VAT fraud include VAT carousel fraud, VAT fraud through missing traders, and VAT fraud committed within a criminal organisation. These forms of fraud create serious threats to the common VAT system and thus to the Union budget. They constitute serious offences against the common system of VAT as established by Council Directive 2006/112/EC (the 'common VAT system').[172] The European Commission's 2016 VAT Plan on countering VAT fraud is one of the organised series of measures taken by the EU and its Member States.

The 2016 VAT Plan emerged on the back of the EU's agenda for 'better regulation' with the aim of rebooting the EU VAT system so as 'to make it simpler, more fraud-proof and business friendly'.[173] This plan provides a 'pathway to the creation of a single EU VAT area' which is not only able to support a deeper and fairer single market, and

(8 June 2020), www.worldbank.org/en/region/eca/brief/global-economic-prospects-europe-and-central-asia, accessed 13 June 2020; R Toplensky, 'The Real Test of Europe's Banks Comes this Fall Lenders face a rough second half as governments unwind the programs that cushioned the initial blow of the coronavirus crisis' (*The Wall Street Journal*, 10 July 2020).

[167] See Eur-lex, 'Communication from the Commission to the European Parliament, the European Council, the Council, the European Economic and Social Committee and the Committee of the Regions the EU budget powering the recovery plan for Europe' (COM/2020/442 final, 27 May 2020), https://eur-lex.europa.eu/legal-content/EN/TXT/?uri=COM%3A2020%3A442%3AFIN, accessed 7 June 2020.

[168] See European Commission, 'Coronavirus response', https://ec.europa.eu/info/live-work-travel-eu/health/coronavirus-response_en, accessed 4 July 2020; also see KPMG, 'European Union: Tax developments in response to Covid-19', https://home.kpmg/xx/en/home/insights/2020/04/european-union-tax-developments-in-response-to-covid-19.html, accessed 13 June 2020.

[169] European Commission, 'Commission Anti-Fraud Strategy: enhanced action to protect the EU budget', COM(2019) 196 final, 29 April 2019).

[170] European Commission, Commission Staff Working Document 'Action Plan accompanying the document Commission Anti-Fraud Strategy' (SWD(2019) 170 final 29 April 2019).

[171] Directive (EU) 2017/1371 of the European Parliament and of the Council of 5 July 2017 on the fight against fraud to the Union's financial interests by means of criminal law [2017] OJ L 198/29–41.

[172] Ibid.

[173] PWC, 'Overview and current state of play – EU VAT Action Plan and OECD VAT/GST developments' (*Tax Policy Bulletin*, 27 August 2018), www.pwc.com/gx/en/tax/newsletters/tax-policy-bulletin/assets/pwc-eu-vat-action-plan-oecd-vat-gst-developments.pdf, accessed 20 February 2020.

help to boost jobs, growth, investment and competitiveness but also that which is fit for purpose in the twenty-first century. These should help the VAT system keep pace with the challenges of today's global, digital and mobile economy. Indeed, the 2016 VAT Plan underscores that the VAT system prior to this plan had the intention to be 'a transitional system'.[174]

> [At the same time the then VAT system was] fragmented, complex for the growing number of businesses operating cross-border and leaves the door open to fraud: domestic and cross-border transactions are treated differently and goods or services can be bought free of VAT within the single market.[175]

In effect, there was the need to pursue an uneasy goal of modernising and rebooting the VAT system that gave rise to VAT fraud. These had to be addressed by making the VAT system:

- simpler for businesses to use;
- able to combat the growing risk of VAT fraud;
- more efficient, particularly at exploiting the opportunities of digital technology and reducing the costs of collecting revenue; and
- based on greater trust – thus, trust between business and tax administrations, and between EU tax administrations.[176]

An interesting observation made by the 2016 Plan is that although reforming the VAT system is challenging and business could no longer be as usual, just 'adding new layers of obligations and checks in order to tackle fraud will add even more compliance costs and legal uncertainty for all businesses'. However, since piecemeal simplification was also unlikely to provide effective remedy, the action urgently required was to create 'a genuine single EU VAT area for the single market' which can be translated into 'a definitive VAT system'.[177]

An overarching instrument which the 2016 VAT Plan rests its success on is the need for 'political leadership' and solidarity to be demonstrably shown by EU Member States towards overcoming what it describes as inherent obstacles that have impeded progress in the past and finally adopt the much-needed reforms to combat fraud, remove administrative barriers and reduce regulatory costs to simplify life for businesses.[178]

The European Parliament and the Council supported by the European Economic and Social Committee were urged to, as soon as possible, provide 'clear political guidance, confirming their willingness to support' the 2016 VAT Plan.[179]

---

[174] Ibid.
[175] Ibid.
[176] Ibid.
[177] Ibid.
[178] European Commission, 'Communication from the commission to the European Parliament, the Council and the European Economic and Social Committee on an action plan on VAT Towards a single EU VAT area – Time to decide' (COM(2016) 148 final, 7 April 2016), https://ec.europa.eu/taxation_customs/sites/taxation/files/com_2016_148_en.pdf, accessed 20 July 2020.
[179] Ibid.

Figure 16 The 2016 VAT Plan as Articulated[180] by the European Commission

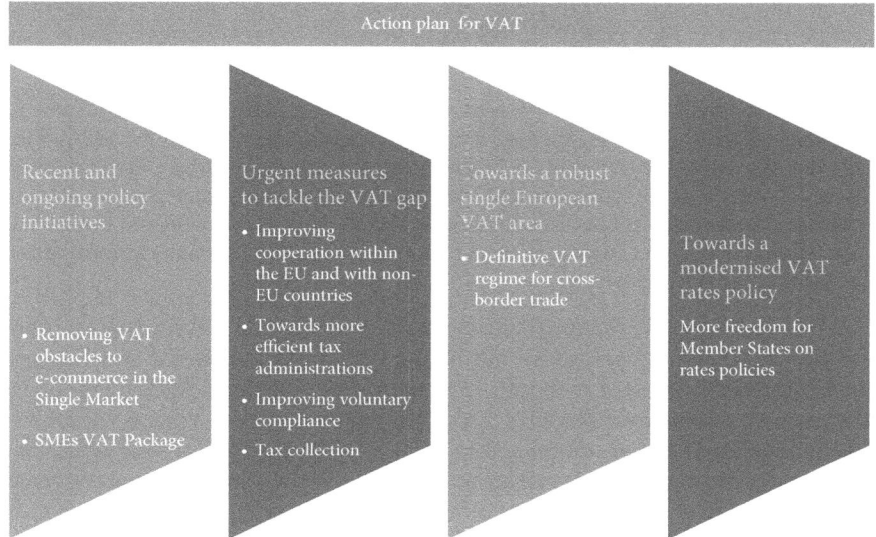

In essence, the intention of the 2016 VAT Plan includes the following elements of modernisation and rebooting:

- Establishment of the definitive VAT Regime.
- Provision of short-term measures to tackle VAT fraud.
- Establishment of 'simplified VAT rules for e-commerce in the context of the EU's Digital Single Market Strategy'.[181]
- Proving 'a comprehensive VAT package to make life easier for small or medium-size enterprises (SMEs)'.[182]
- Establishing an updated framework for VAT rates, and greater flexibility for Member States in setting their own rates.[183]
- Improvement of cooperation both within the EU and with non-EU countries.
- Improvement of efficiency of tax administrations.
- Improvement of voluntary compliance.[184]

The plan thus seeks to 'change rules and improve cooperation between authorities and between Member States to fight VAT fraud'. The strengthening and developing

---

[180] European Commission, 'Action Plan on VAT', https://ec.europa.eu/taxation_customs/business/vat/action-plan-vat_en, accessed 13 April 2020.

[181] PWC, 'Overview and current state of play'.

[182] Ibid.

[183] Ibid.

[184] European Commission, 'Communication from the commission to the European Parliament, the Council and the European Economic and Social Committee – Time to decide'.

cooperation in EUROFISC,[185] which provides a networking platform for EU Member States to cooperate in discovering VAT fraud at an early stage, are part of the critical action points of the EU's plan.[186] In the end, the medium-term outlook of this plan is anchored on adopting

> A unified approach to tackling such fraud that is fully compatible with the requirements of the single market. Even the ambitious administrative actions set out [in the plan] to tackle the VAT gap, while useful, would not be sufficient on their own to put an end to cross-border fraud. A robust single European VAT area would treat cross-border transactions in the same way as domestic transactions, putting an end to the endemic weakness of the system, and would integrate the management and enforcement of VAT through closer cooperation between tax administrations.[187]

As TGP6 would provide for implementation of a strategy for countering tax crimes, the 2016 VAT Plan has been rolled out by the Commission, Council and Parliament of the EU through a series of proposals, directives and regulations. Agreements on most of the main components of the 2016 VAT Plan have so far been reached or are being reached. These include but not limited to the VAT e-commerce package, which was a priority under the digital single market strategy;[188] and the administrative cooperation directives to improve cooperation and information exchange (see details in chapter five) as well as the definitive VAT regime.[189]

For instance, in the European Commission's Communication of 4 October 2017 (COM (2017) 566),[190] where the reform roadmap was articulated, the Commission announced a proposal[191] for a Council Directive to amend the VAT Directive

---

[185] European Commission, Taxation: Anti-fraud network EUROFISC starts operational work, https://ec.europa.eu/taxation_customs/sites/taxation/files/docs/body/2011-02-07_eurofisc_pressrelease_en.pdf, accessed 16 July 2020.

[186] Regeringskansliet, 'Counteracting tax evasion, tax avoidance and money laundering', www.government.se/contentassets/099c10d6502745279ff7a8b11e379c9b/action-plan-counteracting-tax-evasion-tax-avoidance-and-money-laundering.pdf, accessed 16 March 2020.

[187] European Commission, 'Communication from the commission to the European Parliament, the Council and the European Economic and Social Committee on an action plan on VAT Towards a single EU VAT area – Time to decide'.

[188] See European Commission, 'Commission proposes new e-commerce rules to help consumers and companies reap full benefit of Single Market' (Brussels, Press release, 25 May 2016), https://ec.europa.eu/commission/presscorner/detail/en/IP_16_1887, accessed 15 May 2020.

[189] See the Commission's follow-up on the 2016 VAT Plan at: European Commission, 'Communication from the Commission to the European Parliament, the Council and the European Economic and Social Committee on the follow-up to the Action Plan on VAT Towards a single EU VAT area – Time to act' (COM (2017) 566 final, 4 October 2017), https://ec.europa.eu/taxation_customs/sites/taxation/files/communication_-_towards_a_single_vat_area_en.pdf, accessed 15 May 2020.

[190] European Commission, 'Proposal for a Council Directive amending Directive 2006/112/EC as regards harmonising and simplifying certain rules in the value added tax system and introducing the definitive system for the taxation of trade between Member States' (COM(2017) 569 final, 4 October 2017), https://ec.europa.eu/transparency/regdoc/rep/1/2017/EN/COM-2017-569-F1-EN-MAIN-PART-1.PDF, accessed 15 May 2020; this is complemented or followed by: European Commission, 'Communication from the Commission to the European Parliament, the Council and the European Economic and Social Committee on the follow-up to the Action Plan on VAT Towards a single EU VAT area – Time to act'.

[191] European Commission, 'Proposal for a Council Directive amending Directive 2006/112/EC as regards the introduction of the detailed technical measures for the operation of the definitive VAT system for the taxation of trade between Member States' (COM(2018) 329 Final, 25 May 2018), https://eur-lex.europa.eu/legal-content/EN/TXT/?qid=1529052763975&uri=CELEX:52018PC0329, accessed 4 July 2020.

(Directive 2006/112/EC). This proposal[192] seeks to complement the proposal[193] in COM (2017) 569[194] which introduces 'the basic concepts of the definitive VAT system'.[195]

In this proposal,[196] the European Commission put forward a series of principles and key reforms for the EU's VAT area[197] seeking to enhance and modernise the current VAT system in order to:

i.   counter VAT fraud and the huge losses in government revenue due to it;
ii. ensure that life is made simpler for companies that wish to conduct business in the EU Single Market.

This proposal[198] thus entails two components:

- four 'quick fixes' to improve the day-to-day functioning of the current VAT system;[199]
- a series of fundamental principles, or 'cornerstones' (at least three), for a definitive VAT system.[200]

With respect to the quick fixes, four remedies have been proposed to enhance the day-to-day functioning of the current VAT system, until a more permanent regime is agreed and implemented:[201]

i.   *Simplification of VAT rules* for companies moving goods from one EU Member State to another Member State where they are to be stored before being supplied to a customer that is already known in advance. This situation is known as 'call-off stock arrangements'. The simplification is limited to certified taxable persons (CTP)[202] who are accredited for special VAT procedures.[203]

---

[192] Ibid.
[193] Now accepted and completed as: Council Directive (EU) 2018/1910 of 4 December 2018 amending Directive 2006/112/EC as regards the harmonization and simplification of certain rules in the value added tax system for the taxation of trade between Member States ST/12848/2018/COR/1 OJ L 311/3.
[194] European Commission, 'Proposal for a Council Directive amending Directive 2006/112/EC as regards harmonizing and simplifying certain rules in the value added tax system and introducing the definitive system for the taxation of trade between Member States' (COM (2017) 569 Final, 4 October 2017, https://ec.europa.eu/transparency/regdoc/rep/1/2017/EN/COM-2017-569-F1-EN-MAIN-PART-1.PDF, accessed 4 July 2020.
[195] F Martusciello, 'Proposal for a Council Directive Amending Directive 2006/112/EC as Regards the Introduction of the Detailed Technical Measures for the Operation of the Definitive VAT System for the Taxation of Trade Between Member States 2018-06' (Legislative Train Schedule, 24 June 2020), www.europarl.europa.eu/legislative-train/theme-deeper-and-fairer-internal-market-with-a-strengthened-industrial-base-taxation/file-technical-measures-the-definitive-vat-system, accessed 4 July 2020.
[196] COM (2018) 329 Final (25 May 2018).
[197] European Commission, 'Single VAT Area', https://ec.europa.eu/taxation_customs/business/vat/action-plan-vat/single-vat-area_en#heading_3, accessed 13 April 2020.
[198] COM (2018) 329 Final (25 May 2018).
[199] Ibid.
[200] Ibid.
[201] Ibid.
[202] Certified taxable person (CTP) is a new concept referring to a business that has applied to its national tax authority to become a reliable taxpayer with the accompanying benefit of enjoying 'a number of simplified procedures for the declaration and payment of cross-border VAT'. The business applying for CTP approval must prove 'compliance with pre-defined criteria such as: regular payment of taxes, internal controls, and proof of solvency'. Once certified, a CTP is mutually recognised by all the Member States of the EU; see ibid.
[203] European Commission, 'Single VAT Area', https://ec.europa.eu/taxation_customs/business/vat/action-plan-vat/single-vat-area_en#heading_3, accessed 13 July 2020.

ii.   *Simplification provided for chain transaction situations* that identify the supply with
      which the intra-Community transport of goods should be linked. This is limited to
      CTP.[204]

iii. *Simplification of the proof of transport* of goods between two EU Member States
      required to apply for the exemption to intra-Community supplies. This is limited
      to CTP.[205]

iv.   *Clarification* that, in addition to the proof of transport, the VAT number of the
      commercial partners recorded in the electronic EU VIES is needed for application
      of the cross-border VAT exemption under the current rules.[206]

The quick fixes are highly centred on the CTP. These quick fixes essentially attempt to
unpack and simplify some of the complex issues involving movements, transactions,
and certification and accounting processes. This is a smart move, since it takes time
to translate the definitive proposals into concrete actions across EU Member States.
In fact, it may take until 2022 before the definitive proposals would come into effect.
These 'quick fixes' are immediate actions that can be taken by EU Member States within
existing frameworks, particularly EUROFISC and the European Public Prosecutor
Office (EPPO) to control the VAT fraud.[207] EUROFISC[208] provides a mechanism for
EU Member States to enhance their administrative cooperation in combating organised
VAT fraud and especially carousel fraud.

EUROFISC makes it possible for EU Member States to engage in swift and targeted
sharing of information between all Member States on fraudulent activities.[209] The EPPO
is an institution established with competence to fight crimes against the Union budget.
In this regard EPPO will 'investigate, prosecute and bring to judgment crimes against
the EU budget, such as fraud, corruption or serious cross-border VAT fraud'.[210]

In terms of the cornerstones or fundamental principles for a 'definitive VAT regime',
the following elements abound:

i.   The principle of taxation at destination for intra-EU cross-border supplies of
     goods. This principle provides for the VAT rate of the Member State of destination
     to be charged.[211]

ii. The confirmation that the vendor is liable in the case of an intra-EU supply of
     goods as a general rule. Thus, the seller takes responsibility for charging and
     collecting the VAT. The buyer is, however, held liable for payment of the VAT due
     directly to the treasury of the Member State of destination if he/she is a reliable
     taxpayer, a so-called CTP.[212]

---

[204] Ibid.
[205] Ibid.
[206] Ibid.
[207] M Lamensch and E Ceci, 'VAT fraud: Economic impact, challenges and policy issues' (Study requested by the TAX3 Committee, PE 626.076, October 2018).
[208] Regulation on administrative cooperation and combating VAT fraud (Council Regulation 904/2010 ([2010] OJ L268/1).
[209] European Commission, 'Taxation: Anti-fraud network: EUROFISC starts operational work'.
[210] European Commission, 'European Public Prosecutor's Office', https://ec.europa.eu/info/law/cross-border-cases/judicial-cooperation/networks-and-bodies-supporting-judicial-cooperation/european-public-prosecutors-office_en, accessed 16 July 2020.
[211] European Commission, 'Single VAT Area'.
[212] Ibid.

iii. 'The One Stop Shop will be extended. Businesses will be able to make declarations, payments and deductions for cross-border supplies of goods through a single online portal, as is already the case for the supply of e-services. Member States will then pay the VAT to each other directly, as is already the case for the supply of e-services.'[213]

These three cornerstones for a definitive VAT system are by no means exhaustive, since the complex plane of VAT fraud throws up inevitable challenges with time.

In this current proposal,[214] very comprehensive proposed changes are made which go to overhaul the current VAT system. One of the key highlights of the proposed changes is the redefinition of a cross-border business-to-business (B2B) supply of goods.[215] The proposal is designed to discard the transitional VAT system and to introduce a new definitive VAT system still based on the destination principle. This seeks to counter the VAT gap and also to introduce simplifications in the system. It is hoped that there would be reduction in the administrative costs and burden on companies.[216] The proposal eliminates the 'intra-Community acquisition' concept 'from the [VAT] Directive, reviews or deletes all the provisions related to it and defines the concept intra-Union supply of goods.[217]

The proposal[218] was presented to the Council on 25 May 2018.[219] The European Parliament adopted the report on 12 February 2019.[220] The Working Party on Tax Questions (Indirect Taxation – VAT) in the Council is currently conducting assessment on the 25 May 2018 proposal.[221] One of the key priorities in the area of VAT remains the discussion on the definitive VAT system. At the same time, there will be improvement or quick fixes to 'the current VAT system ... until the agreement is reached on the definitive regime.'[222]

The definitive VAT regime proposals include:

- a modernised system of setting VAT rates, which aims at 'modernising the VAT rates framework and give greater flexibility to Member States as regards VAT rates';[223]

---

[213] Ibid.

[214] COM(2018) 329 Final, 25 May 2018.

[215] Martusciello, 'Proposal for a Council Directive Amending Directive 2006/112/EC'.

[216] Ibid.

[217] Ibid.

[218] COM(2018) 329 Final, 25 May 2018.

[219] Ibid; also see European Parliament, 'Detailed technical measures for the definitive VAT system for cross-border goods trade' (20 June 2019), www.europarl.europa.eu/thinktank/en/document.html?reference=EPRS_BRI(2018)625184, accessed 4 July 2020.

[220] European Parliament, 'European Parliament legislative resolution of 12 February 2019 on the proposal for a Council directive amending Directive 2006/112/EC as regards the introduction of the detailed technical measures for the operation of the definitive VAT system for the taxation of trade between Member States' (COM(2018)0329 – C8-0317/2018–2018/0164(CNS), www.europarl.europa.eu/doceo/document/TA-8-2019-0074_EN.html?redirect, accessed 4 July 2020; see also the European Parliament's events on the definitive system here: European Parliament, 'Operation of the definitive VAT system for the taxation of trade between Member States' (2018/0164(CNS), https://oeil.secure.europarl.europa.eu/oeil/popups/ficheprocedure.do?reference=2018/0164(CNS)&l=en, accessed 4 July 2020.

[221] COM (2018) 329 Final (25 May 2018); also see European Parliament, 'Detailed technical measures for the definitive VAT system for cross-border goods trade'.

[222] Martusciello, 'Proposal for a Council Directive Amending Directive 2006/112/EC'.

[223] European Commission, 'The Future of VAT', https://ec.europa.eu/taxation_customs/sites/taxation/files/factsheet_futurevat.pdf, accessed 15 May 2020.

- reinforced administrative cooperation between Member States, to enable EU Member States to more quickly share information and to cooperate more;[224]
- simplifying VAT for SMEs, presenting an update of special VAT rules for smaller companies, including looking at how to ease VAT obligations for small and medium-sized enterprises.[225]

These were followed by another proposal in 2018 which provides 'detailed technical provisions needed to operate the definitive VAT system'. The VAT Directive[226] received full technical adaptation[227] 'to reflect the changes needed to practically implement the VAT definitive regime' proposed. Similar to the EU law-making process in other subject areas,[228] these proposals are first submitted to the European Parliament and the European Economic and Social Committee for consultation and opinions, and the proposals are then sent to the EU Council for unanimous agreement to be reached by all the EU Member States in the Council before the agreement can enter into force. The expectation is that the Single EU VAT area would enter into force in 2022, subject to agreement by the parties.[229]

Lamensch and Ceci posit that the MTIC/carousel VAT fraud 'is the most damaging type of cross-border VAT fraud', with average annual losses amounting to €50 billion.[230] With the efforts to establish the single VAT area upon which the European Commission has proposed 'fundamental principles and key reforms for the EU's VAT area', there appears to be relief in sight. The definitive VAT regime has the potential to significantly mitigate if not eradicate MTIC/carousel VAT fraud in its current modelling. It must be expected, however, that adaptive as tax offenders are, 'new forms of MTIC fraud are likely to arise. Moreover, the one stop shop as currently designed is likely to create severe tensions between the Member States'.[231]

The implementation of the tax crime measures in the definitive VAT regime is guided by four criteria: equality and simplicity, budgetary impact, ease of administration and cost of collection, as well as prevention of fraud and abuse. See these illustrated in Figure 17.[232]

---

[224] Ibid.

[225] Ibid.

[226] Council Directive 2006/112/EC of 28 November 2006 on the common system of value added tax [2006] OJ L 347/1; also see Council Implementing Regulation (EU) No 282/2011 of 15 March 2011 laying down implementing measures for Directive 2006/112/EC on the common system of value added tax [2011] OJ L 77/1; for all the legal instruments constituting the legal framework of VAT, also see European Commission, 'Existing EU legal framework', https://ec.europa.eu/taxation_customs/business/vat/existing-eu-legal-framework_en, accessed 15 May 2020.

[227] See Martusciello, 'Proposal for a Council Directive Amending Directive 2006/112/EC'.

[228] For the law-making process from proposal by the Commission – opinions by the Economic and Social Committee – consultation in the Parliament – to negotiation and acceptance in the Council, see Eur-lex, 'Follow the steps of Procedure 2017/0251/CNS', https://eur-lex.europa.eu/legal-content/EN/HIS/?uri=COM%3A2017%3A569%3AFIN, accessed 4 July 2020.

[229] European Commission, 'The Future of VAT'.

[230] Lamensch and Ceci, 'VAT fraud'.

[231] Ibid, 8.

[232] European Commission, Brussels, 'Commission Staff Working Document on the implementation of the definitive VAT regime for intra-EU trade' (SWD(2014) 338 final, 29 October 2014), https://ec.europa.eu/taxation_customs/sites/taxation/files/resources/documents/taxation/vat/swd_2014_338.pdf, accessed 15 July 2020.

Figure 17 Criteria for Definitive VAT Regime

1. Equality and simplicity

- Same treatment be given to intra-EU and domestic transactions.
- This will result in simple and secure business transactions across EU.

2. Budgetary impact

- Allocation of VAT revenues to MS of final consumption of goods according to its own conditions such as VAT rates. This should lead to genuine level playing field.

3. Ease of administration and cost of collection

- There should be low administrative tax burden for tax administration and business as it is with domestic transactions.
- Ensure tax administration's capacity to conduct crossborder controls.

4. Prevention of fraud and abuse

- Ensure that breaks in the VAT chain with single market is effectively avoided.
- This should ensure that the VAT system continues to be robust and resilient against fraud.

Although fraud and abuse prevention are the more pressing elements in this discourse, it should be noted that the other three criteria are, to a large extent, interconnected with countering of tax fraud and abuse.[233] The VAT Expert Group[234] has applied these criteria in their work. It is hoped that not only would these criteria continue to be used by Commission Staff, EU Member States and other stakeholders, but also other components will be introduced to further enhance the steps towards the implementation of the definitive VAT regime.

With respect to the VAT e-commerce package, the following developments have ensued to date.

The EU Council adopted the VAT e-commerce package on 5 December 2017, which consists of three key legal instruments:

- Council Regulation (EU) 2017/2454;[235]
- Council Directive (EU) 2017/2455;[236]
- Council Implementing Regulation (EU) 2017/2459.[237]

---

[233] Ibid.

[234] See details of the expert group at: European Commission, VAT Expert Group', https://ec.europa.eu/taxation_customs/business/vat/vat-expert-group_en, accessed 23 April 2020.

[235] Council Regulation (EU) 2017/2454 of 5 December 2017 amending Regulation (EU) No 904/2010 on administrative cooperation and combating fraud in the field of value added tax OJ L 348/1.

[236] Council Directive (EU) 2017/2455 of 5 December 2017 amending Directive 2006/112/EC and Directive 2009/132/EC as regards certain value added tax obligations for supplies of services and distance sales of goods OJ L 348/7.

[237] Council Implementing Regulation (EU) 2017/2459 of 5 December 2017 amending Implementing Regulation (EU) No 282/2011 laying down implementing measures for Directive 2006/112/EC on the common system of value added tax OJ L 348/32.

In the same vein, to pave the way for a smooth transition to new VAT rules for e-commerce, the EU Council adopted the implementing measures for the VAT e-commerce package on 21 November 2019, which consist of two main legal instruments:

- Council Directive (EU) 2019/1995;[238]
- Council Implementing Regulation (EU) 2019/2026.[239]

Furthermore, the efforts to formulate a full e-commerce package were materialised in February 2020. The VAT e-commerce package, Commission Implementing Regulation (EU) 2020/194,[240] was adopted on 12 February 2020. This appears to have marked the full completion of the VAT e-commerce package, which lays down details on the working of or registration in the VAT 'One Stop Shop', including the Import One Stop Shop, and for the VAT One Stop Shop return.[241]

However, owing to challenges arising from the Covid-19 pandemic, the EU Commission, on 8 May 2020, made proposal to the EU Council 'to postpone[242] the introduction of new e-commerce VAT rules by six months'. The Council's adoption of this proposal will mean that the rules in Regulation (EU) 2020/194 will apply as of 1 July 2021, rather than the originally intended date of 1 January 2021. This would give enough time for EU Member States and businesses to prepare for the effective implementation of the new VAT rules on e-commerce.[243]

Essentially, the VAT e-commerce package gears towards facilitating cross-border trade, combating VAT fraud and ensuring fair competition for companies in the EU. To this end, the new rules provided by the e-commerce package include the following three key components:

- improvements of the current Mini One Stop Shop (MOSS);[244]
- special provisions applicable to supplies of goods facilitated by electronic interfaces;
- extension of the scope of the MOSS, turning it into a one stop shop (OSS).[245]

---

[238] Council Directive (EU) 2019/1995 of 21 November 2019 amending Directive 2006/112/EC ST/8010/2019/INIT OJ L 310/1.

[239] Council Implementing Regulation (EU) 2019/2026 of 21 November 2019 amending Implementing Regulation (EU) No 282/2011 as regards supplies of goods or services facilitated by electronic interfaces and the special schemes for taxable persons supplying services to non-taxable persons, making distance sales of goods and certain domestic supplies of goods ST/8011/2019/INIT OJ L 313/14.

[240] Commission Implementing Regulation (EU) 2020/194 of 12 February 2020 laying down detailed rules for the application of Council Regulation (EU) No 904/2010 as regards the special schemes for taxable persons supplying services to non-taxable persons, making distance sales of and certain domestic supplies of goods C/2020/657 OJ L 40/114.

[241] European Commission, 'Modernising VAT for cross-border e-commerce', https://ec.europa.eu/taxation_customs/business/vat/modernising-vat-cross-border-ecommerce_en, accessed 15 May 2020.

[242] For series of proposals by the EU Commission to defer tax rules as a result of Covid-19, see European Commission, 'Taxation: Commission proposes postponement of taxation rules due to Coronavirus crisis', https://ec.europa.eu/taxation_customs/news/taxation-commission-proposes-postponement-taxation-rules-due-coronavirus-crisis_en, accessed 15 May 2020.

[243] European Commission, 'Modernising VAT for cross-border e-commerce'.

[244] For the MOSS details, see European Commission, 'MOSS: A simplified system to declare VAT on Telecommunication, Broadcasting and Electronic (TBE) services in the EU', https://ec.europa.eu/taxation_customs/business/vat/telecommunications-broadcasting-electronic-services/, accessed 15 May 2020.

[245] European Commission, 'Modernising VAT for cross-border e-commerce', https://ec.europa.eu/taxation_customs/business/vat/modernising-vat-cross-border-ecommerce_en, accessed 15 May 2020.

The scope of the MOSS is to be extended to:

- business-to-consumer (B2C) supplies of services other than telecommunications, broadcasting and electronic (TBE) services;
- intra-EU distance sales of goods;
- certain domestic supplies of goods facilitated by electronic interfaces;
- distance sales of goods imported from third countries and third territories in consignments of an intrinsic value of maximum €150.[246]

From the foregoing, it can be realised that elements of TGP6 have been diversely integrated into the 2016 VAT Plan, except that the manner in which the procedures of strategic pillars of TGP6 are articulated in the 2016 VAT Plan is not as coherent or clear enough as envisaged in TGP6. There are other EU strategic measures for countering tax crimes in the EU – in fact, these strategies/plans are numerous, which also underlie the challenge of effective coordination of these measures.

The last but not the least two strategic measures to consider are the recent 2019 Commission Anti-Fraud Strategy (CAFS)[247] and 2019 Action Plan[248] of the EU, which provide pathways for countering fraud in the EU including VAT fraud, already treated above. However, while the previous considerations are more to do with both EU and Member States (focusing more on the latter), the 2019 Anti-Fraud Strategy and Action Plan are focused on fraud affecting the Union budget.

2019 Anti-Fraud Strategy and Action Plan

The CAFS of 2019[249] updates the Commission's 2011 CAFS.[250] The Commission adopted its 2011 CAFS with the following components:

- a Communication from the Commission to the other institutions, describing strategic objectives and key operational steps to attain them;[251] and
- a more detailed internal Commission Action Plan[252] to counter fraud.[253]

Thus, both the strategy and action plan were launched. This highlights an idea that although an action plan can be part of a strategy, an action plan can be separated to complement a strategy. Sometimes, also, an action plan can all the more be presented with components that characterise or resonate with the combined force of strategy and

---

[246] Ibid.

[247] European Commission, 'Commission Staff Working Document – Action Plan accompanying the document Commission Anti-Fraud Strategy' (SWD(2019) 170 final 29 April 2019).

[248] European Commission, 'Commission Anti-Fraud Strategy', COM(2019) 196 final.

[249] COM (2019) 196 final (CAFS, 29 April 2019).

[250] 24 June 2011.

[251] European Commission, 'Communication from the Commission to the European Parliament, the Council, the European Economic and Social Committee, and the Committee of the Regions and the Court of Auditors of 24 September 2011 on the Commission Anti-Fraud Strategy' (COM (2011) 376 final).

[252] European Commission, 'Communication to the Commission, Commission Internal Action Plan for the Implementation of the Commission Anti-Fraud Strategy' (SEC (2011) 787/3).

[253] COM (2019) 196 final (CAFS, 29 April 2019).

action plan such as the 2012 Action Plan and 2016 VAT Plan. It all depends on the scope and defining parameters of the term in question. In this context, the action plan is presented as a separate instrument that complements and expatiates on the monitoring and evaluation as well as implementation elements of a strategy as provided by the TGP6.

That said, the 2011 CAFS presented three priorities:

- introducing anti-fraud provisions in Commission proposals on spending programmes under the MFF for 2014–20;[254]
- implementing anti-fraud strategies at service level;[255] and
- revising the public procurement directives.[256]

Essentially, this strategy underscored the need to enhance counter-fraud measures both at the programme's level and service level as well as procurement/transactional level. It thus took a triangular approach to countering fraud – including VAT fraud. The reports that have been generated since 2013 regarding the implementation of the 2011 CAFS in the Reports[257] on Directive (EU) 2017/1371 have established that 'the priority actions and all measures set out in the internal action plan have been completed or are continuing in the case of those of a repetitive nature, eg, training'.[258]

Although the 2019 CAFS recognises the good strategic basis provided by the 2011 CAFS to counter fraud in the EU, the 2019 CAFS is necessitated by the imperative 'to adapt and strengthen [the European Commission's] anti-fraud activities where appropriate' on account of the preparation of the next MFF post-2020. Additionally, the 2019 CAFS strengthens measures 'against fraud that harms the budget on the revenue side (eg, by preventing tax fraud)'.[259]

The 2019 CAFS aims at achieving the following priority objective: 'to equip the Commission with a stronger analytical capability for purposes of prevention and detection and with a more centralised system of oversight for its anti-fraud action'. In this regard, the focus of the 2019 CAFS is on the protection of the financial interests of the EU 'from fraud, corruption and other intentional irregularities and on the risk of serious wrongdoing inside the EU's institutions and bodies', which also attract the legislature.[260] To this end, the 2019 CAFS encapsulates the following four classes of issue:

- Fraud (including VAT fraud), corruption and misappropriation that affect financial interests of the EU, as enshrined in Articles 3 and 4 of Directive (EU) 2017/1371.[261]

---

[254] COM (2019) 196 final (CAFS, 29 April 2019).

[255] Ibid.

[256] Ibid.

[257] See European Commission, 'Report from the Commission to the European Parliament and the Council, 29th Annual Report on the Protection of the European Union's financial interests – Fight against fraud' (2017, COM (2018) 553 final).

[258] Ibid.

[259] COM (2019) 196 final (CAFS, 29 April 2019).

[260] Regulation (EU, Euratom) No 883/2013 of the European Parliament and of the Council of 11 September 2013 concerning investigations conducted by the European Anti-Fraud Office (OLAF) and repealing Regulation (EC) No 1073/1999 of the European Parliament and of the Council, and Council Regulation (Euratom) No 1074/1999, OJ L 248/1, as amended, Art 1, paras 1 and 4.

[261] COM (2019) 196 final (CAFS, 29 April 2019).

- Other criminal offences that affect financial interests of the EU such as offences associated with abuse of procurement procedures where they affect the EU budget.[262]

- Irregularities as defined in Article 1(2) of Regulation (EC, Euratom) No 2988/9523 (insofar as they are intentional[263] but not already captured by the criminal offences referred to above).[264]

- Serious breaches of professional obligations by staff or Members of institutions and bodies of the Union, as referred to in Article 1(4) of the OLAF Regulation[265] and in the second subparagraph of Article 2(1) of Commission Decision (EC, ECSC, Euratom) No 352/199925.[266]

The use of fraud in the 2019 CAFS as provided above connotes a general term characterising various types of criminal and non-criminal wrongdoing.[267] It also provides 'a comprehensive approach to combating fraud affecting the EU's financial interests and guides the Commission, its departments and its executive agencies, as they discharge their legal, political and managerial responsibilities, respectively, to protect the EU budget'.[268]

As provided by TGP6 on the need to conduct threat assessment in strategy development, the fourth AMLD[269] provides that it is obligatory for each Member State of the EU to continuously 'take appropriate steps to identify, assess, understand and mitigate the risks of money laundering and terrorist financing affecting it, as well as any data protection concerns in that regard'. In the same vein, EU Member States shall use risk assessment to 'ensure that appropriate rules are drawn up for each sector or area, in accordance with the risks of money laundering and terrorist financing'.[270] Thus, risk assessment is linked to law-making, with the former providing a basis and guide for the latter. Risk assessment is also used to prioritise and allocate resources. To this end, the European Commission services conducted a fraud risk assessment on the 2011 CAFS so as to provide a guide for reviewing of the anti-fraud policies. Fraud risk assessment is carried out according to the Commission's decentralised model of financial management.[271] As a result, fraud risk assessment and management is conducted 'by authorising officers by delegation' pursuant to Article 74(2) of Regulation (EU, Euratom) 2018/1046.[272] Although this model of fraud risk assessment has a disadvantage of lack of effective centralised coordination of decentralised fraud risk assessment and management, it also has the key advantage of having 'the possibility to tailor anti-fraud strategies to the policy area or field of operations of the individual department concerned'.[273]

---

[262] Ibid.
[263] It is worth noting that although all irregularities appear to be included in the scope of the OLAF Regulation (Regulation (EU, Euratom) No 883/2013), the 2019 CAFS does focus on 'intentional wrongdoing'.
[264] COM (2019) 196 final (CAFS, 29 April 2019).
[265] Regulation (EU, Euratom) No 883/2013.
[266] COM (2019) 196 final (CAFS, 29 April 2019).
[267] Ibid.
[268] Ibid.
[269] Directive (EU) 2015/849, Art 7.
[270] Ibid, Art 7(4)(d).
[271] Ibid.
[272] The second sentence thereof.
[273] COM (2019) 196 final (CAFS, 29 April 2019).

Qualitative risk assessment was conducted by the European Commission services in collaboration with the executive agencies of the EU to determine vulnerability to fraud and fraud patterns. Reported vulnerabilities are identified as:

- insufficient analysis of fraud data, thus limiting the understanding of fraud by the European Commission; and

- certain gaps or weaknesses in the Commission's supervision over fraud risk management at department level – which have also been tackled by the Special Report of the European Court of Auditors (ECA).[274]

Two areas of improvement in fraud risk assessment and fraud risk management were established:

- The necessity of the Commission to be provided with a more comprehensive central analytical capability so that it can scan data on fraud patterns, fraudsters' profiles and vulnerabilities in EU internal control systems. This should support the Commission to develop anti-fraud policies based on facts, statistics and evidence; use its control mechanisms and resources as effectively and efficiently as possible; and enable fraud to be detected.[275]

- It is always critical to ensure that there is consistency and optimised efficiency and effectiveness in the counter fraud framework. But this will only be effectively achieved when 'decentralised assessment and management of fraud risks [are] coordinated and monitored by a strong central review system'. This is lacking in the current model of fraud risk assessment.

The 2019 CAFS also makes use of monitoring and evaluation. The Strategy considers 'the Evaluation of the CAFS for 2011–2017'. It also takes into consideration the results of the recent ECA performance audit known as 'Fighting fraud in EU spending: action needed'.[276] The intention of the European Commission is that it will ensure that its internal monitoring systems for the 2019 CAFS and the 2019 Action Plan are tightened and to 'develop indicators to make anti-fraud action more measurable'. This is a commendable step. It will also be useful to ensure that this exercise is timeously conducted. The Commission features this exercise in the annual reports on the protection of the EU's financial interests wherein the Commission regularly reports on CAFS' implementation.[277]

The overall evaluation[278] of the 2011 CAFS by the European Commission reached a conclusion that despite some shortcomings of the 2011 CAFS, the CAFS instrument 'is still relevant and effective as a policy framework for the Commission in protecting the EU budget'. Going forward, the CAFS is required 'to adapt to an evolving situation [including] new funding schemes and fraud trends, development of IT tools, etc.'[279]

---

[274] ECA, 'Special report No 01/2019: Fighting fraud in EU spending: action needed' (10 January 2019), www.eca.europa.eu/en/Pages/DocItem.aspx?did=48858, accessed 26 April 2020.
[275] COM (2019) 196 final (CAFS, 29 April 2019).
[276] ECA, 'Special report No 01/2019: Fighting fraud in EU spending'.
[277] COM (2019) 196 final (CAFS, 29 April 2019).
[278] Evaluation based on factors such as relevance, effectiveness, efficiency and coherence.
[279] COM (2019) 196 final (CAFS, 29 April 2019).

Obviously, by the mutative and unpredictable nature of fraud, it is imperative to continue to update existing counter-fraud frameworks based on evaluation results of threat/risk assessments.

The 2019 CAFS fits into the developing/current legislation in the anti-fraud framework by considering two key additions[280] made to EU anti-fraud legislation in 2017. While Directive (EU) 2017/1371 provides 'stricter common standards for Member States' criminal laws to protect the EU's financial interests', Regulation (EU) 2017/1939[281] has established the EPPO, to enhance cooperation among EU Member States in investigation and prosecution.

The 2019 CAFS has the following key features of a strategy as provided in TGP6:

- clear priorities;
- two main objectives and other objectives;
- fraud risk assessment;
- principles
- monitoring and reporting;
- accompanying updated 2019 Action Plan.[282]

However, in substance, not all the elements of TGP6 under these features are effectively articulated in the 2019 CAFS. The principles governing counter fraud measures in the 2019 CAFS are shown in Figure 18.

Figure 18   Governing Principles for Countering Fraud in 2019 CAFS

Fight against fraud: Guiding principles and target standards

- Zero tolerance for fraud
- Fight against fraud as an integral part of internal control
- Cost-effectiveness of controls
- Professional integrity and competence of EU staff
- Transparency on how EU funds are used
- Fraud prevention, notably fraud-proofing of spending programmes
- Effective investigation capacity and timely exchange of information
- Swift correction (including recovery of defrauded funds and judicial/administrative sanctions)
- Good cooperation between internal and external players
- Effective internal and external communication on the fight against fraud.

These principles do not effectively cover prosecution as a key principle, as it is done for investigation and prevention. Although prosecution may be captured under an umbrella term such as 'fight against', it does not appear to be enough, since priorities of fighting

---

[280] Directive (EU) 2017/1371, and Regulation (EU) 2017/1939 respectively.
[281] Council Regulation (EU) 2017/1939 of 12 October 2017 implementing enhanced cooperation on the establishment of the European Public Prosecutor's Office ('the EPPO'), OJ L 283/1.
[282] COM (2019) 196 final (CAFS, 29 April 2019).

against fraud can fluctuate along the plane of prevention, investigation/detection and prosecution. Prosecution was found by PROTAX focus groups as one of the effective means of countering tax crimes. This has been highlighted as a characteristic of the principle, 'pursue', in TGP6. Nonetheless, the outsourcing of OLAF that will also handle prosecution in the strategic framework of fraud countering is commendable. It must be noted, however, that the principles provided by the 2019 CAFS are more specific and less evasive than as put forward by TGP6 – but they both present relevant principles for countering tax fraud.

Complementarily, the 2019 Action Plan[283] seeks to improve anti-fraud cooperation and workflows across the EU institutions such as the Commission, OLAF and the EPPO. Additionally, the 2019 Action Plan does carry forward the work of the 2011 CAFS, especially in ensuring the integrity of public procurement and encouraging international cooperation.[284] The 2019 Action Plan demonstrates practical means of implementing the 2019 CAFS while taking account of the 2011 CAFS.[285]

Although EU Member States are not directly addressed by the 2019 CAFS, the Commission urges EU countries to ensure that appropriate steps are taken to prevent, detect and correct fraud affecting the EU's financial interests, in line with their obligation under the Treaty. It is incumbent on the responsible Commission departments and OLAF to continuously grant support to anti-fraud measures taken by the Member States of EU.[286]

At the heart of effective strategy making to counter tax crimes is how, where and when best to change approach or reform in order to succeed in fighting crime. This requires interplay of thought processes and action points, which have generally been covered by the above strategies and action plans. They combine instruments from both the legal framework and socio-political domain. In the legal framework, both criminal and civil/administrative legislative measures are generated and utilised. The general picture presented by the PROTAX focus groups in this regard is that synergistic development and operations of instruments to counter tax crimes should be cardinal in any reform agenda. PROTAX findings evidence that:

> Reforms aimed at strengthening the means of prevention, suppression and prosecution of tax offences must consider all the factors (legal and extra-legal) whereby policies must be integrated and balanced so that the development of reform is not counterproductive.[287]

As a result, it is concluded that tax collection and administrative systems along with the enforcement mechanisms should be reformed with an integrated strategy since no single way is available with the capacity to increase the effectiveness of instruments for preventing and combating tax offences.[288] So far, the EU appears to be increasingly adopting this approach and must continue to rigorously pursue that to the full.

Much as there should be an integrated approach to strategy development in this area, there has to be harmony and clarity that define extra-legal and legal as well as

---

[283] Ibid.
[284] COM (2019) 196 final (CAFS, 29 April 2019).
[285] Ibid.
[286] Ibid.
[287] F Rasmouki et al, 'D2.3 Approaches to tax crimes in the European Union' (EU PROTAX, 2019) 44.
[288] Ibid, 45.

civil/administrative and criminal domains. Turksen and Abukari posit that the confusion drawn from lack of clarity in criminal and civil domains does derive inspiration from the blurry and complicated nature of the strategies to distinguish between criminal tax offences and administrative tax offences at the EU level.[289]

The developments in tax fraud and tax evasion counter-measures mark an unprecedented moment in EU VAT history with so many different proposals in play at the same time.[290] This applies to tax crimes generally. These counter-measures potentially have 'far reaching consequences for businesses trading across the EU'.[291] It is time to gradually pause, take stock and see how the gamut of measures can be harmonised and consolidated while being made easy to implement and coordinate to succeed in fighting tax crimes. Otherwise, the risk of making the counter-crime rules inimical to the fight against tax crimes may be really high.

TGP7: Provision of Adequate Resources for Tax Crime Investigation

Laws without the backing of resources to enforce them (eg, human, financial and technical capacity of the LEAs) can easily become weak or even worthless. Without adequate resources for investigating tax crimes, therefore, the legal provisions to fight against tax crimes will be weak since it will be difficult to generate the required facts and evidence to successfully prosecute and convict tax offenders. The TGP7 advocates for jurisdictions to ensure that tax crime investigation agencies are given adequate resources to conduct investigations.[292] Two domains of resources are considered:

- the level and types of resources particularly relating to the nature, scale and developmental stage of the economy of a jurisdiction;[293]
- the allocation of resources to different functions in an agency.[294]

Thus, variations in approach by jurisdictions in providing adequate resources would primarily originate from these domains. Variation in the level and type of resources that should be provided for tax crime investigations is dependent upon 'the overall budgetary constraints and other budgetary priorities' of jurisdictions. Variation in the type of resources that is needed would depend on the nature, scale and developmental stage of the economy. An instance is given to the urgency to establish the legal and physical infrastructure before acquiring advanced analytical and technological tools. Considering the above factors, systematic, logical and informed decision-making should guide what resources should be provided at what point in time.

In addition, variations in relation to the allocation of resources to different functions within a tax crime investigation agency depends on different factors, including

---

[289] Turksen and Abukari, 'OECD's global principles and EU's tax crime measures'.
[290] PWC, 'Overview and current state of play'.
[291] Ibid.
[292] OECD, *Fighting Tax Crime* 48.
[293] PWC, 'Overview and current state of play'.
[294] Ibid.

the strategic priorities and the organisational structure therein. Whatever the structure and strategy may be, the needed resources should be given to the part of the tax crime agency that can effectively enhance the prospects for conducting successful investigations, which can positively impact prosecution and conviction of tax offenders.

In recognition of the variegated circumstances above, the TGP7 provides that the following are some of the important resources for agencies in charge of countering tax crime:

- financial resources;
- human resources;
- infrastructure resources;
- organisational resources; and
- data and technology resources.

With respect to financial resources, there is the need to have 'the budget and funding to pay for the needs of the agency' responsible for tax crime investigations.[295] Adequacy of human resources refers to ensuring that the tax crime investigation agency has the requisite and competent staff with necessary knowledge and skills. Undoubtedly, high quality and quantity of LEA personnel can have a significant influence on the capacity, capability, efficiency and effectiveness of that tax ecosystem.

PROTAX research revealed an interesting matrix of how the limited number of personnel working under limited resources affect quality and speed of investigations. In the Czech Republic focus group, for instance, the following observation was made:

> When cases are received by the police, time and resources are needed to investigate in the face of an already heavy workload. The police force and the judiciary are overloaded with cases: Last year, the FIU reported 25,000 STRs to the police. The tax administration also reports a high number of cases to the police.[296]

TGP7 is a principle that has been recognised by the EU and its Member States. But recognition is different from moving to implementation. Hardly is there any EU Member State that has not faced the difficulty of availing adequate resources to tax crime investigations.[297] PROTAX case studies found that:

> [T]ax authorities often lack access to specific types of expertise or tools for forensic analysis needed for complex fraudulent schemes. The lack of financial and human resources becomes particularly crucial when under-staffed prosecution is confronted with several lawyers from top-end law firms in court.[298]

---

[295] Ibid.

[296] Rasmouki et al, 'D2.3 Approaches to tax crimes' 45.

[297] C Cross, 'Resourcing and refocusing HMRC' in W Snell, *Tax Takes: Perspectives on building a better tax system to benefit everyone in the UK* (Tax Justice Network, 2017), www.taxjustice.uk/uploads/1/0/0/3/100363766/tjuk_tax_takes_2017.pdf, accessed 24 March 2020; L Buchan, 'Labour condemns "disastrous" HMRC cuts after millions of taxpayer calls go unanswered', *Independent* (30 May 2018), www.independent.co.uk/news/uk/politics/labour-hmrc-cuts-taxpayers-call-contact-helpline-revenue-customs-a8375261.html/, accessed 24 March 2020.

[298] U Turksen and others, 'D1.2: Case Studies of Tax Crimes' 14.

Although different organisational models can be used by jurisdictions and that resources are constrained in most cases, it is imperative that no matter the organisational model and resource envelope, jurisdictions should endeavour to allocate sufficient resources 'to investigate and take enforcement action in respect of tax crimes'.[299] This is crucial, because failure to reasonably allocate sufficient resources to tax crime investigations will mean that investigations will be undermined, which will consequently weaken the ecosystem of countering tax crimes.

An important point to note is that resources should be provided at the right time. This is because, with lackadaisical approach, the tax crime environment is fluidly dynamic to enable tax crime suspects escape well before investigators are granted the needed resources to follow up. Ability to conduct investigations in 'the golden hour' when the evidence is 'fresh and hot' can reduce cost and length of investigations and strengthen the prospects of successful prosecutions, convictions and/or asset recovery.

The EU legal framework does provide relevant legal and policy infrastructure for equipping tax crime investigations with adequate resources. Pursuant to Article 48(2) of the fourth AMLD, Member States were already required to ensure that relevant agencies are given 'adequate financial, human and technical resources to perform their functions'.[300] In particular, Article 32 (3) of the third AMLD provided that EU 'Member States shall provide their FIUs with adequate financial, human and technical resources in order to fulfil their tasks'.[301] The same obligation is imposed on EU Member States with respect to competent authorities.[302] The fifth AMLD provides an additional lever to the resource allocation imperative, which is that Member States of EU shall produce a report on allocated resources.[303] In keeping with this spirit, the sixth AMLD also entreats EU Member States to ensure availability of 'sufficient personnel and targeted training, resources and up-to-date technological capacity' for relevant agencies.[304] While this provision distinguishes human and technological resources from the general resource envelope provided by TGP8, it all boils down to providing the needed tools to investigations of financial crime by criminal law – with TGP8 being more specific on tax crime investigations while the sixth AMLD focuses on 'organised crime or other serious crimes' (which, anyway, would capture some tax crimes such as high-value and cross-border VAT fraud).

Judging by the dimensions of TGP7, the EU counter tax crime framework has the necessary provisions for adequate supply of resources to tax crime investigations. The lingering question, however, is the extent of adequacy of allocations made to both EU investigative institutions and that of relevant institutions of EU Member States. Following FATF Recommendation 2, the EU AML regime makes it mandatory for each Member State to use risk assessment to assist it in the allocation and prioritisation of resources to combat money laundering and terrorist financing.[305] This can be used as

---

[299] OECD, *Fighting Tax Crime* 48.
[300] Directive (EU) 2015/849.
[301] Ibid.
[302] Ibid, Art 1(30).
[303] Ibid, Art 1(4) and (27).
[304] Directive (EU) 2018/1673, recital 19.
[305] Directive (EU) 2015/849 as amended by Directive (EU) 2018/843, Art 7. Also see, Art 44(e) of Directive (EU) 2018/843.

a safeguard for proper allocation of limited resources against which there are several competing needs of the relevant agencies.

The outstanding issue has to do with taking bold steps to ensure that the resources are actually delivered in a way that makes the work of relevant agencies more effective.

TGP8: Establish Organisational Structure with Defined Responsibilities

It can be challenging for tax authorities and other LEAs to effectively and efficiently counter tax crimes if, beyond other factors, they first cannot 'put their house in order' by:

- Ensuring that each agency in the tax crime countering ecosystem is organised with appropriate functional layers that effectively support each other rather than undermine each other.

- Ensuring that the responsibilities for each agency and functional unit or layer are clearly defined. This can go a long way to mitigating part of the challenge in the first point above.

There are different organisational models that can be used to exemplify a best practice scenario for organisations with defined responsibilities. TGP8 provides that jurisdictions should endeavour to design and utilise an organisational model with clearly defined responsibilities for countering tax crimes and other' financial crimes such as money laundering and corruption.[306] The four (alternative) choices of organisational models provided by TGP8 are set out in Table 22.

Table 22 General Organisational Models for Investigating Tax Crimes

Models	Description
1	The tax administration has responsibility for directing and conducting investigations, often through a specialist criminal investigations division. The public prosecutor's office does not have a direct role in investigations, though a prosecutor may provide advice to investigators with respect to matters such as legal process and the laws of evidence.[307]
2	The tax administration has responsibility for conducting investigations, under the direction of the public prosecutor or, exceptionally, examining judges.[308]
3	A specialist tax agency, under the supervision of the Ministry of Finance but outside the tax administration, has responsibility for conducting investigations, which may involve public prosecutors.[309]
4	The police or public prosecutor has responsibility for conducting investigations.[310]

---

[306] Ibid.
[307] OECD, *Fighting Tax Crime* 44.
[308] Ibid.
[309] Ibid.
[310] Ibid.

TGP8 is a principle that is presented as an outstanding challenge for many EU Member States. However, the EU has, through its strategies and action plans, encourage its Member States to recognise and operationalise this principle in their tax crime countering measures. At the same time, a combination of legal provisions obliges EU Member States to act in ways that will result in defined responsibilities for relevant investigative agencies.

The fifth AMLD obliges EU Member States to provide a report on 'the institutional structure and broad procedures of their AML/CFT regime, including, inter alia, the FIU, tax authorities and prosecutors'.[311] One of the key factors informing this obligation is to see and keep track of the defined responsibilities of relevant tax crime agencies in the EU. Recital 44 of the fifth AMLD not only requires the role of public authorities acting as competent authorities with designated responsibilities to be strengthened by Member States, but also that of other relevant authorities including anti-corruption authorities and tax authorities.[312] The regulated entities such as credit institutions and financial institutions of Member States are also required to document their respective responsibilities.[313] These will allow for certainty in roles played and how effective regulation and cooperation between institutions can be achieved.

These provisions do not clearly articulate any of the above organisational models but mainly entreats EU Members to ensure that responsibilities of relevant authorities are defined. EU Member States will therefore draw inspiration from these obligations to define responsibilities of their organisational structures according to their local realities and challenges. PROTAX case studies found that, across the EU, there were differences in responsibilities and division of roles of tax crime agencies. For instance, whereas there are jurisdictions such as Ireland and the United Kingdom in which tax authorities have investigative and prosecutorial powers, there are other jurisdictions such as Finland and Czech Republic in which tax authorities do not have investigative and prosecutorial powers.[314] The thresholds that determine whether a case is investigated through an administrative or criminal procedure are key determinants of the demarcation of the roles (and powers) within a tax ecosystem.[315]

Countries such as Czech Republic, Portugal, Malta, Ireland and Italy were said to have, in their legal frameworks, clearly defined roles for LEAs in respect of investigative and prosecution responsibilities in these jurisdictions. Countries such as Estonia, Finland and the Unitedc Kingdom were said to have a lack of clarity in responsibilities of agencies in charge of investigation and prosecution. However, the PROTAX focus group in Finland reported that the defined responsibilities across the LEA ecosystem do not pose any problems in practice, nor do they lead to any vulnerabilities or weaknesses in the prosecution of tax crimes.[316] This is of course arguable and appears exceptional since clarity of roles not only prevents duplication of goal and performance of activities but also inhibits effective functioning across different layers of the tax crime ecosystem.

---

[311] Directive (EU) 2018/843, Art 1(4) and (27).
[312] Ibid, recital 44.
[313] Directive (EU) 2018/2015/849, Art 19(d).
[314] Rasmouki et al, 'D2.3 Approaches to tax crimes' 54.
[315] Ibid, 57.
[316] Ibid.

In fact, the PROTAX focus group in the United Kingdom posited that 'the current division of responsibilities does lead to weaknesses in the system. These weaknesses do not emanate from lack of legal powers'.[317]

TGP9: Need to have Effective Framework for Domestic Inter-Agency Cooperation

By now, it should be clear that countering tax crimes consists of key stages, strategies, activities and structures in order to frontally face the complexities in the tax crime ecosystem. The stages of countering tax crimes such as 'prevention, detection, investigation and prosecution of offences, and the recovery of the proceeds of crime' involve several stakeholders including government agencies such as 'tax administration, the customs administration, financial regulators, AML authorities including the FIU, the police and specialised law enforcement agencies, anti-corruption authorities and the public prosecutor's office'.[318] In effect, several agencies are responsible for taking steps through the above stages to fight against tax crimes in every jurisdiction. These agencies could also uniquely 'hold information essential to these activities'.[319]

The four models identified in TGP8 above show that each model has distinct features regarding the allocation of competence for the following agencies:

- a tax administration;[320]
- a customs administration;[321]
- AML authorities (including FIUs);[322]
- police and specialised LEAs (including authorities in charge of the investigation of corruption offences);[323]
- a public prosecutor's office;[324] and
- financial regulators;[325] as well as
- magistrates, judges or justices.

Owing to the fact that organisational models for countering tax crimes have distinctive characteristics, the distinctiveness of each needs to be considered when strategies for inter-agency cooperation are being developed. This move will enable achievement of the full benefits of cooperation. The determination and actualisation of the specific agency that is responsible for countering tax crime has the propensity of impacting

---

[317] Ibid.
[318] OECD, *Fighting Tax Crime* 58.
[319] OECD, *Effective Inter-Agency Co-operation in Fighting Tax Crimes*.
[320] Ibid, 11.
[321] Ibid.
[322] Ibid.
[323] Ibid.
[324] Ibid.
[325] Ibid.

directly on the processes and agreements required to achieve a desired benefit from cooperation.[326]

Therefore, the roles of the different government agencies can be more effective if they cooperate to share experiences and information on tax crimes. Cooperation between relevant agencies will thus include:

- information-sharing; and
- other forms of cooperation.[327]

TGP9 advocates that every jurisdiction should have an effective legal and administrative framework to facilitate collaboration between tax authorities and other domestic law enforcement and intelligence agencies.[328]

Cooperation Through Information-Sharing

Key components of an effective information-sharing regime include legal gateways for information-sharing, types of information-sharing, and forms of information-sharing.

The Legal Gateways

Information-sharing has legal gateways. Legal gateways for information-sharing between relevant agencies refer to the laws that stipulate the way agencies can be able to share information between themselves. It is imperative to ensure that there are legal gateways of information sharing between the relevant agencies. The forms of legal gateways for sharing information include those shown in Table 23.

Table 23 Legal Gateways for Information-Sharing

Primary legislation	Usually primary legislation sets out the basic framework for cooperation, whereby an agency could be required to share certain types of information in specified circumstances, or by generally allowing information-sharing between agencies subject to limited exceptions.[329]
Bilateral agreements	As the domestic law would permit, bilateral agreements or 'memoranda of understanding' can be entered into by agencies with the agreement on how information will be shared between them in a certain way, at a given time, as well as on types of information to be shared, circumstances for information-sharing, and any restrictions on sharing information, such as that the information may only be used for specified purposes.[330]

---

[326] Ibid.
[327] OECD, *Fighting Tax Crime* 58.
[328] Ibid.
[329] Ibid, 59.
[330] Ibid.

At the same time, other terms of bilateral agreements between relevant agencies include the information request format, particulars of competent officials that have been authorised to deal with requests, 'agreed notice periods and time limits or a requirement for the agency receiving information to provide feedback on the results of investigations in which the information was used'.[331]

Information-Sharing Types

There are generally four types of cooperation on information-sharing among relevant agencies operating in the tax crime ecosystem:

- Having direct access to information in the records or database of an agency, including being granted direct access to mass or bulk data or specific access rights to a particular case record or file.[332]
- Having in place obligation to provide information automatically or spontaneously.[333]
- Having the ability (not an obligation) to spontaneously provide information.
- Having the obligation or ability to provide information, but only in response to a specific request which is made on a case-by-case basis.[334]

Information-Sharing Forms in Different Contexts

The effectiveness of forms of information sharing will be dependent on the different contexts in which they are used. Three of these contexts are summarised below:

- For purposes of analytics and high-level risk assessment, the most effective forms of information exchange are given as direct access, or automatic or spontaneous exchange of information.[335]
- In situations where a long-standing cooperative relationship exist between the relevant agencies, and there is a clear understanding of the kind of information that could be useful in the activities of the recipient agency, discretionary spontaneous sharing of information has been determined as most effective to be deployed.[336]
- In situations where the information that is required is very specific or needs to be in a certain form, it has been determined that information on request or direct access to a specific case record would be most appropriate.[337]

---

[331] Ibid.
[332] Ibid.
[333] Ibid.
[334] Ibid.
[335] Ibid, 60.
[336] Ibid.
[337] Ibid.

TGP9 advances further that 'it may be most effective if the broadest possible range of information sharing methods is available, both from and to the agency investigating tax crimes'.[338]

Other Cooperation Forms

Apart from the above information-sharing forms, LEAs also use a range of other forms of cooperation, including joint investigation teams, inter-agency centres of intelligence, and secondments and co-location of personnel. With respect to joint investigation teams, agencies with a common interest are enabled to work together in an investigation whereby they can share information, combine and/or benefit from a wider range of skills and experience from investigators with different backgrounds and training.[339]

In terms of inter-agency centres of intelligence, they are usually set up 'to centralise processes for information gathering and analysis for a number of agencies' in to pay attention to 'operational information (case-specific information and investigations) or strategic information (broader assessment of risks and threats, focusing on a specific geographic area or type of criminal activity, or having a wider role in information sharing). The centralised activities enable officials to 'obtain experience of particular legal and practical issues'.[340] This results in developing specialised systems, with the potential of increasing their effectiveness.

Regarding secondments and co-location of personnel (eg, liaison officers), these are presented as an effective way of enabling skills to be transferred while allowing personnel to build contacts with their counterparts in another agency.[341] This form of cooperation also allows LEAs to experience problems in their local contexts and assess subsequent risks that impact their respective jurisdictions. OECD research[342] indicates that such platforms benefit inter-agency cooperation in many ways:

- encouraging officials to recognise opportunities for cooperation;[343]
- bringing about more proactive engagement of seconded officials with counterparts from other agencies;
- improving cooperation effectiveness; and
- increasing the speed and efficiency of information-sharing.[344]

Apart from the strategic formulations of inter-agency cooperation outlined above, other cooperation measures, inter alia using shared databases, disseminating strategic intelligence products (including newsletters and intelligence briefs), establishing joint committees to coordinate policy in areas of shared responsibility, holding inter-agency meetings and training sessions to share information in areas such as financial crime,

---

[338] Ibid.
[339] Ibid.
[340] Ibid.
[341] Ibid, 61.
[342] Ibid.
[343] Ibid.
[344] Ibid.

guidance on investigative techniques and best practice in managing cases, together with involvement in joint research projects can all be instigated.

Based on the foregoing, TGP9 provides nine best practice areas for inter-agency cooperation, shown in Figure 19.

Figure 19 Best Areas of Practice for Inter-Agency Cooperation

Granting	Having	Putting	Developing
• the tax administration access to STRs • the FIU access to certain information held by the tax administration	• a co-ordinated strategy for analysing and responding to STRs • to put obligations on tax officials to report suspicions of non-tax crimes to the police or public prosecutor	• obligations on tax officials to report suspicions of non-tax crimes to the police or public prosecutor • in place a centralised structure for inter-agency co-operation • to use multi-agency task forces to combat financial crimes	• a co-ordinated approach to recovering the proceeds of crime • cooperation with the private sector in the fight against tax crime.

The forms of cooperation provided by TGP9 can be applied alongside each other. The use of any of the forms of cooperation 'does not necessarily exclude the other'. The use of appropriate forms of cooperation depends upon 'the organisational structure in place in a jurisdiction, and which agency has responsibility for investigating tax crimes'.[345]

According to TGP9, jurisdictions should make the best use of cooperation by ensuring that the relevant agencies are given 'identifiable contact points for information sharing and co-operation, as well as a clear understanding of the types of information and powers the other agencies possess'. As with the preceding counter measures, ensuring inter-agency cooperation is subject to the domestic law and the need to prevent any abuse of powers'.[346] An important question to answer is whether agencies in the tax crime countering system in a jurisdiction effectively cooperate among themselves in their activities? A 'yes' to this question is all that the TGP9 seeks to achieve. One wonders how the EU approaches this.

Benchmarking Inter-Agency Domestic Cooperation

The EU has established a legal framework for inter-agency cooperation in EU Member States. Accordingly, most of the EU Member States have also provided some legal, policy

---

[345] Ibid.
[346] Ibid.

and operational framework that allows for inter-agency cooperation domestically and internationally.

With respect to the legal framework, there are several provisions which require and enable inter-agency cooperation in EU Member States.

Article 15 of Directive (EU) 2017/1371, for example, provides that:

> Without prejudice to the rules on cross-border cooperation and mutual legal assistance in criminal matters, the Member States, Eurojust, the European Public Prosecutor's Office and the Commission shall, within their respective competences, cooperate with each other in the fight against the criminal offences referred to in Articles 3, 4 and 5. To that end the Commission, and where appropriate, Eurojust, shall provide such technical and operational assistance as the competent national authorities need to facilitate coordination of their investigations.

Furthermore, the EU AML legal framework[347] includes tax crime in the list of predicate crimes, and Articles 49[348] and 58 of Directive (EU) 2015/849 have provided the clear insights into the foundational requirement of agencies of EU Member States to cooperate nationally or domestically. These provisions have been respectively amended by Articles 1(31) and 1(38) of Directive (EU) 2018/843 to accommodate tax crimes and LEAs in inter-agency cooperation.

Article 1(31) of Directive (EU) 2018/843 replaces Article 49 of Directive (EU) 2015/849 with the following provision:

> Member States shall ensure that policy makers, the FIUs, supervisors and other competent authorities involved in AML/CFT, as well as tax authorities and law enforcement authorities when acting within the scope of this Directive, have effective mechanisms to enable them to cooperate and coordinate domestically concerning the development and implementation of policies and activities to combat money laundering and terrorist financing, including with a view to fulfilling their obligation under Article 7 [on measures for assessing risks].

Essentially, these relatively recent legal instruments have introduced the need for tax authorities and LEAs to be part of the inter-agency cooperation architecture for countering certain financial crimes in EU Member States. This does not appear to be far-reaching enough because the ultimate aim of the cooperation in this provision is to counter 'money laundering and terrorist financing'. Although tax crimes are predicate offences for money laundering, there can be times when the two regimes are put into different silos, thereby creating the need to clearly indicate that this inter-agency cooperation will also target tax crimes. The idea that just because tax authorities 'acting within the scope[349] of Directive (EU) 2015/849' is a sufficient imperative to energise tax authorities to effectively cooperate domestically appears overrated.

---

[347] Mainly consisting of Directive (EU) 2015/849, Directive (EU) 2018/843, and Directive (EU) 2018/1673.

[348] Art 49 provides: 'Member States shall ensure that policy makers, the FIUs, supervisors and other competent authorities involved in AML/CFT have effective mechanisms to enable them to cooperate and coordinate domestically concerning the development and implementation of policies and activities to combat money laundering and terrorist financing, including with a view to fulfilling their obligation under Article 7' (regarding risk assessment measures).

[349] Directive (EU) 2015/849, Art 1.

However, as mentioned above, the EU legal framework also provides further inter-agency domestic cooperation obligations in Article 58 of Directive (EU) 2015/849.[350] Competent authorities[351] are not only obliged to cooperate domestically with other relevant authorities, but also with agencies outside their national borders in the EU. Article 1(38) of the Directive (EU) 2015/849, adds to the above Article 58 as follows:

> Member States shall further ensure that where their competent authorities identify breaches which are subject to criminal sanctions, they inform the law enforcement authorities in a timely manner.

In this amendment, domestic cooperation of competent authorities with other authorities has gone further to highlight the need for competent authorities to timeously cooperate with other LEAs.

From the PROTAX focus groups[352] and conference,[353] a number of countries were said to have in place relevant, if not very effective inter-agency cooperation. However, several challenges were also found, and a number of success factors proffered. Insights into how the challenges and success factors were featured in different EU jurisdictions were highlighted.

Most of the participants in the PROTAX focus groups opined that the legal and operational frameworks in their jurisdictions influence the effectiveness of collaboration and communication between LEAs.[354] As a highlight of the challenges with inter-agency cooperation in most jurisdiction, Portugal was said to have a weak inter-agency cooperation framework particularly owing to the fact that agencies do not receive feedback about the outcome of cases investigated, and the inability of the FIU to freeze accounts.[355] Figure 20 summarises opinions from the PROTAX focus groups. It must be noted that these are both dispersed and synthesised views which represent a

---

[350] Art 58(5).

[351] Competent authorities in EU Member States responsible for disclosure supervision include the following: Financial Market Authority in Austria, Prudential Regulation Authority and Financial Conduct Authority in the United Kingdom, Financial Supervision Authority in Estonia, Central Bank of Ireland in Ireland, Banca d'Italia in Italy, Commission de Surveillance du Secteur Financier in Luxembourg, Banco de Portugal in Portugal, National Bank of Slovakia in Slovakia, Bank of Lithuania in Lithuania, Polish Financial Supervision Authority in Poland, De Nederlandsche Bank in the Netherlands, Malta Financial Services Authority in Malta, Banco de España in Spain, Bank of Slovenia in Slovenia, Finansinspektionen in Sweden, National Bank of Romania in Romania, Financial and Capital Market Commission in Latvia, Central Bank of Hungary in Hungary, BaFin and Bundesbank in Germany, Bank of Greece in Greece, Autorité de contrôle prudentiel et de Resolution in France, Finanssivalvonta (Fin-FSA) in Finland, Bulgarian National Bank in Bulgaria, National Bank of Belgium in Belgium, Central Bank of Cyprus in Cyprus, Czech National Bank in Czech Republic, Finanstilsynet in Denmark, and Croatian National Bank for credit institutions and Croatian Financial Services Supervisory Agency for investment firms in Croatia; see European Banking Authority, 'Competent Authorities', https://eba.europa.eu/supervisory-convergence/supervisory-disclosure/competent-authorities, accessed 16 April 2020; for comprehensive details of EU competent authorities, see also European Securities and Market Authority (ESMA), 'EU Acts and National Competent Authorities', www.esma.europa.eu/rules-databases-library/eu-acts-and-national-competent-authorities, accessed 16 April 2020.

[352] Rasmouki et al, 'D2.3 Approaches to tax crimes' 69.

[353] Hall et al, 'D2.4 Conference Report' 24.

[354] Rasmouki et al, 'D2.3 Approaches to tax crimes' 70.

[355] Ibid.

number of crosscutting issues in several countries, while some of the views may well be limited to just one or two countries.

Figure 20 PROTAX Survey Opinions on Challenges for Inter-Agency Cooperation

Challenges	▪ Lack of legal protection for professionals from the private sector to share information
	▪ Lack of legal frameworks underpinning collaboration mechanisms with obliged entities lack, thereby resulting in lack of legal powers to enforce the need to access relevant information
	▪ Lack of shared databases between LEAs compared to other authorities within the same jurisdiction
	▪ Secrecy obligations creating obstacles to obtaining information from the private sector but also within the LEA eco-system
	▪ Lack of willingness to collaborate from certain categories of enablers such as auditors, lawyers and real estate agents
	▪ The focus of some obliged entities is on ticking boxes rather than intelligence-led flow of information
	▪ Multiplicity of relevant authorities resulting in duplication of effort in some instances
	▪ Restricted access to information of a given authority compared to other authorities.

On the other hand, countries such as Estonia, Malta and Portugal were deemed to have good LEAs cooperation with banks (thus, the private sector/obliged entity). Another seeming good example is the requirement that corporations should 'have a *collegio sindacale* [board of statutory auditors] – a peculiarity of Italy – [which] might entail obligations for the members of such body to report crimes to judicial authorities'. This feature allows corporations to cooperate with judicial authorities.[356]

The PROTAX focus groups rightly opined that it is important for EU Member States to establish solid public-private partnerships since these 'are crucial to the fight against tax crimes especially with regards to benefiting from the expertise of the private sector'. There is continued increase in the appetite of EU jurisdictions to open up more space for inter-agency cooperation, particularly so at the EU level where this imperative has significantly been accentuated in the legal framework for countering financial crime. It can, therefore, be argued that although significant challenge exists relating to private-public cooperation, 'there is considerable potential for improvement of cooperation with the private sector in general'.[357]

Also, the PROTAX focus group in Czech Republic noted that tax crime detection by the FIU is effective owing to its close collaboration with the tax administration. At the same time, conviction rates are published and shared with the media while 'court decisions are stored on an electronic database where selected decisions of the court

---

[356] Ibid.
[357] Ibid.

are published, and other decisions are available upon request'. It also came out that, to ensure data quality across LEAs in the Czech Republic, a platform called Tax Cobra has been created for data exchange. This 'has facilitated inter-agency information exchange and coordination'. Indeed, it is appealing to find that the Tax Cobra platform was used to address 'a problem whereby financial officers (ie, the police) did not have access to information to carry out investigations'.[358]

Additionally, countries such as Finland, Estonia and the Czech Republic were presented as having 'adequate technological platforms for data exchange between various LEAs, which considerably facilitate inter-agency information exchange and co-operation'.[359] As established earlier in this book, the JMLIT with wide public-private participation does place the United Kingdom in an advantageous position compared to other countries.[360] Some of the success factors for overcoming challenges confronting inter-agency cooperation in EU Member States are summarised in Figure 21.

Figure 21   PROTAX survey opinions on success factors for inter-agency cooperation

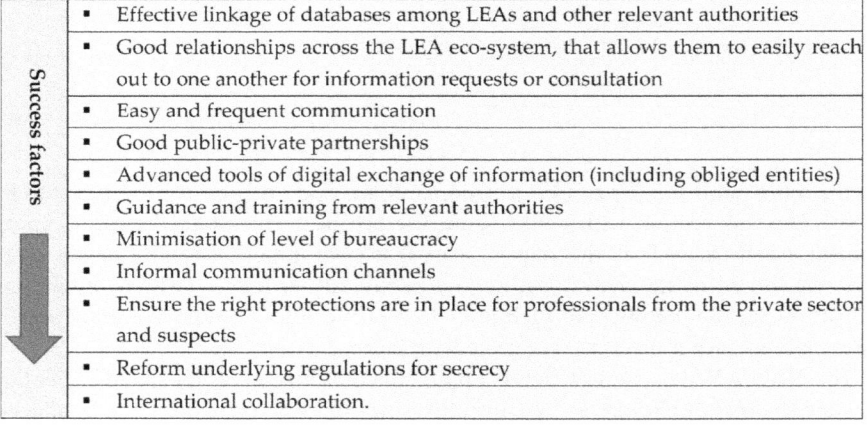

Success factors	• Effective linkage of databases among LEAs and other relevant authorities
	• Good relationships across the LEA eco-system, that allows them to easily reach out to one another for information requests or consultation
	• Easy and frequent communication
	• Good public-private partnerships
	• Advanced tools of digital exchange of information (including obliged entities)
	• Guidance and training from relevant authorities
	• Minimisation of level of bureaucracy
	• Informal communication channels
	• Ensure the right protections are in place for professionals from the private sector and suspects
	• Reform underlying regulations for secrecy
	• International collaboration.

A lot has been achieved in developing the general EU framework for inter-agency cooperation. However, more 'needs to be done in the area of seamless cooperation between agencies involved in the investigation and prosecution of tax crimes'.[361] The details of the forms of domestic inter-agency cooperation established by TGP9 do not appear to be comprehensively drawn up by the EU to be translated into action within national legal frameworks. However, most EU jurisdictions appear to have laid down mechanisms for agencies to cooperate domestically in the fight against tax crimes. At the same time, due to the supranational nature of EU law (being both domestic and international), the EU legal framework on tax crimes provides international cooperation mechanisms that have significant influence on domestic inter-agency cooperation.

---

[358] Ibid, 46.
[359] Ibid, 65.
[360] Ibid, 70.
[361] C Remeur, 'Anti-tax-avoidance directive' (DG EPRS, EU Parliament, July 2016); Turksen and Abukari, 'OECD's global principles and EU's tax crime measures'.

TGP10: Ensuring Availability of International Cooperation Mechanisms

Just like inter-agency cooperation, international cooperation presents a cocktail of significant benefits for countering tax crimes. International cooperation presents even more due to the increasing cross-border nature of tax crimes. For example, foreign jurisdictions and offshore financial centres are often used to hide assets/income, or proceeds from illicit transactions.[362] These would be secured without any declaration made to tax authorities.[363]

While this manipulative feature criss-crosses borders of several countries, it is intriguing that more often than not, investigation agencies and LEAs have powers which are limited by jurisdictional boundaries.[364] Although the EU has a special case of acting as a domestic jurisdiction having its criminal justice frameworks with international outlook, every national jurisdiction needs to participate in designing and implementing cooperation mechanisms that will enable investigation agencies to cooperate in countering tax crimes that evade the individual jurisdictional boundaries of countries. TGP10 therefore provides that:

> Tax crime investigation agencies must have access to criminal legal instruments and an adequate operational framework for effective international co-operation in the investigation and prosecution of tax crimes.[365]

Because of the cross-border and large scale (and volume) of tax crimes, international collaboration is crucial. The OECD has been a global pacesetter on countering tax crimes whereby it has developed strategic collaboration with institutions including the UN, IMF and FATF as well as the EU in developing and implementing tax crime measures. The forms which international cooperation can assume include the following:

- information-sharing;
- facilitation of testimony taking from witnesses;
- service of documents;
- transfer of persons for questioning;
- obtaining evidence;
- joint investigation;
- execution of freezing and seizing orders.[365]

Any serious arrangement between many parties that requires greater legitimacy and sustainability must first be guided by a legal instrument to regulate conduct outside the normal legal framework regulating everyone's conduct. Therefore, for international cooperation to be effectively actioned, TGP10 echoes the need for 'a legal agreement

---

[362] See J Garcia-Bernardo et al, 'Uncovering Offshore Financial Centers: Conduits and Sinks in the Global Corporate Ownership Network (2017) 7(6246) *Science Reports*, https://doi.org/10.1038/s41598-017-06322-9, accessed 12 February 2020.
[363] OECD, *Fighting Tax Crime* 64.
[364] Ibid.
[365] Ibid.
[366] Ibid.

setting out the terms and procedural requirements'. Forms of agreement[367] that could be used and have, so far, been used to authorise international cooperation for crimes such as tax crimes include the following legal gateways:

• Information sharing agreements, including TIEAs.[368]

• Agreements for exchange of information and administrative assistance.

• Agreements for cooperation in using investigative and coercive powers, including MLATs.[369]

• Bilateral tax treaties and other instruments, including the Multilateral Convention on Mutual Administrative Assistance in Tax Matters.[370]

In these legal gateways, information, knowledge, experience, evidence, and culprits (if relevant) are mutually shared among parties. At the same, these also involve elements such as facilitation of witness testimony taking, execution of freezing and seizing orders as well as conducting joint investigations.[371]

Given the complex layers of international engagements (especially regarding differences in legal systems, culture and political considerations) with competing priorities, any legal agreement on international cooperation to counter tax crimes whether at the EU level or beyond, should take not only a balancing approach but also a 'holistic approach'. Successful international cooperation, in this regard, will depend greatly on this imperative. To achieve this, broader stakeholder engagement with a high level of transparency and integrity as well as needs and risk assessments must be at the forefront, to reach a legal agreement. TGP10 adds that it is equally 'of key importance that jurisdictions have a far-reaching and functioning international cooperation network' as a result. Such a cooperation network should be able to feature[372] tenets such as in Table 24.

Table 24 Characteristics of International Cooperation Network

Key terms	International cooperation network should:	Observations
Coverage is geographically wide:	▪ Have a wide geographical coverage of other jurisdictions	▪ All international cooperation networks possess this feature.
Types of assistance covered are wide:	▪ Have a wide range of types of assistance, such as exchange of information and other forms of assistance in investigation and enforcement.	▪ Existing networks have wide assistance types but most of these types still have some restrictions.

(continued)

---

[367] Ibid. 64.
[368] Tax Information Exchange Agreements; see OECD, 'Tax Information Exchange Agreements (TIEAs)', www.oecd.org/ctp/exchange-of-tax-information/taxinformationexchangeagreementstieas.htm, accessed 13 February 2020; see Tax Justice Network, 'Tax Information Exchange Arrangements' (*Tax Justice Briefing*, May 2009), www.taxjustice.net/cms/upload/pdf/Tax_Information_Exchange_Arrangements.pdf, accessed 13 February 2020.
[369] Mutual legal assistance treaties.
[370] Ibid.
[371] Turksen and Abukari, 'OECD's global principles and EU's tax crime measures'.
[372] OECD, *Fighting Tax Crime* 65.

Table 24 *(Continued)*

Key terms	International cooperation network should:	Observations
Domestic legal framework allowing international information sharing:	▪ Have the support of a domestic legal framework that permits sharing of information (both sent and received) under international legal instruments with all relevant domestic criminal investigation, intelligence and enforcement agencies, where appropriate (ie tax authorities, criminal investigation authorities, FIUs, AML authorities).	▪ Many domestic legal frameworks still have unhelpful restrictions in the name of national security and related governmental excuses.
Practically effective – functional operational framework for international cooperation:	▪ Have effect in practice, including having a clear operational framework for international cooperation. This has to entail establishing dedicated and identified contact points that foreign agencies can contact in case of a request for assistance, sufficient resources to fulfil requests for assistance, as well as training and awareness for domestic investigation agencies as to the availability of international cooperation and how to make effective requests.[373]	▪ Because of some of the restrictions suffered in the networks, it sometimes becomes challenging to effectively operationalise some of the networks. EU as a supranational entity is however on course to establish a unitary framework with which all its Member States could be made to comply.

As established by TGP10, there are existing legal gateways and networks for international cooperation in tax matters in general,[374] but developing concrete international frameworks that focus on tax crimes in particular has been a challenge. The framework provided by TGP10 is also bedevilled with factors such as resource limitations, and capacity issues, thereby making 'it difficult for the requirements of this Principle to be appropriately met'.[375] In addition, the constraints that impact on the more effective functioning of these frameworks, based on OECD research,[376] include:

- delays caused by a lack of clear communication channels;[377]
- confusion about the organisational structure or mandate in the counterpart and therefore delays in identifying the correct agency to whom to address the request;[378]

---

[373] Ibid.
[374] See OECD, 'International Co-operation against Tax Crimes and Other Financial Crimes: A Catalogue of the Main Instruments' (2nd Annual Forum on Tax and Crime, 14 June 2012), www.oecd.org/ctp/crime/internationalco-operationagainsttaxcrimesandotherfinancialcrimesacatalogueofthemaininstruments.htm, accessed 4 March 2020.
[375] Turksen and Abukari, 'OECD's global principles and EU's tax crime measures'.
[376] OECD, *Fighting Tax Crime* 65; see also OECD, 'International Co-operation against Tax Crimes and Other Financial Crimes'.
[377] Ibid.
[378] Ibid.

- practical communication difficulties including language or lack of clarity in the presentation of the facts of the request;[379]
- lack of or inadequately detailed data for monitoring the use or impact of the cooperation tools, which may contribute to a lack of or limited awareness or reduced profile of these tools;[380]
- the other impacting challenges include security and political priorities as well as trust issues between countries.

Nonetheless, international efforts have been mobilised to operationalise some of the demands of TGP10. It is part of these efforts that the World Bank, OECD, EU and other stakeholders partnered to develop and encourage the use of 'whole-of-government approach to tackling financial crimes by fostering inter-agency and international cooperation'.[381] This subsequently generated the TGPs in the first place – a feat being used to articulate the benchmarks in this book.

Benchmarking EU Measures on International Cooperation against Tax Crimes

Since the EU plays 'a key role to make international co-operation in tax matters more efficient',[382] it is natural that the EU and its Member States will be patronising or adopting and adapting the international measures against tax crimes. The EU thus entreats its Member States to not only work closely together to mitigate tax crimes in their countries and abroad, but also to work under the collective tax avoidance and evasion frameworks of the Union. Any sustainable remedies would, therefore, have to be effectively aligned to both the similarities and differences of tax crime issues in EU Member States in ways that can generate a coherent pattern of understanding for the collective interest of all Member States of the EU.[383]

The EU has put in place action plans, concrete and binding legal instrument such as Directives and Regulations geared towards international cooperation in the field of tax – including tax evasion and tax fraud. Flowing from the 2012 Action Plan, 2016 VAT Plan, and 2019 Action Plan, the relevant legal and operational framework on cooperation to counter tax crimes are being established and/or strengthened.

The EU AML framework and Directive (EU) 2017/1371 especially provide some good pillars for EU Members to implement. This is equally so with the EU administrative cooperation framework, which addresses some of the bottlenecks in cooperation which, though it is administrative, has some positive consequences on tax crime. The money laundering frameworks provided by FATF are pacesetters from which even some of the

---

[379] Ibid.
[380] Ibid.
[381] The World Bank, 'OECD and World Bank call for whole-of-government approach to combating tax evasion and corruption' (Press Release, 24 October 2018), www.worldbank.org/en/news/press-release/2018/10/24/oecd-and-world-bank-call-for-whole-of-government-approach-to-combating-tax-evasion-and-corruption, accessed 24 April 2020.
[382] OECD, 'International Co-operation against Tax Crimes and Other Financial Crimes' 24.
[383] European Commission, *The European Union explained: Taxation* (European Union, 2015).

tax crime provisions of the EU tax crime countering framework are founded. There are also related legal instruments on judicial cooperation, cooperation of FUIs and EU establishments such as EPPO, EUROPOL, EFECC,[384] OLAF also as well as ECRIS, EUROFISC, VAT forum, Fiscalis Programme, Eurojust, European Judicial Network, and European e-Justice Portal. Some of these frameworks are briefly explored below.

Administrative Cooperation on Information Exchange

Information-sharing is key to the achievement of any of the legal pathways and instruments provided by the TG10. Giving the opportunity for the widest possible cooperation with stakeholders across national frontiers is an essential starting point to sharing relevant information that can counter tax crimes internationally. The EU has thus established that:[385]

> When third parties (i.e. foreign banks, foreign tax authorities) report tax, revenue or financial information to home tax authorities, taxpayers have few opportunities to avoid detection of unreported income.[386]

This narrative highlights the need to encourage and cooperate with third parties to help in preventing tax crimes, in the first place. On the other hand, without 'international information exchange, it is difficult if not impossible to detect international tax evasion through the traditional methods of tax audits'.[387] This proposition re-emphasises the centripetal role played by information-sharing in countering tax crimes internationally. With respect to data exchange cooperation, which is at the heart of outputs of any meaningful international cooperation, the EU and international tax crime framework has traversed three main episodes[388] in countering international tax crimes.

Table 25 Developments in Information Exchange

2004–2005	• Announcement and implementation of the EU Savings Directive. This constituted the first major effort to automatically exchange information between EU Member States and third countries, including Switzerland.[389]

(continued)

---

[384] The European Financial and Economic Crime Centre, which was launched on 5 June 2020, operates under the auspices of EUROPOL, www.europol.europa.eu/newsroom/news/europol-launches-european-financial-and-economic-crime-centre, accessed 25 July 2020.

[385] European Commission, 'Estimating International Tax Evasion by Individuals' (*Taxation Papers*, Working Paper No 76, 2019) 37, https://ec.europa.eu/taxation_customs/sites/taxation/files/2019-taxation-papers-76.pdf, accessed 4 March 2020.

[386] Ibid; see also Henrik Jacobsen Kleven et al, 'Unwilling or unable to cheat? Evidence from a tax audit experiment in Denmark' (2011) 79(3) *Econometrica* 651, https://doi.org/10.3982/ECTA9113, accessed 4 March 2020.

[387] Ibid; see also Treasury Inspector General for Tax Administration, 'A Combination of Legislative Actions and Increased IRS Capability and Capacity Are Required to Reduce the Multi-Billion Dollar U.S. International Tax Gap' (2009-IE-R001, 27 January 2009). Examination of STRs across the EU Member States also reveals that there very few STRs are submitted by auditors and accountants. The Role of Public Auditors in Detecting Fraud – A Critical Review, Forthcoming 2021 in Kassem and Turksen (eds), *Contemporary Issues in Public Sector Accounting and Auditing* – CSEF, Vol 105 (Emerald, 2021).

[388] European Commission, 'Estimating International Tax Evasion by Individuals'.

[389] Ibid.

Table 25 *(Continued)*

2009–2011	▪ Global crackdown on international tax evasion (April 2009 London G20 Summit). This Summit began a worldwide systematic application of the Exchange of Information on Request (EOIR) Standard.[390] ▪ US Congress adoption of FATCA. ▪ DAC 1 adoption.[391]
2014	▪ Adoption of the CRS by the OECD Council and of the enhanced DAC 2[392] which has been amended a couple of times. ▪ FATCA implementation.[393]

There are three main administrative cooperation legal instruments in the EU tax regime:

- Directive 2011/16/EU of 15 February 2011 on Administrative Cooperation in the field of Taxation (which repealed Directive 77/799/EEC) – DAC 1;

- Regulation No 904/2010 of 7 October 2010 on Administrative Cooperation and Combating Fraud in the field of Value Added Tax;[394] and

- Regulation (EC) No 2073/2004 of 16 November 2004 on Administrative Cooperation in the field of Excise Duties.[395]

Council Directive 2011/16/EU provides foundational rules and procedures on information exchange for EU Member States to cooperate among themselves for the administration and enforcement of relevant national laws on tax matters. This Directive covers cooperation on all taxes other than excise duties and VAT. It has been amended five times. For Council Regulation No 904/2010, the EU provides rules and procedures that guide EU Member States to cooperate in the exchange of VAT information between their competent authorities in charge of VAT application. This Regulation has been consolidated.[396] With respect to Council Regulation (EC) No 2073/2004, the EU entreats its Member States to ensure that cooperation between their tax authorities responsible for excise duties is fostered, especially through electronic means in a way that enables them to access relevant information for correctly assessing their excise duties. This Regulation has been repealed by Regulation (EU) No 389/2012[397] but the aims are still current.

---

[390] Ibid.

[391] Directive on Administrative Cooperation (DAC) (2011/16/EU).

[392] Council Directive 2014/107/EU of 9 December 2014 amending Directive 2011/16/EU as regards mandatory automatic exchange of information in the field of taxation OJ L 359/1.

[393] European Commission, 'Estimating International Tax Evasion by Individuals' 9.

[394] See Consolidated text: Council Regulation (EU) No 904/2010 of 7 October 2010 on administrative cooperation and combating fraud in the field of value added tax (recast).

[395] See Council Regulation (EU) No 389/2012 of 2 May 2012 on administrative cooperation in the field of excise duties and repealing Regulation (EC) No 2073/2004 OJ L 121/1.

[396] Consolidated text: Council Regulation (EU) No 904/2010 of 7 October 2010 on administrative cooperation and combating fraud in the field of value added tax.

[397] See Council Regulation (EU) No 389/2012.

EU Cooperation in Criminal Matters

Regarding cooperation in criminal matters, the following legal instruments are applicable:

- Directive (EU) 2017/1371.
- Directive 2014/42/EU.
- Directive (EU) 2015/849.
- Directive (EU) 2018/843.
- Directive (EU) 2018/1673.
- Regulation (EU, Euratom) No 883/2013.[398]
- Directive (EU) 2019/1153.[399]
- Regulation (EU) 2016/794.[400]
- Council Regulation (EU) 2017/1939.[401]
- Council Framework Decision 2006/960/JHA.[402]

This does not mean that information provided under the administrative cooperation instruments do not provide any support for criminal tax matters.

However, all of these EU legal instruments have more significant provisions that seek to enhance and foster cooperation between relevant institutions of the EU and of Member States in relation to tax crimes. For instance, Article 1 of Regulation (EU, Euratom) No 883/2013 sets the pace as to how OLAF[403] can cooperate with other EU institutions, FIUs and competent bodies to step up the 'fight against fraud, corruption and any other illegal activity detrimental to the financial interests of the EU'.

---

[398] Regulation (EU, Euratom) No 883/2013 of the European Parliament and of the Council of 11 September 2013 concerning investigations conducted by the European Anti-Fraud Office (OLAF) and repealing Regulation (EC) No 1073/1999 of the European Parliament and of the Council and Council Regulation (Euratom) No 1074/1999 OJ L 248/1; see also Consolidated text: Regulation (EU, Euratom) No 883/2013 of the European Parliament and of the Council of 11 September 2013 concerning investigations conducted by the European Anti-Fraud Office (OLAF) and repealing Regulation (EC) No 1073/1999 Regulation (Euratom) No 1073/1999 of the European Parliament and of the Council Regulation (EC) No 1074/1999.

[399] Directive (EU) 2019/1153 of the European Parliament and of the Council of 20 June 2019 laying down rules facilitating the use of financial and other information for the prevention, detection, investigation or prosecution of certain criminal offences, and repealing Council Decision 2000/642/JHA PE/64/2019/REV/1, OJ L 186/122.

[400] Regulation (EU) 2016/794 of the European Parliament and of the Council of 11 May 2016 on the European Union Agency for Law Enforcement Cooperation (Europol) and replacing and repealing Council Decisions 2009/371/JHA, 2009/934/JHA, 2009/935/JHA, 2009/936/JHA and 2009/968/JHA, OJ L 135/53.

[401] Council Regulation (EU) 2017/1939 of 12 October 2017, implementing enhanced cooperation on the establishment of the European Public Prosecution Office ('the EPPO'), OJ L 283/1.

[402] Council Framework Decision 2006/960/JHA of 18 December 2006 on simplifying the exchange of information and intelligence between law enforcement authorities of the Member States of the European Union, OJ L 386/89; also see Corrigendum to Council Framework Decision 2006/960/JHA of 18 December 2006 on simplifying the exchange of information and intelligence between law enforcement authorities of the Member States of the European Union (OJ L 386, 29.12.2006) OJ L 75/26.

[403] European Anti-Fraud Office.

Directive (EU) 2017/1371 provides in Recital 23 the

> need for appropriate provision to be made for cooperation to ensure effective action against the criminal offences defined in this Directive affecting the Union's financial interests, including exchange of information between the Member States and the Commission as well as technical and operational assistance provided by the Commission to the competent national authorities as they may need to facilitate coordination of their investigations.

The need for cooperation between the Member States and OLAF and other Union institutions, bodies, offices or agencies is re-emphasised in Article 15 thereof. For Directive 2014/42/EU, the need for international cooperation between relevant institutions to recover assets is provided at Recital 2.

Directive (EU) 2018/1673 has a number of provisions requiring international cooperation including Recitals 2 and 9. Respectively, while individual actions without recourse to international cooperation is warned to have limited effect, it is also provided that cooperation with third countries should be intensified.

Directive (EU) 2015/849, Article 50 provides that 'the competent authorities shall provide the ESAs with all the information necessary to allow them to carry out their duties under this Directive'. Cooperation should also be fostered between FIUs and with the Commission, as established by Articles 51 to 57. Directive (EU) 2015/849 has provided substantial enhancement for 'the Union legal framework that governs the activity and cooperation of FIUs, including the assessment by the Commission of the possibility of establishing a coordination and support mechanism'.[404] Directive (EU) 2018/843 has amended Directive (EU) 2015/849. Among others aspects, the following have been added to the cooperation framework: cooperation between competent authorities of the Member States,[405] and cooperation between competent authorities supervising credit and financial institutions and other authorities bound by professional secrecy.[406]

With respect to Directive (EU) 2019/1153, Articles 1 and 21 as well as recitals 2, 14, 20 and 22 include the key provisions for international cooperation. Article 1, for instance, provides that EU Member States should facilitate access to law enforcement information by FIUs for the prevention and combating of money laundering, associate predicate offences and terrorist financing and measures to facilitate cooperation between FIUs. In recital 22, efforts to establish an 'EU FIU' in order to foster cooperation between FIUs, are envisaged.

Regulation (EU) 2016/794 lays down rules and procedures for Europol to provide support for cross-border investigations by Member States into the money laundering activities of transnational criminal organisations.[407] Council Regulation (EU) 2017/1939 gives a mandate to the European Public Prosecution Office (EPPO) to cooperate and coordinate with relevant institutions in the EU to conduct public prosecutions.

Although a number of instruments support mutual legal assistance in criminal matters between EU countries, including the Convention established by the Council in

---

[404] Directive (EU) 2019/1153, recital 14.
[405] Art 1(32).
[406] Art 1(37).
[407] Directive (EU) 2019/1153, recital 20.

accordance with Article 34 of the Treaty on European Union, on Mutual Assistance in Criminal Matters between the Member States of the European Union.[408]

This convention seeks, inter alia, to enhance 'judicial cooperation in criminal matters between the Member States of the Union, without prejudice to the rules protecting individual freedom'. It entails cooperation forms including 'sending and service of procedural documents, spontaneous exchange of information, placement of articles obtained by criminal means or joint investigation teams'. The convention is supported by Council Act of 29 May 2000 establishing in accordance with Article 34 of the Treaty on European Union the Convention on Mutual Assistance in Criminal Matters between the Member States of the European Union, OJ C 197/2.

At the same time, Council Framework Decision 2006/960/JHA aims[409] to prevent and combat crime through closer cooperation between LEAs in the EU Member States.

In addition to general legal measures to establish and enhance cooperation in criminal matters, there have been specific instruments that address tax crimes.

Further Thematic Analysis of EU in International Cooperation

i. A Quick Reaction Mechanism to Combat VAT Fraud

Directive 2006/112/EC of 28 November 2006 establishes a common system of VAT in the EU (Article 1). The applicable provisions on tax crimes in Directive 2006/112/EC are Articles 11, 19, 80(1), 131, 158(2), 273, 343 and 395(1). These articles provide processes and principles by which the quick reaction mechanism can help combat VAT fraud. The directive has been amended by Directive (EU) 2018/1695 of 6 November 2018 mainly modifying Article 199 that deals with liability of VAT payment and issues of fraud detection vis-à-vis the quick reaction mechanism. What can be gleaned from the directives on VAT relating to tax evasion is that there is a lot of opportunity for possible inconsistencies in implementation because most of the provisions on VAT evasion carry no mandatory terms but only give Member States the prerogative to implement the given measures or not, in whatever manner they deem fit. This does not seem to provide any effective solutions against VAT fraud that has been occasioned by strategies such as VAT carousel.

ii. Cooperation to Combat VAT Fraud through the Use of Information Exchange Systems to Alert Other EU Countries to Fraudulent Activities[410]

VAT evasion or fraud is significantly pervasive across Europe, with more than €46 billion lost to this fraud annually. VAT fraudsters exploit loopholes in the EU's common system

---

[408] Convention established by the Council in accordance with Article 34 of the Treaty on European Union, on Mutual Assistance in Criminal Matters between the Member States of the European Union – Council Declaration on Article 10 (9) – Declaration by the United Kingdom on Article 20, OJ C 197/3.

[409] Recital 2.

[410] European Commission, *The European Union explained: Taxation* (European Union, 2015).

of VAT for cross-border sales of goods – otherwise known as MTIC fraud.[411] Given the fact that this type of tax crime continues unabated, there is an urgent need to foster stronger cooperation between administrations in the EU in order to counter it.

Regulation (EU) 904/2010 of 7 October 2010 is the key administrative instrument designed to achieve this. It was amended by Regulation (EU) 2017/2454 of 5 December 2017. These two regulations were both amended more recently by Regulation (EU) 2018/1541 of 2 October 2018. Fundamentally, these regulations provide Member States with the instruments to support each other on individual taxpayers in order to rightly assess, control and collect VAT. The instruments also enable information exchange on VAT. One of such exchanges is the VAT Information Exchange System (VIES), which avails business information on intra-EU sales of goods and services to Member States.[412]

Even though the amendments have introduced provisions such as the Transaction Network Analysis (TNA) which is granted a certain legal basis for automatically analysing state-held data on businesses using VIES instrument, the opportunities for VAT fraud are still lurking dangerously.[413] VAT carousel is still having some environment to operate. For instance, PROTAX case studies found that the VAT fraud was schematised in two forms: the first form depicts a situation where 'products had never been sold to real consumers but had been imported and exported out of the EU'. This way, on each occasion this transaction took place, affected EU Member States were cheated on VAT. Secondly, the VAT carousel took the form of having a real functioning company that would sell the goods below price to real consumers, in which the interposed missing trader companies cheated the EU jurisdictions on the VAT, while the functioning company filed the VAT that was due. This was found in countries such as Austria, Italy and Estonia.[414] It is difficult to appreciate how the recent amendments to the aforementioned regulations can completely solve these problems. Continuous improvements in VAT legislation and collaboration to eliminate these existential threats in the VAT regime in EU are, therefore, required to sustainably counter VAT fraud and evasion in EU.

iii. A Platform for Tax Good Governance to Monitor EU Countries' Progress in Tackling Aggressive Tax Planning and in Clamping Down on Tax Havens[415]

In 2015, the EU's Corporate Taxation Action Plan[416] fundamentally ushered in what was expected to be an ambitious agenda for fair, effective and growth-friendly corporate

---

[411] UK Parliament, 'VAT fraud: cooperation between tax administrations' (23 May 2018), https://publications.parliament.uk/pa/cm201719/cmselect/cmeuleg/301-xxviii/30116.htm#footnote-013, accessed 23 April 2020.

[412] Ibid.

[413] European Commission, 'Commission Staff Working Document Impact Assessment – Accompanying the document – Amended proposal for a Council Regulation Amending Regulation (EU) No 904/2010 as regards measures to strengthen administrative cooperation in the field of value added tax' (COM (2017) 706 final)–(SWD (2017) 429 final).

[414] Turksen and others, 'D1.2: Case Studies of Tax Crimes'.

[415] G Gimdal, 'Aggressive tax planning' (The TAX 2 report, DG EPRS, EU Parliament, July 2016).

[416] European Commission, 'Communication from the Commission to the European Parliament and the Council: A Fair and Efficient Corporate Tax System in the European Union: 5 Key Areas for Action' (SWD (2015) 121 final) COM (2015) 302 final).

taxation in the EU. This prioritised reform of corporate taxation,[417] in a way that could have positive consequence on countering tax crimes. One of the instruments to achieve this prospect is the Platform for Tax Good Governance. The platform provides a forum where the EU Commission is able to tap the diverse expertise of representatives from business, civil society and national tax administrations towards addressing challenges such as tax crimes in the Union.[418]

This obviously is a unique platform where richer knowledge is consolidated to ensure a good governance framework for addressing challenges associated with tax crimes in the EU.[419] The problem, however, is that the inability of this platform to effectively address the issue of complexities in tax regulations and legislations all the more continues to allow subsistence of unmerited loopholes which aggressive tax planners and tax criminals can exploit to their advantage. A better way for the Platform to sustainably support the EU Council and Commission may be to consult them in consolidating legislations and regulations on tax fraud or evasion.[420]

Apart from the above cooperation measures, there are also rules that govern the assistance between EU countries in recovering claims for taxes, customs duties and certain fees as well as taxes on income, capital and insurance premiums. In addition, the EU institutions and the Member States work collaboratively with non-EU countries and international players to ensure that there are more effective 'global standards' on tax systems and for combating tax crimes. In this context, the EU has established frameworks that enable the Union to cooperate with non-EU states such as Andorra, Liechtenstein, Monaco, San Marino and Switzerland, the dependent and associated territories of the United Kingdom and the Netherlands, as well as some non-European countries.[421] Furthermore, the EU has made it a policy to oblige non-EU Member States to draft into international agreements with the non-EU states the kind of provisions that commit them 'to good governance standards in tax matters' including principal clauses such as obliging them 'to exchange tax information with EU countries and eliminating harmful tax measures'.[422]

The EU is an active contributor to the OECD's work in defining international tax policy. Key successes that have been achieved, in this regard, include 'the new global standard for automatic exchange of financial account information and a project to reshape international corporate tax rules against avoidance'.[423] The OECD and the World Bank have a common understanding that continuous improvement of effective inter-agency cooperation should include the following considerations which states (including EU countries) could observe:

> Availability of widest scope of legal approaches for reporting and sharing of information according to the law; implementation of efficient and effective procedures for operations to make it possible for practical sharing and reporting of information; Utilisation of improved

---

[417] European Commission, 'Platform for Tax Good Governance: Work programme' (Platform/34/2018/EN), https://ec.europa.eu/taxation_customs/sites/taxation/files/work-program-2018_2019-final.pdf, accessed 24 April 2020.
[418] Ibid.
[419] Gimdal, 'Aggressive tax planning'.
[420] European Commission, *The European Union explained: Taxation* (European Union, 2015).
[421] Ibid.
[422] Ibid.
[423] Ibid.

cooperative mechanisms such as joint operations and taskforces; Promotion of cooperation culture at every level of the business, beginning with political leaders and heads of agencies.[424]

On 19 April 2016 four international organisations, the OECD, the UN, the World Bank and the International Monetary Fund (IMF), set out some of the specifics of their joint platform to strengthen their collaboration on matters relating to taxation and tax crimes. Even though their focus has been on developing countries, which may not be a major priority for the EU, the platform has put forward toolkits that resonate with the durable solution demands of the EU.

Therefore, although the EU has a degree of participation in the activities of these institutions and many of its Member States are key players in most of these institutions, it would be beneficial if the EU were to continue to more actively engage in this international collaboration to harness its full potential in tapping the useful international institutional tax experiences. This could significantly help the EU in its efforts towards effectively and efficiently preventing, detecting and prosecuting tax crimes across the EU. The platform is expected to especially give 'capacity-building support [to members], deliver jointly developed guidance, and share information on operational and knowledge activities'. One of the toolkits that will be delivered by the platform is the implementation measures for 'BEPS project and other issues on international taxation'. These are highly relevant for the EU.[425]

The platform culminates in a dossier of dexterity that can sustainably prevent, deter, detect, prosecute, and punish tax-related criminal activities. In addition, the solution box should be able to help in rehabilitating tax offenders after they have been punished. Rehabilitation of offenders who have served their due penalties is a very important component in a criminal justice system that cares to provide holistic socio-legal solutions for criminal activities in which offenders might otherwise return quite easily to their criminal ways after punishment.[426]

The EU has established some remarkable cooperation mechanisms with the OECD and the international community. But much remains to be done in areas such as ensuring a high level of transparency in the exchange of information under this cooperation in order to secure more successful investigations and prosecutions and in respect of fundamental human rights.

Even with all the above instruments for transnational cooperation against tax crime, the reality indicates that stronger cooperation at a global level may still be difficult to reach. International cooperation is one of the major challenges in fighting tax crimes. The challenges include incompatible institutional responsibilities and legal frameworks,

---

[424] OECD and the World Bank, *Improving Co-operation between Tax Authorities and Anti-Corruption Authorities in Combating Tax Crime and Corruption* (CC BY-NC-SA 3.0 IGO 2018); the World Bank, 'OECD and World Bank call for whole-of-government approach to combating tax evasion and corruption' (Press Release, 24 October 2018), www.worldbank.org/en/news/press-release/2018/10/24/oecd-and-world-bank-call-for-whole-of-government-approach-to-combating-tax-evasion-and-corruption, accessed 24 April 2020.

[425] OECD, 'Measuring and monitoring BEPS' (Action 11- 2015, Final report, 2015); the World Bank, 'International Organizations Take Major Step to Boost Global Cooperation in Tax Matters' (Press Release, 19 April 2016), www.worldbank.org/en/news/press-release/2016/04/19/international-organisations-take-major-step-to-boost-global-cooperation-in-tax-matters, accessed 24 April 2020.

[426] FD Greenberg, '"Justice" and Criminal Justice' in FD Hawkins et al (eds), *Crime Control and Social Justice: The Delicate Balance* (Greenwood Press, 2003) 319–54.

the lack of trust-based working relations, as well as communication and language problems between authorities.[427]

Conclusion

The above structural and procedural principles of the OECD have been evaluated along with some of the EU tax crime counter-measures. The chapter concludes on the note that the TGPs have extensive structural measures which the EU could emulate as minimum standards to be leveraged. For instance, the anti-fraud and evasion measures of the EU are to be backed by relevant EU legislation or legal gateways of the TGPs, which are transposed into national legislation of EU Member States. Thus, successful implementation of tax crime measures is dependent upon the effectiveness of using an EU centralised approach to countering tax crimes, along with coordinated efforts from EU Member States.

It is revealing to note that given the complex and overreaching nature of tax crimes, tax crime measures must always endeavour to be interconnected, and inviting appeal to be implemented concurrently and consistently by the EU and its Member States. Thus, tax crime counter-measures are not 'sufficiently effective when applied individually'.[428] The EU has a number of action plans and strategies for countering tax crimes. These include the 2012 Action Plan, the 2016 VAT Plan and the 2019 Action Plan as well as the 2019 Strategy which are being translated into the legal framework for countering tax crimes in the EU.

The next chapter delves further into the interrelationships between the some of the criminal law elements and the administrative law elements on international cooperation. This will underscore just how imperative the administrative cooperation networks are for complementing the criminal law elements on EU and international cooperation for countering tax crimes.

---

[427] Turksen et al, 'D1.2: Case Studies of Tax Crimes in the European Union'.

[428] J Dobrovič et al, 'Action plan on sustainability of fight against tax fraud and tax evasion: EU countries comparison' (2019) 12(4) *Journal of International Studies* 272.

5

Relationship between Criminal and Administrative Mechanisms

Introduction

This chapter interfaces the instruments of the Anti-Tax Avoidance Package (ATAP) of the EU with those of the OECD's TGPs. ATAP is the major EU administrative framework for countering tax avoidance, some of which can be escalated to mitigate some form of tax crime. The extent to which the components of ATAP complement each other is not neatly articulated. This chapter undertakes a rigorous examination of how the components of ATAP contribute to each other, and whether they serve cross-purposes on information exchange or not. The chapter takes a critical look at how tax avoidance measures can be enhanced to support the criminal law instruments on countering tax crimes in the EU.

Anti-Tax Avoidance Strategy and TGPs

The interconnected global environment makes it much easier for taxpayers to evade paying taxes. The reality of cross-border companies using the loopholes created by differences in tax systems amongst EU Member States to shift profits from one country to the other is a glaring issue. At the same, nationals of one EU country can find a way of earning income from abroad yet ensure that such income is not taxed. These approaches to evading tax payment and such related methods are being achieved through non-compliance or avoidance strategies, some of which amount to criminal conduct, just as the results of such strategies equally are. They all the more make it difficult to address tax crimes. That is why tax authorities in the EU regard relevant tax information access, especially regarding earned incomes and overseas assets of resident taxpayers, as a highly valued proposition.[1]

Multinational corporations are notorious for engaging in profit-shifting and aggressive tax planning to limit their tax burden and maximise their profit outturns. Although specific instances of profit-shifting and aggressive tax planning that assume the

---

[1] MP Devereux and J Vella, 'Are we heading towards a corporate tax fit for the 21st century? (2014) 35 *Fiscal Studies* 449–75; Collier et al, 'Dissecting the EU's Recent Anti-Tax Avoidance Measures: Merits and Problems' (*Econ Pol Policy Report*, Vol 2, September 2018).

characteristics of tax evasion and avoidance are considered illegal, profit-shifting and aggressive planning are generally in a legal grey area, apparently still considered lawful activities albeit (arguably) outside the scope of practices intended by legal instruments. The opportunities that exist for companies to engage in these activities are equally common amongst MNCs. Often, these opportunities are sourced from the disparity that exists between MNCs and the disjointed international tax system that consists of separate and inconsistent or contradicting or opposing tax systems.[2]

Both the motives and opportunities have to be addressed by discouraging companies from actualising their willingness to engage in these activities and closing down the opportunities available to businesses in the international tax system. The enduring disposition of the motives and opportunities that translate into profit-shifting is a durable challenge. Three principles have emerged to counter the situation: the source-based taxation of active income of corporations, and the residence-based taxation of passive income of corporations – in combination with a relatively formal residence doctrine; as well as a separate entity approach which requires arm's-length pricing for intra-MNC transactions.[3]

Instead of mitigating the dual problem of willingness or motive of and opportunities for businesses, the three principles have rather succeeded to retain the status quo and allow MNCs to exploit the opportunities for profit-shifting and so on. These principles also tend to promote countries' competition 'over the tax base by reducing their tax rates, by providing special tax regimes ([such as] patent boxes), or by making separate deals with' MNCs.[4]

Nonetheless, there are good opportunities from the interconnectedness of global economic systems that make it difficult to counter tax evasion and avoidance. Closer cooperation amongst Member States gives rise to appropriate access and accountability tools for countering the tax crimes and avoidance. The recognition of the need to foster closer cooperation amongst EU Member States and internationally is, therefore, benchmarked on the need to prevent and punish tax crimes. This need is characterised by the significance of ensuring the achievement of 'fairness of taxation systems both within the EU and internationally' and of harnessing domestic revenue mobilisation potential from tax crimes. The EU has, thus, developed systems of administrative cooperation amongst its Member States to achieve easy cross-border information exchange between tax authorities of the Member States on a variety of income levels of individuals crisscrossing the borders.[5]

There have been suggestions for solutions to profit-shifting for decades, from the Ruding Committee,[6] from the EU Commission[7] that deliberated on the reduction of

---

[2] Collier et al, 'Dissecting the EU's Recent Anti-Tax Avoidance Measures'.

[3] Auerbach et al, 'International tax planning under the destination-based cash flow tax' (2017) 70 *National Tax Journal* 783–802; Collier et al, 'Dissecting the EU's Recent Anti-Tax Avoidance Measures'.

[4] MP Devereux and J Vella, 'Are we heading towards a corporate tax fit for the 21st century? (2014) 35 *Fiscal Studies* 449–75; Collier et al, 'Dissecting the EU's Recent Anti-Tax Avoidance Measures'.

[5] Ibid.

[6] Ruding Committee, 'Report of the committee of independent experts on company taxation' (Commission of the European Communities, 1992).

[7] European Commission, 'Towards an internal market without tax obstacles: A strategy for providing companies with a consolidated corporate tax base for their EU-wide activities' (Communication COM (2001)582, 2001).

tax obstacles in the single market, from the Code of Conduct Group that sought to counter 'harmful tax competition' which eroded revenues,[8] and from the G20/OECD and the EU's recent focus on countering the activities of MNCs in profit-shifting. This recent attention is translated into the ATAP by the EU, which happens to be a move to build on the OECD's Action Plan[9] on Base Erosion and Profit Shifting (BEPS). BEPS is an avoidance strategy employed by companies to evade tax by exploiting the 'gaps and mismatches' associated with tax rules in order 'to artificially shift profits to low or no-tax locations'.[10] BEPS had made recommendations on how individual jurisdictions should design their tax systems to make them more resilient to profit-shifting.[11]

In fact, following the publication of the G20/OECD BEPS action plan in October 2015, the EU was quickly responsive to the implementation of the key anti-tax avoidance measures therein, by coming out with the ATAP and its components.[12] This has exemplified the collaborative effort by the EU to transpose the OECD's anti-tax avoidance rules into EU legislation and rules on profit-shifting.[13] The Anti-Tax Avoidance Directive (ATAD) was, therefore, formulated as part of a broader ATAP framework in response to the call to counter BEPS. In fact, ATAD builds on the Action Plan for Fair and Efficient Corporate Taxation and provides a response to the finalisation of the project against BEPS. ATAD sets out measures in four main areas of specificity, namely: Interest Limitation (IL) rules, Exit Taxation (ET) rules, General Anti-Abuse (GAA) rule, and Controlled Foreign Company (CFC) rules.[14]

In effect, ATAD is purposed to tackle tax practices that amount to tax avoidance by articulating, inter alia, the minimum standards and time frames required of EU Member States to refine their laws on corporate tax in selected areas. ATAD establishes pertinent preventive rules on corporate tax avoidance, paying significant attention to addressing the challenge of aggressive tax planning in the single market of the EU.[15] The EU has particularly adopted ATAD to reduce the scope for profit-shifting.[16]

ATAD was first promulgated in 2016, as Council Directive (EU) 2016/1164, and has since been amended into Council Directive (EU) 2017/952 to accommodate emerging issues of tax avoidance. This new anti-tax avoidance directive was created because it was noticed that Directive (EU) 2016/1164 only provided rules to address hybrid mismatches in the EU without consideration for those that occurred outside the EU.[17]

---

[8] European Commission, 'Towards tax co-ordination in the European Union: A package to tackle harmful tax competition' (Communication from the Commission to the Council, COM (97) 495 final, 1998).

[9] OECD, *Action Plan on Base Erosion and Profit Shifting* (OECD Publishing, 2013).

[10] European Commission, 'Towards tax co-ordination in the European Union'.

[11] Collier et al, 'Dissecting the EU's Recent Anti-Tax Avoidance Measures'.; F Laguna and D Martinez, 'Abuse and Aggressive Tax Planning: Between OECD and EU Initiatives – The Dividing Line between Intended and Unintended Double Non-Taxation' (2017) 9(2) *World Tax Journal* 1–32.

[12] Collier et al, 'Dissecting the EU's Recent Anti-Tax Avoidance Measures'.

[13] Ibid.

[14] Å Johansson et al, 'Anti-avoidance rules against international tax planning: a classification' (Economics department working paper No 1356, OECD, 19 December 2016); A Cédelle, 'The EU Anti-Tax Avoidance Directive: A UK Perspective' (2016) 4 *British Tax Review* 1–14; C Remeur, 'Country-by-country reporting for multinational enterprise groups' (DG EPRS, EU Parliament, June 2017).

[15] Collier et al, 'Dissecting the EU's Recent Anti-Tax Avoidance Measures'.

[16] Ibid.

[17] R Aloys, 'Anti-Tax Avoidance Directive (2016/1164): New EU Policy Horizons, (2016) 56 (11) *EU Taxation* 497–505.

Directive (EU) 2017/952 was adopted to extend the scope of coverage of hybrid mismatches to include that of hybrid mismatches within non-EU states as well.[18]

Hybrid mismatch is associated with an arrangement that is presented to exploit the differences in the tax treatment of instruments, companies or transfers between two or more countries.[19] It is a platform where payers of corporate tax exploit the disparities between tax systems of each of the EU Member States with a view to minimising the overall tax liability of those businesses. The effects of these disparities and the exploitation thereof are the imbalances created and the revenue short-changes effected. The rules on the hybrid mismatches aim at neutralising these adverse effects thereof by establishing appropriate measures or rules whereby one of the two jurisdictions in a mismatch should deny the deduction of a payment leading to such an outcome.[20]

The 'hybrid mismatches' rules of Directive (EU) 2017/952 supersede the hybrid mismatches rules of EU 2016/1164.[21] The amending Directive (EU) 2017/952 entered into force on 27 June 2017 and should become law in EU Member States by 31 December 2019 or 31 December 2021 with respect to the provisions of the hybrid mismatches. The process of implementation and monitoring of ATAD will bring to light the full implications of the new Directive for cross-border transactions and structures that involve EU entities.

ATAP has become one of the key instruments in the EU's toolbox for countering profit-shifting and other practices. Apart from ATAD, ATAP has four complementary components, namely:

- Directive on Administrative Cooperation (DAC) or country-by-country reporting, which has introduced a requirement to report main tax-related information of MNCs, with the aim of enhancing transparency in the process and to give EU Member States the needed information that can help them detect and prevent tax avoidance schemes.[22]

- Tax Treaty Recommendation, aimed at providing EU Member States with necessary information on how to design their tax treaties so as to restrain businesses from engaging in aggressive tax planning to be in accordance with the laws of the EU.

- Communication on External Strategy, aimed at providing EU Member States with a coherent way to work with third countries such as the establishment of a common EU list of third countries for the purposes of taxation.

- Study on aggressive tax planning, aimed at investigating corporate tax rules in EU Member States that may be vulnerable to aggressive tax planning strategies of businesses.[23]

---

[18] C Remeur, 'Hybrid mismatches with third countries' (DG EPRS, EU Parliament, March 2017).

[19] Directive (EU) 2016/1164 of 12 July 2016 laying down rules against tax avoidance practices that directly affect the functioning of the internal market [2016] OJ L 193.

[20] C Remeur, 'Hybrid mismatches with third countries'.

[21] Directive (EU) 2017/952 of 29 May 2017 amending Directive (EU) 2016/1164 as regards hybrid mismatches with third countries (OJ L 144, 7.6.2017).

[22] C Remeur, 'Country-by-country reporting for multinational enterprise groups' (DG EPRS, EU Parliament, June 2017).

[23] European Commission, 'Anti-Tax Avoidance Package', https://ec.europa.eu/taxation_customs/business/company-tax/anti-tax-avoidance-package_en, accessed 10 February 2020; Collier et al, 'Dissecting the EU's

Each of these ATAP measures has, in its respective way, potential and capacity to prevent opportunities in profit-shifting that are available to MNCs. However, they equally have certain defects. To start with, each one of the anti-tax avoidance measures adds to the complexity of the tax system and compliance costs for MNCs and potentially also for non-MNCs.

Secondly, the anti-tax avoidance measures could actually lead to double taxation, especially relating to the CFC, GAAR and interest limitation rule of the ATAD, although it can be alleviated for the latter by allowing carry-forward and carry-back of non-deductible interest expenses.[24]

Thirdly, because CFC allows member countries to come out with 'many important details' of the rules, there is the real possibility for Member States to engage in harmful competition practices amongst themselves so as to create pull factors for MNCs. The measures of GAA rules 'and the interest limitation rule', however, appear to have 'inadequate degrees of freedom'. Fourthly, with hybrid mismatches and the interest limitation rule, there is this lingering potential for non-harmful behaviour or activities of businesses to be restricted unnecessarily. Whereas the rule of interest limitation could be introduced with many additional exemptions for some firm types, that of hybrid mismatch does not allow the possibility of such introduction of additional exemptions.[25]

Fifthly, Directive (EU) 2016/1164 of 12 August 2016 was expected to be transposed into national law, per Article 11, by 31 December 2018, and entered into force on 1 January 2019. A derogation provision was, however, provided by Article 5 to allow transposition to be extended to 31 December 2019 and subsequently entering into force by 1 January 2020. With this, the exit tax measure is likely to be undermined. This derogation for implementation has provided a generous period for companies to conveniently adjust themselves and potentially find means to further avoid taxes.[26]

Another challenge is that ATAP measures elicit or enlist legislations with different shades of complexities as they reflect in domestic legal environments. Undoubtedly, 'this influx of complex new legislations brings about increased costs and reduced economic activity'. There are instances where these new regulations would result in double taxation, while on other occasions, the measures would elicit new distortions to the decisions that corporations make.[27] For instance, the rules on interest limitation can distort corporate decisions or activities. These rules could 'differently affect different sectors and could as well give incentives to multi-sectoral MNCs to locate their activities in a tax-optimal manner'.[28]

It appears that there is too much rigidity in some of the measures that have been introduced, while other measures have too much laxity. The lax measures are open to

---

Recent Anti-Tax Avoidance Measures'; G Gimdal, 'Aggressive tax planning' (The TAX 2 report, DG EPRS, EU Parliament, July 2016).

[24] Johansson et al, 'Anti-avoidance rules'; Collier et al, 'Dissecting the EU's Recent Anti-Tax Avoidance Measures'; Laguna and Martinez, 'Abuse and Aggressive Tax Planning'.

[25] Collier et al, 'Dissecting the EU's Recent Anti-Tax Avoidance Measures'.

[26] Ibid.

[27] Laguna and Martinez, 'Abuse and Aggressive Tax Planning'.

[28] Ibid.

the caprices and 'strategic behaviour of countries' and, therefore, subject to abuse by some jurisdictions. The too rigid measures offer too little opportunity for reasonable adjustments. What is crucial is that these measures appear not to address the incentives or opportunities that are inherent in the current international tax system due to disjointed national tax systems.[29]

It is clear that opportunities for illicit and aggressive tax planning have not been closed down by these measures in a very substantial degree. At the same time, 'the incentives to relocate real economic operations to low-tax countries [have hardly been] touched'. As a result of these limitations, ATAP's anti-tax avoidance rules do not appear to be conducive to creating a stable and sustainable corporate tax system in the long run. Moreover, and quite instructively, the criminalisation of tax offences appears to be largely ignored or poorly placed. The BEPS based on which the EU came out of the ATAP and its components appear, in itself, to be flawed. Murphy and Baker argue that BEPS merely

> placed a sticking plaster on the current system of international taxation instead of standing back and asking for the real weaknesses and spillovers in the current tax system. If the right questions were asked, it would have identified that the current tax treaties and the arm's length pricing method were the issues to be addressed, instead of retaining them. It appears, therefore, that the process of BEPS has experienced a systemic failing.[30]

The outcomes from these aims could have a good attraction for improving the quality of ATAP as it relates to the OECD's action plans. These should also help toward the shaping up of the proposal to establish a Common Consolidated Corporate Tax Base (CCCTB) and the new rules on taxing technology-related transactions. CCCTB is another central instrument in the solution toolbox designed by the EU. It is expected that when the 2016 Commission's proposed directive CCCTB is implemented by 2020, cross-border issues with corporations would be significantly addressed.[31] The EU has also designed new rules to tax digital services.[32] Although these additional new proposals would bring about some improvements in anti-tax avoidance, there are still foundational loopholes to be closed down.

Essentially, as far as it is possible, an exercise should focus on ascertaining costs and benefits of the measures being introduced and to see which outweighs the other. Measures such as compliance that cannot necessarily have the direct costs and benefits completely measured can be evaluated on the basis of the effectiveness the introduction of such measures has brought to or would bring to the tax system. The other part of

---

[29] R Murphy and A Baker, 'A response to the Consultation on an IMF 2019 Analysis of International Corporate Taxation' (City University of London and SPERI of Sheffield, 2018), http://coffers.eu/wp-content/uploads/2018/12/2018-Murphy-Baker.pdf, accessed 4 March 2020; Laguna and Martinez, 'Abuse and Aggressive Tax Planning'.

[30] Ibid.

[31] European Commission, 'Proposal for a Council Directive on a Common Consolidated Corporate Tax Base' COM (2016) 683 final; EU Commission, 'Council Directive on a Common Corporate Tax Base' COM (2016) 685; European Commission, 'Proposal for a Council Directive laying down rules relating to the corporate taxation of a significant digital presence' COM (2018) 147 final.

[32] European Commission, 'Proposal for a Council Directive on the common system of a digital services tax on revenues resulting from the provision of certain digital services', COM (2018) 148 final; OECD, 'About tax and crime', www.oecd.org/tax/crime/about-tax-and-crime.htm, accessed 25 March 2020.

the exercise resonates with ascertaining the 'capability of ATAP to make the tax system stable in the long run'.[33] It is clear that the anti-tax avoidance rules of the EU are not durable. The OECD's rules in this regard are not water-tight either, as they equally suffer certain deficits in the light of the sophistication of the financial system and strategies of tax offenders.

Indeed, Collier and others have demonstrated that the successful implementation of these measures is doubtful. Until the central principles of the international tax system are reviewed and transformed, the EU counter-measures are unlikely to provide durable solutions to profit-shifting or other tax-related problems facing the international community today.

Murphy and Baker tend to be persuaded by the need to reform the international tax system. They have gone as far as describing the current 'international tax architecture as life that is expired' and that it was high time the current tax system was drastically reformed. This is because the current tax system cannot deliver the current tax policy, let alone the tax policy in the future.[34] For instance, the EU counter-measures may help in reducing the 'scope for some profit-shifting channels' as envisaged by the ATAP. At the same time, these counter-measures may succeed in overriding 'the resulting costs for businesses in the form of compliance costs and increased uncertainty due to higher complexity'.[35] Nonetheless, there will still be outstanding problems that will continue to linger on, until the unbridled principles of the international tax system are frontally countered and drastically reformed.

The EU Information Exchange, TGPs and International Cooperation

The administrative cooperation for direct taxation in Europe derived its initial legal basis from Directive77/799/EEC in respect of mutual assistance by competent authorities of EU Member States in the field of direct taxation, certain excise duties and taxation of insurance. This directive was repealed by Directive 2011/16/EU, which, thus, serves as the original directive on administrative cooperation and exchange of information in EU.

Accordingly, Directive 2011/16/EU (DAC 1) is the key legal instrument that supports Member States to ensure that information relating to direct taxation are exchanged harmoniously amongst the EU Member States.[36] This directive is a core pillar of information exchange cooperation because it enables Member States to have 'a new improved framework for commonly structured working methods and

---

[33] Collier et al, 'Dissecting the EU's Recent Anti-Tax Avoidance Measures'.

[34] R Murphy and A Baker, 'A response to the Consultation on an IMF 2019 Analysis of International Corporate Taxation' (City University of London and SPERI of Sheffield, 2018), http://coffers.eu/wp-content/uploads/2018/12/2018-Murphy-Baker.pdf, accessed 4 March 2020.

[35] Collier et al, 'Dissecting the EU's Recent Anti-Tax Avoidance Measures'.

[36] European Commission, *The European Union explained: Taxation* (European Union, 2015) 5.

electronic tools since 2013'.[37] The DAC has since had five amendments in order to strengthen cooperation amongst administrative agencies in the EU. These amendments include:

- Directive 2014/107/EU (DAC 2), which introduced the exchange of financial account data automatically and incorporated the essential elements of the repealed Savings Directive, 2003/48/EC on mutual assistance;
- Directive 2015/2376/EU (DAC 3), which addresses issues appertaining to automatically exchanging amongst Member States tax rulings and advance pricing agreements;
- Directive 2016/881/EU (DAC 4), which deals with automatically exchanging country by country reports; Directive 2016/2258/EU (DAC 5), which enables tax agencies of Member States to 'have access to beneficial ownership information collected pursuant to the anti-money laundering legislation'; and
- Directive 2018/822/EU (DAC 6), which deals with automatically exchanging 'reportable cross border arrangements or tax planning schemes', thus, establishing new disclosure rules on EU tax issues.[38]

Figure 22 demonstrates the trajectory of DAC 1 from adoption to the present.

Figure 22 The Journey so far for the Directive on Administrative Cooperation[39]

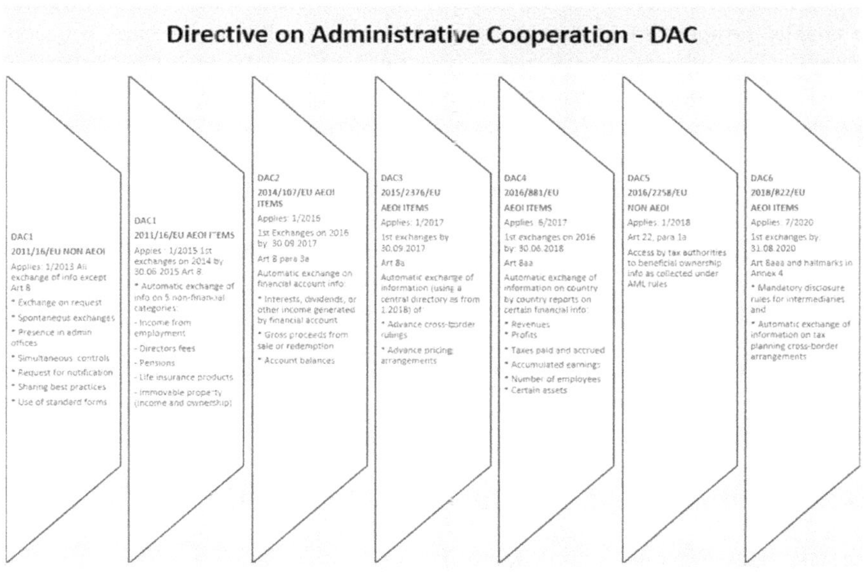

[37] EU Commission, 'Administrative cooperation in (direct) taxation in the EU', https://ec.europa.eu/taxation_customs/business/tax-cooperation-control/administrative-cooperation/enhanced-administrative-cooperation-field-direct-taxation_en, accessed 23 April 2020.
[38] Ibid.
[39] Ibid.

It must also be noted that three forms of information exchange can be appropriated in the DAC. These are:

the exchange of information on request (EOIR) concerning information on specific persons or transactions that have been expressed by the requesting country; the spontaneous exchange of information (SEOI) relating to unsystematic flows of information that is regarded to be of interest to the receiving country; and the automatic exchange of information (AEOI) concerning predefined tax data exchange, using predefined formats and at predetermined times, without prior request from any requesting country in the EU.[40]

AEOI appears to raise higher the level of information exchange. It is executed to address tax information issues relating to taxpayers that happen to be active in a different Member State than the country in which those taxpayers reside. Competent tax authorities are required, under this provision, to automatically supply, in electronic form, the required tax information to the country in which the taxpayer has habitual residence. This process is mandatory and covers information exchange in the following areas of assets, finance and income, namely: 'employment income, pension income, directors' fees, income and ownership of immovable property, life insurance products, financial account information, cross-border tax rulings and advance pricing arrangements, country by country reporting and tax planning schemes' – which basically cover the most parts of DAC 1 to DAC 6.

With respect to tax crimes, DAC 5 especially pierces the veil of company owners and makes it mandatory, according to Article 1, for EU Member States to enact legislation that enables competent tax authorities to have access to the mechanisms, procedures, documents and information referred to in Articles 13, 30, 31 and 40 of Directive (EU) 2015/849 of the European Parliament and of the Council relating to beneficial ownerships. By Article 2 of DAC 5, Member States were also required to have, by not later than 31 December 2017, adopted and published the relevant 'laws, regulations and administrative provisions' for complying with the Directive. Member States were also required to have applied the measures beginning from 1 January 2018.[41]

Complementarily, the fourth AMLD ushered in a regime of Ultimate Beneficial Owner (UBO) that adds an additional layer to the information exchange framework in the criminalisation domain. The UBO regime provides a register that takes custody of information about beneficial owners of both legal and natural persons as well as foundations and trusts that are resident in the EU. This register, which seeks to foster greater transparency, is required to be accessible to the public in EU countries, according to the terms of the fifth AMLD. This is for data of the legal persons, which kicked in at the beginning of 2020, while that of trusts and other legal arrangements were due to be accessible to members of the public who can demonstrate a legitimate interest by March 2020.

Recital 36 of the fifth AMLD establishes some exemptions that border on risk of exposing the beneficial owner to dangers or when the UBO is a minor, or such related

---

[40] EU Commission, 'Report from the Commission to The European Parliament and the Council on Overview and assessment of the statistics and information on the automatic exchanges in the field of direct taxation' (17 December 2018 COM (2018) 844 final), https://ec.europa.eu/taxation_customs/sites/taxation/files/report-automatic-exchanges-taxation-dac-844_en.pdf, accessed 23 April 2020.

[41] European Commission, 'Administrative cooperation'.

issues. But, at least, applicable institutions in the EU may still be open to have access to the register. According to the fifth AMLD, Article 30, it is mandatory for EU institutions such as competent authorities, tax authorities, investigative agencies, and financial intelligence units to consult the UBO register in the course of conducting due diligence on money laundering issues, including tax crimes. This is an important step because the huge reservoir of beneficial owners can easily avail relevant information to LEAs. However, at the time of writing, there is no data available which can inform a commentary on if and to what extent the UBO databases have been established and whether they have yielded any operational value in tax enforcement practices.

Nevertheless, the combination of these measures appears to adequately characterise the OECD's requirements for administrative cooperation. The EU Commission has continued to support the EU Council in its efforts to align EU legislation on automatic information exchange with the OECD Global Standard on automatic exchange of financial account information. The Commission Expert Group is tasked with harmonising EU administrative rules with those of the OECD. It advises the EU Commission as to how to support the EU Council and EU Countries to have EU legislation on automatic exchange of information in direct taxation that is effectively aligned and fully compatible with the OECD Global Standard on automatic exchange of financial account information.

The Expert Group has its meetings' documents placed in a commonly accessible Commission Register of Expert Groups, labelled, 'Expert group on automatic exchange of financial account information'. In effect, while harmonising EU rules with those of the OECD, the group facilitates exchange of information, experience and good practices in the area of mutual assistance for direct taxation amongst EU countries.[42]

This is a good evidence of cooperation between the EU and the OECD in the area of information exchange. As established by recitals 9 and 13 of DAC 2, the Common Reporting Standard (CRS) is a critical common feature of both the OECD automatic information exchange regime and the EU legislation on administrative cooperation for fighting financial crime. CRS allows automatic exchange of financial account information of persons to counterparts in countries that are party to the CRS. The essential information exchanged includes clients' name, date of birth, tax identification number, account number, and balance in the account. Based on the foregoing, it can be said that the information exchange system of DAC 1 to DAC 6 of EU fairly features the needed exchange requirements in the principles 8 and 9 of the TGPs.

Various offshore loopholes still exist, as foreign bank accounts can still be kept secret from tax authorities. Hence, a number of Members of the European Parliament called on the European Commission to revise the rules so that all financial centres and tax havens are required to share information with Member States, with the risk of sanctions if they do not.[43]

---

[42] EU Commission, 'Register of Commission Expert Groups and other similar entities' (2015), http://ec.europa.eu/transparency/regexpert/index.cfm?do=groupDetail.groupDetail&groupID=1711, accessed 22 April 2020.

[43] H Osborne, 'Tax avoidance Offshore wealth: loopholes found in EU anti-tax evasion rules Foreign accounts can still be kept secret from tax authorities, says report', *The Guardian* (15 October 2018), www.theguardian.com/business/2018/oct/15/offshore-wealth-loopholes-found-eu-anti-tax-evasion-rules; and European Greens, 'Halt Tax Avoidance', https://europeangreens.eu/fr/news/greens-call-halt-tax-avoidance, accessed 25 July 2020.

The five amendments so far made to DAC 1 extending the scope thereof have, however, been described as 'loosely based on the common global standards that have been internationally agreed by tax administrations',[44] particularly at the level of the OECD and its TGPs. The DAC's imperatives could sometimes exceed the international standards, such as that of the OECD's TGPs, especially so because the DAC is legally binding with clear legislative parameters, while a number of the OECD's standards on administrative cooperation can be said to be largely based on some sort of 'political agreement without legislative force', which is not compelling enough to be legally binding on states.[45]

Whatever the dynamics may be, there are many ways in which this exchange of information regime can help fight tax crimes in the EU. In the context, transparency and cooperation become a hallmark and suspicious activities of tax crimes in any EU Member States are readily detected and shared with other Member States. Also, potential and real tax fraud schemes in non-EU Member States are likely to be detected and shared with EU Member States. In addition, in investigating and prosecuting tax crimes, the automatic exchange of information of tax mechanism can readily help prosecutors to launch full-scale investigations and acquire relevant information for successful prosecutions, before things get out of control. With regards to the AEOI, especially, it provides a crucial benefit of arming tax administrations with the needed information that is automatically released to 'counter cross-border tax fraud, evasion and avoidance'.[46] Kaye has observed that automatic exchange of information is generally deemed to present the most effective remedy to countering tax evasion.[47] Of course, it still has to be complemented by other measures because it cannot be said to be a holistic or a comprehensive solution.

Partnership and Cooperation

One of the most effective measures against tax crimes is to use high-end research and partnership to explore for sustainable ways to eviscerate both the old and new pathways and strategies which tax criminals use to flout applicable laws, as well as where they hide the profit they generate from illicit financial flows (IFFs). To succeed in doing this, it is important to intensify the building and harnessing of partnerships between countries, partnership across different parts of government, and partnerships between policymakers, operational leaders[48] and multi-disciplinary academia.

The Global Forum on Transparency and Exchange of Information for Tax Purposes presents itself as a global standard that is anchored on partnership with over 160 participating jurisdictions as members and 19 participating international organisations as

---

[44] European Commission, 'Administrative cooperation'.

[45] Ibid.

[46] European Commission, 'Report from the Commission to The European Parliament and the Council on Overview and assessment of the statistics and information on the automatic exchanges in the field of direct taxation'.

[47] AT Kaye, 'Innovations in the War on Tax Evasion' (2014) *Brigham Young University Law Review* 363–413.

[48] OECD, Successful Partnership – A Guide, 2006, www.oecd.org/cfe/leed/36279186.pdf, accessed 25 July 2020.

observers. It leverages goodwill amongst parties to ensure that utilising companies, trusts and partnerships to hide wealth and evading tax is made unattractive to people with such interests. The Global Forum is the leading international institution that works to ensure that 'the internationally agreed standards of transparency and exchange of information in the tax area' resonate well with the international community. Its in-depth peer review mechanism is used to monitor the full implementation of 'the standard of transparency and exchange [of] information' which the members are commited to implementing. The forum also ensures that a level playing field is established for both members and non-members.[49] The work of the OECD has also seen over 100 states establishing 'regular and automatic sharing of bank account and other financial accounts, significantly increasing transparency across the world'.[50]

The fifth OECD Forum, which created the TGPs, generally sought to provide an international platform that will allow for best practice on tax crimes to be shared amongst several countries in order to mobilise a 'whole of government' response to financial crime, capitalise on data and technology potential to detect fraud, deal with professional enablers that tax fraud relies upon, and build the needed capacity that can effectively respond to these issues worldwide.[51] These should be encouraged and actively participated in by EU and its members as the cooperation and transparency measures offer good opportunities for durably fighting tax crimes in the EU. Interestingly, the EU is part of this process, and is travelling in the right direction with its tax crime counter-measures that have been increasingly aligned to the OECD's TGPs. Sustained and closer collaboration with the OECD and customised domestication of the TGPs in the EU's *acquis* is a call too glaringly attractive for the EU to ignore in its efforts to durably counter tax crimes in the Union.

Conclusion

Tax avoidance and tax planning, which are keenly tackled by the ATAP, although not considered strictly illegal as tax fraud, do fall within the letter of the law but outside the spirit of the law.[52] Because of the challenges involved in demarcating the boundaries between tax avoidance and aggressive tax planning, the ATAP measures along with the other cooperation measures are still not able to effectively counter tax avoidance.

There have been encouraging steps, however. For instance, the establishment of beneficial ownership register provision by DAC 5 is particularly instructive towards fighting tax crimes and avoidance. Although this is commendable, the efforts towards

---

[49] OECD, 'Global Forum on Tax Transparency marks a dramatic shift in the fight against tax evasion with the widespread commencement of the automatic exchange of financial information', www.oecd.org/tax/transparency/global-forum-marks-a-dramatic-shift-in-the-fight-against-tax-evasion-with-the-widespread-commencement-of-the-automatic-exchange-of-financial-information.htm, accessed 10 December 2018.

[50] OECD, 'Strengthening the global response to tax crime', www.oecd.org/tax/crime/strengthening-the-global-response-to-tax-crime.htm, accessed 25 March 2020.

[51] Ibid.

[52] Fiscalis Tax Gap Project Group (FPG/041), 'The Concept of Tax Gaps Report on VAT Gap Estimations' (Brussels, European Commission, March 2016), https://ec.europa.eu/taxation_customs/sites/taxation/files/docs/body/tgpg_report_en.pdf, 20 March 2020.

improvements in the administrative legal regime to counter tax crimes in the EU still have end goals of which reasonable achievement is still doubtable.[53]

Knowing that tax avoidance can lay the foundation for tax crimes to be committed, it is imperative that fast-track efforts are mobilised to criminalise the larger chunk of tax avoidance schemes that can predictably fall into or assume the impact of tax crimes. The TGPs have not effectively highlighted the principles that can account for bridging the gap between tax evasion and tax avoidance. However, the international cooperation legal gateways provided by the TGPs can be a springboard for harnessing efforts towards unravelling the intricacies and remedies for tax avoidance especially as it relates to MNCs.[54] The chapter concludes on the note that the EU's administrative tax crime measures, even though not neatly packaged, can be a great source of support for the EU tax crime measures and the TGPs. The next chapter explores whistleblowing and corruption in the tax crime countering ecosystem.

---

[53] T Balco, 'ATAD 2: Anti-Tax Avoidance Directive' (2017) 57(4) *European Taxation* 127–36; N Fowler, 'The European Union, tax evasion and closing loopholes: new report' (Tax Justice Network, 15 October 2018), www.taxjustice.net/2018/10/15/the-european-union-tax-evasion-and-closing-loopholes-new-report/, accessed 23 April 2020.

[54] Fiscalis Tax Gap Project Group (FPG/041), 'The Concept of Tax Gaps'.

6

Other Components of the Tax
Crime Ecosystem

Introduction

There are some essential components of the tax crime ecosystem which have not been effectively covered by the TGPs. These include corruption and whistle-blower protection. These are explored in this chapter.

Corruption and Tax Crimes

Definition

Corruption, just like tax crimes, is difficult to define precisely with universal consensus. It varies in scope and content and from one jurisdiction to another. It can also vary from one scholar, public sector advocate or practitioner to the other. For instance, while the definition provided by Transparency International is that corruption is 'the abuse of entrusted power for private gain',[1] Morris defines it as using public power illegitimately in order to privately benefit.[2] Both definitions deal only with public-sector corruption, which appears to ignore the fact that corruption can also occur in the private sector.

However, Senior has defined corruption as a conduct where someone provides a good or service to another person or third party in a surreptitious manner with the aim or hope that he/she would be able to influence actions or decisions of the third party, owing to the fact that the article of influence would benefit the third party or both parties at a point in time when the third party is in a position of authority or power.[3] This definition captures private-sector corruption too, whereby not only the public official in authority is abusing power for personal gain but also the private person, say a marketing officer, engaging another private person to influence his/her decisions to benefit the marketing officer, with possible benefit accruing to the manager. Kaufmann

---

[1] Transparency International UK, 'Overview: Why Corruption Matters', www.transparency.org.uk/why-corruption-matters, accessed 24 May 2020.
[2] SD Morris, *Corruption and Politics in Contemporary Mexico* (Alabama Press, 1991).
[3] I Senior, *Corruption – the World's Big C: Cases, Causes, Consequences, Cures* (The Institute of Economic Affairs, 2006).

adds to the debate by looking at corruption from the legal perspective also, whereby the abuse of power for personal gain is defined by the law.[4]

No matter how pervasive corruption might appear, however, there is a growing trend towards identifying certain common ingredients that constitute corruption.

Whether the magnitude of corruption is considered petty, grand or systematic, it has a debilitating impact on society, including an increasing scale of tax crimes and difficulty in countering them. According to Interpol, corruption provides 'a fertile ground for organized criminal activities [including serious tax crimes], as criminals are aided in their illegal activities by the complicity of corrupt public officials'[5] and, of course, corrupt private officials too.

It is highly possible that a very corrupt country would give the opportunity for tax crimes to prevail, since officials with a corrupt mentality would like to earn more income from bribes that cannot be accounted for in the tax system. At the same time, a system bedevilled with high degree of tax crime would drive corruption by offering more opportunities for bribes. Moreover, 'larger bribes result in higher levels of evasion'.[6] Indeed, corruption and bribery are some of the established methods to facilitate tax crimes.

There is a lot of literature on separate dimensions of tax crimes[7] and corruption.[8] While both tax crimes and corruption are significant challenges for the EU and the OECD, they are generally approached as distinct phenomena and thus critiqued separately. Although there is a growing interest to establish the layers of linkages or relationships between the two concepts, a lot of grey areas still exist, particularly relating to finding appropriately resilient legal instruments to effectively counter these two phenomena jointly. The OECD and the World Bank have recognised the interrelation between corruption and tax crimes and stressed the importance of promoting cooperation between tax and anti-corruption authorities.[9]

Significant risks have been identified in numerous EU Member States, although the EU as a region scores overall very well in the Perception of Corruption Index.[10] For example, the European Commission's Directorate-General Home Affairs has published reports on corruption in the EU Member States aimed at collecting information

---

[4] D Kaufmann and P Vicente, 'Legal Corruption' (2011) 23(2) *Economics & Politics* 195.

[5] J Alm, J Martinez-Vazquez and C McClellan, 'Corruption and firm tax evasion' (2016) 124 *Journal of Economic Behavior & Organization* 146–63.

[6] Ibid.

[7] In addition to the literature reviewed in this book so far, also see HA Burton, SS Karlinsky and C Blanthorne, 'Perception of a White-Collar Crime: Tax Evasion' (2005) 3 (1) *The ATA Journal of Legal Tax Research* 35–48.

[8] U Turksen and V Chauhan, 'Anti-Bribery and Corruption: Perceptions, Risks and Practice for UK Banks' in N Ryder (ed), *White Collar Crime and Risk* (Palgrave, 2018); N Ryder and L Pasculli (eds), *Corruption in the Global Era – Causes, Sources and Forms of Manifestation* (Routledge, 2019); and N Ryder and L Pasculli (eds) *Corruption, Integrity and the Law – Global Regulatory Challenges* (Routledge, 2020).

[9] OECD and the World Bank, 'Improving Co-operation between Tax Authorities and Anti-Corruption Authorities in Combating Tax Crime and Corruption', www.oecd.org/tax/crime/improving-co-operation-between-tax-authorities-and-anti-corruption-authorities-in-combating-tax-crime-and-corruption.pdf, accessed 25 July 2020.

[10] Transparency International, Corruption Perception Index 2019, www.transparency.org/en/cpi/2019#, accessed 25 July 2020.

published by different international and national institutions and organisations. According to this study, the tax and customs administrations carry a different level of risk for businesses, ranging from high levels of risk in Bulgaria[11] to low risk of corruption in Finland.[12] Another alarming trend is found by the World Bank study, which indicates that there are EU Member States where businesses are expected to provide gifts in meeting with tax officials! According to this study, in 2018–19, over 12 per cent of firms in Croatia and over 5 per cent of firms in Italy expected to give gifts in meetings with tax officials. [13]

Against this background, it can be asserted that there are clear indications of corrupt practices taking place in tax ecosystems of EU Member States. While it is generally accepted that it would be far better to have a world without corruption, the exact definition of corruption is yet to be settled. But, since there is an idea of what it does look like and there already exist numerous legal instruments dealing with specific corrupt practices (eg, bribery), such measures can have some positive effect on countering tax crimes. Thus, in the short term it is imperative to employ the existing (albeit limited) anti-corruption measures available.

Countering Corruption and Tax Crimes

Similar to large-scale tax crimes, corrupt transactions cross many national borders,[14] which fall into different legal systems and enforcement regimes. The need for stronger international cooperation in countering corruption is, therefore, as crucial as that of tax crimes. The OECD has, therefore, been developing instruments that seek to counter these practices that have implications for tax crimes. For example, the OECD provides global leadership for developing instruments to countering bribery that have consequences on tax crimes. Principal ones include:

- the OECD Anti-Bribery Convention 1997;

- the 1994 Recommendation for countries to take effective measures to deter, prevent and combat the bribery of foreign public officials in connection with international business transactions;

- the 1996 Council Recommendation to deny tax deductibility of bribes to foreign public officials and by extension prohibition of tax deductibility of all bribes that are considered as criminal offence which attracts serious penalties;

- the 2009 new Recommendation on Tax Measures for Combating Bribery of Foreign Public Officials in International Business Transactions;

---

[11] Bulgaria Corruption Report (GAN – Business Anti-corruption Portal), www.ganintegrity.com/portal/country-profiles/bulgaria/, accessed 19 July 2020.
[12] Finland Corruption Report (GAN – Business Anti-corruption Portal), www.ganintegrity.com/portal/country-profiles/finland/, accessed 19 July 2020.
[13] World Bank, 'Firms expected to give gifts in meetings with tax officials (% of firms), https://data.worldbank.org/indicator/IC.TAX.GIFT.ZS, accessed 16 July 2020.
[14] Interpol, 'Corruption', www.interpol.int/en/Crimes/Corruption, accessed 2 May 2020.

- the 2009 updated Bribery Awareness Handbook for Tax Examiners to ensure effective detection of bribery; and

- the 2010 new OECD Recommendation on facilitation of cooperation between tax and other law enforcement authorities to fight crimes of serious nature such as tax crimes.[15]

These instruments have not only sought to streamline measures on international bribery and related tax crimes but also attempted to strengthen the role played by tax authorities in effectively countering bribery and tax crimes. For instance, the Tax Awareness Handbook assists tax authorities to fish out questionable transactions that could be bribes in order to enforce the prohibition of tax deductibility of bribes.[16]

Arguably, the Council of Europe's (COE) anti-corruption instruments such as the Civil Law Convention on Corruption (COE, 2003/174) and the Criminal Law Convention on Corruption (COE, 2002/173) as well as the Additional Protocol to the Criminal Law Convention on Corruption (COE, 2005/191)[17] have provided a wider spectrum for countering bribery and corruption, albeit without the kind of concentration OECD's bribery instruments give to tax issues specifically. Ratifications have been suspiciously low, because of the overbearing provisions in these instruments. The EU Member States, as part of both the COE and the OECD, benefit from the combination of legal developments in these platforms and stand a good chance to combat corruption and bribery. This is especially so with the provisions in the Criminal Convention of the COE, which has greater significance in finding durable solutions for tax crimes in the EU. At the same time, the AML legal framework of the EU and Directive (EU) 2017/1371[18] feature corruption with similar approach as tax crimes and other financial crimes.

Globally, however, the United Nations Convention against Corruption 2003 stands as 'the only legally binding universal anti-corruption instrument'.[19] It provides for different forms of corruption including 'bribery, trading in influence, abuse of functions, and corruption in the private sector'. It appears to have a wider coverage of dimensions of corruption but it does not provide for effective concrete enforcement mechanisms nor does it effectively link other financial crimes such as tax crimes to it.

However, the features that make this legal instrument an attractive global anti-corruption tool include not only the far-reaching approach and the mandatory character

---

[15] OECD, 'About tax and crime', www.oecd.org/tax/crime/about-tax-and-crime.htm, accessed 25 March 2020.

[16] Ibid.

[17] COE (2002), "Criminal Law Convention on Corruption" (ETS 173), STE n°173, www.coe.int/fr/web/conventions/full-list/-/conventions/treaty/173?_coeconventions_WAR_coeconventionsportlet_languageId=en_GB, accessed 6 February 2020; COE (2003), Civil Law Convention on Corruption (ETS 174), STE n°174, www.coe.int/fr/web/conventions/full-list/-/conventions/treaty/174?_coeconventions_WAR_coeconventionsportlet_languageId=en_GB, accessed 6 February 2020; COE(2005), Additional Protocol to the Criminal Law Convention on Corruption (ETS 191), STE n°191, www.coe.int/fr/web/conventions/full-list/-/conventions/treaty/191?_coeconventions_WAR_coeconventionsportlet_languageId=en_GB, accessed 6 February 2020.

[18] Directive (EU) 2017/1371 of the European Parliament and of the Council of 5 July 2017 on the fight against fraud to the Union's financial interests by means of criminal law [2017] OJ L 198/29–41.

[19] UNODC, 'United Nations Convention against Corruption', www.unodc.org/unodc/en/corruption/tools_and_publications/UN-convention-against-corruption.html, accessed 6 February 2020.

of many of its provisions but also the unique tool it presents to the global community to be able to develop a comprehensive response to a global problem of destructive corruption.[20] The UN Convention 2003 consists of five key zones:

i.   preventive measures;
ii. criminalisation and law enforcement;
iii. international cooperation;
iv. asset recovery; and
v.   technical assistance and information exchange.

While these zones establish critical areas relevant to the fight against corruption, it does not appear that they provide any meaningful support for countering tax crimes internationally. It is therefore necessary for future developments in the anti-corruption legal framework (the fiscal corruption elements in particular) to include provisions that interconnect the fight against corruption with that against tax crimes.

Whistle-blowing, Corruption and Tax Crimes

Corruption and tax crimes appear to detest whistle-blowing – for obvious reasons. Whistle-blowing shines light on areas where corruption and tax crimes tend to hide. According to the OECD, if employees are encouraged 'to report wrongdoing (to "blow the whistle"), and protecting them when they do', it will serve as an essential instrument to prevent corruption in both the public and private sectors.[21] This proposition is limited to employee whistle-blowers. PROTAX observed that it is not only workers who should be encouraged to report and be protected to expose tax crimes, but also anyone else who has the opportunity to make such disclosures in the public interest. This is the surest way to have all angles of social and economic life covered to be able to effectively uncover the dark alleys that promote tax crimes and corruption.

Whistle-blowing has in fact proven to be an extremely effective tool for countering tax crimes and corruption. This fact has been demonstrated in recent years, which have been marked by notorious whistle-blowing acts conducted against governments, security services, sporting and doping agencies and major financial institutions, which have included, inter alia, LuxLeaks,[22] Panama Papers,[23] Paradise Papers,[24] Football Leaks,[25]

---

[20] Ibid.

[21] OECD, 'Whistle-blower protection', www.oecd.org/corruption/ethics/whistleblower-protection/, accessed 6 February 2020.

[22] S Bowers, 'European Authorities Launch Probe Into Secret Lux Leaks Tax Deal' (*ICIJ*, 7 March 2019), www.icij.org/investigations/luxembourg-leaks/european-authorities-launch-probe-into-secret-lux-leaks-tax-deal/, accessed 11 July 2020.

[23] International Consortium of Investigative Journalists (ICIJ), 'The Panama Papers: Exposing the Rogue Offshore Finance Industry', www.icij.org/investigations/panama-papers/#_ga=2.24674816 4.1276343162.1584385292-1381287180.1584385292, accessed 11 July 2020.

[24] W Fitzgibbon and D Starkman, 'The "Paradise Papers" and the Long Twilight Struggle Against Offshore Secrecy' (*ICIJ*, 27 December 2017), www.icij.org/investigations/paradise-papers/paradise-papers-long-twilight-struggle-offshore-secrecy/, accessed 11 July 2020.

[25] See European Investigation Collaborations, 'About us', https://eic.network/, accessed 11 March 2020.

Danske Bank,[26] Snowden leaks,[27] Cambridge Analytica[28] and Dieselgate.[29] At the same time, given the dire fact that nearly 80 per cent of whistle-blowers face reprisals,[30] the need for viable whistle-blowing policies and laws to help in countering tax crimes has been demonstrated in many instances.[31]

In recent times, various media leaks by the International Consortium of Investigative Journalists (ICIJ) have demonstrated the complexity and dynamics of issues surrounding whistle-blowing and the need to harness efforts to enhance whistleblowing legislations in the EU. *Falciani* and *Deltour* are typical whistle-blowing cases involving taxation and tax evasion issues. While Hervé Falciani from the Swiss Leaks brought to light a controversial tax evasion at HSBC, Antoine Deltour from the Luxembourg Leaks blew off the cover of fraud which enabled a number of EU States to investigate, prosecute and deliver judgements on fiscal fraud.

The significance of these two cases is that, acting as whistle-blowers and revealing information with evidential value, they were able to provide huge support for LEAs and administrations to fight crime. In the case of Hervé Falciani, French LEAs were supported by Falciani's revelations to establish and issue charge of tax fraud and money laundering against HSBC, while prosecutors successfully asked French courts to convict offenders, particularly the heiress of Nina Ricci (Arlette Ricci). She was given a three-year prison sentence (two of which were suspended), a fine of €1 million was issued against her and some of her properties were seized.[32]

Her conviction was based on evading taxes with the support of HSBC. The seriousness of the case was demonstrated not only by being the first successful case out of 50 tax fraud-related cases at HSBC France, but also by the declaration of the Paris court that, in the effort to put a dark cover on the money she inherited that was deposited in Swiss bank accounts, Ricci did exhibit a 'particularly determined willingness for more than 20 years' and that 'the seriousness of the facts are an exceptional threat to public

---

[26] Bruun and Hjejle, 'Report on the Non-Resident Portfolio at Danske Bank's Estonian branch' (19 September 2018), https://danskebank.com/-/media/danske-bank-com/file-cloud/2018/9/report-on-the-non-resident-portfolio-at-danske-banks-estonian-branch.pdf?rev=56b16dfddae94480bb8cdcaebeaddc9b&hash=B7D825F2639326A3BBBC7D524C5E341E, accessed 11 July 2020.

[27] BBC News, 'Edward Snowden: Leaks that exposed US spy programme' (17 January 2014), www.bbc.co.uk/news/world-us-canada-23123964, accessed 11 July 2020.

[28] JC Wong, 'The Cambridge Analytica scandal changed the world – but it didn't change Facebook' (*The Guardian*, 18 March 2019), www.theguardian.com/technology/2019/mar/17/the-cambridge-analytica-scandal-changed-the-world-but-it-didnt-change-facebook, accessed 11 July 2020.

[29] R Parloff, 'How VW Paid $25 Billion for "Dieselgate" – and Got Off Easy' (*Fortune*, 6 February 2018), https://fortune.com/2018/02/06/volkswagen-vw-emissions-scandal-penalties/, accessed 11 July 2020.

[30] The 2019 Report by the UK All Party Parliamentary Group (APPG) reveals a wide spectrum of challenges that whistle-blowers face. Consisting of evidence from over 400 whistle-blowers' responses, the APPG study indicates that the majority of whistle-blowing involved bullying and harassment in the workplace. APPG, 'Whistleblowing – The Personal Cost of Doing the Right Thing and the Cost to Society of Ignoring it', July 2019, https://a02f9c2f-03a1-4206-859b-06ff2b21dd81.filesusr.com/ugd/88d04c_9754e54bc641443db902cd963687cb55.pdf, accessed 16 July 2020.

[31] A Lui and U Turksen, 'Vulnerabilities, Obstacles and Risks in Reporting Financial Crimes: Conundrum of whistle-blowers' in N Ryder and L Pasculli (eds), *Corruption, Integrity and The Law: Global Regulatory Challenges* (Routledge, 2020).

[32] K Willsher, 'Nina Ricci heir convicted of tax evasion in France with help of HSBC' (*The Guardian*, 13 April 2015), www.theguardian.com/world/2015/apr/13/nina-ricci-heir-convicted-of-tax-evasion-in-france-with-help-of-hsbc, accessed 6 February 2020.

order and the republican pact.'[33] In the same vein, in recognition of his revelations, the EU Parliament awarded Deltour a 'European Citizen's Prize' for a remarkable effort to foster 'European cooperation and promotion of common values'.

The challenge, however, is that some whistle-blowers sometimes commit infractions in their effort to break through the dark alleys to reveal the needed information to fight tax crimes. These infractions can include 'stealing data, spying on companies or industrial espionage, and violation of financial secrecy'. These can easily be used by companies against their staff or anyone trying to break through the thick walls and blow the whistle. Whistle-blowers, therefore, have to be reasonably protected against these charges. Otherwise, as Turksen would have us to see, 'when exposing a crime is treated as committing a crime, you are ruled by criminals'.[34]

For instance, Falciani had to suffer for breaches of secrecy and sentenced to five years (*in absentia*) in prison by Swiss Court even though the revelations of Falciani did help in prosecutions and sanctioning of those responsible for series of financial crimes. Other whistle-blowers could be discouraged by these provisions that adversely affected Falciani. However, there are some moral issues with some whistle-blowers, who may act hypocritically where they, at one point, would use information that has been sourced to blackmail perpetrators of suspected crime while, at another time, they submit the information to LEAs and courts/magistrates to help in successful investigation, prosecution and conviction.[35]

According to PROTAX findings, 'greater protection for whistle-blowers may facilitate the detection of tax crimes'.[36] Scholars such as Turksen, Pasculli, Grasso and many others support the idea that whistle-blowing is one of the powerful tools for combating tax crimes and other financial crimes.[37] The EU has in place relevant whistle-blower protection regime especially provided for by Directive (EU) 2019/1937 of the European Parliament and of the Council of 23 October 2019 on the protection of persons who report breaches of Union law.[38] The directive aims at enhancing 'the enforcement of Union law and policies in specific areas by laying down common minimum standards providing for a high level of protection of persons reporting breaches of Union law'.[39] It covers broad spectrum of public life including breaches of tax laws.[40]

Although this directive appears to provide far-reaching guarantees and protections, altogether, it certainly has not been able to give full confidence to a potential whistle-blower. This is because the EU whistle-blower regime still makes it possible for Member States of the EU (or the organisation for which the whistle-blower works for) to penalise a whistle-blower using the reservation mechanisms and the grey areas provided by

---

[33] Ibid.
[34] U Turksen, 'Criminalisation and protection of whistle-blowers in the EU's counter financial crime framework', in Ligeti and Tosla (eds), *Economic and Financial Crime in Europe* (Hart Publishing, 2018).
[35] Ibid.
[36] Ibid.
[37] The Corporate Social Responsibility and Business Ethics Blog, Report on the International Conference, 'Whistle-blowers: Voices of Justice' (London, 10 May 2019), https://corporatesocialresponsibilityblog.com/2019/06/10/conference-on-whistleblowing/, accessed 25 July 2020.
[38] OJ L305/17.
[39] Art 1.
[40] Art 2.

flip-flopping on whether or not to first report to employer or to go directly to the public or competent authorities to make a disclosure. The EU Whistle-blowing Directive is, however, a great feat, despite the lingering grey and missing areas[41] which should be considered in future legal reforms.

Increasingly, EU Member States are legislating to empower the need to use protected whistle-blowers to achieve this feat. The current EU Whistle-blower Directive recognises that 'full commitment and joint efforts of all EU institutions, Member States and stakeholders are required to give protection to whistle-blowers'.[42]

One of the positive steps is that the directive grants some protection for 'facilitators'. There is also now supposed to be a prohibition against compelling whistle-blowers to undergo psychiatric or medical attention. These are all steps in the right direction. However, to draft such whistle-blowing legislation into the durable solutions frame, it is imperative that whistle-blowing laws in the EU are harmonised and inter-agency cooperation both domestically and cross-border is made one of the live wires of whistle-blowing legislation and law enforcement. The EU Whistle-blower Directive provides a consolidated minimum standard which can easily be compatible with different legal environments of the EU jurisdictions. The jurisdictions need to, however, escalate the minimum standards to maximum standards through deliberate proactive legal and policy steps.

Conclusion

In this chapter, it has been established that tax crime and corruption as well as whistle-blowing can be connected. While corruption and tax crimes are intimately related, with each providing support for the other, whistleblowing exposes corruption and tax crimes. It is, therefore, imperative that whistleblowing laws are strengthened to give greater protection to all manner of potential whistle-blowers who could be in a position to make disclosures, which can be used by tax authorities and other LEAs to pursue tax criminals.

The current framework for concomitantly countering corruption and tax crimes in the EU and OECD does still have some loose ends that require tightening up. The UN anti-corruption law has, by far, provided the universally accepted legal instrument for countering corruption, but it lacks the needed attention to effectively consider tax crime as a comfortable bedfellow with corruption. The EU and OECD whistle-blower protection regimes appear to concentrate more on the employee as a whistle-blower instead of everyone as a potential whistle-blower.

Whistle-blowing is a potent instrument for scaling up transparency and demystifying secrecy in corporate and public places wherein many illicit activities which

---

[41] For instance, without legal aid, a whistle-blower (employee) is unlikely to revoke his/her rights or resist reprisals against his/her employer in the courts. Most whistle-blower protection regimes including the one put forward by the EU omit such an important provision.

[42] EU Commission (2018/218), 'Proposal for a Directive of the European Parliament and of the Council on the protection of persons reporting on breaches of Union law' (SWD (2018) 116 final) – (SWD (2018) 117 final) (COM (2018) 218).

undermine tax laws will continue unabated if the hindering structures in whistle-blowing legislation in the EU and OECD are not demolished. At the same time, the recent EU Whistle-blower Directive offers a unique opportunity for whistle-blowers and investigative journalists to improve or harness their efforts at helping unearth illicit behaviours and related criminal acts such as tax fraud, corruption and money laundering. It is reassuring that the directive has made provision for journalists to be protected (albeit indirectly) – being regarded as 'facilitators' in the directive.[43]

The next chapter provides conclusions and recommendations.

---

[43] Art 4(4) provides: 'The measures for the protection of reporting persons set out in Chapter VI shall also apply, where relevant, to: (a) facilitators'; Art 5(8) states: '"facilitator" means a natural person who assists a reporting person in the reporting process in a work-related context, and whose assistance should be confidential'; also see recital 41, Directive (EU) 2019/1937 of the European Parliament and of the Council of 23 October 2019 on the protection of persons who report breaches of Union law PE/78/2019/REV/1 [2019] OJ L 305.

7

Conclusion and Recommendations

The impact tax crimes have on economies and societies is tremendous. Billions of euros and dollars are lost to tax revenue,[1] with attendant consequences on economic growth and the needs of the people.[2] Tax crimes have increasingly been brought to the front burner in top-notch discussions around crime counter-measures whereby they have been featured in 'executive agendas, strategic plans, and legislative priorities of many … global leaders and governing bodies'.[3]

Having comprehensively considered all the TGPs along with the EU tax crime counter-measures and briefly looked at the whistle-blowing and corruption regimes (as missing elements in the TGPs), this chapter draws conclusions and proffers policy recommendations for countering tax crimes.

Conclusion

For years, the Task Force on Tax Crimes and Other Crimes (TFTC) has been drawing expertise from many states, including Member States of the OECD and EU. The aim has been to rejuvenate efforts at developing 'best practices with respect to the legal, institutional and operational frameworks required to fight effectively against tax crimes and other financial crimes'[4] on the global stage.

Riding on the back of the 'Oslo Dialogue', the TFTC operates on the basis of three main pillars: standard-setting, capacity-building,[5] and evaluation and impact measurement.[6] With respect to standard-setting, the OECD provides support to jurisdictions in the identification and overcoming of shortcomings in their legal, operational, and cultural frameworks for deterring, investigating and prosecuting tax crimes and other financial crimes. This support is operationalised by the TFTC through setting standards and identifying best practices and developing tools, with a focus on the TGPs.[7]

---

[1] OECD, 'Technology Tools to Tackle Tax Evasion and Tax Fraud' 6, www.oecd.org/tax/crime/technology-tools-to-tackle-tax-evasion-and-tax-fraud.pdf, accessed 25 February 2020.
[2] Ibid.
[3] Ibid.
[4] APEC/OECD, 'Combatting Tax Crimes More Effectively in APEC Economies, Organisation for Economic Co-operation and Development and Asia-Pacific Economic Cooperation', www.oecd.org/tax/crime/combatting-tax-crimes-more-effectively-in-apec-economies.htm, accessed 12 January 2020.
[5] Ibid.
[6] Ibid.
[7] Ibid.

Through these platforms the standards and best practices of the OECD to counter tax crimes concentrate on four areas:

i. Ten Global Principles for Fighting Tax Crime (ie, the TGPs which have been emphasised in this book).
ii. Enhancing domestic inter-agency cooperation to combat tax crime.
iii. Exchange of information between tax authorities and enhancing international cooperation to combat tax crime.
iv. Prohibiting tax deductions for bribe payments together, these standards equip countries to identify and implement.[8]

Items ii and iii are also featured in the TGPs, except that they are given further attention separately somewhere in their own right. The TGPs contain relevant principles, norms and practices that animate a critical framework for harnessing the efforts of criminal tax administrations and criminal tax compliance across countries of the world. They are also a culmination of participatory bottom-up measures on tax crime which have reasonably provided a global reference guide for launching sustainable path to winning the fight against tax crimes both nationally and globally. Some of the TGPs are, however, lacking any substantive guide as to the best practice or course of action to pursue except to provide experiences of different countries in different classifications. Future developments of the TGPs should not lose fact of the need to give superior direction for all but not some of the TGPs.

That said, the TGPs provide minimum standards for the EU to employ in its tax crime countering toolkit. The benchmarking has shown that the EU has substantially adopted the TGPs into its legal framework and continues to strategise towards improving the anti-fraud regime of the EU – the latest being the 2019 Commission Anti-Fraud Strategy. The EU has demonstrated an exemplary regime for consolidating the TGPs in its legal framework. This would not be surprising because the EU is a significant player in the OECD's work particularly relating to tax crimes – the EU Members are already heavily represented in the OECD apart from the institutional representation by the EU itself. Throughout the benchmarking, the area that EU can be found wanting significantly is the aspect of criminalisation of tax crimes that require common definition of tax crimes.

At the EU level, tax crimes have been somewhat legislatively defined but it still gives EU Member States the liberty to define tax offences in their individual national terms. This is, of course, challenging due to differences in legal systems and cultures – which undergird the reason for transposition difficulties faced by some EU Member States in respect of EU level tax crime counter-measures that have already incorporated the TGPs. However, it can present a source of tension in certain areas of cooperation to counter tax crimes. The solace that can be found is that there appears to be an increasing appetite and solidarity among EU Members to make tax offences criminal and without sloppy and weak thresholds. If that is achieved, it would not matter how tax offences are defined.

Corruption has an intimate relationship with tax crimes as well as money laundering. Joint efforts should, therefore, be mobilised to counter these 'twin evils'. It appears

---

[8] Ibid.

that the current framework for pushing the frontiers towards defeating the 'twin evils' is not yet strong enough, either internationally or in the EU. The whistle-blower protection regime, which is receiving favourable attention, should be effectively utilised to counter both corruption and tax crimes, as well as money laundering. The grey and inadequate provisions for whistle-blower protection particularly with regards to channels of making disclosures should be addressed. However, the good news is that the AML regime in the EU and internationally as provided by FATF and others appears to have impressive provisions. There can always be room for improvements given the increasing sophistication of tax crime, corruption and money laundering methods.

As a criminal law measure, 'countering tax crimes has had two basic functions: to deter and punish criminality. The overall disposition of the TGPs and other measures adopted by the OECD and EU tend to be inclined to achieve deterrence, punishment, and criminal justice. The third pillar arguably sometimes attempts to vitiate the vitality of the traditional dual functions of criminal law by trying to connect the two purposes to rule of law and justice. This is a process by which LEAs and tax authorities develop a strategy of transiting from controlling tax crimes to the management of tax crimes for a higher good of society.

Most of the policy measures for combatting tax crimes in the EU and even in the OECD are currently in a flux – trekking along the unsettled contours of the three purposes of law on tax crimes. The purposes are to deter and punish criminality as well as to connect the first two purposes to rule of law and justice. EU legal frameworks as obtained in Member States for countering tax crimes have had a mixture 'of administrative and criminal offences and sanctions'[9] in which the criminalising domain was widely conflictual and not stringent. The TGPs, particularly TGP1, arguably give a framework within which criminal justice can be articulated, even if not secured.

The foregoing analysis of the relationship between the legal regime of tax crimes in the EU and OECD's TGPs demonstrates the fast-developing nature of a varied and multi-layered legal framework for countering tax crimes in the EU. It also illustrates the closely related nature of the relationship between the OECD and the EU in the fight against tax crimes internationally.

Policy and Legal Recommendations

Although there are several issues confronting tax crimes in the EU and OECD, the following recommendations are made with the view that implementing them will have some rippling effects on the other underlying issues. At the same time, without the risk of repeating the TGPs as recommendations, a careful balancing approach is used. A future edition of this book will likely dedicate more space to specific recommendations, as empirical research conducted by PROTAX in 18 EU Member States starts to yield the results in the second half of 2021.

---

[9] E Thirion and A Scherrer, 'Member States' capacity to fight tax crimes: Ex-post impact assessment' (European Parliamentary Research Service (EPRS), EU Parliament, 2017) 7, www.europarl.europa.eu/RegData/etudes/STUD/2017/603257/EPRS_STU(2017)603257_EN.pdf, accessed 9 July 2020.

Strategy Development

The following strategy is sound for approaching tax crimes:

- Promoting compliance by designing it into systems and processes, helping customers get things right from the very start.[10]
- Preventing non-compliance by using available data to detect mistakes, personalise services and support, block fraudulent claims, and automate calculations.[11]
- Responding by identifying and targeting the areas where there may be tax risk – and using tough measures to tackle those who deliberately try to cheat the system.[12] Robust investigation and prosecution mechanisms are critical in this approach.
- Integrated strategy for countering tax crimes be used where legal, institutional, operational, human, cultural, and environmental factors are all targeted.[13]
- The deployment of advanced IT solutions for countering tax crimes should be prioritised.[14]

Criminalisation of Tax Offences

- Three key elements should be, at the minimum, included in the offence of tax fraud and evasion: false representation, failure to disclose information and abuse of position.
- Tax offences should be defined in a way that they can be effectively proven in criminal proceedings.
- Excessive fragmentation of criminal tax legislation should be avoided and thus be coordinated with tax legislation.
- Civil, administrative and criminal offences should be coordinated following the principles of *ne bis in idem* and proportionality.
- The definitions of tax offences at European level should be harmonised in order to strengthen the common fight against tax evasion.
- The OECD should generate a model tax crime legislation that integrates the TGPs and other tax crime standards for easy use by jurisdictions.
- A system should be provided for monitoring the quality of criminal tax legislation.[15]

---

[10] HM Treasury and HM Revenues & Customs, *Tackling tax avoidance, evasion, and other forms of non-compliance* (Crown, March 2019) 7, https://assets.publishing.service.gov.uk/government/uploads/system/uploads/attachment_data/file/785551/tackling_tax_avoidance_evasion_and_other_forms_of_non-compliance_web.pdf, accessed 18 November 2019.
[11] Ibid.
[12] Ibid.
[13] F Rasmouki et al, 'Approaches to tax crimes in the European Union' (EU PROTAX, 2019) 25.
[14] Ibid.
[15] Ibid.

Future Legislation

- Rather than being thinly covered under AMLDs, it would be more piercing and targeted if criminal law legislation on EU taxation were to be enacted to focus specifically on the varied connotations of tax crimes with specific and common definitions.
- This legislation on tax crimes in the EU could only be a detailed form of the provisions of tax crimes as predicate offences established in the fifth AMLD and sixth AMLD, for instance.
- It follows that the provisions in the AMLDs targeting tax crimes could still be maintained, with the exception of any detected disjointed provisions that require amendment to be in harmony with the detailed legislation on countering tax crimes in the EU.

Ensuring Highest Degree of Transparency and Stakeholder Engagement

Commitment to delivering transparency can help a great deal in delivering the other principles of countering tax crimes. Drastic improvement, if not overhaul, of the regulatory and legal framework of the current global financial system (GFS) is very necessary. This is because the GFS has been 'characterised by laggard or outdated regulation and particularly by inadequate transparency' which has 'made it fairly easy for wrongdoers (including multinationals engaging in unfair tax agreements) to benefit from [tax crimes], by hiding and mixing themselves, their assets and their transactions within legitimate uses of the global financial and tax system'.[16]

Multi-stakeholder and multi-layered approaches are required at all times in policy development, regulation and law enforcement spheres. The major players in the rather opaque GFS, such as major financial centres and tax havens must be enticed into agreeing to the transparency and regulatory measures in order for them to change their systems for the best. The reactive disposition of just blacklisting or blocking such players does not appear to provide a durable solution for tax crimes in the EU.[17]

Continued fostering of stakeholder collaboration, communication, cooperation and partnership in the counter tax crime ecosystem is essential not only for fighting tax crimes but also for combating illicit financial flows and financial crime generally. The TGPs can serve as one of the reflective pillars for organisations responsible for the criminal tax offences across the world.

---

[16] A Knobel, 'Reporting taxation: Analysing loopholes in the EU's automatic exchange of information and how to close them' (report commissioned by the GREENS/EFA Group in the European Parliament, 15 October 2018), http://extranet.greens-efa-service.eu/public/media/file/1/5729, last accessed 15 January 2020.
[17] Ibid.

BIBLIOGRAPHY

Books

Allen SD, *The World of Prometheus: The Politics of Punishing in Democratic Athens* (Princeton University Press, 2003).

APEC/OECD, *Combatting Tax Crimes More Effectively in APEC Economies, Organisation for Economic Co-operation and Development and Asia-Pacific Economic Cooperation* (OECD, 2019), www.oecd.org/tax/crime/combatting-tax-crimes-more-effectively-in-apec-economies.htm, accessed 12 January 2020.

Arp R, *1001 Ideas that Changed the Way We Think* (Atria Books, 2013).

Arrow KJ, *Essays in the Theory of Risk-bearing* (Markham Publishing Co, 1971).

Barnard C, *The Substantive Law of the EU: The Four Freedoms Paperback,* 4th edn (OUP, 2013).

Barnard C and Peers S (eds), *European Union Law,* 2nd edn (Oxford University Press, 2017).

Beccaria C, *On Crimes and Punishment* (Bobbs-Merrill, 1980).

Bentham J, 'Punishment and Utility' in Murphy J (ed), *Punishment and Rehabilitation* (Wadsworth, 1995).

Bernard T, *The Consensus – Conflict Debate: Form and Content in Social Theories* (University Press, 1983).

Black D, *The Behaviour of Law* (Academic Press, 1976).

Black W, *The Best Way to Rob a Bank is to Own One: How Corporate Executives and Politicians Looted the S&L Industry* (University of Texas Press, 2013).

Bongardt A and Torres F, 'Lisbon Strategy' in Jones E, Menon A and Weatherill S (eds), *The Oxford Handbook of the European Union* (Oxford University Press, 2012).

Brederode FvR, *Systems of General Sales Taxation: Theory, Policy and Practice* (Kluwer Law International, 2009).

Burg FD, *A World History of Tax Rebellions: An Encyclopaedia of Tax Rebels, Revolts, and Riots from Antiquity to the Present* (Taylor & Francis, 2004).

Cerioni L, *The European Union and Direct Taxation: A Solution for a Difficult Relationship* (Routledge, 2015).

Copeland P and Papadimitriou D (eds), *The EU's Lisbon Strategy: evaluating success, understanding failure* (Palgrave Macmillan, 2012).

Craig P and Burca DG, *EU Law: Text, Cases and Materials,* 6th edn (Oxford University Press, 2015).

Cross C, 'Resourcing and refocusing HMRC', in Snell, W (ed) *Tax Takes: Perspectives on building a better tax system to benefit everyone in the UK* (Tax Justice Network, 2017), www.taxjustice.uk/uploads/1/0/0/3/100363766/tjuk_tax_takes_2017.pdf, accessed 14 January 2019.

Dani AJ and Mohen J-P, *History of Humanity: From the third millennium to the seventh century BC,* Vol II (Routledge, 1996).

Deflem M, *Economic Crisis and Crime* (Emerald Publishing, 2011).

Doig A, *Fraud* (Crime and Society Series, Routledge, 2008).

Doig A (ed), *Fraud: The Counter Fraud Practitioner's Handbook* (Routledge, 2012).

Douma S, *Legal Research in International and EU Tax Law* (Kluwer, 2014).

Dvořáček J and Tyll L, *Outsourcing and Offshoring Business Activities* (CH Beck, 2010).

Duff A and Garland D, 'Introduction: Thinking about Punishment' in Duff RA and Garland D (eds), *A Reader on Punishment* (Oxford University Press, 1994).

Durkheim E, *The Division of Labor in Society* (Free Press, 1964).

European Commission, *The European Union Explained: Taxation* (European Union, 2015).

European Union, *Consolidated Treaties: Charter of Fundamental Rights* (March, 2010), https://europa.eu/european-union/sites/europaeu/files/eu_citizenship/consolidated-treaties-en.pdf, accessed 18 January, 2020.

Eurostat, *Smarter, greener, more inclusive? Indicators to support the Europe, 2020 Strategy* (European Union, 2019).

Everest-Phillips M, 'The Political Economy of Controlling Tax Evasion and Illicit Flows' in Reuter P (ed), *Draining Development? Controlling Flows of Illicit Funds from Developing Countries* (The World Bank, 2012) 69.

Fabbrini F, *Fundamental Rights in Europe: Challenges and transformations in comparative perspective* (Oxford University Press, 2014).

FATF, *International Standards on Combating Money Laundering and the Financing of Terrorism & Proliferation* (FATF, 2012–19), www.fatf-gafi.org/recommendations.html, accessed 24 March, 2020.

Fletcher C, 'Social value or social harm? The impact of the Proceeds of Crime Act, 2002 upon the defendant and their families' in Benson K, King C and Walker C (eds), *Assets, Crimes and the State: Innovation in 21st Century Legal Responses* (Routledge, 2020) 79.

Frunza M-C, *Value Added Tax Fraud* (Routledge, 2019).

Gelemerova YL, *The Anti-Money Laundering System in the Context of Globalisation: a Panopticon built on quicksand?* (Wolf Legal Publishers, 2011).

Greenberg FD, 'Justice and Criminal Justice' in Hawkins FD et al (eds), *Crime Control and Social Justice: The Delicate Balance* (Greenwood Press, 2003) 319.

Harrison K and Ryde N, *The Law Relating to Financial Crime in the United Kingdom*, 2nd edn (Routledge, 2016).

Hetherington S, *Halsbury's Laws of England Centenary Essays* (LexisNexis Butterworths, 2007).

HM Government, *Serious and Organised Crime Strategy* (October, 2013), https://assets.publishing.service. gov.uk/government/uploads/system/uploads/attachment_data/file/248645/Serious_and_Organised_Crime_Strategy.pdf, accessed 17 April, 2020.

HM Treasury and HM Revenues & Customs, *Tackling Tax Avoidance, Evasion, and other Forms of Non-compliance* (Crown, March, 2019), https://assets.publishing.service.gov.uk/government/uploads/system/uploads/attachment_data/file/785551/tackling_tax_avoidance_evasion_and_other_forms_of_non-compliance_web.pdf, accessed 18 November, 2019.

Horspool M et al, *European Union Law*, 10th edn (Oxford University Press, 2018).

IBFD, *International Tax Glossary*, 6th edn (IBFD, 2009).

Lang M et al (eds), *Introduction to European Tax Law on Direct Taxation*, 5th edn (Linde, 2018).

Letsas G, 'Autonomous Concepts, Conventionalism, and Judicial Discretion' in *A Theory of Interpretation of the European Convention on Human Rights* (Oxford University Press, 2007) 2.

Levi M, *The Phantom Capitalists: The Organisation and Control of Long-Firm Fraud* (Heinemann, 1981).

Levi M, *Regulating Fraud: White-Collar Crime and the Criminal Process* (Routledge, 1987).

Levi M (ed), *Fraud: Organisation, Motivation and Control* (Dartmouth, 1999).

Ligeti K and Tosza S (eds), *White Collar Crime: A Comparative Perspective* (Hart Publishing, 2018).

Lui A and Turksen U, 'Vulnerabilities, Obstacles and Risks in Reporting Financial Crimes: Conundrum of whistle-blowers' in Ryder N, Pasculli L (eds), *Corruption, Integrity and The Law: Global Regulatory Challenges* (Routledge, 2020).

Marx K, 'Theories of Surplus Value' in Bottomore TB and Rubel M (eds), *Karl Marx: Selected Writings in Sociology and Social Philosophy* (McGraw-Hill, 1964).

Medecigo A, *Rule of Law and Fundamental Rights: Critical Comparative Analysis of Constitutional Review in the United States, Germany and Mexico*, (Springer, 2016).

Michalowski R, *Order, Law and Crime* (Random House, 1985).

Moore SM, *Placing Blame: A Theory of the Criminal Law* (Oxford University Press, 2010).

Morris DS, *Corruption and Politics in Contemporary Mexico* (Alabama Press, 1991).

Morris N, 'Dangerousness and Incapacitation Record of the Association of the Bar in the City of New York' in Duff A and Garland D (eds), *A Reader on Punishment* (Oxford University Press, 1994).

Oberson X, *International Exchange of Information in Tax Matters: Towards Global Transparency* (Edward Elgar Publishing, 2015).

OECD, *Money Laundering Awareness Handbook for Tax Examiners and Tax Auditors* (OECD Publishing, 2009), www.oecd.org/ctp/crime/money-laundering-awareness-handbook-for-tax-examiners-and-tax-auditors. pdf, accessed 9 October, 2020.

OECD, *Action Plan on Base Erosion and Profit Shifting* (OECD Publishing, 2013).

OECD, *Effective Inter-Agency Co-operation in Fighting Tax Crimes and Other Financial Crimes*, 3rd edn (OECD Publishing, 2017), www.oecd.org/tax/crime/effective-inter-agency-co-operation-in-fighting-tax-crimes-and-other-financial-crimes.htm, accessed 12 March, 2020.

OECD, *Fighting Tax Crime: The Ten Global Principles* (OECD Publishing, 2017), www.oecd.org/tax/crime/fighting-tax-crime-the-ten-global-principles.htm, accessed 26 October, 2019.

OECD, *Money Laundering and Terrorist Financing Awareness Handbook for Tax Examiners and Tax Auditors* (OECD, 2019), www.oecd.org/tax/crime/money-laundering-and-terrorist-financing-awareness-handbook-for-tax-examiners-and-tax-auditors.pdf, accessed 19 December, 2019.

Olmert M, *Milton's Teeth and Ovid's Umbrella: Curiouser and Curiouser Adventures in History* (Simon and Schuster, 1996).

Panayi HJIC, *Advanced Issues in International and European Tax Law* (Hart Publishing, 2015).

Panayi HJIC, Haslehner W and Traversa E (eds), *Research Handbook on European Union Taxation Law* (Edward Elgar, 2020).

Reiman J, *The Rich Get Richer and the Poor Get Prison* (Wiley, 1998).

Robinson J, *The Sink: Terror, Crime and Dirty Money in the Offshore World* (Constable & Robinson, 2003).

Rotman E, *Beyond Punishment: A New View of the Rehabilitation of Offenders* (Greenwood Press, 1990).

Ryder N, *The Financial Crisis and White-Collar Crime: The Perfect Storm?* (Edward Elgar, 2014).

Ryder N and Pasculli L (eds), *Corruption in the Global Era – Causes, Sources and Forms of Manifestation* (Routledge, 2019).

Schütz D, *The Fall of UBS: The Forces that Brought Down Switzerland's Biggest Bank* (Pyramid Media Group Inc, 2006).

Schütze R, *European Union Law,* 2nd edn (Cambridge University Press, 2018).

Sellen T, *Culture, Conflict and Crime* (Social Science Research Council, 1938).

Senior I, *Corruption – the World's Big C: Cases, Causes Consequences, Cures* (The Institute of Economic Affairs, 2006).

Shavitt S, Lee YA and Johnson PT, 'Cross-cultural consumer psychology' in Haugtvedt PC, Herr MP and Kardes RF (eds), *Handbook of Consumer Psychology* (Routledge, 2008), 1103.

Shute S and Simester A (eds), *Criminal Law Theory: Doctrines of the General Part* (Oxford Scholarship Online, 2010).

Steinkeller P and Hudson M, *Labor in the Ancient World,* Vol V (ISLET-Verlag, 2015).

Suso, AM, 'The Boundaries of Abusive Practices: The Grey Zone', in Lang, M et al (eds), *ECJ – Recent Developments in Value Added Tax: The Evolution of European VAT Jurisprudence and its Role in the EU Common VAT System* (Linde, Schriftenreihe, 2014).

Tobler C and Beglinger J, *Essential EU Law in Charts,* 4th edn (HVG-ORAC, 2018).

Turk A, *Criminality and Legal Order* (Rand McNally, 1969).

Turksen U, 'Implications of Anti-Money Laundering Law for Accountancy in the European Union – A Comparative Study' in Ryder N, Turksen U and Hassler S (eds), *Fighting Financial Crime in the Global Economic Crisis* (Routledge, 2015).

Turksen U, 'Criminalisation and protection of whistle-blowers in the EU's counter financial crime framework' in Ligeti and Tosla (eds), *Economic and Financial Crime in Europe* (Hart Publishing, 2018).

Turksen U, *EU Energy Relations with Russia – Solidarity and the Rule of Law* (Routledge, 2018).

Turksen U and Chauhan V, 'Anti-Bribery and Corruption: Perceptions, Risks and Practice for UK Banks' in Ryder N (ed), *White Collar Crime and Risk* (Palgrave, 2018).

Unger B et al, *The Economic and Legal Effectiveness of the European Union's Anti Money Laundering Policy* (Edward Elgar Publishing, 2014).

Vold G, *Theoretical Criminology* (Oxford University Press, 1958).

Walker N, *Punishment, Danger and Stigma: The Morality of Criminal Justice* (Blackwell, 1980).

Wilson QJ, *Thinking about Crime* (Basic Books, 1979).

Journals/Research Papers/Reports

Allain C, Fraudeau J and Martin A-G, 'Facing tax fraud in the European Union – Challenges and perspectives' (European Judicial Training Network, International Cooperation in Criminal Matters, 2016).

Allingham MG and Sandmo A, 'Income tax evasion: A theoretical analysis' (1972) 1 *Journal of Public Economics* 323, www3.nccu.edu.tw/~klueng/tax%20paper/1.pdf, accessed 11 November 2019.

Alm J, Jackson RB and McKee M, 'Fiscal exchange, collective decision institutions, and tax compliance' (1993) 22(3) *Journal of Economic Behavior & Organization* 285.

Alm J, Martinez-Vazquez J and McClellan C, 'Corruption and firm tax evasion' (2016) 124 *Journal of Economic Behavior & Organization* 146.

Aloys R, 'Anti-Tax Avoidance Directive (2016/1164): New EU Policy Horizons' (2016) 56 (11) *EU Taxation* 497.

Auerbach JA et al, 'International tax planning under the destination-based cash flow tax' (2017) 70(4) *National Tax Journal* 783.

Balco T, 'ATAD 2: Anti-Tax Avoidance Directive' (2017) 57(4) *European Taxation* 127.

Becker GS, 'Crime and punishment: an economic approach' (1968) 76 *Journal of Political Economy* 169.

Besley T, Jensen A and Persson T, 'Norms, Enforcement, and Tax Evasion' (NBER Working Paper No 25575, February 2019), www.lse.ac.uk/economics/Assets/Documents/personal-pages/tim-besley/working-papers/norms-enforcement-and-tax-evasion.pdf, accessed 15 March 2020.

Boadwaya R, Marchand M and Pestieau P, 'Towards a Theory of the Direct–Indirect Tax Mix' (1994) 55(1) *Journal of Public Economics* 71.

Bonch-Osmolovskiy M et al, 'Study and Reports on the VAT Gap in the EU-28 Member States: 2018 Final Report' (Institute for Advanced Studies, IHS, TAXUD/2015/CC/131, 11 September 2018).

Bonch-Osmolovskiy M et al, 'Study and Reports on the VAT Gap in the EU-28 Member States: 2019 Final Report' (TAXUD/2015/CC/131, 04 September 2019).

Bowers S, 'European Authorities Launch Probe Into Secret Lux Leaks Tax Deal' (ICIJ, 7 March 2019), www.icij.org/investigations/luxembourg-leaks/european-authorities-launch-probe-into-secret-lux-leaks-tax-deal/, accessed 11 July 2020.

Browning L, 'Names Deal Cracks Swiss Bank Secrecy', *The New York Times* (Global Business, August 2009), www.nytimes.com/2009/08/20/business/global/20ubs.html, accessed 11 March 2020.

Bruun & Hjejle, 'Report on the Non-Resident Portfolio at Danske Bank's Estonian branch' (19 September 2018), https://danskebank.com/-/media/danske-bank-com/file-cloud/2018/9/report-on-the-non-residen t-portfolio-at-danske-banks-estonian-branch.pdf?rev=56b16dfddae94480bb8cdcaebeaddc9b&hash=B7D 825F2639326A3BBBC7D524C5E341E, accessed 11 July 2020.

Buchan L, 'Labour condemns "disastrous" HMRC cuts after millions of taxpayer calls go unanswered', *The Independent* (30 May 2018), www.independent.co.uk/news/uk/politics/labour-hmrc-cuts-taxpayers-cal l-contact-helpline-revenue-customs-a8375261.html/, accessed 14 January 2019.

Bulgaria Corruption Report (GAN – Business Anti-corruption Portal), see, www.ganintegrity.com/portal/country-profiles/bulgaria/, accessed 19 July 2020.

Burton H, Karlinsky S and Blanthorne C, 'Perception of a White-Collar Crime: Tax Evasion' (2005) 3 (1) *The ATA Journal of Legal Tax Research* 35–48.

Cédelle A, 'The EU Anti-Tax Avoidance Directive: A UK Perspective' (2016) 4 *British Tax Review* 1.

Christie N, 'Conflicts as Property' (1977) 17 *British Journal of Criminology* 1.

Collier R et al, 'Dissecting the EU's Recent Anti-Tax Avoidance Measures: Merits and Problems' (2018) 2 *Econ Pol Policy Report*.

Collovà C, 'Prevention of the use of the financial system for the purposes of money laundering or terrorist financing' (DG EPRS, EU Parliament, October 2016).

Cross C, 'Resourcing and refocusing HMRC' in W Snell, *Tax Takes: Perspectives on building a better tax system to benefit everyone in the UK* (Tax Justice Network, 2017), www.taxjustice.uk/uploads/1/0/0/3/100363766/tjuk_tax_takes_2017.pdf, accessed 24 March 2020.

Devereux MP and Vella J, 'Are we heading towards a corporate tax fit for the 21st century?' (2014) 35 *Fiscal Studies* 449.

Dobrovič J et al, 'Action plan on sustainability of fight against tax fraud and tax evasion: EU countries comparison' (2019) 12(4) *Journal of International Studies* 272.

Endresen C, 'Taxation and the European Convention for the Protection of Human Rights: Substantive Issues' (2017) 45 (8/9) *Intertax* 508–26.

EU Parliament, 'The Impact of Schemes revealed by the Panama Papers on the Economy and Finances of a Sample of Member States' (DG IPOL 2017).

European Commission, 'Assessment of the application and impact of the optional 'Reverse Charge Mechanism' within the EU VAT system' (EY Final Report, November 2014), https://ec.europa.eu/taxation_customs/sites/taxation/files/docs/body/kp_07_14_060_en.pdf, accessed 23 April 2020.

European Commission, 'Commission Staff Working Document on the implementation of the definitive VAT regime for intra-EU trade' (SWD (2014) 338 final, 29 October 2014), https://ec.europa.eu/taxation_customs/sites/taxation/files/resources/documents/taxation/vat/swd_2014_338.pdf, accessed 15 May 2020.

European Commission, 'Communication to the Commission, Commission Internal Action Plan for the Implementation of the Commission Anti-Fraud Strategy' (SEC (2011) 787/3).

European Commission, 'Estimating International Tax Evasion by Individuals' (Taxation Papers, Working Paper No 76, 2019).

European Commission, 'Green Paper on the future of VAT – Towards a simpler, more robust and efficient VAT system', https://ec.europa.eu/taxation_customs/consultations-get-involved/tax-consultations/green-paper-future-vat-towards-a-simpler-more-robust-efficient-vat-system_en, accessed 16 March 2020.

European Commission, 'Report from the Commission to the European Parliament and the Council, 29th Annual Report on the Protection of the European Union's financial interests – Fight against fraud' (COM (2018) 553 final).

EU Commission, 'Report from the Commission to The European Parliament and the Council on Overview and assessment of the statistics and information on the automatic exchanges in the field of direct taxation' (COM (2018) 844 final).

European Investigation Collaborations, 'About us', https://eic.network/, accessed 2 March 2020.

European Parliament, 'Report on financial crimes, tax evasion and tax avoidance: European Parliament resolution of 26 March 2019 on financial crimes, tax evasion and tax avoidance' (2018/2121(INI)), www.europarl.europa.eu/doceo/document/TA-8-2019-0240_EN.html, accessed 10 February 2020.

Financial Reporting Council (FRC), 'International Standard on Auditing (UK and Ireland) 240: The auditor's responsibilities relating to fraud in an audit of financial statements' (October 2009) 35, www.frc.org.uk/getattachment/6cb0c88e-b11e-4b03-81b6-527e992d4f0e/ISA-240.pdf, accessed 13 December 2019.

Fowler N, 'The European Union, tax evasion and closing loopholes: new report' (Tax Justice Network, 15 October 2018), www.taxjustice.net/2018/10/15/the-european-union-tax-evasion-and-closing-loopholes-new-report/, accessed 23 April 2020.

Garcia-Bernardo J et al, 'Uncovering Offshore Financial Centers: Conduits and Sinks in the Global Corporate Ownership Network' (2017) 7(6246) *Science Reports*, https://doi.org/10.1038/s41598-017-06322-9, accessed 12 February 2020.

Gimdal G, 'Aggressive tax planning' (The TAX 2 report, DG EPRS, EU Parliament, July 2016).

Global indirect tax management, 'Standard Audit File for Tax Purposes (SAF-T)' (Tax assurance research, 23 May 2015).

Hadzhieva E, 'Impact of Digitalisation on International Tax Matters: Challenges and Remedies' (Study Requested by the TAX3 Committee, European Parliament, PE 626.078 – February 2019).

Hakelberg L, 'The power of states and business: Explaining transformative change in the fight against tax evasion and avoidance', COFFERS Project, D3.2, p 29, http://coffers.eu/wp-content/uploads/2019/11/D3.2-Conference-Paper.pdf, accessed 22 July 2020.

Hall M et al, 'D2.4 Conference Report summarising and documenting contributions from T2.7' (EU PROTAX, 2020).

ICC, 'Using Mutual Legal Assistance Treaties (MLATs) To Improve Cross-Border Lawful Intercept Procedures', Document No. 373/512 – (12 September 2012), Policy Statement.

Johansson Å et al, 'Anti-avoidance rules against international tax planning: a classification' (Economics department working paper No 1356, OECD, 19 December 2016).

Kastanakisa NM and Voyerab GB, 'The effect of culture on perception and cognition: A conceptual framework' (2014) 67(4) *Journal of Business Research* 425.

Kaye AT, 'Innovations in the War on Tax Evasion' [2014] *Brigham Young University Law Review* 363.

Kaufmann D and Vicente P, 'Legal Corruption' (2011) 23(2) *Economics & Politics* 195.

Kleven JH et al, 'Unwilling or unable to cheat? Evidence from a tax audit experiment in Denmark' (2011) 79(3) *Econometrica* 651.

Knobel A, 'Reporting taxation: Analysing loopholes in the EU's automatic exchange of information and how to close them' (A Report Commissioned by the GREENS/EFA Group in the European Parliament, 15 October 2018).

Korauš A et al, 'The impact of monetary variables on the economic growth and sustainable development: case of selected countries' (2017) 6(3) *Journal of Security and Sustainability Issues* 383.

Kreissl R et al, 'D1.1 – The Case Study Design: Guideline and template for case studies on tax crimes in Europe' (EU PROTAX, 2018).

Kreissl R et al, 'Austrian Focus Group – Synthesis of discussions: Focus groups to explore institutional practices in anti-money laundering and tax evasion' (EU PROTAX, 2019).

Laguna F and Martinez D, 'Abuse and Aggressive Tax Planning: Between OECD and EU Initiatives – The Dividing Line between Intended and Unintended Double Non-Taxation' (2017) 9(2) *World Tax Journal* 1.

Lamensch M and Ceci E, 'VAT fraud: Economic impact, challenges and policy issues' (Study requested by the TAX3 Committee, PE 626.076, October 2018) 29.

Lederman L, 'Does Enforcement Reduce Voluntary Tax Compliance?' (2018) 395 Research Paper *BYU L REV* 627.

Lederman L, 'The Fraud Triangle and Tax Evasion' (2019) 398 Research Paper, Working Paper, https://papers.ssrn.com/sol3/papers.cfm?abstract_id=3339558, accessed 20 May 2020.

Levi M, 'The Investigation, Prosecution, and Trial of Serious Fraud' (Royal Commission on Criminal Justice Research Study No 14, 1993).

Luttmer EFP and Singhal M, 'Tax Morale, Journal of Economic Perspectives' (2014) 28 *Journal of Economic Perspectives* 149.

MacLennan S, 'The Questionable Legality of the Diverted Profits Tax Under Double Taxation Conventions and EU Law' (2016) 44 (12) *Intertax* 903–12.

Markovits SR, 'The General Theory of the Second Best and Economic Efficiency Analysis' (2015) 49 (2) *Akron Law Review* 9.

Markus RH and Kitayama S, 'Cultures and Selves: A Cycle of Mutual Constitution' (2010) 5(4) *Perspectives on Psychological Science* 420.

Michel C, 'The Old Assyrian Trade in the light of Recent Kültepe Archives' (2008) *Journal of the Canadian Society for Mesopotamian Studies* 71.

Mitsilegas V and Vavoula N, 'The Evolving EU Anti-Money Laundering Regime: Challenges for Fundamental Rights and the Rule of Law' (2016) 23(2) *MJ* 261.

Mossin J, 'Aspects of rational insurance purchasing' (1968) 76 *Journal of Political Economy* 553.

Murphy R, 'The European Tax Gap' (A report for the Socialists and Democrats Group in the EU Parliament, Tax Research UK, January 2019), www.socialistsanddemocrats.eu/sites/default/files/2019.01.23%20 EU%20Tax%20Gap%20%28003%29.pdf?utm_source=S%26D+Group%3A+MEP%27s+Assistants+and +staff+in+Mailchimp&utm_campaign=66d0debcca-EMAIL_CAMPAIGN_2019_01_22_10_51&utm_ medium=email&utm_term=0_726ea1fd8d-66d0debcca-111480441, accessed 4 March 2020.

Murphy R and Baker A, 'A response to the Consultation on an IMF 2019 Analysis of International Corporate Taxation' (City University of London and SPERI of Sheffield, 2018), http://coffers.eu/wp-content/uploads/ 2018/12/2018-Murphy-Baker.pdf, accessed 4 March 2020.

Nelson CS, 'American Bar Association Section of International Law and Practice Reports to the House of Delegates' (1990) 24 (3) *The International Lawyer* 872–79, https://scholar.smu.edu/cgi/viewcontent. cgi?article=2759&context=til, accessed 26 January 2020.

OECD, 'International Co-operation against Tax Crimes and Other Financial Crimes: A Catalogue of the Main Instruments' (2nd Annual Forum on Tax and Crime, 14 June 2012).

OECD, 'Measuring and monitoring BEPS' (Action 11-2015, Final report, 2015).

OECD, 'Coronavirus: The World Economy at risk' (OECD Interim Economic Assessment, 2 March 2020).

OECD and the World Bank, 'Improving Co-operation between Tax Authorities and Anti-Corruption Authorities in Combating Tax Crime and Corruption' (CC BY-NC-SA 3.0 IGO, 2018).

Perdriel-Vaissière M, Brillaud L and Portela C, 'Into the void: The EU's struggle to recover the proceeds of grand corruption' (Transparency International EU, 2019), http://transparency.eu/wp-content/uploads/2019/09/ Asset_recovery_report.pdf, accessed 20 April 2020.

Posner EA, 'Law and Social Norms: The Case of Tax Compliance' (2000) 86 *Virginia Law Review* 1781.

Rasmouki F et al, 'D2.3 Approaches to tax crimes in the European Union' (EU PROTAX, 2019).

Reed Q and Fontana A, 'Corruption and Illicit Financial Flows: The Limits and Possibilities of Current Approaches' (U4 Anti-Corruption Resource Centre, U4 Issue, January No 2, CMI, 2011).

Remeur C, 'Anti-tax avoidance Directive' (DG EPRS, EU Parliament, July 2016).

Remeur C, 'Hybrid mismatches with third countries' (DG EPRS, EU Parliament, March 2017).

Remeur C, 'Country-by-country reporting for multinational enterprise groups' (DG EPRS, EU Parliament, June 2017).

Richupan S, 'Measuring tax evasion: A brief description of the major techniques' (International Monetary Fund, External Relations Dept, December 1984) 38.

Rothstein B, 'Trust, Social Dilemmas and Collective Memories' (2000) 12(4) *Journal of Theoretical Politics* 477.

Ruding Committee, 'Report of the committee of independent experts on company taxation' (Commission of the European Communities, 1992).

Spreutels J and Grijseels C, 'Interaction between money laundering and tax evasion' (2001) 10(1) *EC Tax Review* 3.

Tax Justice Network, 'Tax Information Exchange Arrangements' (*Tax Justice Briefing*, May 2009), www.taxjustice.net/cms/upload/pdf/Tax_Information_Exchange_Arrangements.pdf, accessed 13 February 2020.

Thirion E and Scherrer A, 'Member States' capacity to fight tax crimes: Ex-post impact assessment' (European Parliamentary Research Service (EPRS), EU Parliament, 2017), www.europarl.europa.eu/RegData/etudes/STUD/2017/603257/EPRS_STU(2017)603257_EN.pdf, accessed 9 October 2019.

Toplensky R, 'The Real Test of Europe's Banks Comes this Fall Lenders face a rough second half as governments unwind the programs that cushioned the initial blow of the coronavirus crisis' (*Wall Street Journal*, 10 July 2020).

Treasury Inspector General for Tax Administration, 'A Combination of Legislative Actions and Increased IRS Capability and Capacity Are Required to Reduce the Multi-Billion Dollar U.S. International Tax Gap' (2009-IE-R001, 27 January 2009).

Tulkens H and Jacquemin A, 'The cost of delinquency: a problem of optimal allocation of private and public expenditure' (1971) 7133 CORE Discussion Paper.

Turksen U et al, 'D1.2: Case Studies of Tax Crimes in the European Union' (EU PROTAX, 2018).

Turksen U et al, 'D4.1 – Report on conviction rates in selected Member States' (EU PROTAX, 2020).

Turksen U and Abukari A, 'OECD's global principles and EU's tax crime measures' (2020) *Journal of Financial Crime*, www.emerald.com/insight/content/doi/10.1108/JFC-09-2019-0118/full/html, accessed 26 June 2020.

Turksen U and Ryder N, 'The fight against fraud: A critical review and comparative analysis of the Labour and Conservative government's anti-fraud policies in the United Kingdom' (2015) 4(2) *Law and Economics Yearly Review* 369.

Tyler RT, 'Psychological Perspectives on Legitimacy and Legitimation' (2006) 57 *Annual Review of Psychology* 375.

White D, 'Taxes in the Ancient World' (2002) 48(28) *University of Pennsylvania Almanac*, https://almanac.upenn.edu/archive/v48/n28/AncientTaxes.html, 20 March 2020.

Williams CC, 'Elements of a preventative approach towards undeclared work: an evaluation of service vouchers and awareness raising campaigns' (European Platform Undeclared Work, May 2018).

Zourek H, 'Fighting tax fraud and evasion' (European Commission, https://ec.europa.eu/taxation_customs/sites/taxation/files/resources/documents/taxation/tax_fraud_evasion/2013-12-05_press-briefing.pdf, accessed 22 January 2020.

Webpages

ACCA, 'Economic crime in a digital age' (January 2020), www.accaglobal.com/content/dam/ACCA_Global/professional-insights/EconomicCrime/JasonPiper.EconomicCrime.pdf, accessed 18 April 2020.

Agnew H, 'Guy Wildenstein cleared of tax fraud charges in Paris', *The Financial Times* (12 January 2017), www.ft.com/content/c8e383d8-d8b8-11e6-944b-e7eb37a6aa8e, accessed 15 December 2018.

All Party Parliamentary Group (APPG) 'Whistleblowing – The Personal Cost of Doing the Right Thing and the Cost to Society of Ignoring it', July 2019, https://ac2f9c2f-03a1-4206-859b-06ff2b21dd81.filesusr.com/ugd/88d04c_9754e54bc641443db902cd963687cb55.pdf, accessed 16 July 2020.

BBC News, 'Edward Snowden: Leaks that exposed US spy programme' (17 January 2014), www.bbc.co.uk/news/world-us-canada-23123964, accessed 11 July 2020.

BBC, 'Ronaldo fined €18.8m over tax evasion', *BBC News* (22 January 2019), www.bbc.co.uk/news/world-europe-46957605, accessed 06 February 2020.

Cannon P, 'What are the penalties for tax evasion (UK)? www.patrickcannon.net/tax-evasion-penalties-uk/, accessed 27 March 2020.

Charlemagne, 'Do Europeans want a dynamic economy?' *The Economist* (European politics, 8 January 2010), www.economist.com/charlemagne/2010/01/08/do-europeans-want-a-dynamic-economy, accessed 18 April 2020.

Cobham A, 'Taxation Policy and Development', Oxford Council on Good Governance, Economy Analysis 2, www.taxjustice.net/cms/upload/pdf/OCGG_-_Alex_Cobham_-_Taxation_Policy_and_Development.pdf, accessed 17 December 2019.

COFFERS, 'About Coffers' (EU Horizon 2020 Project: Combating Fiscal Fraud and Empowering Regulators), https://coffers.eu/, accessed 16 March 2020.

Cordella P, 'Criminal Sanctions' (Cengage, Encyclopedia.com, Updated 3 May 2020), www.encyclopedia.com/social-sciences/encyclopedias-almanacs-transcripts-and-maps/criminal-sanctions, accessed 7 May April 2020.

Corporate Social Responsibility and Business Ethics Blog, 'Report on the International Conference Whistle-blowers: Voices of Justice' (London, 10 May 2019), https://corporatesocialresponsibilityblog.com/2019/06/10/conference-on-whistleblowing/, accessed 25 July 2020.

Council of the European Union, 'Code of Conduct Group (Business Taxation)', www.consilium.europa.eu/en/council-eu/preparatory-bodies/code-conduct-group/, accessed 4 May 2020.

Council of the European Union, 'ECOFIN Report to the European Council on Tax Issues' (9 December 2019), https://data.consilium.europa.eu/doc/document/ST-14863-2019-INIT/en/pdf, accessed 4 July 2020.

Cox SM, McLure EC and Neumark F, 'Taxation' (Encyclopædia Britannica, 18 October 2019), www.britannica.com/topic/taxation, accessed 14 April 2020.

Credit Industry Fraud Avoidance System (CIFAS), https://www.cifas.org.uk/.

Crumbley LD and Apostolou N, 'America's first (and most fearless) high-profile forensic accountant' (September/October 2007) *The Value Examiner* 16, 18, www.bus.lsu.edu/accounting/faculty/lcrumbley/AlCapone.pdf, accessed on 11 March 2020.

Department of Finance, 'The Europe 2020 strategy' (Gov.UK), www.finance-ni.gov.uk/articles/europe-2020-strategy#toc-1, accessed 18 April 2020.

DW staff (sp), 'Liechtenstein Tax Scandal Spreads across Europe' (*Business*, 25 February 2008), www.dw-world.de/dw/article/0,3148308,00.html, accessed 11 March 2020.

DW, 'Spain calls for binding EU economic goals – and penalties' (*Business*, 8 January 2010), www.dw.com/en/spain-calls-for-binding-eu-economic-goals-and-penalties/a-5098907, accessed 18 April 2020.

ECA, 'Special report No 01/2019: Fighting fraud in EU spending: action needed' (10 January 2019), www.eca.europa.eu/en/Pages/DocItem.aspx?did=48858, accessed 26 April 2020.

Europa, 'Taxation' (EU), https://europa.eu/european-union/topics/taxation_en, accessed 1 November 2019.

EU Open Data Portal, 'Taxpayer Identification Number (TIN)', https://data.europa.eu/euodp/en/data/dataset/taxpayer-identification-number-tin, accessed 23 April 2020.

Eur-lex, 'Follow the steps of Procedure 2017/0251/CNS', https://eur-lex.europa.eu/legal-content/EN/HIS/?uri=COM%3A2017%3A569%3AFIN, accessed 4 July 2020.

Eurodad et al, 'Analysis: EU Action plan to strengthen the fight against tax fraud and tax evasion' (December 2012), https://eurodad.org/files/integration/2012/12/EC-Action-Plan-analysis2.pdf, accessed 18 April 2020.

Europarl, 'Member States capabilities in fighting tax crimes: Relevant legal definition(s) of tax-related offences' (Spain fiche), www.europarl.europa.eu/cmsdata/124716/Spain%20fiche.pdf, accessed 12 January 2020.

European Banking Authority, 'Competent Authorities', https://eba.europa.eu/supervisory-convergence/supervisory-disclosure/competent-authorities, accessed 16 April 2020.

European Commission, '6 Commission priorities for 2019–24' (Priorities), https://ec.europa.eu/info/strategy/priorities-2019–2024, accessed 18 April 2020.

European Commission, 'A deeper and fairer economic and monetary union: Policies areas', https://ec.europa.eu/info/strategy/priorities-2019–2024/economy-works-people/deeper-and-fairer-economic-and-monetary-union_en, accessed 19 April 2020.

European Commission, 'A huge problem: How big is the tax fraud and tax evasion problem?', https://ec.europa.eu/taxation_customs/fight-against-tax-fraud-tax-evasion/a-huge-problem_en, accessed 14 March 2020.

European Commission, 'Action Plan on Corporate Taxation' (June 2015), https://ec.europa.eu/taxation_customs/business/company-tax/action-plan-corporate-taxation_en, accessed 18 April 2020.

European Commission, 'Action Plan on VAT', https://ec.europa.eu/taxation_customs/business/vat/action-plan-vat_en, accessed 13 April 2020.

European Commission, 'Administrative cooperation in (direct) taxation in the EU', https://ec.europa.eu/taxation_customs/business/tax-cooperation-control/administrative-cooperation/enhanced-administrative-cooperation-field-direct-taxation_en, accessed 23 April 2020.

European Commission, 'An economy that works for people: Working for social fairness and prosperity' (Priority), https://ec.europa.eu/info/strategy/priorities-2019-2024/economy-works-people_en, accessed 18 April 2020.

European Commission, 'Anti-Tax Avoidance Package', https://ec.europa.eu/taxation_customs/business/company-tax/anti-tax-avoidance-package_en, accessed 10 February 2020.

European Commission, 'Boosting jobs', https://ec.europa.eu/info/strategy/priorities-2019-2024/economy-works-people/jobs-growth-and-investment/boosting-jobs_en, accessed 19 April 2020.

European Commission, 'Commission adopts the report "Asset recovery and confiscation: Ensuring that crime does not pay"' (Migration and Home Affairs, 2 June 2020), https://ec.europa.eu/home-affairs/news/20200602_commission-adopts-report-asset-recovery-confiscation-ensuring-crime-does-not-pay_en, accessed 16 June 2020.

European Commission, 'Commission proposes new e-commerce rules to help consumers and companies reap full benefit of Single Market' (Brussels, Press release, 25 May 2016), https://ec.europa.eu/commission/presscorner/detail/en/IP_16_1887, accessed 15 May 2020.

European Commission, 'Commission Expert Group on automatic exchange of financial account information', https://ec.europa.eu/taxation_customs/business/tax-cooperation-control/administrative-cooperation/commission-expert-group-automatic-exchange-financial-account-information_en, accessed 22 April 2020.

European Commission, 'Commissioner Šemeta launches Tax Policy Group to push forward fundamental issues in taxation' (P/10/1312, 12 October 2010), https://ec.europa.eu/commission/presscorner/detail/en/IP_10_1312, accessed 4 May 2020.

European Commission, 'Common Consolidated Corporate Tax Base (CCCTB)', https://ec.europa.eu/taxation_customs/business/company-tax/common-consolidated-corporate-tax-base-ccctb_en, accessed 10 February 2020.

European Commission, 'Confiscation & asset recovery', https://ec.europa.eu/home-affairs/what-we-do/policies/organized-crime-and-human-trafficking/confiscation-and-asset-recovery_en, accessed 16 June 2020.

European Commission, 'Confiscation and freezing of assets', https://ec.europa.eu/info/law/cross-border-cases/judicial-cooperation/types-judicial-cooperation/confiscation-and-freezing-assets_en, accessed 25 April 2020.

European Commission, 'Coronavirus response', https://ec.europa.eu/info/live-work-travel-eu/health/coronavirus-response_en, accessed 4 July 2020.

European Commission, 'Economy, finance and the euro: Policies' (Policy), https://ec.europa.eu/info/strategy/economy-finance-and-euro_en, accessed 19 April 2020.

European Commission, 'EU country-specific recommendations', https://ec.europa.eu/info/business-economy-euro/economic-and-fiscal-policy-coordination/eu-economic-governance-monitoring-prevention-correction/european-semester/european-semester-timeline/eu-country-specific-recommendations_en, accessed 19 April 2020.

European Commission, 'EU Economic governance: monitoring, prevention, correction', https://ec.europa.eu/info/business-economy-euro/economic-and-fiscal-policy-coordination/eu-economic-governance-monitoring-prevention-correction_en, accessed 19 April 2020.

European Commission, 'EU joint transfer pricing forum: a coordinated approach to transfer pricing Controls within the EU' (Taxud/D2, October 2018), https://ec.europa.eu/taxation_customs/sites/taxation/files/jtpf_report_on_a_coordinated_approach_to_transfer_pricing_controls_within_the_eu_en.pdf, accessed 26 April 2020.

European Commission, 'EU VAT Forum', https://ec.europa.eu/taxation_customs/business/vat/eu-vat-forum_en, accessed 23 April 2020.

European Commission, 'EU VAT forum voluntary disclosure and related issues' (26 May 2015), https://ec.europa.eu/taxation_customs/sites/taxation/files/resources/documents/taxation/vat/key_documents/eu_vat_forum/voluntary_disclosure.pdf, accessed 25 April 2020.

European Commission, 'European Public Prosecutor's Office', https://ec.europa.eu/info/law/cross-border-cases/judicial-cooperation/networks-and-bodies-supporting-judicial-cooperation/europea n-public-prosecutors-office_en, accessed 16 July 2020.

European Commission, 'European Semester Thematic Factsheet: Curbing Aggressive Tax Planning', https://ec.europa.eu/info/sites/info/files/file_import/european-semester_thematic-factsheet_curbing-agressive-tax-planning_en_0.pdf, accessed 19 April 2020.

European Commission, 'European Semester Thematic Factsheet: Fight against Corruption', https://ec.europa.eu/info/sites/info/files/file_import/european-semester_thematic-factsheet_fight-against-corruption_en_0.pdf, accessed 19 April 2020.

European Commission, 'European Semester Thematic Factsheet: Taxation', https://ec.europa.eu/info/sites/info/files/file_import/european-semester_thematic-factsheet_taxation_en_1.pdf, accessed 19 April 2020.

European Commission, 'Fraud prevention: Policies' (Policy), https://ec.europa.eu/info/strategy/fraud-prevention_en, accessed 19 April 2020.

European Commission, 'Guidelines for a Model for A European Taxpayers' Code' (Reference Ares (2016)6598744–24/11/2016, European Union, 2016).

European Commission, 'Harmful Tax Competition', https://ec.europa.eu/taxation_customs/business/company-tax/harmful-tax-competition_en, accessed 23 April 2020.

European Commission, 'Internal Market', https://ec.europa.eu/info/strategy/priorities-2019–2024/economy-works-people/internal-market_en, accessed 18 April 2020.

European Commission, 'Jobs, growth and investment: Policies', https://ec.europa.eu/info/strategy/priorities-2019–2024/economy-works-people/jobs-growth-and-investment_en, accessed 19 April 2020.

European Commission, 'List of the organisations appointed as members of the EU VAT Forum (2018–2022)', https://ec.europa.eu/taxation_customs/sites/taxation/files/resources/documents/taxation/vat/key_documents/eu_vat_forum/vat-forum_membres_en.pdf, accessed 23 April 2020.

European Commission, 'Modernising VAT for cross-border e-commerce', https://ec.europa.eu/taxation_customs/business/vat/modernising-vat-cross-border-ecommerce_en, accessed 15 May 2020.

European Commission, 'MOSS: A simplified system to declare VAT on Telecommunication, Broadcasting and Electronic (TBE) services in the EU', https://ec.europa.eu/taxation_customs/business/vat/telecommunications-broadcasting-electronic-services/, accessed 15 May 2020.

European Commission, 'Multiannual financial framework 2014–2020'< https://ec.europa.eu/info/strategy/eu-budget/documents/multiannual-financial-framework/2014–2020_en, accessed 22 April 2020.

European Commission, 'Multiannual financial framework 2021–2027', https://ec.europa.eu/info/strategy/eu-budget/documents/multiannual-financial-framework/2021–2027_en, accessed 12 May 2020.

European Commission, 'New framework in the EU for Administrative Cooperation', https://ec.europa.eu/taxation_customs/sites/taxation/files/docs/body/administrative_coop.pdf, accessed 23 April 2020.

European Commission, 'Online services and databases for Taxation', https://ec.europa.eu/taxation_customs/online-services-and-databases-taxation_en, accessed 25 April 2020.

European Commission, 'Platform for Tax Good Governance', https://ec.europa.eu/taxation_customs/business/company-tax/tax-good-governance/platform-tax-good-governance_en#:~:text=The%20Platform%20for%20Tax%20Good,identify%20and%20address%20double%20taxation, accessed 23 April 2020.

European Commission, 'Platform for Tax Good Governance: Work programme' (Platform/34/2018/EN), https://ec.europa.eu/taxation_customs/sites/taxation/files/work-program-2018_2019-final.pdf, accessed 24 April 2020.

European Commission, 'Policy: Taxation', https://ec.europa.eu/info/policies/taxation_en, accessed 18 April 2020.

EU Commission, 'Register of Commission Expert Groups and other similar entities' (2015), http://ec.europa.eu/transparency/regexpert/index.cfm?do=groupDetail.groupDetail&groupID=1711, accessed 22 April 2020.

EU Commission, 'The concept of the Tax Gap' (2018), https://ec.europa.eu/taxation_customs/news/vat-gap-report_en%20-%20accessed%20at%2001/06/2020, accessed 22 July 2020.

European Commission, 'Role of the EU: An action plan to combat tax fraud and evasion', https://ec.europa.eu/taxation_customs/fight-against-tax-fraud-tax-evasion/role-eu_en, accessed 14 March 2020.

European Commission, 'SEED on Europa', https://ec.europa.eu/taxation_customs/dds2/seed/seed_home.jsp?Lang=en, accessed 26 April 2020.

European Commission, 'Single Market initiatives overview', https://ec.europa.eu/commission/publications/single-market-initiatives-overview_en, accessed 18 April 2020.

European Commission, 'Single VAT Area', https://ec.europa.eu/taxation_customs/business/vat/action-plan-vat/single-vat-area_en#heading_3, accessed 13 April 2020.

European Commission, 'Strategic plan 2016–2020 – Economic and Financial Affairs' (Planning and Management Document), https://ec.europa.eu/info/publications/strategic-plan-2016–2020-economic-and-financial-affairs_en, accessed 19 April 2020.

European Commission, 'Tax Co-operation and control', https://ec.europa.eu/taxation_customs/business/tax-cooperation-control_en, accessed 19 April 2020.

European Commission, 'Taxation: Anti-fraud network EUROFISC starts operational work', https://ec.europa.eu/taxation_customs/sites/taxation/files/docs/body/2011-02-07_eurofisc_pressrelease_en.pdf, accessed 16 July 2020.

European Commission, 'Taxation: Commission proposes postponement of taxation rules due to Coronavirus crisis', https://ec.europa.eu/taxation_customs/news/taxation-commission-proposes-postponement-taxation-rules-due-coronavirus-crisis_en, accessed 15 May 2020.

European Commission, 'Taxation: Policies' (Policy), https://ec.europa.eu/info/policies/taxation_en, accessed 19 April 2020.

European Commission, 'Tax Transparency Package' (March 2015), https://ec.europa.eu/taxation_customs/business/company-tax/tax-transparency-package_en, accessed 10 February 2020.

European Commission, 'TEDB – "Taxes in Europe" database', https://ec.europa.eu/taxation_customs/economic-analysis-taxation/taxes-europe-database-tedb_en, accessed 26 April 2020.

European Commission, 'The Future of VAT', https://ec.europa.eu/taxation_customs/sites/taxation/files/factsheet_futurevat.pdf, accessed 15 May 2020.

European Commission, 'The European Semester', https://ec.europa.eu/info/business-economy-euro/economic-and-fiscal-policy-coordination/eu-economic-governance-monitoring-prevention-correction/european-semester_en, accessed 24 April 2020.

European Commission, 'The European Semester: why and how', https://ec.europa.eu/info/business-economy-euro/economic-and-fiscal-policy-coordination/eu-economic-governance-monitoring-prevention-correction/european-semester/framework/european-semester-why-and-how_en, accessed 24 April 2020.

European Commission, 'The fight against tax fraud and tax evasion', https://ec.europa.eu/taxation_customs/fight-against-tax-fraud-tax-evasion_en, accessed 19 April 2020.

European Commission, 'The Fiscalis 2020 Programme', https://ec.europa.eu/taxation_customs/fiscalis-programme_en, accessed 3 May 2020.

European Commission, 'The impact of the Covid-19 pandemic on global and EU trade' (Chief Economist Team, DG Trade, European Commission, 17 April 2020), https://trade.ec.europa.eu/doclib/docs/2020/april/tradoc_158713.pdf, accessed 26 April 2020.

European Commission, 'The Single Market Strategy', https://ec.europa.eu/growth/single-market/strategy_en, accessed 18 April 2020.

European Commission, 'Thematic factsheets', https://ec.europa.eu/info/business-economy-euro/economic-and-fiscal-policy-coordination/eu-economic-governance-monitoring-prevention-correction/european-semester/thematic-factsheets_en, accessed 19 April 2020.

European Commission, 'Time to get the Missing Part Back: What does it mean – Tax avoidance', https://ec.europa.eu/taxation_customs/fight-against-tax-fraud-tax-evasion/missing-part_en, accessed 25 March 2020.

European Commission, 'Time to get the Missing Part Back: What does it mean – Tax fraud', https://ec.europa.eu/taxation_customs/fight-against-tax-fraud-tax-evasion/missing-part_en, accessed 25 March 2020.

European Commission, 'TIN – Taxpayer Identification Number', https://ec.europa.eu/taxation_customs/business/tax-cooperation-control/administrative-cooperation/tax-identification-numbers-tin_en, accessed 26 April 2020.

European Commission, 'Value added tax-based own resource', https://ec.europa.eu/info/strategy/eu-budget/revenue/own-resources/value-added-tax_en, accessed 19 April 2020.

European Commission, 'VAT', https://ec.europa.eu/taxation_customs/business/vat_en, accessed 8 January 2020.

European Commission, 'VAT Expert Group', https://ec.europa.eu/taxation_customs/business/vat/vat-expert-group_en, accessed 23 April 2020.

European Commission, 'VIES VAT number validation', https://ec.europa.eu/taxation_customs/vies/vieshome.do?locale=en, accessed 26 April 2020.

European Economic and Social Committee, 'VAT fraud – Quick reaction mechanism', www.eesc.europa.eu/en/our-work/opinions-information-reports/opinions/vat-fraud-quick-reaction-mechanism, accessed 23 April 2020.

European Parliament, 'Detailed technical measures for the definitive VAT system for cross-border goods trade' (20 June 2019), www.europarl.europa.eu/thinktank/en/document.html?reference=EPRS_BRI (2018)625184, accessed 4 July 2020.

European Parliament, 'Lisbon European Council 23 and 24 March 2000: Presidency Conclusions', www.europarl.europa.eu/summits/lis1_en.htm, accessed 18 April 2020.

European Parliament, 'Operation of the definitive VAT system for the taxation of trade between Member States' (2018/0164(CNS), https://oeil.secure.europarl.europa.eu/oeil/popups/ficheprocedure.do?reference=2018/0164(CNS)&l=en, accessed 4 July 2020.

European Securities and Market Authority (ESMA), 'EU Acts and National Competent Authorities', www.esma.europa.eu/rules-databases-library/eu-acts-and-national-competent-authorities, accessed 16 April 2020.

European Union, 'EU law', https://europa.eu/european-union/law_en, accessed 8 May 2020.

European Union, 'EU member countries in brief' (last published 01 February 2020), https://europa.eu/european-union/about-eu/countries/member-countries_en, accessed 13 April 2020.

European Union, 'Living in the EU' (last published 29 April 2020), https://europa.eu/european-union/about-eu/figures/living_en, accessed 7 May 2020.

Europol, 'Joint Investigation Teams – JITs: Numerous successes across the board', www.europol.europa.eu/activities-services/joint-investigation-teams, accessed 11 April 2020.

Europol, 'MTIC Fraud Investigation and LEA's Cooperation Improving' (06 March 2018), www.europol.europa.eu/publications-documents/mtic-fraud-investigation-and-leas-cooperation-improving, accessed 22 July 2020.

Eurostat, 'Europe 2020 – Overview', https://ec.europa.eu/eurostat/web/europe-2020-indicators#:~:text=The%20Europe%202020%20strategy%20is%20the%20EU%27s%20agenda,areas%3A%20Employment%3B%20Research%20%26%20Development%3B%20Climate%20change%20, accessed 19 April 2020.

Eurostat, 'Europe 2020 Targets' (Updated on 07 March 2017), https://ec.europa.eu/eurostat/documents/4411192/4411431/Europe_2020_Targets.pdf, accessed 19 April 2020.

Eurostat, 'Gross domestic product at market prices', https://ec.europa.eu/eurostat/tgm/refreshTableAction.do?tab=table&plugin=1&pcode=tec00001&language=en, accessed 7 May 2020.

Fiscalis Tax Gap Project Group (FPG/041), 'The Concept of Tax Gaps Report on VAT Gap Estimations' (Brussels, European Commission, March 2016), https://ec.europa.eu/taxation_customs/sites/taxation/files/docs/body/tgpg_report_en.pdf, 20 March 2020.

Fitzgerald A and Guevara WM 'New Leak Reveals Luxembourg Tax Deals for Disney, Koch Brothers Empire, LuxLeaks expands' (2014) *ICIJ*, www.icij.org/investigations/luxembourg-leaks/new-leak-reveals-luxembourg-tax-deals-disney-koch-brothers-empire/ >accessed 23 November 2018).

Fitzgibbon W and Starkman D, 'The "Paradise Papers" and the Long Twilight Struggle Against Offshore Secrecy', www.icij.org/investigations/paradise-papers/paradise-papers-long-twilight-struggle-offshore-secrecy/, accessed 11 July 2020.

GFI, 'Illicit Financial Flows Analytical Methodologies Utilized', www.gfintegrity.org/wp-content/uploads/2014/09/GFI-Analytics.pdf, accessed 4 December 2019.

Gov.UK, 'Serious and Organised Crime Strategy' (Collection, last updated 25 April 2019), www.gov.uk/government/collections/serious-and-organised-crime-strategy, accessed 17 April 2020.

GT Offshore Shield, 'Numbered Bank Account in Andorra 2020: Asset Protection', https://offshoreshield.globaltradersacademy.org/en/numbered-bank-accounts/andorra/, accessed 26 March 2020.

HM Government, 'Serious and Organised Crime Strategy' (October 2013), https://assets.publishing.service.gov.uk/government/uploads/system/uploads/attachment_data/file/248645/Serious_and_Organised_Crime_Strategy.pdf, accessed 17 April 2020.

International Consortium of Investigative Journalists (ICIJ), 'Giant Leak of Offshore Financial Records Exposes Global Array of Crime and Corruption', *The Panama Papers*, www.icij.org/investigations/panama-papers/20160403-panama-papers-global-overview/, accessed 20 December 2019.

ICIJ, 'The Panama Papers: Exposing the Rogue Offshore Finance Industry', www.icij.org/investigations/panama-papers/#_ga=2.246748164.1276343162.1584385292-1381287180.1584385292, accessed 11 July 2020.

ICIJ, 'An ICIJ Investigation Swiss Leaks: Murky Cash Sheltered by Bank Secrecy: Private Bank Secrets Revealed', www.icij.org/investigations/swiss-leaks/, accessed 2 March 2020.

Interagency-agency tax force on financing for development (IATF, no date), 'Tax policy effectiveness and transparency', https://developmentfinance.un.org/tax-policy-effectiveness-and-transparency, accessed 10 December 2019.

International Monetary Fund, '4. Report for Selected Country Groups and Subjects', www.imf.org/external/pubs/ft/weo/2016/02/weodata/weorept.aspx?pr.x=56&pr.y=8&sy=2016&ey=2016&scsm=1&ssd=1&sort=country&ds=.&br=1&c=001,998&s=NGDPD&grp=1&a=1, accessed 7 May 2020.

Interpol, 'Corruption', www.interpol.int/en/Crimes/Corruption, accessed 2 May 2020.

JITs Network, 'Joint Investigation Teams Practical Guide' (Council of the European Union, 14 February 2017).

KPMG, 'European Union: Tax developments in response to Covid-19', https://home.kpmg/xx/en/home/insights/2020/04/european-union-tax-developments-in-response-to-covid-19.html, accessed 13 June 2020.

Martusciello F, 'Proposal for a Council Directive Amending Directive 2006/112/EC as Regards the Introduction of the Detailed Technical Measures for the Operation of the Definitive Vat System for the Taxation of Trade Between Member States / 2018-06' (Legislative Train Schedule, 24 June 2020), www.europarl.europa.eu/legislative-train/theme-deeper-and-fairer-internal-market-with-a-strengthened-industrial-base-taxation/file-technical-measures-the-definitive-vat-system, accessed 4 July 2020.

Mazur R, 'A Plan to End Global Money Laundering: Whitepaper' (KYC360, RiskScreen), www.riskscreen.com/kyc360/requestamlwhitepaper/, accessed 4 December 2019.

Ministry of Justice, 'Corporate liability for economic crime: call for evidence' (Consultation, 31 January 2018), www.gov.uk/government/consultations/corporate-liability-for-economic-crime-call-for-evidence, accessed 26 July 2018.

Morgan T, 'Football Leaks revelations: The standout stories broken down', *Daily Telegraph*, www.telegraph.co.uk/football/2018/11/09/football-leaks-series-defining-headlines-may-happen-next/, accessed 7 December 2019).

Murray J, 'What Is the Difference Between Tax Avoidance and Tax Evasion? How to Avoid Tax Fraud Charges', *The Balance – Small Business* (29 April 2020), www.thebalancesmb.com/tax-avoidance-vs-evasion-397671, accessed 8 October 2020.

National Crime Agency (NCA), www.nationalcrimeagency.gov.uk.

NCA, 'National Economic Crime Centre: Joint Money Laundering Intelligence Taskforce', www.nationalcrimeagency.gov.uk/what-we-do/national-economic-crime-centre, accessed 11 April 2020.

OECD, 'About tax and crime', www.oecd.org/tax/crime/about-tax-and-crime.htm, accessed 25 March 2020.

OECD, 'Fifth OECD Forum on Tax and Crime', www.oecd.org/tax/crime/forum-on-tax-and-crime.htm, accessed 25 March 2020.

OECD, 'Global Affairs: Participation plans', www.oecd.org/global-relations/partnershipsinoecdbodies/participations-plans.htm, accessed 15 May 2020.

OECD, 'Global Forum members', www.oecd.org/tax/transparency/who-we-are/members/, accessed 23 April 2020.

OECD, 'Global Forum on Tax Transparency marks a dramatic shift in the fight against tax evasion with the widespread commencement of the automatic exchange of financial information', www.oecd.org/tax/transparency/global-forum-marks-a-dramatic-shift-in-the-fight-against-tax-evasion-with-the-widesp read-commencement-of-the-automatic-exchange-of-financial-information.htm, accessed 11 March 2020.

OECD, 'Global Forum on Transparency and Exchange of Information for Tax Purposes: Putting an end to offshore tax evasion', www.oecd.org/tax/transparency/, accessed 23 April 2020.

OECD, 'Glossary of statistical terms: Fraud', https://stats.oecd.org/glossary/detail.asp?ID=4781, accessed 23 March 2020.

OECD, 'Gross domestic product (GDP)', https://data.oecd.org/gdp/gross-domestic-product-gdp.htm, accessed 7 May 2020.

OECD, 'History', www.oecd.org/about/history/, accessed 7 May 2020.

OECD, 'Negotiating Group on the Multilateral Agreement on Investment (MAI)' (Expert Group No 3 on Treatment of Tax Issues in the MAI, 19 April 1996), www.oecd.org/daf/mai/pdf/eg2/eg2963e.pdf, accessed 21 December 2019.

OECD, 'Population and Migration', www.oecd.org/sdd/01_Population_and_migration.pdf, accessed 13 May 2020.

OECD, 'Save the date: Sixth OECD Forum on Tax and Crime: Strengthening our Foundations: Intensifying the Global Response to Tax Crimes and Other Financial Crimes, 15–17 December 2020, Ottawa, Canada' www.oecd.org/tax/forum-on-tax-and-crime.htm, accessed 28 March 2020.

OECD, 'Strengthening the global response to tax crime' (8 November 2017), www.oecd.org/tax/crime/strengthening-the-global-response-to-tax-crime.htm, accessed 25 March 2020.

OECD, 'Technology Tools to Tackle Tax Evasion and Tax Fraud' (2017) 6, www.oecd.org/tax/crime/technology-tools-to-tackle-tax-evasion-and-tax-fraud.pdf, accessed 25 February 2020.

OECD, 'Where: Global reach', www.oecd.org/about/members-and-partners/, accessed 29 April 2020.

OECD, 'Whistleblower protection' < www.oecd.org/corruption/ethics/whistleblower-protection;, accessed 6 February 2020.

Offshore Manual, 'Swiss Numbered Bank Account', www.offshore-manual.com/SwissNumbered.html, accessed 11 March 2020.

OLAF (European Anti-Fraud Office), 'Report fraud', https://ec.europa.eu/anti-fraud/olaf-and-you/report-fraud_en, accessed 23 March 2020.

Osborne H, 'Tax avoidance Offshore wealth: loopholes found in EU anti-tax evasion rules Foreign accounts can still be kept secret from tax authorities, says report', *The Guardian* (15 October 2018), www.theguardian.com/business/2018/oct/15/offshore-wealth-loopholes-found-eu-anti-tax-evasion-rules, accessed 22 April 2020.

Parloff R, 'How VW Paid $25 Billion for "Dieselgate" – and Got Off Easy' (*Fortune*, 6 February 2018), https://fortune.com/2018/02/06/volkswagen-vw-emissions-scandal-penalties/, accessed 11 July 2020.

PROTAX, 'PROTAX provides solutions for the prevention and prosecution of tax crimes' (EU Horizon 2020 Project), https://protax-project.eu/, accessed 16 March 2020.

PWC, 'Overview and current state of play – EU VAT Action Plan and OECD VAT/GST developments' (*Tax Policy Bulletin*, 27 August 2018), www.pwc.com/gx/en/tax/newsletters/tax-policy-bulletin/assets/pwc-eu-vat-action-plan-oecd-vat-gst-developments.pdf, accessed 20 February 2020.

Rediker AD and Maio De G, 'Order from chaos: Europe and the existential challenge of post-COVID recovery' (*Brookings*, 20 April 2020), www.brookings.edu/blog/order-from-chaos/2020/04/20/europe-and-the-existential-challenge-of-post-covid-recovery/, accessed 26 April 2020.

Regeringskansliet, 'Counteracting tax evasion, tax avoidance and money laundering', www.government.se/contentassets/099c10d6502745279ff7a8b11e379c9b/action-plan-counteracting-tax-evasion-tax-avoidance-and-money-laundering.pdf, accessed 16 March 2020.

Savona E and Riccardi M, 'Assessing the risk of money laundering in Europe' (Final Report of Project IARM, April 2017), www.transcrime.it/wp-content/uploads/2017/05/ProjectIARM-FinalReport.pdf, accessed 8 October 2020.

Serious Fraud Office, https://www.sfo.gov.uk.

Tax Justice Network, 'Financial Secrecy Index 2020'< www.taxjustice.net/2020/02/18/financial-secrecy-index-2020-reports-progress-on-global-transparency-but-backsliding-from-us-cayman-and-uk-prompts-call-for-sanctions/, accessed 15 May 2020.

Tax Justice Network, 'Financial Secrecy Index 2020: Narrative Report on Switzerland', https://fsi.taxjustice.net/PDF/Switzerland.pdf, accessed 24 March 2020.

Transparency International UK, 'Overview: Why Corruption Matters', www.transparency.org.uk/why-corruption-matters, accessed 24 May 2020.

UK Parliament, 'VAT fraud: cooperation between tax administrations' (23 May 2018), https://publications.parliament.uk/pa/cm201719/cmselect/cmeuleg/301-xxviii/30116.htm#footnote-013, accessed 23 April 2020.

UNODC, 'United Nations Convention against Corruption', www.unodc.org/unodc/en/corruption/tools_and_publications/UN-convention-against-corruption.html, accessed 6 February 2020.

United States Senate, 'Constitution of the United States 1788', www.senate.gov/civics/constitution_item/constitution.htm#amdt_16_%281913%29, accessed 20 March 2020.

Vella M, 'What are the Malta Files?', *Malta Today*, https://www.maltatoday.com.mt/news/national/77384/what_are_the_malta_files#.XC7ufVz7RPZ, accessed 4 December 2019.

Working Minds, 'Quotations from Ayn Rand [1905–1982]', www.working-minds.com/ARquotes.htm, accessed 16 April 2020.

Willshe K. 'Nina Ricci heir convicted of tax evasion in France with help of HSBC', (*The Guardian*, 13 April 2015), www.theguardian.com/world/2015/apr/13/nina-ricci-heir-convicted-of-tax-evasion-in-f rance-with-help-of-hsbc, accessed 8 November 2019.

Wilson-Chapman A and Fitzgibbon W, 'The Paradise Papers: What do you want to know?', Question Time, ICIJ,www.icij.org/blog/2018/10/the-paradise-papers-what-do-you-want-to-know/, accessed 11 December 2019.

Wong J, 'The Cambridge Analytica scandal changed the world – but it didn't change Facebook' (*The Guardian*, 18 March 2019), www.theguardian.com/technology/2019/mar/17/the-cambridge-analytica-scanda l-changed-the-world-but-it-didnt-change-facebook, accessed 11 July 2020.

World Bank, 'Global Economic Prospects: Europe and Central Asia' (8 June 2020), www.worldbank.org/en/ region/eca/brief/global-economic-prospects-europe-and-central-asia, accessed 13 June 2020.

World Bank, 'Illicit Financial Flows (IFFs)' (Brief, 7 July 2017), www.worldbank.org/en/topic/financialsector/ brief/illicit-financial-flows-iffs, accessed 12 December 2019.

World Bank, 'International Organizations Take Major Step to Boost Global Cooperation in Tax Matters' (Press Release, 19 April 2016), www.worldbank.org/en/news/press-release/2016/04/19/internationa l-organisations-take-major-step-to-boost-global-cooperation-in-tax-matters, accessed 24 April 2020.

World Bank, 'OECD and World Bank call for whole-of-government approach to combating tax evasion and corruption' (Press Release, 24 October 2018), www.worldbank.org/en/news/press-release/2018/10/24/ oecd-and-world-bank-call-for-whole-of-government-approach-to-combating-tax-evasion-and-cor ruption, accessed 24 April 2020.

Wyplosz C, 'The failure of the Lisbon strategy' (*VOX*, 12 January 2010), https://voxeu.org/article/ failure-lisbon-strategy, accessed 18 April 2020

INDEX

Lightning Source UK Ltd.
Milton Keynes UK
UKHW020810190722
406053UK00003B/79